KNIGHTS OF THE CLOISTER

KNIGHTS OF THE CLOISTER

Templars and Hospitallers in
Central-Southern Occitania
c.1100–c.1300

Dominic Selwood

THE BOYDELL PRESS

First published 1999
The Boydell Press, Woodbridge

ISBN 0 85115 730 0

The Boydell Press is an imprint of Boydell & Brewer Ltd
PO Box 9, Woodbridge, Suffolk IP12 3DF, UK
and of Boydell & Brewer Inc.
PO Box 41026, Rochester, NY 14604–4126, USA
website: http://www.boydell.co.uk

A catalogue record for this book is available
from the British Library

Library of Congress Cataloging-in-Publication Data
Selwood, Dominic, 1970–
    Knights of the cloister : Templars and Hospitallers in central
-southern Occitania, c.1100–c.1300 / Dominic Selwood.
        p.   cm.
    Includes bibliographical references and index.
    ISBN 0–85115–730–0 (alk. paper)
    1. Templars – France, Southern – History.   2. Hospitalers – France,
Southern – History.   3. France, Southern – History.   I. Title.
CR4755.F7S45   1999
944'.8 – DC21   99–12004

This publication is printed on acid-free paper

Printed in Great Britain by
St Edmundsbury Press Ltd, Bury St Edmunds, Suffolk

CONTENTS

PLATES

To the Memory of

EVA ELISABETH HÜTTER
née Hese

Dr Phil. (Breslau)
1906–1995

A medieval scholar, tireless enthusiast for life,
inspiration,
and irreplaceable friend

Lignum Crucis
Signum Ducis
Sequitur exercitus
Quod non cessit
Sed processit
In vi Sancti Spiritus

ACKNOWLEDGEMENTS

This book is the fruition of three rewarding and happy years research conducted at Oxford, the Sorbonne and in the south of France (1993–1996). For the opportunity to immerse myself in the subject, my greatest debt and deepest thanks are owed to the late Right Honourable the Lord Craigmyle, President of the English Association of The Sovereign Military Hospitaller Order of St John of Jerusalem, of Rhodes and of Malta. Without his help, interest and support the research would not have been conducted.

The funding of my time in France was provided by the Banque Nationale de Paris, on the recommendation of the committee of the Oxford-Paris Programme and the Académie de Paris. For this scholarship to the Centre de Recherches d'Histoire et Civilisation Byzantines et du Proche Orient Chrétien at the Sorbonne, I am grateful.

The advice, help and enthusiasm of my parents, David and Barbara Selwood, and my inspirational medievalist grandmother, Eva Hütter (who did not live to see the research completed), cannot be quantified, and gratitude cannot be adequately expressed.

The staff of the libraries, museums and archives in whose debt I lie include those of the Bibliothèque Méjanes at Aix, the Bibliothèque Sainte-Geneviève in Paris, the Bodleian Library, the British Library, the Burrel Collection in Glasgow, the Cambridge University Library, the French Dominicans' Bibliothèque Saulchoir in Paris, the Maison Française at Oxford, the National Archives of France, the National Library of France, New College Library, Oxford History Faculty Library, Rhodes House Library (Scicluna Collection) and Saint Gregory's Monastery Library, Downside Abbey near Bath. Most importantly, I particularly need to express my gratitude to all at the Institut de Recherche et d'Histoire des Textes of the CNRS at both Paris and Orléans, the staff of Duke Humphrey's Library in Oxford, and those of the manuscript room at the Departmental Archives of the Bouches-du-Rhône in Marseille.

All research is dependent on the guidance and expertise of others. Those who have given me their assistance are legion, and in naming the following I do not mean to thank any the less the others: Ian Agnew, Malcolm Barber, Daniel le Blévec, Caroline Bourlet, Jessalynn Bird, Eric Christiansen, James Clarke, Hannah Cole, Annie Dufour, Jean Dunbabin, Peter Edbury, Alan Forey, Rev. David Forrester, Thomas Iglesias, Dom. Philip Jebb, O.S.B., Sarah Kay, Maurice Keen, Anne-Marie Legras, Anthony Luttrell, Sophia Menache, Alexander Murray, Dom. Daniel Rees, O.S.B., Jonathen Riley-Smith, Paul Santoni, Oliver Selwood and Richard Sharpe. I am particularly grateful to Michel Balard and Alain Demurger for their encouragement whilst I was working in France.

For invaluable guidance, encouragement, scholarship, enthusiasm and interest throughout the project, I cannot thank enough my doctoral supervisor: Miri Rubin of Pembroke College, Oxford. Her many contributions have been devoted, indefatigable and always wise.

To the examiners of the original thesis, Alexander Murray and Malcolm Barber, I owe gratitude for their keen remarks, observations and perception.

Finally, I must thank all at Boydell & Brewer for their patience, understanding and commitment.

Friendship and its value must have pride of place, and this is owed to Ignacio de Murtinho-Braga, Mark-Antony Conti, my brother Andreas Selwood and all my family.

To all I am grateful. For all errors I apologize. They are entirely my own.

Dominic Selwood
Temple
London

Feast of Saint Louis, 1998

NOTE ON TRANSLATIONS AND CITATIONS

The sources used in this study are in the main Latin and Occitan. Translations are my own with the original in the corresponding footnote, unless indicated otherwise.

Because of the high incidence of Occitan, names have been anglicized, except where this goes against accepted practice. Therefore, William Hare-lip instead of Guilhem Lavia-corta, and Raymond the Under-nourished instead of Ramón Malnourri. Place names are in the language of origin, but have been put into the modern rendering if there is one. Therefore, les Saintes-Maries-de-la-Mer and not la Sainte-Marie-de-la-Mer (*Sancta Maria de mari*), or Martigues and not Saint-Geniès. Church names, however, are in English; thus, Saint Mary of Alet, and not Sainte-Marie of Alet.

For the few Arabic words used, long and short vowels (a and ā) and normal and aspirated consonants (d and ḏ) are distinguished, thus Ḥiṭṭīn not Hittin. The definite article has been rendered phonetically, thus as-Ṣakhrah, and not al-Ṣakhrah.

Biblical quotations are taken from the *Revised Standard Version (Catholic Edition)*, Ignatius Press, San Francisco, 1966.

The wars against the Albigensians have been styled 'the Albigensian Crusade' following common usage.[1]

With regard to citations, the dates of charters have been given in the footnote as well as in the text. If an act is undated, the footnote will stipulate (undated). For dates which fall within a range, the convention of using an x has been observed, thus 1099x1105 denotes any time between, and including, these dates.

Citations from charters in archives follow the pattern of:

collection/number (year)[2]
thus: 56H5168 (1202)

---

[1] Arguments as to what constituted a 'Crusade' abound in almost all studies of the Crusades. A concise argument for limiting this terminology solely to those expeditions which had Jerusalem and the Holy Land as their objective is to be found in H. Mayer, *The Crusades*, J. Gillingham (tr.), Oxford, 1972, pp. 283–286. The alternative definition, the 'broad' view (taking the legal formalities and papal pronouncements as the test), is fully argued by N. Housely, *The Later Crusades, 1274–1580*, Oxford, 1992.

[2] In the Midi acts were dated according to the *calculus Pisanus* (year began on 25 March), except in Narbonne, Foix and Provence where it was on the 25 December, J. Garrigues, 'Les Styles du commencement de l'année dans le Midi. L'Emploi de l'année pisane en pays Toulousain et Languedoc', *AM* 53(1941), p. 239.

Charters which are from manuscript cartularies follow the pattern:

commandery, folio (year)
thus: *Saint-Gilles(Temple)*, fol. 97v (1170)

For charters which are drawn from printed cartularies, the pattern is:

title, volume number, document
thus: *CH*, I, no. 31, p. 30 (1113).

If there is a running sequence in a footnote from a particular source, volume numbers are not repeated. Equally, to avoid repetition, acts from the same year are grouped, with the date at the end of the sequence; thus:

Richerenches(Temple), no. 210, p. 187; no. 211, p. 188; no. 216, pp. 192–193; no. 225, pp. 200–220; no. 226, pp. 201–202 (1175); no. 214, pp. 190–191; no. 217, pp. 193–194 (1176); no. 220, pp. 196–197 (1177); no. 243, p. 216 (1180)

means that the first five acts date from 1175, the second two from 1176, the next from 1177, and the last from 1180.

ABBREVIATIONS

AM	*Annales du Midi*, Toulouse, 1889–
Avignon(Hospital)	Marseille, departmental archives of the Bouches-du-Rhône, 56H1281
Barber, *Knighthood*	M. Barber, *The New Knighthood*, Cambridge, 1994
BN	Bibliothèque nationale (National Library of France)
Carcenac, *Larzac*	A.-R. Carcenac, *Les Templiers du Larzac*, Nîmes, 1994
CF	*Cahiers de Fanjeaux*, Toulouse, 1966–
CH	*Cartulaire général de l'ordre des Hopitaliers de Saint Jean de Jérusalem (1100–1310)*, J. Delaville le Roulx (ed.), 4 vols., Paris, 1894–1906
CT	*Cartulaire de l'ordre du Temple 1119?–1150. Recueil des chartes et des bulles relatives à l'ordre du Temple*, Marquis d'Albon (ed.), Paris, 1913
Demurger, *Temple*	A. Demurger, *Vie et mort de l'ordre du Temple*, Paris, 1989
Douzens(Temple)	*Cartulaires des Templiers de Douzens*, P. Gérard and E. Magnou (eds.), Collection de documents inédits sur l'histoire de France 3, Paris, 1965
Forey, *Aragón*	A. Forey, *The Templars in the Corona de Aragón*, Oxford, 1973
Forey, *Orders*	A. Forey, *The Military Orders*, Basingstoke, 1992
Gap(Hospital)	*Origine des chevaliers de Malte et rôle des donations de la commanderie de Gap (XIe–XIIe siècles)*, P. Guillaume (ed.), Paris, 1881
GC	*Gallia christiana*, D. de Sainte-Marthe *et al.* (eds.), 16 vols., Paris, 1812–1896
GCN(various)	*Gallia christiana novissima*, U. Chevalier and J. H. Albanès (eds.), 7 vols., Montbéliard and Valence, 1895–1920
H	Toulouse, departmental archives of the Haute Garonne, charters of the Hospital and Temple
La Selve(Temple)	*Le Cartulaire de la Selve*, P. Ourliac and A. Magnou (eds.), Paris, 1985
MGHSS	*Monumenta Germaniæ Historica Scriptores*, G. H. Pertz *et al.* (eds.), Hanover, 1896–

Montsaunès(Temple)	'Cartulaire des Templiers de Montsaunès', C. Higounet (ed.), *Bulletin philologique et historique* (1957), pp. 225–293
PH	*Provence Historique*, Marseille, 1950–
PL	*Patrologiæ cursus completus, series latina*, J.-P. Migne (ed.), 221 vols., Paris, 1844–1865
Prov	*Les Plus anciennes chartes en langue provençale*, C. Brunel (ed.), 2 vols., Paris, 1926 and 1952
RA	Augustine of Hippo, *Regulæ*, in J. Dickinson, *The Origins of the Austin Canons and their Introduction into England*, London, 1950, appendix 2, pp. 273–279
RB	Benedict of Nursia, *Regula sancti Benedicti*, in *RB 1980, The Rule of Saint Benedict in Latin and English with Notes*, T. Fry (ed.), Collegeville, 1981
RHC Occ.	*Recueil des historiens des croisades. Historiens occidentaux*, Académie des inscriptions et belles lettres (ed.), 5 vols., Paris, 1844–1895
RHC Or.	*Recueil des historiens des croisades. Historiens orientaux*, Académie des inscriptions et belles lettres (ed.), 5 vols., Paris, 1872–1906
Richerenches(Temple)	*Cartulaire de la commanderie de Richerenches de l'ordre du Temple (1136–1214)*, Marquis de Ripert-Monclar (ed.), Marseille, 1978
Riley-Smith, *Knights*	J. Riley-Smith, *The Knights of Saint John in Jerusalem and Cyprus 1050–1310*, London, 1967
Roaix(Temple)	*Chartularium domus Templi Hierosolymitani de Roais diocesis Vasionensis*, in *Cartulaires des Hospitaliers et des Templiers en Dauphiné* 3, U. Chevalier (ed.), Vienne, 1975, pp. 61–136
RTemp.	*La Règle du Temple*, H. de Curzon (ed.), Paris, 1886
Saint Eulalia(1308)	'L'Inventaire des biens de la commanderie du Temple de Sainte-Eulalie du Larzac en 1308', A. Higounet-Nadal (ed.), *AM* 68(1956), pp. 255–262
Saint-Gilles(Hospital)	Arles, municipal archives, GG 89
Saint-Gilles(Temple)	Arles, municipal archives, GG 90
Saint-Paul(Hospital)	*Chartularium domus Hospitalis Hierosolymitani Sancti Pauli prope Romanis*, in *Cartulaires des Hospitaliers et des Templiers en Dauphiné* 3, U. Chevalier (ed.), Vienne, 1975, pp. 3–58
Saint Victor	*Cartulaire de l'abbaye de Saint-Victor de Marseille*, B. Guérard (ed.), Collection des cartulaires de France 9, 2 vols., Paris, 1857

Trinquetaille(Hospital)	*Cartulaire de Trinquetaille*, P. Amargier (ed.), Aix-en-Provence, 1972
Vaour(Temple)	*Cartulaire des Templiers de Vaour*, C. Portal and E. Cabié (eds.), Albi, 1894
William of Tyre, *Chronicon*	*Chronicon*, R. Huygens (ed.), Corpus christianorum. Continuatio mediævalis, 2 vols., Turnhout, 1986
1G	Marseille, departmental archives of the Bouches-du-Rhône, charters of the archbishopric of Aix-en-Provence
3H	Marseille, departmental archives of the Bouches-du-Rhône, charters of the Cistercian abbey of Silvacane
56H	Marseille, departmental archives of the Bouches-du-Rhône, charters of the Hospital and Temple

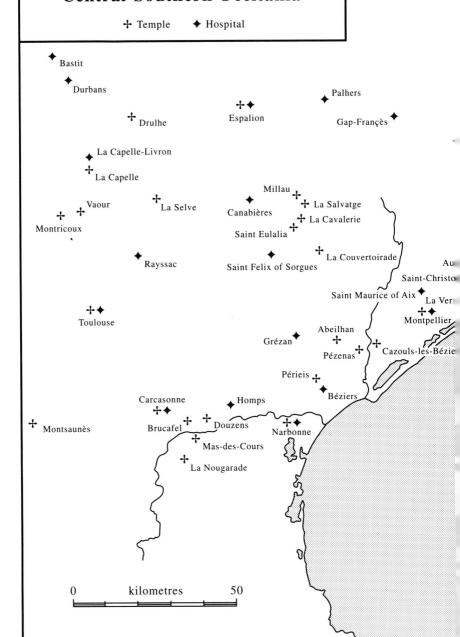

'Principal Commanderies in Central-Southern Occitania'

✝ Temple   ◆ Hospital

◆ Bastit

◆ Durbans

✝ Drulhe

✝◆ Espalion

◆ Palhers

Gap-Françès ◆

◆ La Capelle-Livron

✝ La Capelle

✝ Vaour   ✝ La Selve

Millau ✝

◆ Canabières

✝ La Salvatge

✝ La Cavalerie

✝ Montricoux

Saint Eulalia ✝

◆ Rayssac

◆ Saint Felix of Sorgues

✝ La Couvertoirade

Au

Saint-Christo

Saint Maurice of Aix ◆

La Ver

✝◆ Montpellier

Abeilhan

◆ Grézan

✝ Pézenas

✝ Toulouse

✝ ✝ Cazouls-les-Bézie

Périeis ✝

◆ Béziers

Carcasonne

✝◆

◆ Homps

✝ Montsaunès

Brucafel ✝ ✝ Douzens

✝ ✝ Narbonne

✝ Mas-des-Cours

✝ La Nougarade

0   kilometres   50

Echirolles

Valence

Saint Maurice of Trièves

Embrun

Col-de-Cabres

Gap

Montélimar

Pöet-Laval

Boynessac

Valdrôme

urg Saint-
Andéol

Richerenches

Trignan

Roaix

Saint-Paul-
Trois-Châteaux

Lachau

Orange

Montfrin

Avignon

Manosque

Puimoisson

Nice

Joucas

Nîmes

Comps

Bonpas

Barbentane

Rué

nérac

Argence

lès

Trinquetaille

Cavaillon

Arles

Saliers

Aix

Bailles

Bras

Astros

La Favillane

Saint Maurice
of Régusse

Peirassol

Plan de la Peyre

Biot

Marseille

Beaulieu

Grasse

Toulon

Hyères

INTRODUCTION

> Listen carefully, my son, to the master's instructions, and attend to them with
> the ear of your heart. This is advice from a father who loves you; welcome it,
> and faithfully put it into practice. The labour of obedience will bring you back
> to him from whom you had drifted through the sloth of disobedience. This
> message of mine is for you, then, if you are ready to give up your own will,
> once and for all, and armed with the strong and noble weapons of obedience to
> do battle for the true King, Christ the Lord.
>
> *The Rule of Saint Benedict*, in *RB*, Prologue,
> caps. 1–3, p. 157

THE Crusades of the central Middle Ages (1099–1291) have a perennial interest for historians of differing religious denominations, cultures and countries.

No account of Western Christendom's conquest of, and struggle to retain land in, the near-East is complete without an understanding of the backbone of the Crusader states from the Second Crusade onwards: the Military and Religious Orders. A number of such Orders were later formed, increasingly based on geography and/or nationality. But the two prototypes (each in its own way) were the Order of the Temple (founded 1120) and the Order of the Hospital (founded c.1099). This work is limited to these two Military Orders.

This study addresses two aims normally subservient to the Orders' military histories. The first is to move the emphasis away from the Crusader states and towards Western Europe, where most of the brethren of the Orders lived. Whilst it is well known that the Military Orders were supported by immense networks in Europe, the activities of the brethren in European commanderies outside the theatre of war have not formed the basis of any intensive, contextual studies. The second aim is to concentrate on their role as religious Orders, for whilst fighting was emphasized amongst their activities, and central to their image, these were principally religious, cloistered Orders.

By studying the life led by brethren in Dèçamer (Europe; the opposite of Outremer), a picture emerges which places the Military Orders into the context of main-stream European religious culture. For whilst the purpose of these commanderies was constantly to look to the Crusader states, and respond to their needs, the daily life led by a European brother was one of a monk following a religious life. His was a vocation as real as that of a Benedictine, Cistercian, or any other member of the *ordo monasticus*.

Evidently, as members of a support structure, the brethren living in Europe were concerned with the vicissitudes of the Crusader states, and this study is

I

accordingly focused on analysing the mechanisms developed by the Orders to ensure that their brethren in the East could at all times be effective standing armies. The Orders achieved this partly by innovation, and partly by engaging in the financial and social activities already devised and developed by established religious communities.

The Military Orders are habitually ignored by most works on monasticism, even those dedicated to the Crusader states;[1] whilst Crusade historians have dealt with the Military Orders mainly in the context of their activities in Outremer. An extreme expression of this attitude is that regional, European studies of

> [the Temple] . . . throw limited light on the active practice of the Templar vocation, a vocation only fully permissible in the Latin East and the Iberian peninsula.[2]

This view reflects a fundamental misunderstanding of the phenomenon of the Military Order, for more commanderies of the Temple and Hospital were founded in Occitania alone than in Outremer. The Military Orders were like icebergs. Their visible tips were the battle-outposts in the Crusader states, but the structures that kept them afloat were the enormous support mechanisms working ceaselessly from within European society.

The last thirty years have witnessed the rebirth of interest in the Military Orders, and a series of scholarly works have been devoted to separate histories of the Orders. The study of the Order of the Temple has been inspired by the work of Malcolm Barber and Alain Demurger, whilst the Hospitallers have been the domain of Jonathan Riley-Smith. The study of Military Orders as a phenomenon has been led by Alan Forey, who has also conducted the sole extensive regional study of a Military Order in Europe: *The Templars in the Corona of Aragón* (1973).[3] In this tradition, and reflecting a modern trend towards regional studies, this work concentrates on an important area of the Military Orders' implantations. Yet, unlike works devoted to the Military Orders in the Crusader states, or indeed, the Iberian peninsula, this study explores a society where the Military Orders lived as non-combatant religious. As such, the primary emphasis is on the Military Orders as European religious organizations. Whilst this aspect of their networks has been dealt with by most works on the Orders, it has been subordinated to their military activities, and

---

[1] The most recent of such works to ignore them is A. Jotischky, *The Perfection of Solitude. Hermits and Monks in the Crusader States*, Pennsylvania, 1995.

[2] S. Rovik, 'The Templars in the Holy Land in the Twelfth Century', Oxford D.Phil. thesis, 1986, p. 3.

[3] Forey, *Aragón*.

has never formed the basis of an in-depth survey drawing on local archives. To achieve such an enquiry is the aim of this study.

Central-southern Occitania has been chosen as the *pays* for this study for three principal reasons. First, both Military Orders accorded a primacy to Occitania over the rest of Europe. Second, the area was in constant contact with the eastern and western Mediterranean. And third, there remain sufficient sources to make the study feasible and rewarding. J. Delaville le Roulx remarked at the turn of the century that little research had been conducted into the Hospitallers of the grand-priory of Saint-Gilles.[4] Whilst articles have appeared since then, research into the Military Orders in Occitania is fragmented, dealing with small areas of enquiry. Moreover, many of the studies are outdated, and do not reach the critical standards required by modern scholarship.

The other reasons which single out Occitania as worthy of study are precisely those which led the Military Orders to grant it an elevated status. It was economically advanced, cosmopolitan, tolerant, had exceptionally well developed trade links with the eastern and western Mediterranean, a markedly urban coastal belt with a rich agricultural hinterland, and strong links with pilgrimage and Crusade.

The sources used for this study are varied, but the core is made of the collections of charters housed principally in the Departmental archives of the Bouches-du-Rhône in Marseille, of the Haute-Garonne in Toulouse and in the Municipal archives in Arles. Together with these, charters of other monastic and ecclesiastical establishments in the region have been used, and consultation of this material has permitted the activities of the Military Orders to be examined in the context of Occitanian religious life and organization.

The Orders' activities can only be reconstructed by such close charter work. Indeed, there are few other sources from which to build a picture of the lives the Orders led in Occitania. Yet, additional sources have been used where relevant. Thus, chronicles, the Orders' Rules, seals, and architecture have been studied and used where they offer contributions to the discussion.

These enquiries have not been conducted without difficulty. The first problem lies in the charters themselves, for to a certain degree they are stylized. To imbue meaning to standard repetitious formulæ could lead to inconclusive results. Yet, in the Occitanian culture of Roman law and developed notariats, variations in the wording of charters are significant, and their often unique individuality can render them valuable, and offer important insights.

A second problem is that charters are notoriously ambiguous. Sales were camouflaged as donations, loans as sales, pledges as donations, and so on. This

---

4 *CH*, I, p. xxviii n. 1.

study has not attempted to create charts and percentage calculations of the frequency of donations as compared to sales and the such like, for this very reason: conclusions would be deceptive.

A more fundamental problem in such a comparative work is the lower survival rate of Templar charters as compared with those of the Hospitallers. Whilst this lack is not prohibitive to conducting a comparative study, it predisposes the structure to be one of themes and mechanisms, rather than numerical comparisons. Therefore, unless it is unambiguous, there is no suggestion of predominantly Templar, or predominantly Hospitaller, activities.

The charters which have been consulted emanate from two sources: original acts and medieval cartulary copies (transcriptions of charters into books or onto rolls). There is no consistent reason why some commanderies (or monasteries, for that matter) left cartularies, and others did not. For example, the abbey of Saint Victor of Marseille drew up a cartulary, but the Cluniac abbey of Saint-Gilles did not. There are no Cistercian cartularies from Occitania, nor are there any Carthusian. Likewise, the archbishopric of Aix left a cartulary, but the bishopric of Cavaillon did not. Either they have been lost, or they were never compiled. There are no general explanations, but the suggested effect of the Albigensian Crusade in prompting the copying of cartularies has been disproved, for many were compiled before the invasion.[5]

No identifiable group of scribes penned the charters of the Military Orders, or was commissioned to compile the cartularies. At cities such as Saint-Gilles, Arles and Avignon, as well as many others, the renaissance of Roman law had created a need for workshops of licensed public notaries.[6] Sometimes the Orders used such notaries and associated scribes, but never exclusively. At the Hospitaller commandery of Trinquetaille charters were drawn up by notaries from Arles,[7] whereas at Saint-Gilles the work was sometimes executed by Hospitaller priests.[8] At Templar Douzens the commandery had its own *scriptorium*,[9] whilst at Richerenches the charters were drawn up within the commandery.[10] Moreover, it was not uncommon for the cartularies to be the work of more than one scribe.[11]

5 D. le Blévec and A. Venturini, 'Cartulaires des ordres militaires xiie–xiiie siècles (Provence occidentale–Basse vallée du Rhône)', *Mémoires et documents de l'Ecole des Chartes* 39(1993), pp. 458–465.
6 A. Gouron, 'Diffusion des consulats méridionaux et expansion du droit romain aux xiie et xiiie siècles', *Bibliothèque de l'Ecole des Chartes* 121(1963), pp. 26–77; R. Aubenas, *Etude sur le notariat provençal*, Aix-en-Provence, 1951.
7 *Trinquetaille(Hospital)*, p. ii.
8 *Saint-Gilles(Hospital)*, fols. 160v–161v (1168).
9 *Douzens(Temple)*, p. xii, n. 2; E. Delaruelle, 'Templiers et Hospitaliers en Languedoc pendant la croisade des Albigeois', *CF* 4(1969), p. 318.
10 *Richerenches(Temple)*, p. xi.
11 For example, Paris, BN, lat. 11082.

This study spans two centuries in its thematic analysis of the Occitanian commanderies of the Military Orders. In some instances recourse has even been had to early fourteenth century material. This must be justified by the historical value of certain sources from the 1300s which illuminate important areas such as the 1308 inventory of Saint Eulalia (the basis of chapter seven).

The underlying theme which emerges during this study is that of the striking similarity in the mode of implantation and behaviour of the two main Military Orders. Crusade historiography has long laid emphasis on the antagonism and hostility of the Military Orders.[12] Yet, the Orders at times stressed the harmony between themselves, and medieval writers were aware of their fundamental similarity. John of Ypres, abbot of Saint-Bertin (d.1383), wrote that the people (*vulgus*) called the Hospitallers 'Templars' in those places where there had been a Templar commandery which the Hospital had taken over after the suppression of the Temple, and he cited the symbolic commandery of Ypres, which traced its origins to Brother Godfrey of Saint-Omer, co-founder of the Order of the Temple.[13] Moreover, co-operation between the two Orders in the West was not uncommon. A convincing example of this is that after the dedication of the choir extension of the London Temple (attended by King Henry II), it was none other than the London Hospitallers who laid on the celebratory banquet.[14]

One way of describing the relationship is to say that the Orders experienced co-evolution. In Occitania at least, there was widespread interaction between the Orders. Much of their land abutted,[15] they witnessed each other's acts,[16]

[12] For example, H. Mayer, *The Crusades*, J. Gillingham (tr.), Oxford, 1972, p. 266; Riley-Smith, *Knights*, pp. 151–152.

[13] John of Ypres, *Chronicon Sythiense S. Bertini*, in *Thesaurus novus anecdotorum*, E. Martène (ed.), III, Paris, 1717, col. 427.

[14] Matthew Paris, *Chronica majora*, Rolls Series 57, H. Luard (ed.), IV, London, 1877, p. 11.

[15] *Douzens(Temple)*, A no. 135, p. 125 (1157); no. 120, pp. 113–114 (1167); no. 162, pp. 145–146 (1178); no. 133, pp. 123–124 (1163); no. 161, pp. 144–145 (1182); *Richerenches(Temple)*, no. 122, p. 177 (1172); *Saint-Gilles(Hospital)*, fols. 30r (1188); 173v–174r (1191); *Saint-Gilles(Temple)*, fols. 125rv (1171); 20v–21v (1175); 62v–63r (1180); 105rv (1184); 197rv (1187); 22v–24r (1190); 56v–57r (1193); *Trinquetaille(Hospital)*, no. 164, pp. 148–149 (1192); no. 179, pp. 172–173 (1194); 56H5174 (1206); 56H5196 (1271); 56H5289 (1202).

[16] *Avignon(Hospital)*, fols. 59r–60r (1200); *Douzens(Temple)*, A no. 127, pp. 119–120 (1156); B no. 28, p. 210 (1168); A no. 169, p. 151 (1181); *Saint-Gilles(Hospital)*, fols. 174v (1158); 153v–154r (1187); 102r (1201); *Saint-Gilles(Temple)*, fols. 106rv (1167); 63r–64r (1187).

exchanged realty,[17] were involved in litigation as well as in agreements,[18] were included together in individual testaments,[19] and the Hospitallers even kept a register of privileges granted to both Orders by the counts of Provence of Barcelona.[20] This is a very different picture to that as seen in England, where for the most part the two Orders lived wholly separately, without even adjoining territories.[21]

A significant factor in the historiography of the rivalry between the Orders has been the need to find a *casus offensionis* for the loss of the Holy Land and for the subsequent frustration of the West's efforts to regain control.[22] This is evident in writing which followed the loss of Acre in 1291.[23] The welter of individual and conciliar proposals regarding union between the Orders is a logical continuation of this type of reasoning.[24] An example of a symbolic manifestation of the unity of the Military Orders is that unlike other monastic Orders, which took their inspiration from the lives of the Apostles, the Military Orders came to be likened to biblical warriors: the Macabees.[25]

The Templar Brother James of Molay (c.1293–1314) was the last of his Order to express his views on the relationship that existed between his Order

---

[17] *Saint-Gilles(Hospital)*, fols. 37v–38r (1202); 38rv (1202); 92rv (1203); 92v (1203); 93v–94r (1203); 98rv–99r (1204); 98r (1204); *Saint-Gilles(Temple)*, fol. 214rv (1202); *Trinquetaille(Hospital)*, no. 179, pp. 172–173 (1194); no. 177, pp. 169–171 (1197); 56H5286 (1258).

[18] *Douzens(Temple)*, A no. 167, pp. 149–150 (1183); *Saint-Gilles(Hospital)*, fols. 22r (1184); 15rv (1193); 37rv (1197); 38rv (1202); 174r (1209); *Saint-Gilles(Temple)*, fol. 214v–215v (1202); *Trinquetaille(Hospital)*, no. 175, pp. 163–168 (1197 and 1198); no. 172, pp. 159–160 (1198); no. 173, pp. 161–162 (1199).

[19] *Saint-Gilles(Hospital)*, fol. 143v (1170); *Saint-Gilles(Temple)*, fols. 209v–211r (1202); *Trinquetaille(Hospital)*, no. 183, pp. 177–178 (1201); 56H4107 (1194); 56H5028 (1227).

[20] 56H4050 (undated).

[21] M. Gervers, '*Pro defensionis Terre Sancte*: the Development and Exploitation of the Hospitallers' Landed Estate in Essex', in *The Military Orders. Fighting for the Faith and Caring for the Sick*, M. Barber (ed.), Aldershot, 1994, p. 19.

[22] H. Nicholson, *Templars, Hospitallers and Teutonic Knights: Images of the Military Orders 1128–1291*, Leicester, 1993, p. 130.

[23] *De excidio urbis Acconis*, in *Veterum scriptorum et monumentorum amplissima collectio*, E. Martène and U. Durand (eds.), v, Paris, 1729, cols. 766, 770, 771; Bartholemew of Neocastro, *Historia Sicula*, in *Rerum italicarum scriptores*, L. Muratori (ed.), Milan, 1928, cols. 1159–1160; *Annales prioratus de Dunstaplia*, in Rolls Series 36, H. Luard (ed.), iii, London, 1866, p. 366; Eberhard, *Annales*, in *MGHSS* 17, P. Jaffé (ed.), p. 594.

[24] Forey, 'The Military Orders in the Crusading Proposals of the late-Thirteenth and early-Fourteenth Centuries', *Traditio* 36(1980), pp. 320 *et. seq.*

[25] *CT, Milites Templi Hierosolimitani*, bull no. 8, p. 381 (1144); *CH*, i, no. 1536, p. 211 (1217); ii, no. 2928, pp. 877–878 (1259); iii, no. 3153, pp. 107–108 (1265); for identifications between Crusaders and the Macabees see S. Menache, *The Vox Dei*, New York and London, 1990, pp. 114–115.

and that of the Hospital. His most revealing remark stressed the benefits of their rivalry:

> Item, if one wished to object that to extinguish the rivalry which is said to exist between the Templars and Hospitallers, the two should be fused, I reply that it would be to the greatest detriment of the Holy Land to suppress this rivalry, and would be to the great advantage of the Saracens; for it has always procured honour and advantage to the Christians, and the contrary to the Saracens, because when the Hospitallers ride armed against the Saracens, the Templars have no rest until they have done the same, or more, and *vice versa*.[26]

Elsewhere in his petition he emphasized the competitive stimulus a further three times.[27] Moreover, it would be a mistake to believe that the suppression of the Order of the Temple reflected a disillusionment with Crusade, for the early fourteenth century saw concerted efforts to create a new Order to act as a foil for the Hospital, so that it could once again hone itself by the stimulus of competition.[28] Just as Christendom had fought to regain lost land in the Crusader states before, now the role of the Military Orders was even more crucial, for they had the whole of their former territories to recapture.

More revealing still of the Orders' similarities were the roles Brother James ascribed to the two Orders. He reminded the Holy See that the Hospital was founded to provide hospitality, whilst the Temple was based on military service.[29] Yet, his examples demonstrated how blurred the distinction had become in the matter of the Orders' lives, for he repeatedly spoke of the military activities of the Hospital, and particularly how the two Orders provided the vanguard and rearguards for all military expeditions:

> they covered and enveloped the strangers who lay between them, as a mother with her child.[30]

---

[26] 'Item, si aliquis vellet objicere quod pro extinguenda invidia que inter Templarios et Hospitalarios esse dicitur esset unio facienda, respondeo quod maximum dampnum esset Terre Sancte tollere talem invidiam et ex hoc proveniret magnum commodum Saracenis. Nam talis invidia semper attulit et honorem et commodum Christianis et contrarium Saracenis, quia si Hospitalarii faciebant aliquid bonum exercitium armorum contra Saracenos, Templarii numquam cessabant nisi fecissent tantumdem, vel plus et a converso', James of Molay, *De unione Templi et Hospitalis ordinum*, in *Le Dossier de l'affaire des Templiers*, G. Lizerand (ed.), Paris, 1923, p. 8.

[27] *ibid.*, p. 8.

[28] *Clément VI, 1342–1352, Lettres closes, patentes et curiales se rapportant à la France*, E Déprez (ed.), *Bibliothèque des Ecoles françaises d'Athènes et de Rome* 1, Paris, 1901, no. 341, cols. 129–132 (1343).

[29] 'Nam religio Hospitaliorum super hospitalitate fundata est . . . Templarii vero super milicia proprie sunt fondati', James of Molay, *De unione*, p. 6.

[30] 'et sic extraneos inter ipsos cooperiunt et involvunt sicut mater infantem', *ibid.*, p. 10.

He also emphasized that the Temple was as much of a hospitaller Order as the Hospitallers, for:

> the Lord's pilgrims who come to the Holy Land, whomsoever they might be, great or small, always find refreshment, comfort, help and support with one of the two Orders.[31]

This petition to the Holy See by Brother James has been criticized by modern scholars as the intellectually weak protestations of an aged man, unable to cope with reform and change.[32] Whilst his arguments may not have been of the highest calibre, the overall tenor of the relationship between the Temple and Hospital emerges clearly, as does the public perception of the similarities between the Orders.

Mention will frequently be made in this study to the 'Rules' of the Military Orders. This term is used in its broadest sense to incorporate the Rules proper and various capitular statutes, customs, *esgarts* and *retrais*.[33] It is quite clear that the traditional view that the Hospitaller Rule was of Augustinian origin, and the Templars' was of reformed Cistercian inspiration, is too simplistic.[34] First,

---

[31] 'Item, quicunque peregrini majores Domini vel minores venerunt ad Terram Sanctam, semper invenerunt refrigerium, recreacionem, auxilium et succursum sive ab una sive ab altera religionum,' *ibid.*, p. 10.

[32] H. Prütz, *Die geistlichen Ritterorden, Ihre Stellung zur kirchlichen, politischen, gesellschaflichen und wirtschaftlichen Entwicklung des Mittelalters*, Berlin, 1908, p. 467; M. Barber, 'James of Molay, the last Grand Master of the Order of the Temple', *Studia monastica* 14(1972), p. 106; Demurger, *Temple*, pp. 283–285; Barber, *Knighthood*, pp. 284–294; *cf.* Forey, 'The Military Orders in the Crusading Proposals', p. 324.

[33] The Rule of the Temple has been published in *RTemp.*; L. Daillez, *La Règle du Temple*, Nice, 1977 is a beautiful work comprising photographs of the entire Bruges ms. as well as various other documents relating to the Order. His translations are not wholly reliable. The constituent parts of the Rule of the Hospital appear in *CH, passim*.

[34] For the Hospitaller Rule and its links with the Rule of Saint Augustine see Riley-Smith, *Knights*, pp. 46, 48–9; J. Delaville le Roulx, *Les Hospitaliers en Terre Sainte et à Chypre (1100–1310)*, Paris, 1904, p. 32; M. Ambraziejuté, *Studien über die Johanniterregel*, Freiburg, 1929, pp. 6–7. There is medieval authority for this view, 'Postea de mandato Honorii papæ patriarcha Stephanus statuit eis regulam B. Augustini canonicorum regularium tenendam, et habitum albam sine cruce', John of Ypres, *Chronicon*, III, col. 427. The relationship between the Rule of the Templars and the Rule of Saint Benedict has been analysed by G. Schnürer, *Die ursprüngliche Templerregel*, Freiburg, 1933, pp. 130–153; P. Cousin, 'Les Débuts de l'ordre des Templiers et Saint-Bernard', *Melanges Saint Bernard, XXIVe congrès de l'association Bourguignonne des sociétés savantes*, Dijon, 1953, p. 44. The main works on the Rule of the Temple, in addition to Schnürer, are H. Prütz, *Die Anatomie der Templerordens*, Sitzungsberichte der Münchner Academie, 1903; Dr Knöpfler, 'Die Ordensregel der Tempelherren', *Historisches Jahrbuch* 8(1877), pp. 666–695; J. Gmelin, 'Die Regel des Templeordens kritisch untersucht', *Mitteilungen des Instituts für Österreichische Geschichsforschung* 14(1893), pp. 237–284.

there is the problem of the identity and status of the Rule of Saint Augustine itself in the central Middle Ages.[35] It must then be accepted that there are traces of the Augustinian Rule in the Templars',[36] and of the Benedictine Rule in the Rule of the Hospitallers.[37] Further, the Rules of both Military Orders bear traces of each other, as well as of their respective sources.[38] This is not remarkable. Even Rules of thirteenth century non-military hospitaller Orders reflect an affinity with the Rule of the Temple.[39]

It is unsurprising that the Orders cast their nets wide in seeking inspiration

[35] 'on ne sait plus aujourd'hui, même dans le monde de l'érudition, en quoi consiste ou a consisté la règle de Saint Augustin', P. Mandonnet, *Saint Dominique, l'idée, l'homme et l'œuvre*, II, Paris, 1937, p. 107. However, it is accepted that to medieval people the Austin Rule meant the *Regula secunda* and the *Regula tertia*, which can be found in *RA*.

[36] The Templar Primitive Rule evinces none of the spiritual guidance of the Rule of Saint Benedict. Of direct similarities there are seven: the taking of counsel (*RB*, cap. 3, pp. 178–180 and *RTemp.*, cap. 36, pp. 42–43), obedience to the master (*RB*, cap. 5, pp. 186–190 and *RTemp.*, cap. 39, pp. 44–45), the nocturnal candle in the dormitory (*RB*, cap. 22, p. 218 and *RTemp.*, cap. 21, pp. 31–32), the prohibition on association with the excommunicate (*RB*, cap. 26, p. 222 and *RTemp.*, cap. 12, pp. 23–4), the respect for the elderly (*RB*, cap. 37, pp. 234–236 and *RTemp.*, cap. 60, pp. 60–61), the permission to drink wine (*RB*, cap. 40, pp. 238–240 and *RTemp.*, cap. 30, pp. 38–39) and the keeping of silence after Compline (*RB*, cap. 42, p. 242 and *RTemp.*, cap. 31, pp. 39–40). For the Templar Rule and its links with the Rule of Saint Benedict and the Cistercians see Schnürer, *Templerregel*, p. 57; *The Rule of the Templars*, J. Upton-Ward (ed. and tr.), Woodbridge, 1992, p. 3; *RTemp*, p. xj; see also *Monasticon Anglicanum*, W. Dugdale (ed.), VI, London, 1830, p. 814 for the belief that the Templar Rule is Austin.

[37] Whilst the broad variety of Austin hospitaller Rules attests to the breadth of possible interpretations, the number of articles in the Rule of Brother Raymond of Le Puy which are strictly Austin are few. Of the fifteen probable original articles, only the commandments to embrace poverty (*CH*, I, *Rule of Brother Raymond of Le Puy*, no. 70, cap. 1, pp. 62–3), always to go about in pairs (*ibid.*, cap. 4, p. 63), not wear bright clothes (*ibid.*, cap. 8, p. 64), keep silence at the table (*ibid.*, cap. 11, pp. 63–64) and attempt to correct brothers amongst themselves before approaching the master (*ibid.*, cap. 12, pp. 65–66) are directly traceable to the Rule of Saint Augustin, whereas of the remainder, only cap. 17 (*ibid.*, p. 67), an elaborated form of the correctional cap. 12 (*ibid.*, pp. 65–66), bears any resemblance to the Rule of Saint Augustin. It was not, in fact, uncommon, for Austin Rules to bear traces of the Rule of Saint Benedict, C. Lawrence, *Medieval Monasticism*, London and New York, 1989, p. 166. See also Ambraziejuté, *Johanniterregel*, pp. 7–9; *Statuts d'hotels-Dieu et de léproseries*, L. Le Grand (ed.), Paris, 1904, p. vii.

[38] *RTemp.*, p. xi; Riley-Smith, *Knights*, p. 49, admits that Cîteaux may have had an influence on the Rule of the Hospital, but points to only one similarity between the Rules of the Military Orders; but *ibid.*, p. 51 states that parts of the Rule of Raymond of Le Puy were drawn up in 'an environment conditioned by Cistercian Clairvaux . . . and influenced by the growth of the Templars'.

[39] 'Fratres sint tonsurati ut Templarii, sorores ut moniales', Statutes of the Paris hotel-Dieu (c.1220), in *Statuts*, cap. 8, p. 44; 'fratres vero laici tonsorati sint velut Templarii', Statutes of the Hotel-Dieu-le-Comte at Troyes (1263), *ibid.*, p. 105.

for their Rules. The Rule of Saint Benedict alone was too restrictive. Monks had to profess stability of location and obedience to an abbot.[40] Moreover, on a structural scale, one of the fundamental precepts of the Rule of Saint Benedict was that it was a sacred, untouchable rule by which all were bound.[41] Yet, the Templar master needed to be able to vary the Order's rule, a power expressly granted to him.[42] Likewise, the Hospitaller Rule of Master Raymond of Le Puy claimed no authority save that Raymond, a layman, had 'instituted these precepts and statutes'.[43] The Military Orders were not looking back to a conception of religious purity alone; the Templars defined their purpose: to create an *ordo militaris*,[44] and Saint Bernard was sure that what had been created was not a revived form of religious life, but something unprecedented: 'a new knighthood'.[45]

The Hospitallers were initially less innovative than the Templars in their written regulations. The first surviving Hospitaller Rule, the Rule of Master Raymond of Le Puy (1120–1158x60), was drawn up in the period during which the Hospital became militarized.[46] Although the original Rule of Brother Gerard (1099–1120) was probably Benedictine in inspiration,[47] Brother Raymond's Rule can only be dated to 1120x1153,[48] a period when the Order was becoming as militarized as the Temple. James of Vitry (c.1160x70–1240) described this process:

> For the aforesaid brothers of the Hospital, in imitation of the brothers of the knighthood of the Temple, have taken up physical arms, receiving knights and sergeants into their Order.[49]

---

[40] 'promittat de stabilitate sua et conversatione morum suorum et obœdientia', *RB*, cap. 58, p. 268.

[41] 'Ecce lex sub qua militare vis; si potes observare, ingredere; si vero non potes, liber discede', *RB*, cap. 58, pp. 266–267; Lawrence, *Monasticism*, pp. 27–28.

[42] 'Tous les comandemens qui sont dis et ecris dessus en ceste presente regle sont en la discretion et en l'esgart dou Maistre', *RTemp., Primitive Rule*, cap. 73, p. 71.

[43] 'statui hec precepta et statuta', *CH*, i, *Rule of Brother Raymond of Le Puy*, no. 70, p. 62.

[44] 'In ipsa namque refloruit iam et revixit ordo militaris', *RTemp., Primitive Rule*, cap. 2, p. 12.

[45] 'Novum militiæ genus ortum nuper auditur in terris', Bernard of Clairvaux, *Liber ad milites Templi de laude novæ militiæ*, in *Sources Chrétiennes* 367, P.-Y. Emery (ed.), Paris, 1990, book 1, ch. 1, p. 50.

[46] Delaville le Roulx, *Les Hospitaliers*, pp. 44–47; Riley-Smith, *Knights*, pp. 52–59; A. Forey, 'The Militarisation of the Hospital of Saint John', *Studia monastica* 26(1984), pp. 75–89.

[47] Riley-Smith, *Knights*, p. 50.

[48] Brother Raymond of Le Puy acceded to the magistracy in 1120. The *Cronica magistrorum defunctorum* recounted that the Rule was confirmed by Pope Eugenius III, whose pontificate ended in 1153, *Monasticon*, vi(ii), 1830, p. 796.

[49] 'Prædicti enim Hospitalis fratres, ad imitationem fratrum militiæ Templi, armis

and scholars accept the influence of the Temple on the Hospital in this matter.[50]

The rivalry between the Orders does not preclude the possibility of influence between the Orders. Competitiveness between siblings does not deny their common ancestry, and might even be the greatest indicator of similarities. This study argues for such a state of inter-relationship between the Temple and Hospital, and bases the comparison on information drawn from records of their daily lives in an area which constituted a central zone for their European implantation and activity.

This study dwells on a variety of focal points. As a prerequisite to any discussion of the Military Orders, an examination of Occitanian society permits an understanding of why it was likely to have attracted, and been responsive to, the Orders. This focuses on the factors mentioned above, but also discusses other areas. Thus, the impact of the Iberian *Reconquista* on Occitanian society is examined, as are the roles the Military Orders came to play in it. The Albigensian Crusade is also addressed, for the predominant non-activity of the Templars and Hospitallers in the Languedoc is anomalous (chapter one).

A chronology of the Military Orders' move to Occitania demonstrates two principal factors. The Orders settled Occitania quickly, and did so very shortly after their foundations. The detailed charting of the waves of activity which constituted this settlement demonstrates that both Orders wished to establish houses in the politically and religiously important urban centre, as well as the agricultural hinterland of central-southern Occitania. Moreover, the Military Orders settled areas controlled by all the rival factions in Occitania, thus ingratiating themselves with the Roman Empire, the counts of Toulouse, the counts of Barcelona, and the lesser viscomital families such as the Trencavel and the Baux (chapter two).

The relationship between the Church, both secular and monastic, and the Military Orders is of prime interest in assessing the attitude of the established religious communities towards these near-Eastern creations. It demonstrates that the sour relationship presumed to exist between the Church and the

materialibus utentes, milites cum servientibus in suo collegio receperunt', James of Vitry, *Historia Hierosolymitana*, in *Gesta Dei per Francos*, J. Bongars (ed.), book 65, p. 1084.
[50] Forey, *Orders*, p. 20; Riley-Smith, *Knights*, p. 54 notes that this was probable, but suggests that the Templars may well not have been in a condition to exert an influence at this date, but see D. Selwood, '*Quidam autem dubitaverunt*: The Saint, the Sinner, the Temple and a Possible Chronology', *Autour de la première croisade, Actes du colloque de la Society for the Study of the Crusades and the Latin East (Clermont-Ferrand, 22–25 juin 1995)*, M. Balard (ed.), Paris, 1996, pp. 221–230 and Forey, 'Militarisation', who believes that the Templars played a role; see also E. King, *The Knights Hospitallers in the Holy Land*, London, 1931, p. 37; J. Prawer, *The Latin Kingdom of Jerusalem*, London, 1972, p. 253.

Military Orders is an over simplification, for a distinction between the secular clergy and the monastic religious is necessary. The former was on broadly amicable terms with the Military Orders, sometimes markedly so, whilst the latter attempted to curtail the fostering of deep relationships between the laity and the Military Orders, for such relationships were losing the monasteries their highly valued *spiritualia* (chapter three).

The relationships the Orders fostered with the laity are also discussed at length, and permit an insight into the hearts and priorities of the people of Occitania. A picture emerges of a people strongly attached to Crusade and pilgrimage, and welcoming to the Military Orders, with which they found an affinity. This comes across in the success of the Orders' recruitment policies, the numbers of the laity who sought to participate in the spiritual benefits the Orders could offer, and their general popularity as the objects of pious donations. This was all nurtured by the Military Orders' insistence on local recruitment. Such discussion yields a picture of a society firmly attached to the idea of Crusade, and of the opportunities afforded by the Military Orders in their role as representatives of the Crusader states (chapter four).

The hierarchies and administrative systems developed by the Orders are of key interest in demonstrating their particular and specific needs. Unlike other religious Orders, the Military Orders were international concerns with a need for responsive and efficient methods of communication between Jerusalem and Europe. The structures and models they developed evince their innovation in creating unprecedented systems of organization suited to their requirements. At a more localized level, discussion of their structures permits the examination of a previously unstudied area: the Courts of the Commanders, tribunals in which the local commanders of the Temple and Hospital exercised various seigneurial jurisdictions (chapter five).

The purpose of all the European activities of the Military and Religious Orders, their fundamental *raison d'être*, is then examined. The commodities they shipped to the Outremer are discussed, as are the primary methods by which they raised their income. This demonstrates that whilst the Military Orders were fully integrated into Europe as monastic religious, they had a constant eye on the needs and demands of the Crusader states, and accordingly tended to the provisions required by their brethren fighting the Crusades (chapter six).

Whilst a commandery was a place where brethren lived a religious life together, it was also the focal point of their efforts. Often fortified and well guarded, it controlled the surrounding lands belonging to the Order. Urban commanderies were show-pieces, where visiting dignitaries could be entertained. Rural commanderies were essentially farms, but nevertheless were built around a chapel where the brethren heard the daily Offices. A tour around one such rural house, Saint Eulalia, concludes this study by a portrait of the buildings, and a description of the property to be found within its walls (chapter seven).

Conclusions follow and bring out an emphasis on the Orders' requirement to elaborate and create systems and practices which suited their particular, and quite specific, needs. Their European mission was unprecedented, for they needed to make themselves attractive and effective as religious houses, but also to promote Crusade and encourage awareness of the Crusader states. To achieve this effectively they had to appeal to several social groups simultaneously: to the great comital houses, to the bishops and to neighbouring monastic houses, to the merchants and town-dwellers and to the rural populations. A study of the Military Orders' achievements is therefore of necessity an exploration into Occitanian society.

This study, therefore, straddles various divisions within medieval history. It combines the disciplines of Crusade history, Church history, and social history in such a way as to give the fullest possible account of the lives led by the European brethren of the Military Orders, and their reception into one European society.

CHAPTER I

Central-Southern Occitania

Segnour Jèsu,
Tu qu'as clafi de pèis li fielat de tis Aposto,
Tu qu'as fa camin sus lis aigo de la mar,
Tu qu'as fa cala la tempèsto:
benessisse nosto mar.
Ansin se chalaran li pescaire,
e li navigaire faran si viage dins la bono,
aro, e toustème, vers li siècle di siècle. Amen

Quaqui benedicioun: De la mar, in *Missau e rituau
en lengo nostro*, Traductions officielles AEL (ed.),
Marseille, 1976, p. 257

Throughout the twelfth and thirteenth centuries the Military Orders settled and established close relationships with local communities throughout Christendom. Of those areas in Europe to which the Orders moved, one stood out as having a privileged status: Occitania. The aim of this chapter is two-fold. It describes the many facets of Occitania and Occitanian culture, and suggests why the Military Orders were attracted to it. This is effected through a geographical description of Occitania, a survey of its powerful comital families, and an overview of its religious links with the Holy Land. The emphasis then moves to a discussion of the Military Orders' involvement in the *Reconquista* and Albigensian Crusade.

Geography and Economy

Occitania, a medieval term,[1] was the land stretching from the mouth of the river Ebro in the Iberian peninsula, around the Gulf of the Lion, and on to the Ligurian Gulf. It not only hugged the coast, but stretched north beyond Clermont and Le Puy. The Pyrenees were not a frontier, as can be seen by an 1187

---

[1] It gained widespread use in the fourteenth century, L. Paterson, *The World of the Troubadours*, Cambridge, 1993, p. 3.

letter from King Guy of Jerusalem to the 'men of the provincial parts from Marseille to Barcelona'.[2] Yet, although Catalonia should be included in a political map of Occitania, it was not a part of linguistic Occitania,[3] a land defined and confined by its people's language: the romance language of Oc.[4] From *Niço* (Nice) to *Baiouno* (Bayonne), and *Marsiho* (Marseille) to *Engoulèime* (Angoulême), the language of Occitan was spoken, albeit with variations in dialect.

This study explores central-southern Occitania, concentrating on the lands around the Gulf of the Lion, essentially the Languedoc and Provence. This was a land of geographical extremes. From the alluvial plains of the Albigeois and Lauraguais, the limestone plateaux of the Aveyron, the fertile Vaucluse, the tough inhospitableness of the Camargue, the undulations of the Lubéron, Alpilles, Trévarasse and Nerthe, and the harshness of the 3,000-metre Provençal Alps, the fundamental of central-southern Occitania was its variety. In Toulouse the prevailing weather was Atlantic, foggy and wet.[5] Past the mountains to the east, in the Aude valley olives were as much a part of the economy as around the Gulf of the Lion and along the Côte d'Azur, where the vegetation was strongly Mediterranean. Journeying eastward from the Rhône the fertile plains gave way to the foothills of the Alps, with Aix-en-Provence marking the turning point. The weather here was sun soaked in summer, dry and dusty. But, violent storms in the autumn were commonplace around the Rhône, and west of Toulon the *Mistral* had free reign. The climate and land-scape ensured that the economy was based on the vine, the olive and wheat,[6] although dyed woollen cloth, honey and furs were produced and exported. Yet, the fertile soil of the region was limited by the mountainous terrain of the various ranges which penned in Occitania, leaving the most fertile areas in the Garonne and Aude valleys, the Rhône delta and the Alpine tributaries.[7] Mirroring the geographical diversity of Occitania was the variety of the composition of its peoples, for once stability had returned after the barbarian invasions

---

[2] 'homines provincialium partium a Massilia usque Barchinonam', A. Germain, *Histoire du commerce de Montpellier*, I, Montpellier, 1861, p. 180.

[3] R. Lafont, *Histoire d'Occitanie*, Paris, 1979, pp. xi–xv; Paterson, *World*, pp. 1–3.

[4] Its Romance or neo-Latin cognates are French, Catalan, Franco-Provençal, Castilian, Portuguese, Italian, Sardinian, Romanian, Rheto-Romansh and Dalmatian, Paterson, *World*, p. 2.

[5] J. Madaule, *Le Drame albigeois et l'unité française*, Saint-Amand, 1973, p. 23.

[6] R. Busquet, *Histoire de Provence des origines à la révolution française*, Monaco, 1954, pp. 17–22.

[7] A. Lewis, 'Patterns of Economic Development in Southern France, 1050–1271', *Studies in Medieval and Renaissance History* 3(1980), p. 58.

which had ended Roman rule, Jews, Greeks and Syrians had all re-established themselves throughout its trading centres.[8]

The main resource in the Occitanian economy was the Mediterranean. It yielded salt, traded in many places along the coast, particularly at Hyères, Aigues-Mortes, Peccais, Les Saintes-Maries-de-la-Mer and La Vernède.[9] This rivalled the main trade in wine and grain.[10] But, the strongest point of the Occitanian economy was its maritime activity, for Occitania boasted the most active ports to the west of the Alps. In the twelfth century ships could be put to sea from Perpignan, Narbonne, Sérignan (the port of Béziers), Agde, Frontignan, Montpellier, Saint-Gilles, Martigues, Toulon, Nice, Villefranche and, most importantly, from the giant sister cities of Barcelona and Marseille. Moreover, the maritime economy of Occitania was more stable than that of the Italian peninsula, where political disunity made the soliciting of privileges complicated, and commercial relationships less secure. For example, the Order of the Temple found itself denied access to the Adriatic in 1220 owing to disputes with Emperor Frederick II.[11]

Competition with the Italian peninsula was nevertheless fierce. As early as 1109 the Genoese attempted to gain a monopoly on river trade between Saint-Gilles and the Mediterranean, a privilege refused them by the count of Saint-Gilles.[12] In 1150 the Genoese tried to prevent the merchants of Narbonne, Montpellier and Marseille from trading by sea, and in 1154 they procured a ban on all Provençal ships docking in Sicily.[13] Although Marseille and Barcelona dominated trade, such Genoese activity demonstrates the importance of traffic from the lesser ports. Arles, for example, had a strong tradition of maritime trade going back to Classical Antiquity and Celto-Ligurian times, and in 921 Emperor 'Louis the Blind' had ratified the right of the Arlésians to collect tolls from Greeks and Jews at its harbour.[14] In the twelfth century it was one of the

---

[8] R.-H. Bautier, *The Economic Development of Medieval Europe*, H. Karolyi (tr.), London, 1971, p. 22.

[9] A. Dupont, 'L'Exploitation du sel sur les étangs de Languedoc (ixe–xiiie siècles)', *AM* 70(1958), pp. 7–25; *idem*, 'Un Aspect du commerce du sel en Languedoc oriental au xiiie siècle: la Rivalité entre Lunel et Aigues-Mortes', *PH* 18(1968), pp. 101–112.

[10] Bautier, *Economic*, p. 218. In the fourteenth century some 25,000 tons *per annum* were being produced in Provence, *ibid.*, p. 219.

[11] Barber, *Knighthood*, p. 238.

[12] Bautier, *Economic*, p. 104 states that it was Count Raymond of Saint-Gilles who refused this petition. This is not possible. Raymond died in 1105. The Count in 1109 was his son, Bertrand.

[13] *ibid.*, p. 104.

[14] *ibid.*, p. 70.

largest cities in Provence, having some six thousand inhabitants at the end of the century, served by around twenty charitable hospitals.[15]

In central-southern Occitania the key port was Marseille, the *ville Phocéene*. Founded by Phoceans around the *Lagune de Lacydon* over half a millennium before Christ,[16] it was protected on its landward side by the mountains of the Chaîne de l'Etoile, and from the sea by the islands of If, Saint-Etienne (now Ratonneau) and Pommègues. Its maritime tradition stretched back to c.600 B.C., and had survived the city's destruction by Gaius Julius Cæsar in 49 B.C.[17] Rebuilt, it weathered the break up of the Roman Empire, and in the time of Saint Gregory the Great (590–604) it was booming. The seventh century *Gesta Dagoberti* recorded that monks from as far afield as Saint-Denis came here to collect oil for lighting their church.[18] It has for long been the only non-Italian medieval city to be ranked in importance for its maritime trade along with Genoa, Pisa and Venice, although it has been suggested that the intensity of Marseillais trade has been over-emphasized.[19] Whatever the extent of its mercantile activities, its maritime traffic in humans, principally pilgrims, was highly developed, particularly after the Second Crusade. It was, after all, from Marseille that the two merchants, Hugh Fer and William Porc, exploited the 1212 Children's Crusade.[20] Marseille was a significant trading centre, and amongst the principal imports can be listed luxury goods such as spices, sugar, silks, incense and Egyptian cotton.[21]

The Military Orders quickly came to appreciate the maritime possibilities afforded by the Gulf of the Lion. They were not alone, for the Capetians lost

---

[15] G. Giordanengo, 'Les Hôpitaux arlésiens du XIIe au XIVe siècle', *CF* 13(1976), pp. 189, 192.

[16] F. Benoit *et al.*, *Villes épiscopales de Provence: Aix, Arles, Fréjus, Marseille et Riez de l'époque gallo-romaine au moyen-age*, Paris, 1954, p. 34.

[17] *ibid.*, p. 34.

[18] *Gesta Dagoberti*, in *MGHSS rerum Merovingicarum* 2, B. Krush (ed.), ch. 18, p. 406.

[19] These doubts are based on the dubious authenticity of the pre-1187 Marseillais privileges in Acre, D. Abulafia, 'Marseilles, Acre and the Mediterranean, 1200–1291', *Coinage in the Latin East: the Fourth Oxford Symposium on Coinage and Monetary History*, P. Edbury and D. Metcalf (eds.), Oxford, 1980, pp. 19–39; H. Mayer, *Marseilles Levantehandel und ein akkonensisches Fälscheratelier des* XIII. *Jahrhunderts*, Tübingen, 1972; E. Baratier, 'Marquisat et comtés en Provence', *Histoire de la Provence*, E. Baratier (ed.), Toulouse, 1969, p. 145.

[20] Aubri of Trois Fontaines, *Chronica*, in *MGHSS* 23, G.-H. Pertz (ed.), pp. 893–894. Generally, H. Mayer, *The Crusades*, J. Gillingham (tr.), Oxford, 1972, pp. 202–205; C. Pallenberg, *La Crociata dei bambini*, Milan, 1983; N. Zacour, 'The Children's Crusade', *A History of the Crusades*, K. Setton (ed.), II, Madison, Milwaukee and London, 1969, pp. 325–342.

[21] Y. Dossat, 'La Société méridionale à la veille de la croisade albigeoise', *Revue historique et littéraire de Languedoc* 1(1944), pp. 76–81.

little time in developing holdings in Occitania following their conquests in the Albigensian campaigns. Narbonne, then on the river Aude, became a Capetian favourite, and in 1241 Saint Louis founded the port of Aigues-Mortes on land belonging to the abbey of Psalmodi,[22] departing from there in both 1248 for the Egypt campaign, and in 1270 for Tunis.[23] Aigues-Mortes had a strong role as a valve for trade in the remainder of the thirteenth century, for the Capetians attempted to make it the national trading port on the Gulf. Italian merchants seeking to do business as far afield as Champagne were required to bring their produce into Capetian lands at Aigues-Mortes, and store it at Nîmes. Aigues-Mortes had become Catalan-Montpellier's Capetian rival.[24]

With regard to pilgrimage and Crusading, ports in Occitania were an ideal point of departure, for the passage from the Gulf of the Lion to the Holy Land took only around a month, ships travelling at an average speed of six or seven knots, more in the favourable summer conditions typified by dry weather and moderate winds. Sailing was possible in winter, but strong winds and gales made it ill advised, especially in January.[25] For Military Orders which wished for a European centre of operations, and to keep naval contact with both the Latins in Outremer and with the Christians engaged in the Iberian *Reconquista*, no area could have suggested itself so well.

Political Power

Although the Pyrenees were a geographical border, they were not a political frontier,[26] for the two great power bases of Occitania were the counties of Barcelona and Toulouse. Both had large interests as far east as Provence, and wars between them over property and influence were a common feature of the twelfth century.[27] As with the comital houses of Cerdagne, Narbonne, Béziers

[22] A. Fliche, *Aigues-Mortes et Saint-Gilles*, Paris, 1934, p. 5. See J. Le Goff, *Saint Louis*, Paris, 1996 for an exposition of Saint Louis' view of the importance of the Mediterranean.
[23] C. Dufourcq, *La Vie quotidienne dans les ports méditerranéens au moyen age (Provence, Languedoc, Catalogne)*, Biarritz, 1975, p. 20.
[24] Bautier, *Economic*, p. 117.
[25] R. Morris (Rear Admiral), *The Hydrographer of the Navy, Ocean Passages for the World*, Crown Copyright, 1987, pp. 56–58; valuable opinions from Captain O. Selwood (Merchant Navy, Extra Master).
[26] J. Ventura, *Alfons el Cast*, Barcelona, 1961, has stressed the unity of the Catalano-Occitan empire by its geography, economy and demography; as has S. P. Bensch, *Barcelona and its Rulers, 1096–1291*, Cambridge, 1995, pp. 1, 402–403, and generally for cultural and mercantile links pp. 82, 118, 166, 211, 228–229, 213, 278, 288, 293, 296, 300, 315; *cf.* R. d'Abdal, 'A Propos de la domination de la maison de Barcelone sur le Midi français', *AM* 76(1964), pp. 315–316.
[27] J. Dunbabin, *France in the Making, 843–1180*, Oxford, 1985, p. 299.

and Foix, the house of Barcelona was at root Occitanian, descended from Roger I 'the Old' of Carcassonne (d.1002).[28] Although the Iberian counts used men from the west of the Pyrenees as their representatives in Occitania,[29] few Spaniards settled in hostile cities such as Toulouse.[30]

By the death of Count Raymond IV of Toulouse of Saint Gilles (1088–1105), the principal possessions of the house of Toulouse were the county of Toulouse itself, the duchy of Narbonne (the old Carolingian marquisate of Septimania, comprising the dioceses of Narbonne, Béziers, Agde, Carcassonne, Lodève, Maguelone, Nîmes and Uzès),[31] and the marquisate of Provence, which embraced all land between the Rhône, Isère, Durance and the Alps. Additionally, Count Raymond IV had received half of the bishoprics of Nîmes, Argence and Saint-Gilles from his father, and before becoming count of Toulouse had fashioned the county of Saint-Gilles out of these lands.

When he succeeded his brother to the county of Toulouse in 1088, Raymond IV kept as his major title 'count of Saint-Gilles', despite its relative insignificance beside that of the county of Toulouse. To the Arab chronicler 'Izz-al-Dīn ibn al-Athīr (1160–1234), he was simply S̱andjīl.[32] By the dawn of the First Crusade Raymond had campaigned in the Iberian peninsula,[33] and was ruler of thirteen counties.[34] As one of the richest men in Europe he was without doubt the 'uncrowned king of the Midi'[35] and certainly the richest Crusader, *Christiane milicie excellentissimus princeps*,[36] leading the largest host. Although he never saw Occitania again, he did not forget it, for he gifted property in his newly won lands in Outremer to those still in Provence.[37]

Crusading links between the counts of Toulouse and the Holy Land

---

[28] *ibid.*, p. 171; d'Abdal, 'A Propos', table pp. 322–323.

[29] M. Aurell i Cardona, 'Le Personnel politique Catalan et Aragonais d'Alphonse ier en Provence (1166–1196)', *AM* 93(1981), pp. 138–139.

[30] C. Higounet, 'Le Peuplement de Toulouse au xiie siècle', *AM* 55(1943), p. 493.

[31] This came to Count Raymond IV by his 1066 marriage with the daughter of Count Bertrand I of Provence, *L'Art de vérifier les dates*, a Benedictine (ed.), ii, Paris, 1784, pp. 294–295.

[32] Ibn al-Athīr, *al-Kāmil fi at-Ta'rīkh*, in *RHC Or.* 1, *passim*.

[33] There is no direct evidence of this, but it is thought more likely than not, J and L. Hill, *Raymond IV Count of Toulouse*, Syracuse, 1962, pp. 19–20; R. Lejeune, 'L'Esprit de croisade dans l'épopée occitane', *CF* 4(1969), p. 166 claims that Raymond IV led a host into the Iberian peninsula.

[34] *ibid.*, p. 166.

[35] Hill, *Raymond IV*, p. 3.

[36] J. and L. Hill, 'Justification historique du titre de Raymond de Saint-Gilles: "Christiane milicie excellentissimus princeps" ', *AM* 66(1954), pp. 102–112.

[37] *GCN(Marseille)*, no. 1086, col. 689 (1103).

remained strong for a generation after the death of Count Raymond. Count Bertrand (1105–1112), Raymond's son by his first wife, emigrated to the Holy Land in 1109, and handed over the great house of Tripoli to his son, Count Pons. Raymond's second son by his third wife, Elvira, was born Outremer, in the castle of Mount Pilgrim.[38] Baptized in the Jordan, he took the name Count Alfonso Jordan (1112–1148). He was at Vézelay in 1146 where he took the Cross. He departed for the Holy Land in 1147 and, after a spell in Italy, arrived in Acre. Pausing at Cæsarea whilst on his way to Jerusalem, he died, suddenly, of an acute illness. Many suspected poison administered by Queen Melisende.[39]

There were many claims to the county of Toulouse through Carolingian ancestry, and Counts Alfonso Jordan and Raymond V (1148–1194) had to repel repeated attacks by the counts of Poitiers and the royal families of both France and England,[40] notably in a sustained campaign by King Richard I of England.[41] The most frequent participants in these wars were the counts of Barcelona, who allied themselves with the aggressors. There was no love lost between Toulouse and Barcelona, who waged a particularly acrimonious war over Provence for more than a century.[42] The rivalry began in 1112 when Count Raymond Berenger III 'the Great' of Barcelona (1093–1131) married Dolça (daughter of Viscount Gilbert of Milhaud and Gévaudan, and of Countess Gerberge of Provence), who brought him the county of Provence and the suzerainty of Carcassonne as a dowry.[43] This new territory comprised the land east of the Petit-Rhône, west of the Turbie and south of the Durance, as well as half of the cities of Avignon, Sorgues, Caumont and Le Thor in the marquisate of Provence.

Conflict over these lands ensued, but the house of Toulouse was weakened by the minority of the young Alfonso Jordan, restrained under the tutelage of

---

[38] S. Runciman, *A History of the Crusades*, Harmondsworth, II, p. 61.

[39] *ibid.*, II, p. 280. An alternative view was taken by his son, Count Bertrand, who accused Count Raymond of Tripoli, *ibid.*, p. 280.

[40] Dunbabin, *France*, p. 301.

[41] Richard had first begun the attacks against Count Raymond V. They continued against Count Raymond VI (1194–1222), and were not concluded until 1196, when Richard renounced his claims to Toulouse, and gave Count Raymond VI his sister, Joanna, in marriage. For a detailed analysis of the struggles inherited by Richard from his father King Henry II, and the background to the peace of 1196, see R. Benjamin, 'A Forty Years War: Toulouse and the Plantagenets, 1156–96', *Historical Research, The Bulletin of the Institute of Historical Research*, 61(1988), pp. 270–285. Joanna brought Count Raymond the Agenais as a dowry, T. Bisson, *Medieval France and her Pyrenean Neighbours*, London, 1989, p. 4.

[42] Baratier, 'Marquisat', p. 135.

[43] Bensch, *Barcelona*, pp. 117, 223; Bisson, *Medieval Crown*, p. 26; *L'Art de vérifier*, II, pp. 295, 436.

Count William IX of Aquitaine.[44] When he attained his majority in 1119 Count Alfonso Jordan revolted against his tutor, and attacked the by now consolidated Catalan holdings in Provence,[45] land which the counts and nobles of Barcelona viewed as a substitute for their losses in al-Andalus.[46] In 1125 Counts Alfonso Jordan and Raymond Berenger III (now also Raymond Berenger I of Provence) concluded a treaty by which Provence was divided for the very first time. Large parts of the dioceses of Avignon, Vaison, Cavaillon, Carpentras, Orange, Saint-Paul-Trois-Châteaux, Valence and Dié were retained by the house of Toulouse, whilst all that was south of the Durance and east of the Rhône passed to Barcelona.[47] On the death of Raymond Berenger, the cadet branch of his family under his younger son, Berenger Raymond (1131–1144), acceded to the county of Provence, whilst his elder son, Raymond Berenger IV 'the Saint', retained the county of Barcelona.[48]

Although land around the Rhône, and specially in the Camargue, was often contested by the two houses, all that lay south of the Durance between Arles and Nice was under the control of Catalan-Barcelona, following the same borders as it had under the Roman Empire.[49] Other Provençal cities were later added to the Catalan possessions, but by that branch of the comital family of Barcelona which had become the royal house of Aragon, not the cadet Provençal branch. For instance, in 1204 Peter II 'the Catholic', count of Barcelona and king of Aragon, married Mary of Montpellier, and so brought this city, too, under Catalan control.[50] Thus, in the early thirteenth century, Barcelona controlled the three great maritime cities of Barcelona, Marseille and Montpellier.[51]

Although the counts of Toulouse and Barcelona had made peace over Provence in 1125, within forty years Barcelona went to war over it again; for the viscounts of Marseille (the family of Baux) were perennially in revolt over the control of their land, which stretched from Marseille to Aix, and Brignolles to Toulon.[52] The power-base of Barcelona was too far away for the

---

44 Baratier, 'Marquisat', p. 136.

45 ibid., p. 136.

46 Bensch, Barcelona, pp. 117, 170.

47 Bisson, Medieval Crown, p. 26; L'Art de vérifier, II, pp. 297, 436.

48 F. Portal, La République marseillaise du XIIIe siècle, Marseille, 1907, p. 214; L'Art de vérifier, II, p. 295; Bisson, Medieval Crown, p. 27.

49 Receuil des actes des comtes de Provence appartenant à la maison de Barcelona, F. Benoit (ed.), I, Paris, 1925, p. xxiv.

50 Bisson, Medieval Crown, p. 38. In the ninth century there were two villages, Montpellier and Montpellieret, on the site of Montpellier. Its period of real development was in the twelfth and thirteenth centuries, J. Russell, Medieval Demography, New York, 1987, p. 156.

51 Bensch, Barcelona, p. 279.

52 ibid., p. 224; J.-P. Poly, La Provence et la société féodale (879–1166), Paris, 1976, pp. 325–329; Baratier, 'Marquisat', pp. 133, 138.

control of the Catalans to be effective, and their suzerainty was thus nominal. Peace was broken when Frederick II, overlord of the county of Provence, invested the Baux with the county over the claims of the counts of Barcelona. Accordingly, Raymond Berenger IV rode east to Provence in 1159 to support the claim of the cadet branch of his family; and he died on this campaign in 1162.[53] Three years later the Empire resumed its support of the claims of Barcelona in Provence.[54]

Relationships between Toulouse and Barcelona were often strained, yet an alliance struck between Peter II of Barcelona and Count Raymond VI of Toulouse in the early thirteenth century grouped them against Simon of Montfort.[55] After the death of King Peter at the battle of Muret (1213), the Catalan county of Provence gave the count of Toulouse much needed support against the French invaders,[56] for the Albigensian Crusade had clearly become a question of the independence of Occitania, more than a religious war.[57] The situation was complicated by the presence of the Trencavel clan, the viscounts of Carcassonne and Béziers. This family held a wedge of land from Albi to Perpignan, and from Castelnaudary to Agde, cutting through the territories of the count of Toulouse.

The viscounty of Carcassonne had become disputed between the houses of Barcelona and Toulouse in the late eleventh century, and in 1112, the year of his marriage to Dolça of Provence, Count Raymond Berenger III of Barcelona travelled to Carcassonne to persuade Viscount Bernard Atton IV (d.1130) to pay proper homage to Barcelona.[58] Yet, it was only following the death of the viscount that Barcelona succeeded in imposing its will.[59] This sparked new hostilities, for in 1153 Count Raymond V of Toulouse declared war on the Trencavel for having recognized the suzerainty of Barcelona.[60] Peace had returned by 1187 when Viscount Bernard Atton VI gave Count Raymond V the viscounty of Nîmes, and Raymond married his daughter, Adelaïde, to Viscount Roger II Trencavel of Carcassonne (1167–1193).[61]

[53] Bisson, *Medieval France*, p. 133.
[54] Baratier, 'Marquisat', p. 139.
[55] Bisson, *Medieval Crown*, p. 38.
[56] B. Hamilton, *The Albigensian Crusade*, London, 1974, p. 21.
[57] Baratier, 'Marquisat', p. 153. In 1212 Simon de Montfort had engineered his papal and royal recognition as count of Toulouse, Bisson, *Medieval France*, p. 393.
[58] The crux of the problem was the sale of Carcassonne to Count Raymond Berenger I 'the Old', by the counts of Carcassonne in the eleventh century, d'Abdal, 'A Propos', pp. 319–327. Count Raymond Berenger III had accepted the fealty of the men of Carcassonne in 1107, but it took until 1113 for the viscount to do likewise, Bisson, *Medieval Crown*, p. 26.
[59] *Douzens(Temple)*, p. xxii.
[60] *L'Art de vérifier*, II, p. 297.
[61] *ibid.*, II, p. 298.

The count of Barcelona may have married into the comital house of Provence, but he had acquired an extremely powerful neighbour and suzerain: the Roman Emperor.[62] Much of Provence was part of the imperial kingdom of Burgundy, which comprised the provinces of Besançon, Lyon, Tarentaise, Vienne, Embrun, and most importantly Aix and Arles. Aix had grown from the oldest Roman settlement (*Aquæ Sextiæ Saluviorum*) in Gaul,[63] but Arles claimed the special status, for it was the seat of the kingdom, and its king was the emperor.[64] By the mid-twelfth century the emperor's power in the kingdom was somewhat more *de jure* than *de facto*, and the indifference of its people towards the Empire was a source of acute embarrassment to Emperor Lothar III of Supplinburg, who complained in strong terms to the archbishop of Arles in 1132.[65] Under Frederick I 'Barbarossa' an effort was made to bring the kingdom into line, and in 1156 Frederick married Beatrix, heiress of the county of Burgundy, as a way of coaxing the Burgundians to grant him more cooperation. Little changed, and his policy towards Provence became more hard line. In 1162 he met the young count of Barcelona, and exacted an avowal from him that Barcelona held the county of Provence as a fief of the Empire.[66]

To stress his view of the importance of Provence, Emperor Frederick had himself re-crowned in Arles on 30 July 1178 according to an ancient practice that had fallen into disuse.[67] However, despite the high-powered entourage which attended, the ceremony did not succeed in impressing the power of the Empire on its Provençal vassals.[68] Frederick enacted little that was sensitive to the Provençaux, although in August of 1178 he issued a special charter from Montélimar putting the Avignonais Jews under the protection of Bishop Pons.[69]

Under his son, Emperor Henry VI, the kingdom became somewhat of a pawn for imperial use against the French. This was one of the prime reasons for a plan hatched to give Provence to King Richard I of England.[70] In reality this was a demonstration of the ingenuity of the emperor, for he feared French involvement in Provence following the alliance that had been struck between

---

62 The prefix 'Holy' was added to the imperial title in 1157.

63 M. Clerc, *Aquae Sextiae, histoire d'Aix-en-Provence dans l'antiquité*, Aix-en-Provence, 1916, p. 1; Benoit, *Villes*, p. 7.

64 P. Fournier, *Le Royaume d'Arles et de Vienne*, Grenoble, 1884, p. 3.

65 *Veterum scriptorum et monumentorum historicum, dogmaticorum, moralium, amplissima collectio*, E. Martène and U. Durand (eds.), I, Paris, 1724, col. 717 (1132).

66 *ibid.*, I, cols. 860–863 (1162).

67 *GCN(Arles)*, no. 285, col. 82 (1178).

68 Fournier, *Royaume*, p. 44.

69 *GCN(Avignon)*, no. 287, col. 82 (1178).

70 Roger of Hovendon, *Chronica*, Rolls Series 51, W. Stubbs (ed.), III, London, 1870, p. 225.

King Philip Augustus and John of England.[71] This elaborate and tactical arrangement finally came to nothing, for in early 1194 Richard returned straight home to England, ushering in the further decline of imperial power in the area. After the reign of Emperor Henry VI Roman authority in the kingdom of Arles became even more of a phantom. The worst fears of the Empire arrived within twenty years in the guise of the northern French knights' invasion of Occitania in the Albigensian wars.

The introduction of French claims to parts of Occitania in the wake of the conquests of the Albigensian campaigns created problems of administration which remained unsettled for much of the century. Marseille, for instance, was staunchly loyal to the counts of Toulouse,[72] even though it had been part of the Catalan holdings for over a century. In 1230 the Catalan Count Raymond Berenger V of Provence unsuccessfully besieged Marseille for two months, whilst simultaneously the commune of Marseille elected Count Raymond VII of Toulouse as its overlord.[73]

The balance of power in western Occitania shifted radically after the Albigensian Crusade. A clause of the Peace of Paris had stipulated that when the line of the house of Toulouse came to an end, all the comital lands would pass to the French crown. It only took a generation, for Raymond VII's daughter, Jeanne, and Saint Louis' brother, Count Alfonso of Poitiers, died leaving no issue, so the county escheated to the crown in 1271.[74] Barcelona lost, too, for in the Treaty of Corbeil in 1258 James I of Aragon renounced Catalan claims to Provence in return for Saint Louis' renunciation of French claims to various Aragonese Pyrenean dependencies.[75]

More devastating for the Provençal way of life was the accession by marriage of Saint Louis' youngest brother, Charles of Anjou (1227–1285), to the

---

[71] The fate of Provence now looked all but sealed, for Richard wrote from his prison to the archbishop of Canterbury in September 1193 informing him that he would be free by Christmas, and would shortly afterwards be crowned king of Provence. However, underlying the scheme was a degree of imperial intrigue, for Richard was under the impression that he was also to have certain jurisdictions, as Roger of Hovendon was swift to point out, not in the gift of the Empire: 'Præterea prædictus imperator dedit regi Angliæ, et carta sua confirmavit has terras subscriptas: scilicet, Provinciam, et Vianam, et Vienais, et Massiliam, et Nerbonam, et Arleblanc, et Leun supra Rodanum usque ad Alpes, et quicquid imperator habet in Burgundia et homagium regis Aragoniæ, et homagium comitis de Disders, et homagium comitis de Sancto Ægidio', Roger of Hovendon, *Chronica*, III, p. 225.

[72] *L'Art de vérifier*, II, p. 300.

[73] L de Santi, 'Relations du comte de Toulouse Raymond VII avec la ville de Marseille', *AM* 11(1899), p. 201; J. Pryor, *Business Contracts of Medieval Provence*, Toronto, 1981, pp. 55–56.

[74] Hamilton, *Albigensian*, p. 29.

[75] *ibid.*, p. 30.

counties of Provence and Forcalquier in 1246.[76] He and his *franciots* met with resistance from the 'imperial' cities of Marseilles, Arles and Avignon, and an anti-Angevin alliance led by Barral of Les Baux and Boniface of Castellane emerged.[77] The disquiet lasted for half a century,[78] but all effective resistance was smashed by the public execution of the then leading rebels (including Hugh of Les Baux, the former *podestà* of Arles) in Marseille in 1264.[79] However, the Provençaux soon came to realize the opportunities afforded by Charles' ambition, and their large presence in his Italian and Sicilian campaigns and administrations attest to this.[80] Their optimism was not unfounded, for Charles also rewarded them with substantial mercantile rights in Messina, Naples, Palermo, Syracuse, Trani and Trapani.[81]

With regard to the local administration of authority, it became common in the fourteenth and fifteenth centuries for villages to have a rudimentary assembly, the *universitas*, but up until then there are very few sources for charting the history of such authority.[82] In the more developed areas consulates representing the urban aristocracy and merchant class had become widespread in the wake of the re-awakening of Roman law,[83] although those in Provence were to be quashed by Charles of Anjou in the mid-thirteenth century. For example, Arles, Avignon, Grasse, Tarascon, Forcalquier, Marseille and Hyères all lost their consulates, and had to submit to a *viguier*.[84] Along with these consulates came an increase of local fairs. New ones at Nîmes, Carcassonne, Gard, Maguelone and Beaucaire vyed with the traditional September fair at Saint-Gilles.[85]

The debate as to whether the appearances of these local bodies was due to influence from Italy or to an indigenous re-awakening of Gallo-Roman systems of public administration has yet to be settled. However, it is clear that the first consulates to appear in Occitania did so in the 1130s in trading cities

---

[76] Generally, see R. Sternfeld, *Karl von Anjou als Graf von Provence*, Berlin, 1888.

[77] E. Léonard, *Les Angevins de Naples*, Paris, 1954, p. 48; S. Runciman, *The Sicilian Vespers*, Cambridge, 1992, p. 73.

[78] *ibid.*, pp. 73–76.

[79] *ibid.*, p. 82; Léonard, *Angevins*, p. 53.

[80] Runciman, *Vespers*, pp. 76, 96, 130.

[81] Léonard, *Angevins*, pp. 100–101.

[82] *Le Village de Provence au bas moyen âge*, Cahiers du centre d'études des sociétés méditeranéens, Série no. 2, Aix en Provence, 1987, pp. 34–35.

[83] A. Gouron, 'Les Etapes de la pénétration du droit romain au xiie siècle dans l'ancienne Septimanie', *AM* 69(1957), pp. 103–120; R. Saint-Jean, 'Les Origines du consulat en Vivarais méridional au Moyan Age', *AM* 88(1965), pp. 353–370.

[84] Léonard, *Angevins*, p. 78; E. Baratier, 'Rois Angevins et papes d'Avignon (xiiie–xve siècles), *Histoire de la Provence*, E. Baratier (ed.), Toulouse, 1969, p. 170.

[85] J. Combes, 'Les Foires en Languedoc au moyen âge', *Annales* 13(1958), pp. 231–259.

between the Rhône and Aude valleys.[86] The first consulate to be established was in Avignon in 1129. The expansion occurred in the 1130s and 1140s when Arles, Béziers, Narbonne, Montpellier, Saint-Gilles, Nîmes, Nice and Tarascon all developed consulates.[87] As a corollary, the establishment of the public notariat inevitably followed this pattern.[88] Consulates did not appear solely in the larger towns, for example, Les-Saintes-Maries-de-la-Mer acquired one in 1233.[89] In the case of Marseille, the city even became a republic. Although Catalan controlled, the influence of Italy can be seen by the fact that between 1221 and 1228 the city was headed by a *podestà*, and five out of the six consuls were Italian.[90] In the lesser towns such as Avignon, Montpellier, Saint-Gilles, Arles, Narbonne and Carcassonne civil statutes were in force by c.1250.[91]

The composition of the bourgeois which emerged in the late twelfth century in the coastal towns in Occitania comprised a patriciate descended from urban knights, and *prud'hommes* made up of the wealthier merchants, artisans and lawyers. The remainder of the inhabitants were lesser artisans, merchants and large Jewish communities.[92] The strength of the Jewish presence is attested to not only by charters and chronicles, but also by the emergence of the Judeo-Provençal language.[93] A city could even have more than one Jewish quarter. Narbonne had two,[94] and in 1166 Benjamin of Tudela found two, each of some three hundred people, in the upper and lower towns of Marseille.[95] Moreover, Occitan Christian amulets, such as the twelfth century seventy-two names of God to be used to ward off fire, water, death in

---

[86] A. Gouron, 'Diffusion des consulats méridionaux et expansion du droit Romain aux xiie et xiiie siècles', *Bibliothèque de l'Ecole des Chartes* 121(1963), pp. 26–32.

[87] Toulouse (1152), Grasse (1155), Marseille (1178), Cervera (1182), Millau (1187), Carcassonne (1192), Montauban (1195), Perpignan (1197), Lérida (1197), Alès (1200), Lodève (1202), Uzès (1206), Cahors (1207), Limoux (1218), Albi (1220) and Barcelona (1249), Gouron, *Diffusion*, pp. 33–45; Portal, *République*, p. 11 believes that a consulate was established in Marseille in 1128.

[88] Gouron, *Diffusion*, p. 55.

[89] *Village*, p. 34.

[90] Pryor, *Business Contracts*, p. 53.

[91] A. Gouron, 'Aux Origines de l'"émergence" du droit; glossateurs et coutumes méridionales (xiie-milieu du xiiie siècle)', *La Société du droit dans le Midi de la France au Moyen Age*, Variorum (ed.), London, 1984, p. 255; *idem*, ' "Libertas hominium Montispessulani", Rédaction et diffusion des coutumes de Montpellier', *AM* 90(1978), pp. 289–318; H. de Tarde, 'La Rédaction des coutumes de Narbonne', *AM* 85(1973), pp. 371–395.

[92] Baratier, 'Marquisat', pp. 146–147.

[93] M.-C. Viguier, 'Le "Sermon des juifs" à Carpentras: carnaval ou pourim', *AM* 101 (1989), pp. 279–287.

[94] R. Emery, *Heresy and Inquisition in Narbonne*, New York, 1941, p. 23.

[95] Benjamin of Tudela, *The Itinerary of Benjamin of Tudela*, M.-N. Amor (tr.), London, 1907, p. 5; J. Schatzmiller, 'Structures communales juives à Marseille. Autour d'un contrat de 1278', *PH* 28(1979), pp. 33–45.

battle, child-birth tragedies and evil,[96] evince not only corruptions of Hebrew words, but also of Jewish mysticism.

Occitania had a large number of cities where bishops resided. Since the Carolingian period Occitania had become more populous as more land was cleared for agriculture by *medium plantum* and *aprisios*.[97] The Gallo-Roman *mansum* was the principal unit,[98] still preserved today in the innumerable *mas* which dot the Midi. The vast majority of agglomerations were simple *villæ* or *castra* (*castel* or *villa* in Occitan), the two being synonymous in Provençal sources.[99] *Castra* were not necessarily fortresses with *villæ* as their associated burghs, although during the twelfth century it became common to use the word *castrum* for a *villa* with rudimentary ramparts.[100] By the thirteenth century a *villa* was exclusively a village.[101] Yet, by 1150 nobles and castellans were becoming ever more numerous in Occitania, each carving out their own domains. The countryside was thus strewn with a great number of castles and fortresses housing the new bellicose aristocracy, descendants of those who had been the prime stimulus for the Peace of God activity.[102] This pattern was to

[96] 'Elei ✠ Homo ✠ Salvator ✠ Primogenitus ✠ Principium ✠ Finis ✠ Via ✠ Veritas ✠ Vita ✠ Sapiensia ✠ Virtus ✠ Paroclitus ✠ Mediator ✠ Agnus ✠ Hovis ✠ Vitulus ✠ Aries ✠ Leo ✠ Serpens ✠ Vermis ✠ Os ✠ Verbum ✠ Ymage ✠ Sol ✠ Lux ✠ Splendor ✠ Panis ✠ Fons ✠ Utis ✠ Lapis ✠ Petra ✠ Angelus ✠ Sponsus ✠ Pastor ✠ Profeta ✠ Sacerdos ✠ Immortalis ✠ Christus ✠ Jesus ✠ Pater ✠ Filius ✠ Deus ✠ Spiritus ✠ Sanctus ✠ Omnipotens ✠ Mizricordie ✠ Caritas ✠ Creator ✠ Redemptor ✠ Theragramaton ✠ Primus ✠ Novissimus ✠ Samaritanus ✠ Iaef ✠ Hic geren ✠ Hic geronay ✠ Gey ✠ Iamo ✠ Zachias ✠ Cazarny ✠ Ydonay ✠ Conditor ✠ Esmutabilis ✠ Fortis ✠ Heleyson ✠ Gloria ✠ Bonum ✠ Sacyo ✠ Sacraton ✠ Sacratorium ✠ May ✠ Pax', 'Los LXXII noms de nostre senhor Jhesu Crist, trobat escrig per salut de tots fidelz crestians', *Ecrivains anticonformistes du moyen-âge occitan, hérétiques et politiques*, R. Nelli (ed. and tr.), Paris, 1977, pp. 137–141.

[97] *Medium plantum* was a system under which the peasantry cleared lands and divided them with the original owners; *aprisios* refers to wastelands which were cleared and given to those who bought them under cultivation in full allodial ownership, Lewis, 'Patterns', p. 60.

[98] C. Higounet, 'Observations sue la seigneurie rurale et l'habitat en Rouergue du IXe au XIVe siècle', *AM* 62(1954), p. 126.

[99] E. Baratier, 'Les Communautés de Haute-Provence au moyen age: problèmes d'habitat de population', *PH* 21(1971), p. 237. The word *castrum* became more prevalent in the twelfth century, and places which had formerly been *villæ* were designated *castra*. Research has shown that out of 230 localities mentioned in the cartulary of Saint Victor, 91 received the appellation *castra/villæ*, 80 were *villæ/villulæ* and 59 were both, *Village*, p. 6; see also, Carcenac, *Larzac*, pp. 95–98.

[100] *Village*, pp. 5–8.

[101] Higounet, 'Observations', p. 126.

[102] Lewis, 'Patterns', pp. 61–62; S. Weinburger, 'Les Conflits entre clercs et laïcs dans la Provence du XIe siècle', *AM* 92(1980), p. 272.

remain the norm until the imposition of Capetian suzerainty in the thirteenth century.[103]

Large numbers of new villages, *salvetats*, were founded in the twelfth century by religious Orders. These were the forerunners of the *bastides* of the thirteenth century, and the equivalent of the *villes neuves* of northern France.[104] The Military Orders were involved in this urbanization. The Order of the Hospital alone created around forty *salvetats* in the valley of the Moyenne-Garonne between Muret and Saint-Gaudens.[105] In the towns landlords emerged in the thirteenth century, and the leasing of houses contributed in large part to the growth of the nascent monetary economy by the creation of this group,[106] despite the fact that money had been in circulation even in the remotest reaches of Occitania in the twelfth century.[107]

The great families managed to retain their estates through primogeniture, but amongst the lesser nobility partible inheritance was the norm. Accordingly, co-lordship was prevalent in the Languedoc and Provence. Thus, at Mirepoix in 1207 co-lordship was shared by thirty-five people.[108] This tendency, coupled with the large number of nobles, led to substantial poverty amongst this group.[109] Accordingly, as in England and the Dauphiné, an increasing number of 'noble lands' came to be held by non-nobles.[110]

The systems of Occitanian land tenure are not, as yet, fully understood. Carolingian style tenure in the form of multiple subinfeudations cemented by homage and vassalic obligations did not exist. Rather, there was a 'fidelity unbacked by realty, a feudality with no sworn support, an aristocracy with no vassals'.[111] Land was based upon the fief, but it brought no obligations. Transactions were *convenientiæ*, or non-reciprocal promises. The words *homagium* or *hominium* only appear in rare cases, for the system was one of bilateral accords. Yet classic feudalism began to make an impact in the lands controlled by

---

[103] Bensch, *Barcelona*, p. 398.

[104] Lewis, 'Patterns', p. 63.

[105] E. Delaruelle, 'La Ville de Toulouse vers 1200 d'après quelques travaux récents', *CF* 1(1966), p. 110.

[106] Bautier, *Economic*, p. 159.

[107] M. Castaing-Sicard, *Monnaies féodales et circulation monétaire en Languedoc (Xe–XIIIe siècles)*, Toulouse, 1967, pp. 90 *et seq.*

[108] Peter of les Vaux-de-Cernay, *Hystoria albigensis*, P. Guébins and E. Lyon (eds.), I, Paris, 1926, p. 120, n. 2.

[109] Bautier, *Economic*, p. 156.

[110] *ibid.*, p. 157.

[111] E. Magnou-Nortier, 'Fidélité et féodalité méridionales d'après les serments de fidélité (xe–début xiie siècle), *AM* 80(1968), p. 476.

Barcelona.[112] Thus, in a Catalan-controlled city such as Montpellier, the two systems could co-exist.[113]

It becomes evident that within the linguistic unity of the Occitanian world there was much political disunity, hinging around the rival claims of the houses of Toulouse and Barcelona. In the larger towns comital authority was exercised by representatives, but much of the population lived in small towns and villages where the castellans and knights had more sway than the comital overlords. Nevertheless, the degree of the urbanization of the coastal regions and the fertile areas, coupled with the small size of the major fiefs, singled Occitania out as a civilization markedly distinct from its northern neighbour.

Religious Life

Aside from the firm links between Occitania's major comital house and Syria-Palestine, there was a strong tradition of pilgrimage in Occitania. Not only did pilgrims pass through on their way to Jerusalem, Rome and Santiago de Compostela, but there were many pilgrimage sites in Occitania itself. A strong tradition existed that Saint Mary Magdalene was buried in the basilica of Saint-Maximin near Aix,[114] and despite the claims of Vézelay,[115] many, including Saint Louis, visited this shrine.[116] Further north, in the Lot, was the most famous Marian shrine of the Midi; and the *Miracles of Our Lady of Rocama-dour* (c.1172) testify to its importance to both Occitanians and those from as far afield as Acre.[117] Indeed, one lady lost her sight whilst giving birth in the Hospital in Jerusalem and, having tried all the holy sites in Outremer, was only re-granted it at Rocamadour.[118]

Of even greater resonance and attraction was the pilgrimage to Santiago, and the twelfth century pilgrim's guide to the tomb of Saint James laid emphasis on

---

[112] G. Giordanengo, *Le Droit féodal dans les pays du droit écrit. L'Exemple de la Provence et du Dauphiné XIIe–début XIVe siècle*, Rome, 1988, p. 244 and *passim*.

[113] H. Katsura, 'Serments, hommages et fiefs dans la seigneurie des Guilhem de Montpellier (fin XIe–XIIIe siècle)', *AM* 104(1992), pp. 141–161.

[114] J. Albanès, *Le Couvent royal de Saint-Maximin en Provence de l'ordre des frères prêcheurs*, Marseille, 1882, pp. 1–58; H. Garth, *Saint Mary Magdalene in Mediaeval Literature*, Baltimore, 1950, pp. 101–104.

[115] The Vézelay claim is based on a translation of her relics from Saint-Maximin in the eighth century, V. Saxer, *Le Culte de Marie Madeleine en Occident*, Paris, 1959, p. 264.

[116] John of Joinville, *Histoire de Saint-Louis*, N. de Wailly (ed.), Paris, 1868, p. 238.

[117] *Les Miracles de Notre-Dame de Roc-Amadour au XIIe siècle*, E. Albe (ed. and tr.), Paris, 1907, *passim*; pp. 72–79 for John of Acre, who visited Rocamadour on his way to, and return from, Santiago.

[118] *ibid.*, pp. 212–213.

the sites to be visited on the route that began at Arles.[119] Pilgrims came from Paris, Clermont, Brioude, Le Puy, assembled at Arles, went on to Saint-Gilles, Nîmes, Montpellier, Toulouse, and then into the Iberian peninsula.[120] The cult of Saint Giles was in the ascendent,[121] and the city of Saint-Gilles itself blossomed, for it was a principal stopping point on the *via Tolosana*.[122] In the first decade of the twelfth century the increase in pilgrim traffic at Saint-Gilles led to the demolition of its three churches dedicated to Saint Giles, Saint Peter and the Blessed Virgin to provide the raw material for the new church of Saint Giles, the first stone of which was laid on the Monday of Easter week 1116.[123] The city comprised nine parishes,[124] minted its own money (the *moneta egidiensis* or *giliensis*), between 1095 and 1144,[125] and was also to become, in the time of Saint Louis, the location for a courtly romance: *The Châtelaine of Saint-Gilles*.[126]

On the eve of the First Crusade the abbey of Saint-Gilles was already a powerful force. It had gained its independence from secular control under Pope Benedict VIII in the early eleventh century.[127] In 1066 Count Raymond IV of Saint-Gilles, together with his mother Almodis, had subjected the abbey to Hugh of Cluny.[128] It was, accordingly, ruled by Cluniac abbots from 1076–1125.[129] However, the abbey did not perceive itself as dependent from any institution other than the papacy.[130] Much of its influence stemmed from a gift by Count Raymond IV of Saint-Gilles of Toulouse. Before departing on Crusade he attended the Council of Nîmes, and declared in front of Pope Urban II that a vast array of his rights in the *vallée Flavienne* (the site of the

---

[119] *Le Guide du pèlerin de Saint-Jacques de Compostelle*, J. Vielliard (ed. and tr.), Macon, 1950.

[120] The *Via Tolosana* was a composite of the *Viæ Podensis* and *Regordana*, Lejeune, 'L'Esprit', p. 166.

[121] R. de La Coste-Messelière and G. Jugnot, 'L'Acceuil des pèlerins à Toulouse', *CF* 15(1980), p. 118.

[122] Dunbabin, *France*, p. 172.

[123] M Ménard, *Histoire civile, écclesiastique, et litteraire de la ville de Nismes avec les preuves*, Paris, 1744, p. 197; de la Coste-Messelière and Jugnot, 'L'Acceuil', p. 118.

[124] Fliche, *Aigues-Mortes*, p. 56.

[125] H. Rolland, 'La Monnaie de Saint-Gilles', *PH* 5(1955), pp. 32, 38.

[126] *La Châtelaine de Saint-Gilles*, in *Les Amours du bon vieux tems*, de Sainte Palaye (ed.), Paris, 1756, pp. 66–80.

[127] Fliche, *Aigues-Mortes*, p. 54.

[128] A. Remensnyder, *Remembering Kings Past, Monastic Foundation Legends in Medieval Southern France*, Ithaca, 1995, p. 236.

[129] *ibid.*, pp. 236–237.

[130] Generally, *ibid.*, pp. 236–242.

abbey) and elsewhere was to be vested in the abbot.[131] This was to be the cause of hostility between Raymond's sons, Counts Bertrand and Alfonso Jordan, and the abbey.[132] In 1107 Pope Paschal II wrote to Archbishop Gibelin of Arles, later to become patriarch of Jerusalem, instructing him to punish Count Bertrand for his activities against the abbey.[133] In 1112 Count Alfonso Jordan succeeded his half brother as count, and inherited the grievance against the abbey. In 1121 Pope Calixtus II enjoined Archbishops Atton of Arles and Fulcaud of Aix to excommunicate Alfonso Jordan and others within forty days if they did not make reparation to the abbey for damages done.[134] Not only did the count not take any action, but neither archbishop implemented the wishes of the Holy See. So the following year Pope Calixtus wrote to the archbishop of Arles, Count Raymond Berenger III of Barcelona (and newly Provence) and a local noble informing them that he had excommunicated Count Alfonso Jordan for his violence against the monks.[135]

Saint-Gilles' growing importance is attested to by its urban and major ecclesiastical institutions. Pope Urban II had passed through Saint-Gilles in 1095 on his way to preach the First Crusade at Clermont, and he passed there again in 1096 on his return, consecrating the new altar of the abbatial church.[136] In 1115 there was an ecclesiastical council at Saint-Gilles whose purpose is unclear.[137] In November 1118 Pope Gelasius II docked in Saint-Gilles on his flight from the Emperor Henry V;[138] and a native of Saint-Gilles, Guy Fulquois, after a successful legal career with the counts of Toulouse, became bishop of Le Puy, archbishop of Narbonne, cardinal of Sabina and finally Pope as Clement IV (1265–1268).[139] It was also here that the most significant councils were held during the Albigensian Crusade. The papal legate, Peter of Castelau, was assassinated when leaving Saint-Gilles.[140] Count Raymond VI was publicly flogged and pardoned by the Church here on 18 June 1209;[141] and at the council held here in 1211 he was once again excommunicated.[142]

---

[131] *Les Coutumes de Saint-Gilles*, E. Bligny-Bondurand (ed.), Paris, 1915, p. 275; C. Devic and J. Vaissete, *Histoire générale de Languedoc*, III, Toulouse, 1872, pp. 488, 492.

[132] For an overview of the relationship between the abbey and the counts of Toulouse, see Remensnyder, *Remembering*, pp. 221–229.

[133] *GCN(Arles)*, no. 468, col. 189 (1107).

[134] ibid., no. 504, col. 199 (1121).

[135] ibid., no. 506, col. 199 (1122).

[136] R. Crozet, 'Le Voyage d'Urbain II en France', *AM* 49(1937), pp. 4, 68.

[137] It was probably related to a dispute between the abbots of Grasse and Alet, who both claimed the abbey of Polycarpe as a dependency, Ménard, *Histoire*, p. 197.

[138] ibid., p. 198.

[139] Fliche, *Aigues-Mortes*, pp. 54–55; Runciman, *Vespers*, p. 83.

[140] *L'Art de vérifier*, II, p. 298.

[141] ibid., II, p. 299.

[142] ibid., II, p. 299.

The strong links between Occitanian prelates and the Crusader states were varied and wide-ranging. Thus, Gibelin, who rose to be archbishop of Arles, was subsequently made papal legate in Palestine in the first decade of the twelfth century, and then elected patriarch of Jerusalem.[143] This link between the see of Arles and the Crusader states was given fresh impetus in 1190 when the then archbishop, Peter Isnard, himself departed on Crusade.[144] The see of Marseille also allied itself to events in Outremer. When the Templars regained possession of the castle of Safet in 1240, the initiative for its rebuilding came from the bishop of Marseille, who devoted himself to raising money for the project.[145] Financial contributions for the effort in Outremer were also more generally demanded from ecclesiastics in the West; as in 1198 when Pope Innocent III wrote to the archbishops and their suffragans in Provence requesting money for the 'Holy War against the Saracens'.[146]

Whilst it is the case that ecclesiastical authority was not as developed in Occitania as it was in the north, it is a mistake to portray the area as an ecclesiastical backwater. It was, after all, an Occitanian, Bishop Adhémar of Le Puy, who played such a key role in the early stages of the First Crusade; and the regard in which the Occitanian Church was held is amply demonstrated by the enormous success of the Military and Religious Orders. Moreover, even in the hinterlands piety was developed, an example being a gift of a chapel by the canons of Aix in 1126 to the monks of Lure where the monks could provide for the faithful who wished to hear a daily Mass.[147]

The Reconquest and the Crusading Orders

On that same day (17 July 1178) the present city of Toulon was destroyed by Saracens, three hundred Christians and more perished by fire and the sword.[148]

This is an extract from the martyrology of Arles/Toulon. It recorded not only the destruction of Toulon, but also the taking into captivity of Viscount Hugh

---

[143] *GCN(Arles)*, no. 470, col. 189 (1109x1110).

[144] *ibid.*, no. 676, col. 262 (1190).

[145] Forey, *Orders*, p. 129; D. Metcalf, 'The Templars as Bankers and Monetary Transfers between West and East in the Twelfth Century', *Coinage in the Latin East: the Fourth Oxford Symposium on Coinage and Monetary History*, P. Edbury and D. Metcalf (eds.), Oxford, 1980, p. 2.

[146] *GCN(Marseille)*, no. 1118, col. 701 (1198).

[147] C. Blanc, 'Les Pratiques de piété des laïcs dans les pays du Bas-Rhone aux xie et xiie siècles', *AM* 72(1960), p. 138.

[148] 'Eodem die presens civitas Toloni a Sarracenis destructa fuit, in qua cccti christianorum et eo amplius, igne et gladio perierunt', *GCN(Toulon)*, no. 93, col. 62 (1178).

Geoffrey of Marseille, his nephew, Reforciat, and many others. A Muslim fleet had embarked from Mallorca, taking the city by surprise during the night of the 16/17 July.

Devastating as this attack was, Islam was no strange enemy to the Occitanians, but an old sparring partner. Following the sacks of Narbonne (720) and Toulouse (721), the Muslims had not been driven south of the Pyrenees in the aftermath of the battle of Poitiers (732).[149] They seized Avignon two years later, pillaged Lyons nine years after that, and only relinquished Narbonne and the Languedoc in 759.[150] The legacy of fear they left was deep-rooted, and it took until the tenth century for the Languedoc to become substantially re-populated.[151]

Although it has recently been suggested that the 'French' role in the Iberian peninsula before the First Crusade has been exaggerated,[152] the *Reconquista* had indisputably involved Occitanians from an early date. The *Reconquista* was initially a process of resettlement. But, following the siege of Barbastro in 1064, conquest became the chief priority. By the early twelfth century the *convivencia* was over, and both sides heightened the aggression.[153] Occitanians became involved on a greater and wider scale. For example, the early twelfth century *Miracles of Saint Giles* include two that are linked to Occitanian knights in the *Reconquista*;[154] and at Rocamadour a miracle-story circulated concerning the knight William Fouquier, freed from his chains in a Muslim prison on Mallorca by the intercession of Our Lady of Rocamadour.[155]

The taking of Zaragoza in 1118 involved hosts led by the counts of Bigorre and Béarne,[156] and was masterminded from Toulouse, with the viscount of Carcassonne playing a leading role.[157] In 1128 Roger II of Sicily struck an agreement with Count Raymond Berenger III of Barcelona that Roger would provide fifteen ships for a joint campaign down the Iberian coast, and that they would divide the spoils.[158] Count Raymond fought in the *Reconquista* many times. He attacked Mallorca in 1114 with the help of Catalan and Pisan

---

[149] Bisson, *Medieval Crown*, p. 8; Mayer, *Crusades*, p. 4. The battle of Poitiers, between ʿAbd-al-Raḥmān and Charles Martel, took place between Poitiers and Tours at the juncture of the rivers Clain and Vienne, P. Hitti, *History of the Arabs*, Basingstoke, 1994, p. 500.

[150] C. Dufourcq, *La Vie quotidienne dans l'Europe médiévale sous domination arabe*, Biarritz, 1978, p. 11; Hitti, *History*, p. 501.

[151] Bautier, *Economic*, p. 80.

[152] M. Bull, *Knightly Piety and the Lay Response to the First Crusade*, Oxford, 1993, pp. 70–115.

[153] R. Fletcher, *Moorish Spain*, London, 1994, p. 116.

[154] Peter William, *Miracula beati Egidii*, in *MGHSS* 12, P. Jaffé (ed.), pp. 318, 321.

[155] *Miracles*, Albe (ed.), pp. 162–164.

[156] Bisson, *Medieval Crown*, p. 15.

[157] Lejeune, 'L'Esprit', p. 166.

[158] *Storia del musulmani di Sicilia*, M. Amari (ed.), III, Catania, 1938, no. 1, pp. 396–398.

flotillas,[159] and the Muslims retaliated by laying siege to Barcelona in his absence. He returned to Barcelona, and slaughtered the Muslim army.[160] Still with his eye on the Balearics, he took Ibiza with Genoese and Pisan help, and on 3 April 1116 he conquered Mallorca.[161] His eldest son, Count Raymond Berenger IV, also gained a reputation for his military exploits against the Muslims.[162]

By the early thirteenth century the Military Orders had come to play an ever more important role in the Iberian peninsula. What lay west of the Pyrenees had assumed a character distinct from the rest of Europe. Both the Orders of the Temple and Hospital had a presence in the Iberian peninsula at extremely early dates in their histories. Most importantly, however, they were not military presences. The Hospitallers had a commandery at Cervera by 1111.[163] The Templars received their first castle in the peninsula in 1128 when Queen Teresa of Castile, countess of Portugal, gave them the castle of Soure near Coïmbra.[164] This was the first gift of a fortification in the peninsula, but it is clear that the Templars did not garrison it at this pre-Council of Troyes stage.[165] The gift was confirmed the following year by her son, Alfonso, who was already a *confrater* of the Order.[166] On the other side of the peninsula the Catalan Count Raymond Berenger III of Barcelona professed as a brother of the Templar house of Barcelona in 1130,[167] giving the Templars another castle in the peninsula: Grañena, close to the Muslim frontier. Once again, the Order chose not to install a garrison.[168]

The event which sparked the Templars' entry into the *Reconquista* is one of the most puzzling in the history of twelfth century Iberian politics. It stemmed from the testament of Alfonso I 'el Batallador', king of Aragon and Navarre, who died leaving no heirs.[169] This need not have created a power vacuum, as Aragon was a fief of the Holy See. The Pope was, therefore, free to choose

---

[159] Bensch, *Barcelona*, p. 116; Bisson, *Medieval Crown*, p. 27.
[160] *L'Art de vérifier*, II, p. 294.
[161] *ibid.*, II, p. 295.
[162] *ibid.*, II, p. 296.
[163] *CH*, I, no. 21, pp. 22–23 (1111); I, no. 22, pp. 23–24 (1111).
[164] *CT*, no. 10, p. 7 (1128).
[165] Barber, *Knighthood*, p. 32.
[166] *CT*, no. 24, p. 17 (1129).
[167] *ibid.*, no. 33, p. 24 (1130). See Chapter 4, p. 136 for a discussion of this.
[168] Nor did they garrison a castle at Barbará given to them by the count of Urgel in 1132, *ibid.*, no. 47, pp. 36–37 (1132).
[169] The majority of the information in this section has been highlighted in a series of contentious articles between A. Forey and E. Lourie: E. Lourie, 'The Will of Alfonso I, "El Batallador", King of Aragon and Navarre: a Reassessment', *Speculum* 50(1975), pp. 635–651; A. Forey, 'The Will of Alfonso I of Aragon and Navarre', *Durham University Journal* (1980), pp. 59–65; E. Lourie, 'The Will of Alfonso I of Aragon and Navarre. A

a king. Commentators are agreed that this would certainly have been Alfonso VII of Léon and Castile. But, fearing the Castilians, the Aragonese chose Alfonso's younger brother, Ramiro, who had entered the monastery of Saint Pons of Thomières in 1093, and also became bishop-elect of Burgos, Pamplona, Roda-Barbastro, and prior of San Pedro el Viejo in Huesca. He was brought out of his cloister, and a marriage to Agnes, daughter of the count of Aquitaine, was arranged to produce an heir. The Navarrese, however, disagreed with the choice of Ramiro, and elected a nobleman by the name of García Ramírez instead.

Both Aragon and Navarre were acting in strict violation of the terms of Alfonso's will, for he had made detailed provision for his kingdom. It was an extraordinary wish. He stipulated that the kingdom be split between the Orders of the Temple (the knights of the Temple of the Lord), the Hospital and the Holy Sepulchre.[170] This will was first drawn up at the siege of Bayonne in October 1131, and he intended it to be taken seriously, for he confirmed it four days before his death. In 1137 his brother, Ramiro (the Aragonese choice, who had by now become king, sired a child, and returned to his monastery), split Aragon from Navarre, and joined it to Catalonia by the simple expedient of marrying his very young daughter, Petronilla, to Count Raymond Berenger IV of Barcelona, who thus became king of Aragon.

A controversial hypothesis is that this is exactly what 'the Battler' had wished to happen when he made his unusual will. That is, that his will was designed to be unimplementable, creating the necessary time for Ramiro to come out of his monastery, and sire a child. The reference to the Orders would, and did, block the Holy See from intervening with its own choice of king.[171] If this is true, it credits King Alfonso with a political acumen and powers of foresight that are quite extraordinary. But it is a touch fanciful. It degrades King Alfonso's manifest respect for the Church,[172] and underestimates his esteem for the Orders. King Alfonso was a militant enthusiast of the Order of the Temple. He created two Military Orders himself in the space of a decade, one of which, the militia of Monreal del Campo, was designed

---

Reply to Dr Forey', *Durham University Journal* (1981), pp. 165–172; A. Forey, 'A Rejoinder', *Durham University Journal* (1981), p. 173; see also Forey, *Aragón*, pp. 15–26.

[170] 'Sepulcrum Domini quod est Iherosolimis et eos qui observant et custodiant illud et ibidem serviunt Deo, et Ospitale pauperum quod Iherusalemis est, et Templum Domini cum militibus qui ad defendendum christianitas nomen ibi vigilant. His tribus totum regnum meum concedo'. The full text appears in S. García Larragueta, *El Gran priorado de Navarra de la orden de San Juan de Jerusalén*, ii, Pamplona, 1957, no. 10.

[171] Thesis of E. Lourie, *supra*.

[172] *Crónicas anónimas de Sahagún*, A. Ubierto Arteta (ed.), Textos Medievales 75, Zaragoza, 1987, ch. 29, p. 52; *Chronica Adefonsi imperatoris*, L Sánchez Belda (ed.), Escuela de estudios medievales, Textos 14, Madrid, 1950, ch. 52, p. 43.

specifically in emulation of the Order of the Temple.[173] It is not likely that such a man would have used the Temple as a decoy, risking its reputation by ensnaring it in a clandestine manœuvre to snub the papacy.

The position of the Orders in the affair was not surprising; they were loath to become involved, and for good reason. The Temple was a Military Order devoted to combat, but in the Holy Land, not elsewhere. There was no precedent for its engaging in warfare anywhere but in Outremer. It did not relish the prospect of joining the *Reconquista*, just as seventy years later it would show no desire to become involved in the Albigensian campaigns.[174] Neither Queen Teresa of Castile's gift of the castle of Soure (1128) nor Count Raymond Berenger III's gift of the castle of Grañena (1130) had spurred it into action in the *Reconquista*. Nor did Alfonso's will. The Hospital and the Holy Sepulchre were not Military Orders, and were, therefore, not expected to perform a combat role in the *Reconquista*. Nevertheless, they did not desire to become embroiled in Iberian politics. Significantly, the master of the Hospital acted for his own Order and that of the Holy Sepulchre,[175] whereas the Temple acted alone. This underscores the distinction at this date between their respective non-military and military orientations.

The Hospitallers and the Order of the Holy Sepulchre renounced their claims to the legacy in 1140,[176] whilst the Temple did not conclude its negotiations with Count Raymond Berenger until 1143. By this it was agreed that the Templars would join the *Reconquista*, thereby implementing in part the spirit of the will. The arrangement brought the Temple into play by creating a new knighthood:

I [Count Raymond Berenger] have decided to create a knighthood for the defence of the western Church which is in Spain, to suppress, subdue, and expel the Moorish people, and to exalt the holy Christian faith and religion, on the model of the knighthood of the Temple of Solomon in Jerusalem, which defends the eastern Church, in subjection and obedience to it, following the rule and the customs of that knighthood.[177]

---

[173] 'quemadmodum ut Ierosolimis ordinare et constituere militiam Christi', *CT*, no. 6, pp. 3–4 (1126x1130). As with Belchite, there is only one source relating to this confraternity.
[174] E. Delaruelle, 'Templiers et Hospitaliers en Languedoc pendant la croisade des Albigeois', *CF* 4(1969), pp. 315–334.
[175] The documents are published in C. Odriozola y Grimaud, *Ramón Berenguer IV, conde de Barcelona, caballero del Santo Sepulcro de Jerusalén. Memorias históricas referentes a la cesión en su favor de la Corona de Aragón, hecha por la Orden militar del Santo Sepulcro, la del Hospital y del Temple en el año 1140*, Barcelona, 1911.
[176] *CH*, 1, no. 136, pp. 111–112 (1140).
[177] 'ad defendendam occidentalem ecclesiam que est in Ispaniis, ad deprimendam et debellandam et expellendam gentem maurorum, ad exaltandam sancte cristianitatis fidem et religionem, ad exemplum milicie Templi Salomonis in Iherusalem, que orientalem

PLATE I: Twelfth century Templar doorway. Church of *Santa Maria la Blanca*, Villacázar de Sirga (Palencia, Castile–Leon, Spain).

The Templars gained extensive possessions and privileges as a result of these protracted negotiations with the count of Barcelona, and were soon campaigning on a broad geographical scale in the peninsula.[178] This became widely known; the troubadour Marcabru (c.1129–1150) even sang of the burdensome weight the Templars bore by this involvement.[179] And in the fourteenth century Peter of La Palud composed a sermon, part of which recounted that certain captive Moors from the Iberian peninsula wanted to know what had happened to the white-clad knights with crosses on their shoulders.[180] In time the Hospitallers, too, began to campaign militarily in the peninsula. Brethren were present at the siege of Tortosa in 1148,[181] and in 1149 Count Raymond Berenger IV gave them the castle of Amposta:

> for the exaltation of the church of Christ, for the propagation of the holy Chritian faith and religion, and the suppression and confusion of the Moorish people.[182]

Yet, in the main, little is known of the Hospitallers military activities in the peninsula, for the sources are sparse,[183] although Count Alfonso II of Barcelona (King of Aragon) did exempt the Hospital from paying one fifth of all they conquered from the Moors to the crown.[184] An unusual role ascribed to the Orders in the peninsula was to act as an international penal administration, providing letters of proof that those who had been sentenced to fight in Spain, for example, five Narbonnais guilty of murder, carried out their sentence.[185]

---

defendit ecclesiam, in subjectione et obedientia illus secundam regulam et ejusdem milicie instituta beate obedientie miliciam constituere decrevi', *CT*, no. 314, p. 204 (1143).

[178] Forey, *Orders*, p. 24; J. Phillips, *Defenders of the Holy Land, Relations between the Latin East and the West 1119–1187*, Oxford, 1996, p. 111.

[179] 'En Espagna sai, Lo Marques,/ e cill del temple Salamo, safron lo pes/ e-l fais de l'orguoill paganor', Marcabru, 'Pax in Nomine Domini', in *La Poesia dell'antica Provenza*, G. Sansone (ed.), Milan, 1984, pp. 112–117.

[180] J. Dunbabin, *A Hound of God. Pierre de La Palud and the Fourteenth Century Church*, Oxford, 1991, p. 176.

[181] A. Forey, 'The Military Orders and the Spanish Reconquest in the Twelfth and Thirteenth Centuries', *Traditio* 40(1984), p. 200.

[182] 'ad exaltandam Christi ecclesiam, ad propagandam sancte christianitatis fidem et religionem, ad deprimendam et confundendam gentem maurorum', *CH*, I, no. 181, pp. 141–143 (1149).

[183] M. Ledesma, 'Notas sobre la actividad militar de los hospitalarios', *Principe de Viana* 25(1964), pp. 51–56; S. García Larraguete, 'La Orden de San Juan en la crisis del imperio hispánico del siglo XII', *Hispania* 12(1952), pp. 483–524; Forey, 'Spanish Reconquest', p. 200. Phillips, *Defenders*, p. 210 emphasizes the Hospitaller's strong presence in the Peninsula.

[184] *CH*, I, no. 980, pp. 621–622 (1195).

[185] Emery, *Heresy*, p. 87.

King Alfonso's militia of Monreal del Campo was not a success. It had probably become defunct by 1131 despite the support of dignitaries such as William, archbishop of Auch.[186] Alfonso's other military creation was the Aragonese confraternity of Belchite.[187] This was founded in 1122, and confirmed at the Council of Burgos in 1136. The idea behind the confraternity was to create a castle garrisoned by those willing to fight the expansion of Islam within an approved confraternity. The confraternity was open to any Christian, clerk or lay. It offered full remission of sins after confession to those who joined for life, or the same remission of sins as if a pilgrimage to Jerusalem had been undertaken for those who served only for a year. Donations of arms and horses earned the same remission of sins as if the gift had been made to the Temple or Hospital. It was not a successful enterprise either, for its existence was short-lived, and Count Raymond Berenger IV gave the castle of Belchite to the Temple along with other possessions as part the 1143 settlement of the will of 'the Battler'.[188]

Nevertheless, the Iberian peninsula was ripe ground for the activities of Military Orders. Amongst the plethora of such Orders which evolved there to aid in the *Reconquista*, the vast majority remained west of the Pyrenees.[189] Yet, at least one, the Order of Saint James of the Sword, had a presence in Provence. A Spanish official, Peter Bernard, master of the Order in Provence, was given permission to build a house in Marseille in 1190.[190] Other new Orders were also settling and developing in Occitania at the time the Hospital and Temple were developing their networks. For instance, before the First Crusade, Joscelin, seigneur of Châteauneuf de l'Albene, son of the magnate baron William Cornu, returned home to the Dauphiné in 1076 with the relics

186 Forey, 'Spanish Reconquest', p. 198.
187 The document from the Council of Burgos (4 October 1136) which relates to the confraternity is reproduced in P. Rassow, 'La Cofradia de Belchite', *Anuario de historia del derecho espanol* 3(1926), pp. 200–226. It is the only source relating to the confraternity.
188 M. Pallarés Gil, 'La Frontera sarracena en tiempo de Berenguer IV', *Boletin de historia y geografia del Bajo-Barcelona* 1(1907), pp. 150–151; Forey, *Aragón*, p. 67.
189 The principle Orders being the Order of Santiago (1170), S. Castro, *Los Comendadores de la ordern de Santiago*, Madrid, 1949; D. Lomas, *La Orden de Santiago 1170–1275*, Madrid, 1965; the Order of Calatrava (1158), F. Gutton, *L'Ordre de Calatrava*, Paris, 1955, J. O'Callaghan, *The Spanish Military Order of Calatrava and its Affiliates*, London, 1975; the Order of Alcantara (pre-1176), F. Gutton, *L'Ordre d'Alcantara*, Paris, 1975; the Order of Avis; the Order of Mountjoy (1173), A. Forey, 'The Order of Mountjoy', *Speculum* 46(1971), pp. 250–266; the Order of San Jorge de Alfama (c.1200); the Order of Santa Maria de España (c.1270), J. Torres-Fontes, 'La Orden de Santa Maria de España', *Miscelánea medieval Murciana*, 3(1977), pp. 73–119, J. Menéndez Pidal, 'Noticias acerca de la Orden militar de Santa Maria de España', *Revista de archivos, bibliotecas y museos* 17(1907), pp. 161–207; generally Forey, *Orders*.
190 *GCN(Marseille)*, no. 1190, cols. 736–738 (1248).

of Saint Antony. These had been presented to him by Emperor Romanus Diogenes of Constantinople in thanks and recognition for his efforts against the Turks. Joscelin founded a church, which still stands, to house the relics at Motte-Saint-Didier. When c.1100 an outbreak of disease (either streptococcal erysipelas or ergotism)[191] hit the region, his son and successor, Guigues, built a hospital there. This illness became known as 'Saint Antony's Fire', for sufferers invoked the saint for cure. Ten local notables led by Gaston, lord of Valloire, and his son banded around Guigues, and the hospitaller Order of Saint Antony of Vienne was formed (1095).[192] Almost simultaneously with the Order of the Temple, the church of Motte-Saint-Didier gained the Apostolic blessing of Calixtus II in 1119. As with most hospitaller Orders its brethren were lay, but they were given as spiritual guides the Benedictine monks of Montmajour near Arles. This was unusual for a hospitaller Order, for whom the Rule of Saint Augustine was normally the base.[193] They expanded rapidly in both Europe and Outremer, and by the end of the thirteenth century Pope Boniface VIII declared them to be a Military and Religious Order, giving them an Austin Rule.[194] Their implantation throughout Occitania was widespread, but not as striking as that of the Temple or Hospital.[195]

There were other specifically Military Orders in Occitania at the time. For example, the militia of the Faith of Jesus Christ was in existence in 1221. It had as its aim the destruction of the Cathar heresy, and wished for Pope Honorius III to grant it a Rule along the lines of that of the Templars.[196] It failed as an Order, for no more was heard of it. Another local Order was that of the militia of Saint James (or alternatively of the Sword or of Faith and Peace), established by Archbishop Amanieu of Auch c.1231 to fight in the west Toulousain not against heretics, but for faith and peace which were, to the

---

[191] *Dorland's Illustrated Medical Dictionary*, Philadelphia (28th edition), 1994. See *ergot* (p. 574), *ergotism* (p. 574) and *erysipelas* (p. 575).

[192] D. Le Blévec, 'Aux Origines des hospitaliers de Saint-Jean de Jérusalem: Gérard dit "Tenque" et l'établissement de l'ordre dans le Midi', *AM* 89(1977), p. 145.

[193] See *Statuts d'hotels-Dieu et de léproseries*, L. Le Grand (ed.), Paris, 1904.

[194] L. Blancard, *Inventaire-sommaire des archives départementales antérieures à 1799, Bouches-du-Rhone, archives écclésiastiques, série H*, Paris, 1869, pp. 38–39.

[195] The Archives of the Bouches-du-Rhône contain material from the following houses of the Order: Le Bastic, Canabières, La Capelle-Livron, Capette, Douzens, Durbans, Espalion, Espinas, La Favillane, Homps, Lugan, Montpellier, Narbonne, Pézenas, Plan de La Peyre, Rayssac, Sainte-Anne d'Argence, Sainte-Eulalie, Saint-Félix de Sorgues, Vabres, Sainte-Marguerite de Lusseran, La Selve, Thorenc-la-Gaude, La Tronquière, Vaour, Blancard, *Inventaire*, pp. 40–46.

[196] G. Meersseman, 'Etudes sur les anciennes confréries dominicaines, 4, Les milices de Jésus-Christ', *Archivum fratrum predicatorum* 23(1953), p. 286; see A. Forey, 'The Military Orders and Holy War against Christians', *English Historical Review* 104(1989), pp. 6–8.

archbishop's mind, rare commodities in the area.[197] In 1267 Pope Clement IV deposed its master for malice and neglect but, despite an attempt at resuscitation by the see of Auch, the Order did not survive.[198] Mention should also be made of the Teutonic knights who, unusually for this exclusively German Order, had a small number of commanderies in Occitania; for example, a house at Arles.[199]

Two other institutions born in Jerusalem were present in Occitania. The church of the Holy Sepulchre had been staffed with Augustinian canons in 1099 by Godfrey of Bouillon, advocate of the Holy Sepulchre, and by 1101 an almoner of the Order was in the Lauraguais.[200] Priests of the Holy Sepulchre were drawn to Occitania not only by the possible revenue, but also by the strong tradition of pilgrimage in northern Iberia and southern Occitania. A bull of Pope Honorius II, *Habitantes in domo Domini* (1128), confirmed to Prior William of the Holy Sepulchre around sixty churches with their dependencies, two hospitals, and various properties in this part of Europe.[201] Some local regional administration was put into place, for in 1146 there was a prior of the Order in Catalonia, Peter Bernard, a canon of the see of Barcelona.[202] In 1204 there was a hospital of the Holy Sepulchre in Marseille, and by 1241 there was a prior of the Holy Sepulchre of Marseille.[203]

The canons of the Temple of the Lord also had a presence in Occitania. In 1174 Stephen, a canon of the Temple of the Lord, 'administrator of the provincial houses belonging to that same Temple',[204] was involved in litigation in Sisteron. The act clearly referred to the Temple of the Lord, but paradoxically spoke of 'brothers (*fratres*) of the Temple' and 'the other brothers', terminology not normally associated with canons. This can only be explained if the act is a fabrication, or if Stephen was acting on behalf of the Templars. This

[197] *Les Registres de Grégoire IX, Recueil des bulles de ce Pape*, i, L. Auvray (ed.), Paris, 1890, no. 753. p. 476; see Forey, 'Holy War', pp. 7–8.

[198] *ibid.*, pp. 7–8.

[199] *Inventaire chronologique et analytique des chartes de la maison de Baux*, L. Barthélemy (ed.), Marseille, 1882, no. 434, p. 125 (1258).

[200] *CH*, i, no. 6, pp. 9–11 (probably 1101).

[201] *Le Cartulaire du chapitre du Saint-Sépulcre de Jérusalem*, C. Bresc-Bautier (ed.), Documents relatifs à l'histoire des croisades 15, Paris, 1984, no. 6, pp. 39–44; see generally N. Jaspert, 'La Estructuración de las primeras posesiones del capítulo del Santo Sepolcro en la península Ibérica: la génesis del priorado de Santa Ana en Barcelona y sus dependencias', *I. Jornadas de estudio la orden del Santo Sepulcro*, Calatayud – Zaragoza, 1991, pp. 93–108.

[202] Jaspert, 'Estructuración', p. 97.

[203] P. Amargier, 'La Situation hospitalière à Marseille', *CF* 13(1978), p. 239; *Bullaire de l'église de Maguelone (1030–1303)*, J. Rouquette and A. Villemagne (eds.), ii, Montpellier, 1911, no. 392, pp. 519–521 (1241).

[204] 'Stephanum canonicum Templi Domini administratorem domorum provincialium ad idem Templum pertinentium', *GCN(Sisteron)*, no. 16, cols. 421–422 (1174).

poses a question which might be answered by an argument that the links between the Temple and the Temple of the Lord were much closer than the foundation outlined by William of Tyre would suggest.[205]

The Occitanians' awareness of the *Reconquista* cannot be doubted, nor can their participation in it. This is a factor which made the people susceptible and responsive to both Crusade in Outremer, and to those Orders which were its representatives in Europe. The phenomenon of the creation of indigenous Military Orders only confirms this. It is a double irony, then, that a Crusade was launched into their heartland.

The Albigensian Crusade

The most singular series of events to occur in Occitania in the thirteenth century were the campaigns led by the French against the Cathar heresy of the Midi. The position of the Military Orders in these campaigns is of the greatest interest. Having been lured into combat on the European mainland in the *Reconquista*, it would be expected that their networks of commanderies, local knowledge and expertise in warfare would have made them ideal forces in these engagements. Yet the Orders played a strikingly minimal role in these campaigns. The contemporary record, William of Tudela's pro-Catholic, but anti-French, *Song of the Albigensian Crusade*, made few references to the Orders, none of them in military contexts. Whilst he related that northern Templars were amongst those who marched on Toulouse, he significantly listed them amongst the ecclesiastics, and not the combatants.[206]

The Military Orders did not support the heresy, but the Hospital was not hostile toward certain 'heretics'. For instance, the Order welcomed the excommunicate Count Raymond VI of Toulouse. The count sent the prior of the Hospital to Rome as his ambassador,[207] and during the siege of Toulouse in 1218 Count Raymond became a *confrater* of the Hospital whilst still

---

[205] There are certainly sources from which to draw such a conclusion. In particular, James of Vitry, *Historia Hierosolymitana*, in *Gesta Dei per Francos*, J. Bongars (ed.), Hanover, 1611, books 64–65, pp. 1082–1084; John of Ypres, *Chronicon Sythiense S. Bertini*, in *Thesaurum novus anecdotorum*, E. Martène (ed.), III, Paris, 1717, cols. 625–626, 627–628; William of Tyre, *Chronicon*, I, book 12, chs. 6–7, pp. 553–555; Michael the Syrian, *Chronique de Michael le Syrien*, J. Chabot (ed. and tr.), Paris, 1840, pp. v, x; *idem*, *Chronicle*, in *RHC Ar.* 1, pp. 309–409; Ernoul, *Chronique d'Ernoul et de Bernard le trésorier*, L. de Mas-Latrie (ed.), Paris, 1871, ch. 2, p. 7.

[206] 'E'l cardenals de Roma e'ls prelatz dels mostiers,/ Arsavesques, avesques e abatz e templiers', William of Tudela, *La Chanson de la croisade albigeoise*, H. Gougaud (ed.), Paris, 1989, verse 213, lines 14–15, p. 538.

[207] 'Lo priors de l'Ospital, us bos feziciare:/ Aicestz iran a Roma e pois a l'enperaire;/ Parlaren am lo papa, car cilh son bon gramaire,' *ibid.*, verse 10, lines 11–13, p. 50.

excommunicate, stating his wish to become a brother in the future.[208] He was received into the Hospital *ad succurrendum* in 1222, and buried in the church of Saint Remigius.[209] A story related by the monk Peter of Les Vaux-de-Cernay, who supported the Crusade, suggested that perhaps the Hospitallers were perceived as having sided with the heretics, for after the victory at Castelnaudary crosses appeared in the sky, and the only person not to see them was a chaplain, a Hospitaller.[210]

Local Templars also became involved, but unlike the Hospitallers, on the side of the Crusaders. After Count Raymond had his brother, Baldwin, hanged for treachery in revenge for the death of the King of Aragon at Muret in 1213,[211] the Templars of La Villedieu near Montauban took down his body from the tree, and gave it a Christian burial in the commandery cemetery.[212] In 1228 the commander of La Villedieu, on hearing of a plot against the bishop of Toulouse, whom he was sheltering, had the conspirators tortured and banished from his commandery.[213] Put simply, the Orders fought the infidel, and none other. Thus, combat against non-Christians in the Iberian peninsula was permissable, as it was in Eastern Europe against the Mongols in 1241 when the Orders fought under King Bela of Hungary.[214] But fighting Christians was not an option exercised by the Orders, even though writers such as James of Vitry (1170–1240), and later Thomas Aquinas (c.1225–1275), thought such engagement to be well within the reasonable tasks of a Military Order.[215]

---

208 *CH*, II, no. 1617, p. 246 (1218); H319 has a copy of this act in an *Authenticum* (1639) of the old cartulary of the counts of Toulouse from Raymond III to Alfonso of Poitiers.

209 William of Puylaurens, *Historia albigensium*, in *Recueil des Historiens des Gaules et de la France* 19, M.-J.-J. Brial (ed.), Paris, 1880, pp. 214–215; Delaruelle, 'Templiers', p. 330.

210 Peter of les Vaux-de-Cernay, *Hystoria*, I, pp. 163–164.

211 *L'Art de vérifier*, II, p. 299.

212 William of Puylaurens, *Historia*, p. 209.

213 *ibid.*, p. 218.

214 Demurger, *Temple*, p. 254.

215 'ad hoc igitur fratres ordinis militaris ordinati sunt, ut Christi Ecclesiam gladio materiali defendant, maxime contra eos qui extra sunt, id est contra Sarracenos in Syria, contra Mauros in Hispania, contra paganos in Prutia, Livonia et Comania, et nihilominus de mandato superioris contra schismaticos in Græcia, et contra hæreticos ubique dispersos in universali Ecclesia', James of Vitry, *Sermo* XXXVII *ad fratres ordinis militaris*, in *Analecta novissima: Spicilegii Solesmensis altera continuatio*, J. Pitra (ed.), II, Paris, 1888, p. 405. Thomas of Aquinas went further: 'Potest autem officium militare ordinari ad subventionem proximorum, non solum quantum ad privatas personas, sed etiam quantum ad totius reipublicæ defensionem . . . convenienter institui potest aliqua religio ad militandum, non quidem propter aliquid mundanum, sed propter defensionem divini cultus et publicæ salutis, vel etiam pauperum et oppressorum . . . religio non sic instituitur ad militandum quod religiosis auctoritate liceat bella gerere', Thomas of Aquinas, *Summa theologiæ* 47, J. Aumann (ed.), London, 1973, quæstio 188, art. 3, pp. 190–192; generally, see Forey, 'Holy War', pp. 1–24.

It is difficult to assess the precise role of the Orders during the Albigensian Crusade. From the sources left by the Orders, one would not even know that the Albigensian campaigns had ever happened. The numbers of *perfecti* and *perfectæ* were small,[216] and it is hard to know how deep the support for the Cathars really ran. It can be said that they did not represent a sizeable part of those who had property to gift, for there is no marked decline of pious donations to the Military Orders in the half century leading up to the sack of Béziers. This is maybe to be expected, and it is clear that in some areas, such as Montpellier, there were no Cathars at all. Neither is it the case that families were either Cathar or Catholic. Count Roger of Foix was a Catholic, but his wife and sister had both received the *consolamentum*, and were thus 'clothed' Cathars (*perfectæ*).[217] Bernard Raymond of Roquefort, bishop of Carcassonne, mediated at the siege of Termes (1210), where his mother and brother were both Cathar heretics holding out in the castle.[218]

With regard to any involvement by the Orders, there are simply no references in charters at all. Whilst commentators have stated that the Orders played a small but invaluable role in provisioning and sharing their local knowledge with the French armies,[219] there is no proof for this. The most likely explanation is the most obvious. The Orders did not perceive themselves as constituted to fight Christian heresy, but rather the infidel, in whatever guise he may come. Late in the thirteenth century the Orders did become involved against Christians, but these ventures were localized exceptions. They never involved the entire Order. For example, the Templar Brother Brian of Jay led a detachment of Welsh archers at the battle of Falkirk in 1298,[220] and some thirty years earlier a contingent of Hospitallers fought under Brother Philip of Egly alongside Charles of Anjou in Italy at the request of Pope Clement IV,[221] but not without complaint from Master Hugh Revel, who mourned the destruction of Hospitaller properties in Sicily by opponents to the Angevins.[222]

---

[216] The term *bonhommes* has been avoided, for the early Grandmontese were also so styled, and confusion is therefore possible, Lawrence, *Monasticism*, p. 159.

[217] Hamilton, *Albigensian*, p. 16.

[218] Peter of les Vaux-de-Cernay, *Historia*, I, p. 188; M. Barber, 'Catharism and the Occitan Nobility: the Lordships of Cabaret, Minerve and Termes', *The Ideals and Practice of Medieval Knighthood* 3, Papers from the Fourth Strawberry Hill Conference (1988), C. Harper-Bill and R. Harvey (eds.), Woodbridge, 1990, p. 17.

[219] Delaruelle, 'Templiers', pp. 315–334.

[220] 'ad quod bellum dictus magister nomine Brianus de Jais se diposuit et adduxit de Anglia secum magnam comitiam de gente Cambrensi', Hospitaller charter of Brother Thomas of Lindesay (1354), transcribed in J. Edwards, 'The Templars in Scotland in the Thirteenth Century', *Scottish Historical Review* 5(1907), pp. 13–25; see also R. Aitkin, 'The Knights Templars in Scotland', *Scottish Review* 32(1898), p. 25.

[221] *Licet vestri ordinis*, *CH*, III, no. 3279, p. 164 (1267).

[222] *CH*, IV, no. 3308, pp. 291–293 (undated).

The Orders were deeply entrenched in communities, reinforced by their policies of local recruitment. Individual's professions into a Military Order could not have expunged from their minds personal knowledge of Cathars amongst friends, family and neighbours. Such Christians were unlikely to have perceived neighbours as a similar threat to that posed by the Muslims. There is no question that the Orders had heretical leanings, or that there was any specific link between the Orders and the Cathars, but it is inconceivable that the Orders lived in total ignorance of local feeling. Just as some Occitanian seigneurs refused to turn on their people, so, too, did the local Orders.

One of the few thirteenth century comments on the inactivity of the Orders during the Albigensian campaigns came from a troubadour, Bernard Sicard of Marvejols, who fulminated against the Hospital for not having taken part. He was not incensed that the Order had not crushed the Cathars, but rather, that they had not fought with the Cathars against the northern French.[223] One should not read too much into one man's opinion, but it is possible that he was reflecting a general sentiment that the Order was part of the communities in Occitania, and was well enough integrated to be expected to show some loyalty. Perhaps it is in this light that an understanding can be gained of the profession of the heretic William of Minerve into the Hospitaller commandery of Campagnolles in 1215 after he had been reconciled to the Church in the wake of the burning of his followers. His career as a Hospitaller was, however, short-lived, for the following year he was back in the fray, fighting at the siege of Marmande against the army of Prince Louis.[224] However, the Hospital was not a haven for heretics, for one Cathar, Alaman of Roaix, was brought before the Inquisition, and instructed to make good his plunderings of the Order of the Hospital's property.[225]

Interesting as the role of the Orders during the Albigensian Crusade is, it should not be overemphasized. Although the political ramifications were far-reaching, the areas actually besieged and attacked by the Crusading armies in no way covered all of Occitania. Combat was confined to certain parts of the Languedoc. Although the Church used Saint-Gilles as the head-quarters for its negotiations, the military activity did not spill this far east. Yet Hospitallers in Saint-Gilles were politically involved, testified to by four acts in the Hospitaller cartulary from Saint-Gilles relating to Raymond of Toulouse's 1209

---

[223] Bernard Sicard of Marvejols, 'Ab greu cossire', in *Choix des poésies originales des troubadours*, M. Renouard (ed.), IV, Paris, 1819, no. 27, pp. 191–193.
[224] Barber, 'Catharism', pp. 17–18.
[225] W. Wakefield, *Heresy, Crusade and Inquisition in Southern France 1100–1250*, London, 1974, pp. 239–240.

absolution.[226] However, for the majority of the brethren of the Military Orders in Occitania, the events of the Albigensian Crusade unfurled outside their lives and responsibilities.

Conclusion

A description of the Provençaux Crusaders given by Ralph of Caen, chronicler of Tancred during the First Crusade, gives a humorous twelfth century impression of the people of Occitania. Written by a Norman, its emphasis and conclusions are slanted, but instructive:

> These people have a proud eye, a bellicose spirit, prompt to take up arms, light to scatter and listless to regroup. As the hen is different from the duck, so the Provençaux by nature differ [from the Normans] in spirit, manner, and way of life: living off little, examining all thoroughly, dogged at their work but, no need to be silent on this point, less warlike.[227]

He continued by telling of their favourite trick, demonstrating their cunning. If starving on Crusade they would covertly select a healthy pack animal and, unobserved, repeatedly jab a sharpened stick into it from the rear. As a result of the ensuing internal hæmorrhage, it would die. All around would be amazed that an animal so healthy could have suddenly expired with no visible cause. Reaching the inevitable conclusion, with the advice of the Provençaux, that an evil spirit had possessed the animal, all present would distance themselves from the cadaver. At this the Provençaux, magnanimously, would come to the decision that they would taste the food to see if it was all right, for 'better to die than to starve'.[228]

Between this comical caricature and the portrait given by Emmanuel Le Roy Ladurie of the libidinous and heretical villagers of Montaillou,[229] it is difficult to gain a picture of the Occitanians. Yet central-southern Occitania had important features. Its society was more cosmopolitan and urbanized than in the north, and the people were turned towards the sea, not northern Europe. For those principal cities which hugged the Gulf of the Lion, or were built on the Rhône, Durance or any of the other rivers connected to the sea, the

---

[226] *Saint-Gilles(Hospital)*, fols. 165r–176r (1209).
[227] 'Gentis hujus sublimis est oculus, spiritus ferox, promptæ ad arma dexteræ, ceterum ad spargendum prodigæ, ad congregandum ignavæ. His, quantum anati gallina, Provinciales moribus, animis, cultu, victu adversabantur: parce vivendo, sollicite perscrutando, laboriferi: sed, ne verum taceam, minus bellicosi', Ralph of Caen, *Gesta Tancredi in expeditione Hierosolymitana*, in *RHC Occ.* 3, cap. 61, *Provincialium mores*, p. 651.
[228] *ibid.*, p. 651.
[229] E. Le Roy Ladurie, *Montaillou, village occitane de 1294 à 1324*, Paris, 1975.

Mediterranean was not only their future, but also their past. The trading and cultural influences which had shaped their society were all linked to the sea: Greek, Roman, Catalan, Ligurian, Muslim and Jewish; many of which were reflected not only in the activities and in the language of the Occitanians, but also in their spirit and nature. The cities of the coast were technologically and intellectually half a century in advance of the inland cities such as Aix or Avignon, and a good century ahead of the rural hinterland.[230]

For Military Orders seeking an area of Europe which was relatively affluent, well-governed, possessing good trade links, and an established maritime reputation, as well as one which bred men physically prepared for service in the twin extremes of the Mediterranean climate of the Holy Land,[231] Occitania provided all these things and more. It lay sandwiched between Rome and Santiago de Compostela, the Holy Land and the *Reconquista*, the Empire and powerful Capetian France. It was, in very many ways, the crossroads of Europe,[232] and its appeal to the Orders was inevitable. This was not an unrequited relationship, but rather symbiotic, for the Occitanians were to be as welcoming to the Orders as the Orders were keen to become integrated into Occitanian communities. The following chapter will discuss the chronologies of the earliest commanderies of the Military Orders, implantations which are testimony to the Occitanian response to the opportunities and challenges the Military Orders offered.

---

230 Baratier, 'Marquisat', p. 160.
231 See G. Smith, *The Historical Geography of the Holy Land*, London, 1908, pp. 64–76.
232 See R.-H. Bautier, 'Recherches sur les routes de l'Europe médiévale. I. De Paris et de foires de Champagne à la Méditerranée par le Massif Central', *Bulletin philologique et historique* (1960), pp. 99–143; *idem*, 'Recherches sur les routes de l'Europe médiévale. II. Le grand axe routier est-ouest du Midi de la France: d'Avignon à Toulouse', *Bulletin philologique et historique* (1961), pp. 277–308.

CHAPTER II

Early Activity in Occitania

Consider now what duties are performed in the service of God. . . . Christ's garrisons struggle manfully against the devil. . . . [with] vigils, their hymns and psalms, their prayer and alms, and their daily offerings of masses with tears. The followers of Christ devote themselves wholly to this, sacrificing themselves to be found truly acceptable to God. . . . [in] a citadel of God against Satan, where the cowled champions may engage in ceaseless combat against Behemoth . . .

Orderic Vitalis, *The Ecclesiastical History of Orderic Vitalis*,
M. Chibnall (ed. and tr.), III, Oxford, 1975, book 5, 14,
pp. 144–147

THIS chapter presents the first wave of the Military Orders' activities in Occitania by examining the commanderies founded in the initial phase of expansion. The two themes are chronological and geographical.

The Orders did not use monastic vocabulary to describe their buildings. Thus, 'monastery' is not a proper term for their houses. Rather, the sources refer to a building complex of either Order as a 'house' (*domus* or *la maio/mayso*), although the Hospitallers frequently used the word 'hospital' (*ospitalis*), regardless of the size or activities of the house. It is normal modern usage to call such a building a 'commandery'. This term incorporates all the house's possessions and rights. Presiding over a commandery was a 'commander' (*commendator* or *lo comendaire, magister* or *lo maistre*). In Latin he is sometimes called a *preceptor*, which has led some to adopt the term 'preceptory' for a commandery. Evidently, consistency is desirable; and thus, in this work, the terms house and commandery will be used interchangeably, with the senior brother styled as commander.

It is not always simple to recognize a commandery. Small, dependent, agricultural developments (*grangiæ*)[1] are easily identifiable. But three problems complicate matters. First, there are sometimes insufficient references to a holding to allow an appraisal of its size and importance. Second, a small house might have a commander at its head even though it depended upon another

---

[1] These were also a part of Cistercian monasteries, C. Lawrence, *Medieval Monasticism*, New York, 1992, p. 179.

49

commandery. Third, a commandery could be affiliated to another even though it possessed its own dependencies.[2] Yet, there is no doubt about the status of the major commanderies, and, in the main, they provide most information.

The Hospital

For protocol, the Hospital ranked its geographic units by precedence: Provence, Auvergne, France, Italy, Aragon, England, Germany and Castile. Provence had primacy because it was the first to have been created. The importance of Provence had little to do with the Provençal tradition that Brother Gerard, the 'founder' of the Order, was himself from Martigues (then Saint-Geniès).[3] Rather, he came from the region of Amalfi.[4] This is confirmed by numerous sources.[5]

The moment when the Hospital first came to Europe is unclear, but it was long before it became a Military Order. The areas for its activity were dictated by charitable considerations. In the bull *Pie postulatio voluntatis* of 15 February 1113 Pope Paschal II referred to Hospitals at Saint-Gilles, Asti, Bari, Messina, Pisa, Otranto and Taranto.[6] All these, save Asti, were ports from which pilgrims sailed for the Holy Land. Saint-Gilles itself being a pilgrimage site in its own right, and significantly placed at the head of Pope Paschal's list. This date of 1113 is certain, but clearly the hospices were older. Moreover, there had been earlier activity in Europe, for the Order had possessions not mentioned in the bull.

---

[2] For a discussion of ambiguities see E. Bonnet, 'Les Maisons de l'ordre du Temple dans le Languedoc méditerranéen', *Cahiers d'histoire et d'archéologie* 7(1934), p. 516.

[3] There is a modern inscription to this effect outside the Town Hall in Martigues: 'L'an dou sant Crist MXL/ Dins nosto cieuta dou Martegue/ Nasqué lou benurous/ Gerard Tenque/ Foundatour di mounge espitalie/ De Sant Jan de Jerusalem', in D. Le Blévec, 'Aux Origines des Hospitaliers de Saint-Jean de Jérusalem: Gérard dit "Tenque" et l'établissement de l'ordre dans le Midi', *AM* 89(1977), p. 151.

[4] A memorial to him exists at Scala: 'Anno Christi MOXX, nobiles regiones Amalphiæ fundaverunt in sanctam Hyerusalem civitatem militarem religionis equitum S. Johannis Hyerosolimitani qui nunc Melitenses dicuntur. Cujus religionis primus electus magister fuit beatus Gerardus ordinis fundator civitatis Scalarum', in M. Camera, *Memorie storico-diplomatiche dell'antica città e ducato di Amalfi*, II, Salerno, 1881, p. xlviii.

[5] William of Tyre, *Chronicon*, II, book 18, ch. 4, pp. 815–517; Sicard of Cremona, *Chronicon*, in *Rerum italicarum scriptores*, L. Muratori (ed.), VII, Milan, 1725, col. 586; Aimatus of Monte Cassino, *L'Ystoire de li Normans*, J. Champollion-Figeac (ed.), Paris, 1835, p. 231; Anonymous in *De prima origine Hospitalariorum Hierosolymitanorum*, J. Delaville le Roulx (ed.), Paris, 1885, p. 268; J. Delaville le Roulx, *Les Hospitaliers en Terre Sainte et à Chypre*, Paris, 1904, p. 37 agrees, as does Le Blévec, 'Aux Origines', pp. 137–151.

[6] *CH*, I, no. 30, pp. 29–30 (1113).

On the day that Paschal promulgated *Pie postulatio voluntatis*, he published another bull to the prelates, abbots, nobles and faithful of the Iberian peninsula, recommending Brother Palaic, a representative sent by Brother Gerard to collect alms for the Hospital in Jerusalem, which 'sincerely, devotedly [and] assiduously administered to the concerns of pilgrims and the poor'.[7] Such activity in the Iberian peninsula may have begun very early in the twelfth century. A letter dating possibly from 1102 from Bishop Richard of Albano, Apostolic legate, instructed the bishops of the Iberian peninsula to take the Hospital under their protection, and to allow it to enjoy the gifts it received from the faithful.[8]

The Hospital may have come to Europe together with the Order of the Holy Sepulchre, for a chaplain of the Sepulchre was in the Lauraguais c.1101 receiving a gift to the Hospital and the Holy Sepulchre, 'being mindful of the suffering, injuries, sadnesses, and needs, which are sustained by Christ's poor in the city of Jerusalem'.[9] Excluding a purported gift by Duke William of Normandy in 1060 because it appears in a very late register,[10] there are three charters from the area around Albi which are suggestive of even earlier activity.[11] The charters are dated to 1083, 1084 and 1085. They record the gifts of the churches of Saint Antonin of Lacalm, Saint Michael of Ambialet, and Our Lady of Rouairoux and the *mas* of Nizolers to Ancelin and to the 'master of the Hospital'. Ancelin might be the Brother Aiselmus present for the donation of the commandery of Trinquetaille 1115x1126, but this is not certain.[12] Although the consensus on the dates of these acts is now 1108x1110,[13] based

---

[7] 'quod sincere, devote, assidue, peregrinorum et pauperum curam gerat', *ibid.*, I, no. 31, p. 30 (1113).

[8] *ibid.*, I, no. 8, pp. 12–13 (1102x1114).

[9] 'cogitantes de passionibus et de injuriis, et de doloribus et de penuriis quas sustinent pauperes Christi in civitate Jerosolima', *ibid.*, I, no. 6, pp. 9–11 (c.1101).

[10] Paris, National archives, S5512, fol. 12; J. Delaville le Roulx thought that the duke concerned may have been Geoffrey, duke of Normandy and Anjou (1144–1151), but gave no reasons, *CH*, I, p. 1, n. 1.

[11] H, Saint-Antonin, 1; *CH*, I, no. 12, p. 15; no. 13, pp. 15–16; no. 14, pp. 16–17 (1108x1110).

[12] *ibid.*, I, no. 42, p. 36 (1118x1126); *Trinquetaille(Hospital)*, no. 257, p. 272 (1115x1126); *GCN(Arles)*, no. 487, col. 196 (1118); Brother Ancelin appears with the styling of 'master' in the second and third of these acts.

[13] H. Blaquière, 'Les Hospitaliers en Albigeois à l'époque de la croisade: la commanderie de Rayssac', *CF* 4(1969), p. 343; Le Blevec, 'Aux Origines', p. 148; P. Santoni, 'Les Deux premiers siècles du prieuré de Saint-Gilles de l'ordre de l'Hôpital de Saint-Jean de Jérusalem', *Actes du colloque de Barroux, Des Hospitaliers de Saint-Jean de Jérusalem, de Chypre et de Rhodes hier aux chevaliers de Malte aujourd'hui*, Paris, 1983, p. 116; *CH*, I, p. 1, n. 1; E. Cabié, 'Sur trois chartes albigeoises concernant les origines de l'ordre de Saint-Jean de Jérusalem', *AM* 10(1891), pp. 145–156.

on the episcopal and regnal information they should be dated to 1102x1108.[14] In any event, to have donations so far into the hinterland of the Toulousain at this early date demonstrates a wide and successful effort on the part of the Hospitallers to promote the Order.

This view is borne out by other documents. Already in Provence c.1101 was John Bonioli, 'prior of Jerusalem'.[15] A gift from William Alferic of the church of Saint Roman with some land where the Order could build a house with a courtyard, could also date from this year.[16] In 1102 Brother Gerard the Hospitaller received land at Pexiora (then Puysubran) close to Castelnaudary.[17] In 1109 William Pons of Campagnolles and others gave the Orders, with the local bishop's blessing, the churches of Saint Andrew of Campagnolles and Saint Peter of Polignan in the diocese of Béziers.[18] At some time in the first decade of the twelfth century, possibly before, an official in Outremer presented Brother Gerard with a list of donations to the Hospital and the Sepulchre by Count Sancho of Asterac.[19] Brother Gerard declined this gift, and sent word to Brother Durand in Saint-Gilles of this decision.[20] It is not possible to infer that Brother Durand was the prior of Saint-Gilles, as there is no mention of this title until 1142,[21] but he was an official of the Order. He may be the Constable Durand in Outremer in 1125–1126.[22]

In 1113 Brother Palaic was not a lone Hospitaller in the Iberian peninsula, for in 1111 there was already a commandery at Cervera accepting men and women into confraternity.[23] Links were also being forged with the royal houses. In 1116 Queen Uracca of Castile, remembered by the Order in a prayer to be read in the Hospital at Acre recording her generosity,[24] drew up two charters in 1116.[25] Further to the west in Portugal, in 1122 the prior of the

---

[14] Bishop Aldegar's known dates are 1102, and 1109–1115, P. Gams, *Series episcoporum*, Ratisbon, 1873, p. 484; *GC* I, cols. 11–12; King Philip I died in 1108.

[15] *CH*, I, no. 6, pp. 9–11 (c.1101).

[16] 56H4509; *CH*, I, no. 7, p. 12 (1101x1119).

[17] *ibid.*, I, no. 9, p. 13 (1102).

[18] *ibid.*, I, no. 17, pp. 18–19 (1109).

[19] *ibid.*, I, no. 3, pp. 2–3 (1100x1110); A du Bourg, *Histoire de grand-prieuré de Toulouse*, Toulouse, 1883, no. 28, pp. xxi–xxii, puts the date at 1096.

[20] J. Delaville le Roulx thought that this might be Saint-Gilles in Syria-Palestine, but as the act was drawn up at Simorres (Gers), it alludes to Saint-Gilles in Provence, *CH*, I, no. 3, pp. 2–3 (1100x1110).

[21] Santoni, 'Deux premiers', p. 121.

[22] *CH*, I, no. 72, pp. 69–70 (1125); no. 74, p. 71; no. 77, pp. 72–73 (1126).

[23] *ibid.,* I, no. 21, pp. 22–23; no. 22, pp. 23–24 (1111).

[24] 'Proés pour dama Uracca d'Espaigna: que Dieu li rende le bien que elle a fait en la sainte maison de l'Hospital', in 'La Prière des malades dans les hôpitaux de l'ordre de Saint-Jean de Jérusalem', L. Le Grand (ed.), *Bibliothèque de l'Ecole des Chartes* 57(1896), p. 336.

[25] *CH*, I, no. 38, p. 34; no. 39, p. 35 (1116).

Hospital of Barosa had so successfully offered up prayers of intercession for the victory of Afonso (later King Afonso I of Portugal) over King Ibucazan of Badajoz, that Afonso gave the Order a number of *casals* near Trancoso in gratitude.[26]

The earliest records from a commandery originate from the Provençal Alps, where the Order had a commandery beyond the city walls of Gap on the banks of the Laye. Its cartulary roll contains sixty-three charters,[27] only two of which are dated (1111 and 1112).[28] The dates of the remaining charters are uncertain, but tentative extremes of pre-1100 to the 1140s have been suggested.[29] A conclusion as to the dates of the earliest charters in the roll is impossible,[30] but it remains a possibility that some of the charters date from before the conquest of Jerusalem. They are certainly earlier than 1104.[31]

There is thus a strong possibility that the commandery of Gap preceded that of Saint-Gilles. At the very least it was contemporary. There are two other principal arguments in support of this view. First, one based on a tracing of the names from the charters; and second, by 1114 the Order was rafting goods from Gap down the river Durance to Orgon, then into the Rhône, the Petit-Rhône, and finally to Saint-Gilles.[32]

Turning to Saint-Gilles, the Hospitaller house there was founded sometime before 1113. Either Count Raymond IV of Saint-Gilles or his son, Count Bertrand, granted the Order permission to build there. Given Count Bertrand's long running disputes over his father's gifts of property to the abbey of Saint-Gilles,[33] such a project is unlikely to have attracted him, and he never associated himself with the Military Orders.[34] The building permission is likely to have been granted by Count Raymond IV, who had ample opportu-

---

[26] *ibid.*, I, no. 60, pp. 49–50 (1122).

[27] 56H4382; The hand is twelfth century. The roll consists of three skins stitched together, 1800x145mm. It has 344 lines of writing.

[28] *Gap(Hospital)*, no. 22, p. 23 (1111); no. 25, p. 25 (1112).

[29] *ibid.*, p. 10.

[30] For a discussion of arguments, see D. Selwood, '*Ultra vel Citra Mare?* The Expansion of the Orders of the Temple and the Hospital into Occitania', *I. Templari: La Guerra è la Santità*, S. Cerrini (ed.), Piacenza, forthcoming.

[31] Bishop Isoard appeared in *Gap(Hospital)*, no. 1, p. 15; no. 18, p. 21; no. 29, p. 25 (all undated). He held the see from 1090 until 1092, 1099 or 1104, Gams, *Series episcoporum*, p. 552; *GC* 1 (Paris, 1870), col. 461; *GC* (Paris, 1715), col. 462; *CH*, I, p. 6 suggests that Isoard was still Bishop in 1099.

[32] *Trinquetaille(Hospital)*, no. 261, p. 276 (1114); *CH*, I, no. 33, pp. 31–32 (1114); *Trinquetaille(Hospital)*, no. 260, pp. 274–275 (1114x1150); *CH*, I, no. 24, pp. 24–25 (1112x1128); on contextual grounds it is reasonable to date the undated privilege to 1114.

[33] See Chapter 1, pp. 31–2.

[34] However, a gift of his to the Hospital is known from two confirmations by his son, Pons of Tripoli, *CH*, I, no. 79, pp. 74–75 (1126); no. 82, pp. 76–78 (1128).

nity to meet with brothers of the Order in Outremer.[35] This would have been before 28 February 1105, the date of his death whilst besieging Tripoli, 'that Provence of the Levant'.[36] He certainly made gifts concerning Provence during this period.[37]

Both Saint-Gilles and Gap may thus date from the period of the First Crusade, or very soon after. The commandery at Pexiora, founded in 1102,[38] has left few records until 1120; but it, too, was undoubtedly one of the earliest commanderies in the West.[39] The intensity of the Hospital's activities in Europe at this time is supported by foundations elsewhere: Clerkenwell in London dates from 1100,[40] Messina and Altenmünster from 1101, and Pisa from 1112.[41]

The next major Hospitaller house was founded in a suburb of Arles, then one of the largest cities in Provence,[42] home not only to the archbishop of Arles, but also capital of the imperial kingdom of Burgundy. Whilst Saint-Gilles benefitted from the fluvial activity on the Petit-Rhône, the new commandery of Trinquetaille could concern itself with the Grand-Rhône, and it too, was involved in the carriage of goods from Gap.[43] It was founded by the gift from Atton, archbishop of Arles, of the church of Saint Thomas of Trinquetaille in 1115x1126,[44] and was confirmed in 1129 by Archbishop Bernard Guérin.[45] This commandery rose in power and prestige, becoming the most important central-Occitanian commandery after the grand-priory of Saint-Gilles. Shortly after 1146 reference was made to a communal chapter of brethren from Saint-Gilles and Trinquetaille.[46]

---

[35] C. Devic and J. Vaissete, *Histoire générale de Languedoc*, III, Toulouse, 1872, p. 602 favour Count Bertrand.

[36] R. Grousset in P. Deschamps, 'Raymond de St Gilles et sa sépulture au chateau de Tripoli (Liban)', *Etudes de civilisation médiévale (IXe–XIIe siècles), Mélanges offerts à E.-R. Labande*, CESCM (ed.), Poitiers, 1975, p. 211.

[37] *GCN(Marseille)*, no. 1086, col. 689 (1103).

[38] *CH*, I, no. 9, p. 13 (1102).

[39] R. Guimbail, 'Les Hommes et la terre dans une communauté du Lauraguais: Puysubran (Pexiora) du XIIe au début du XVIe siècle', *AM* 99(1987), p. 431.

[40] However, unlike the Temple, the Hospital did not become popular in England until the Second Crusade, M. Gervers, '*Pro defensionis Terre Sancte*: the Development and Exploitation of the Hospitallers' Landed Estate in Essex', in *The Military Orders. Fighting for the Faith and Caring for the Sick*, M. Barber (ed.), Aldershot, 1994, p. 3.

[41] *CH*, I, no. 1, pp. 1–2 (c.1100); Delaville le Roulx, *Gap*, p. 2.

[42] G. Giordanengo, 'Les Hôpitaux arlésiens du XIIe au XIVe siècle', *CF* 13(1978), p. 189.

[43] *Trinquetaille(Hospital)*, no. 261, p. 276 (1114); no. 260, pp. 274–275 (1114x1150).

[44] *CH*, I, no. 42, p. 36 (1118x1126); *Trinquetaille(Hospital)*, no. 257, p. 272 (1115x1126); *GCN(Arles)*, no. 487, col. 196 (1118).

[45] *Trinquetaille(Hospital)*, no. 258, pp 272–273 (1129); *GCN(Arles)*, no. 516, col. 201 (1129).

[46] *Trinquetaille(Hospital)*, no. 110, pp. 95–96 (after 1146).

As with all religious endowments,[47] two fundamental mechanisms led to the foundation of a house. Either the Order was given land, or the Order chose an area and began purchasing rights over it. In the former case it could be that the donor did not even intend for the land to be of great use. There may have been pressing reasons for the sale, as in 1168 when the widow Bernarda and her children were forced to sell possessions to avoid starvation.[48] The Orders built commanderies on some sites which reached them in this way. In 1116 Odilon Guérin swore homage to the Hospitallers, promised to sell them the castle of Montrillon, and gave them donations at Salarial, Alpier, Gariel, Malavieille, Lauran, Grussinas and Gap-Françès.[49] All of these remained simple possessions, except Gap-Françès, which became the controlling commandery, increasing its possessions throughout the twelfth century by a concerted effort on behalf of the Order.[50] Evidently, many early houses remained small, like the house mentioned at Capestang in 1115, administered by a brother from Jerusalem.[51]

When no foundation charters survive, it can only be determined by what date the Orders held possessions in a given place through mention in a legal act. Accordingly, the further implantation of the Orders in the twelfth century must mainly be reconstructed in this way. The Hospitaller in control of developments c.1115–c.1120 was Brother Pons, probably the first prior of Saint-Gilles.[52] During this period the most important acquisition was Saint-Nazaire-d'Aude.[53] The 1120s brought a small increase in the Order's possessions at Aix-en-Provence and Manosque,[54] but it was not until the 1140s that major donations of sites began to proliferate. The priory of Nébian, near Béziers, was founded in 1147,[55] and the acquisition of interests at Aix and land

---

[47] Lawrence, *Monasticism*, p. 98.

[48] 'inopia et necessitate famis coacti', *Saint-Gilles(Hospital)*, fol. 137v (1168).

[49] 56H4444 (1116).

[50] Including the priory of Saint-Privat-de-Frugères (1187), Saint-Maurice de Ventalon (1190), Cubières (1155) and Saint-Sauveur-de-Ginestoux (1179); 56H1917–2087 and 56H4443–4496.

[51] 'Wirallo ospitalario sancte civitatis Iherusalem', 56H4505 (1115).

[52] Santoni, 'Deux premiers', pp. 124, 183.

[53] This was later to belong to the commandery of Grézan; 56H2088–2165 and 56H4497–4519.

[54] Marsolargues, Salazac, La Calmette, Saint-Martin-de-Ligaujac, Saint-Etienne-de-l'Olm, Vezenobres, Malons, Bagard, Calvas, Alès and Arnassan (1126). These were later to be grouped under the commandery of Saint Maurice of Aix (or of Casesvielles); 56H4892–4964; 56H4676 (1127); F. Reynaud, *La Commanderie de l'Hôpital de Saint-Jean de Jérusalem de Rhodes et de Malte à Manosque*, Gap, 1981, p. 8; 56H4676(1127).

[55] This was later to be part of the commandery of Béziers; 56H1560–1700 and 56H4338–4366.

at Jalès begun.[56] In 1149 Mabille, wife of Stephen Lafon, presented a gift to both the prior and commander of Saint-Christol, between Nîmes and Montpellier, which suggests that this house was already well established;[57] while the counts of Forcalquier gave more in the series of donations which were to result in the Order owning the entire town of Manosque.[58] This growth continued well into the 1150s. In 1150 Count Raymond of Barcelona, together with his nephew Raymond Berenger, unreservedly gave the Order the town of Saint Michael of Puimoisson in the Provençal Alps;[59] and by 1158 the Order had a house in Marseillan on the Etang de Thau.[60] The previous year the building of the commandery, as distinct from the grand-priory, of Saint-Gilles had been commenced; and by the following year the house had a commander.[61] The 1160s saw the first mention of a commandery at Nice.[62] In 1175 the commandery of Trignan (later joined to Jalès) was first mentioned,[63] and in 1178 the abbot and the chapter of Psalmodi granted the Templars land at Barbentane. Templar officials from Montpellier exchanged it with the Hospitallers of Montpellier for land at Contreirargues.[64] This land became the Hospitaller commandery of Barbentane, or Mas de Liviers. The following decade saw the Order's establishment at Saint-Didier in 1186, and the first act mentioning the commandery at Avignon (1187).[65] Substantial donations in the surrounding area soon followed; the priory of Bonpas in 1189, Martigues in 1198 and Saint-Symphorien in 1199.[66] The commandery of Grézan had also first been mentioned in 1181.[67] In the last decade of the century the commandery of Palliers (or Palhers) was founded by a donation by Richard of Grèzes, who gave the Order land on the condition that he be received as a *confrater* of the Order.[68] Two further commanderies, Homps and Rayssac, were also founded in the twelfth century, but the dates are unknown.

In many of the early Occitan charters there is mention of a Brother

[56] Montaren, which was to be incorporated into the commandery of Saint Maurice of Aix, 56H4892–4964; L. Blancard, *Inventaire-sommaire des archives départementales antérieures à 1790, archives ecclésiastiques, série H*, Paris, 1869, p. 25.

[57] 56H4870 (1149).

[58] 56H4626 (1149).

[59] 56H4825 (1150).

[60] 56H4501 (1158).

[61] 56H4101 (1157); The commander appears in *Saint-Gilles(Hospital)*, fols. 118v–119r (1158).

[62] 56H4784 (1164).

[63] 56H4567 (1175).

[64] Blancard, *Inventaire*, p. 20.

[65] 56H4219 (1187).

[66] 56H1262–1419; 56H4219–4320.

[67] 56H4497 (1181).

[68] 56H4813 (1191).

Gerard.[69] Whilst this may, infrequently, have been Master Gerard, and was, on occasions, a Provençal brother named Gerard,[70] the majority of instances are symbolic.[71] Many gifts in Europe were given for the benefit of the Hospital in Jerusalem. Thus, a charter would be made out:

> to the house of the Hospital of Jerusalem, and the brethren living there, [given] into your hands, Raymond the Under-nourished, preceptor of the Hospital built at Saint-Pierre[-de-Camp-Public].[72]

This was standard practice for the Order of the Temple, too; gifts would be given:

> to Lord God, the Blessed Mary his mother, to the knights of the Temple of Jerusalem, which is called of Solomon, and to the house of Richerenches, which is built for them and for their sustenance.[73]

Reference to Jerusalem and the mother houses is a symbolic link; the laity saw in their donations a benefit not only for their own souls and the commandery to which they were giving, but also for the maintenance of the Holy Land. It brought them closer to the fundamental ideals of the Orders.

These foundations demonstrate a willingness on the part of the Hospital to acquire and administer properties over a very wide area. From the Pyrenees to the Alps, the officials at Saint-Gilles were responsible for setting up a network that ran the length and breadth of Occitania. It not only developed the coast, but exploited the hinterland, too. The formal administration was begun at an early date. Already by 1123 there was mention of a Pentecostal chapter held in the region of Saint-Gilles.[74]

---

[69] *inter alia*, *CH*, I, no. 7, p. 12 (1101x1119); no. 10, pp. 13–14 (1106x1110); no. 11, pp. 14–15 (1106x1123); no. 18, p. 20 (c.1110); no. 32, 36 (1118x1126); *Trinquetaille(Hospital)*, no. 257, p. 272 (1115x1126); *GCN(Arles)*, no. 3, pp. 3–4; no. 4, p. 4; no. 264, p. 278; no. 271, p. 281 (1110x1116); no. 487, col. 196 (1118); *Gap(Hospital)*, no. 9, p. 16; no. 12, p. 18; no. 18, p. 21 (1100x1120).

[70] Santoni, 'Deux premiers', p. 121.

[71] See also p. 61.

[72] 'domui Hospitalis Jherosolimitani et fratribus ibidem habitantibus in manu de te Raimundo malo nutrito preceptor domus Hospitalis hedificate apud Sanctam Petrum', *Saint-Gilles(Hospital)*, fols. 71v–80r (1184).

[73] 'Domino Deo, et Beate Marie genitrici ejus, et militibus Templi Iherosolimitani quo dicitur Salomonis, et domui de Richarensis, quę edificatur pro illis, et sustentacione illorum', *Richerenches(Temple)*, no. 13, p. 17 (1141).

[74] *CH*, I, no. 69, pp. 61–62 (1123).

The Temple

Although better documented than that of the Hospital, the Temple's expansion into Europe is equally as riddled with uncertainty. There were three distinct periods to note. The first, a lone act of 1124. The second, the activity surrounding the preparation for the Council of Troyes in 1129; and the third, the true move to Europe. Whilst the first and third of these directly concern Occitania, there is much in the second that does not, and this will not be examined here.[75]

As with the Order of the Hospital, there is a tradition that the Order of the Temple was founded by two Provençaux;[76] it is fantasy. However, the earliest European Templar act was drawn up, and concerned property, in Provence. It related to what may have been a failed commandery. In the same way that in 1110 Brother Gerard of the Hospital gave back the church of the Blessed Virgin of Dalbade to Pons of Melgueil, abbot of Cluny, and Abbot Ansquilin of Moissac,[77] so the Templar act of 1124 witnessed the Temple divesting itself of the church of Saint Bartholemew of La Motte Palayson (canton of Fréjus) on the Côte d'Azur. It had been given to them at an unknown date by Bishop Berenger of Fréjus (c.1090–1131)[78] as a source of revenue, for it came with its tithes. There were no Templars present in 1124 when the Order gifted it to the church of the Blessed Virgin of Palayson, a dependency of the abbey of Saint Victor in Marseille.[79]

There was no question of the Temple supplying a priest for the church at this date, for the privilege to retain their own priests was not granted until 1139, but it would doubtless have envisaged presenting a secular priest. This was a costly procedure, for a secular priest expected to be granted a living from the tithes of a church to which he had been presented.[80] Acting for the Temple was William of Poitiers of the comital house of Valentinois.[81] He did

---

[75] Generally, V. Carrière, 'Les Débuts de l'ordre du Temple', *Le Moyen âge* 18(1914), pp. 308–335; Barber, *Knighthood*, pp. 12–14; Demurger, *Temple*, pp. 55–59.

[76] A. Blès, *Dictionnaire historique des rues de Marseille*, Marseille, 1989, p. 361.

[77] *CH*, I, no. 18, p. 20 (c.1110).

[78] Gams, *Series*, p. 551, believes this Bishop Berenger to have been Berenger IV of Fréjus; *GC* 1, cols. 427–428 deems him to have been Berenger III, although both agree on the dates of his episcopacy.

[79] *CT*, no. 2, pp. 1–2 (1124); *Saint Victor*, no. 1102, pp. 574–575 (1124); *GCN(Marseille)*, no. 141, col. 65 (1124).

[80] G. Constable, 'Monasteries, Rural Churches and the Cura Animarum in the Early Middle Ages', *Settimane di studio del centro italiano de studi sull'altro medioevo, XXVIII: Cristainizzazione ad organizzazione ecclesiastica delle compagne nell'alto medioevo: espansione e resistenze*, II, Spoleto, 1982, p. 352.

[81] Barber, *Knighthood*, p. 11.

not sever all Templar links with the church, but retained a rent of eight sextaries of wheat 'for the works of the knights every year'.[82] This is a small quantity, a Provençal sextary of wheat being worth around 2 *sous* for most of the century, and equivalent to one fifth of a charge (*saumata* or *asinata*), a measure based on the amount with which a beast of burden could be laden.[83] This is hardly enough to warrant being shipped to Outremer, so the use to which it was put remains something of a mystery. Perhaps it was William's fee for acting for the Order. How long the Temple continued to receive these eight sextaries is unknown, for in the records of Saint Victor no more is heard of the church of Saint Bartholemew. Yet there is much that is revealing in that between 1120 and 1124 Bishop Berenger of Fréjus had already entrusted a church to the Order.

The next wave of activity surrounded the Council of Troyes in 1129. Sometime before 1126 King Baldwin II of Jerusalem had sent Brothers Gundomar and Andrew to Abbot Bernard at Clairvaux.[84] They carried with them a letter from the king which related that the Templars wished for Apostolic approval, and a Rule.[85] A reason why the king may have written to Saint Bernard, aside from his repute, was that Brother Andrew was Saint Bernard's uncle.[86] Preparations were under way soon, and in 1127 Brother Hugh of Payns, master of

---

[82] 'in quam ecclesiam retinuit supradictus Guilelmus, ad opus militum, VIII sextaria frumenti vendentis mensure Roche Brune, sine ullo alio retinaculo, omni anno', *CT*, no. 2, pp. 1–2 (1124).

[83] *Richerenches(Temple)*, p. cxxxvi.

[84] The dates for this letter are 1120x1126, excluding the period April 1123–August 1124 (Baldwin's imprisonment).

[85] *CT*, no. 1, p. 1 (1120x1126).

[86] Brother Andrew of Montbard, Saint Bernard's uncle, was master of the Order from 1153–1156. *Dictionnaire de biographie française*, J. Baltheau, M. Barroux and M. Prevost (eds.), II, Paris, 1936, pp. 962–963; Andrew of Montbard was the son of Bernard of Montbard, and the brother of Saint Bernard's mother, Aleth. Three letters of relevance from Saint Bernard survive, one to his uncle Andrew (1153), and two to Queen Melisende of Jerusalem (undated and 1153) in which he refers to this uncle, Bernard of Clairvaux, *Epistolæ*, in *PL* 182, letters 288, 206 and 289, cols. 493–493, 373 and 491–493. It is probable that the Andrew sent to Saint Bernard was this Andrew, for it explains, in part, the choice of Saint Bernard as one to secure Apostolic approval of the Rule; G. de Valous, 'Quelques observations sur la toute primitive observance des Templiers et la *Regula pauperum commilitonum Christi Templi Salomonici* rédigée par Saint-Bernard au concile de Troyes (1128)', *Mélanges Saint Bernard, XXIVe congrès de l'association bourguignonne des sociétés savantes*, Association des amis de Saint-Bernard (ed.), Dijon, 1953, p. 32 is clear that Andrew was one of the founding nine; J. Richard, 'Le Milieu famial', *Bernard de Clairvaux*, Commission d'histoire de l'ordre de Cîteaux (ed.), Paris, 1953, p. 14 proposed that Andrew of Montbard was still a layman in 1129. This would discount him from being a member of the Clairvaux party. Richard's suggestion is based on the Abbé Jobin, *Saint-Bernard*, p. 47 who suggested that since Andrew was present at Saint-Pierre-le-Vif in 1129,

the Order, brought a handful of knights with him to Europe with a fourfold objective: to recruit for the Damascus campaign,[87] on royal business to Count Fulk V of Anjou, to prepare for the Council of Troyes, and to publicize and receive donations for the Order.[88]

At some time between April 1127 and 1128 Brother Hugh was in Anjou at the court of Count Fulk V, where he presented the proposition of King Baldwin II that Fulk marry the heiress Melisende, and so be invested king of Jerusalem.[89] He followed Fulk to Le Mans where the latter took the Cross on Ascension Day 1128 (31 May), and by 31 May 1129 he had returned to Fulk's court in Anjou.[90] From here Brother Hugh travelled to Flanders in the company of Brothers Godfrey of Saint-Omer, Pagan of Montdidier and others. Brother Godfrey was active here in this, his home region. From there they took a passage to England, and their visit merited a lengthy entry in the Anglo-Saxon Chronicle.[91] From England they made for the continent once again. By January 1129 Brothers Hugh, Godfrey and Pagan were at Troyes preparing for the Council.[92] Other Templars, too, converged on Troyes. Brothers Roland, Geoffrey Bisol and Archambaud of Saint-Amand were all present, and Andrew of Baudemont, cited at the Council of Troyes as a layman, appeared soon after as 'master' of the Temple.[93]

Following the Council Brother Hugh undertook a journey to oversee developments in Occitania, culminating in his embarkation at Marseille along with

---

witnessing a charter together with many of his kin, he had not yet joined the Temple. This does not necessarily follow.

[87] William of Tyre, *Chronicon*, I, book 13, ch. 15, p. 620; J. Phillips, 'Hugh of Payns and the 1129 Damascus Crusade', in *The Military Orders. Fighting for the Faith and Caring for the Sick*, M. Barber (ed.), Aldershot, 1994, pp. 346–357.

[88] J. Phillips, *Defenders of the Holy Land, Relations between the Latin East and the West 1119–1187*, Oxford, 1996, pp. 24–26 emphasizes the Royal nature of the venture, together with King Baldwin II's implicit understanding of the importance of a well-resourced Military Order.

[89] *CT*, no. 8, pp. 5–6 (1127x1128).

[90] *ibid.*, no. 12, pp. 8–9 (May 1128).

[91] 'In the course of the same year Hugh of the Temple came from Jerusalem to the king in Normandy, and the king received him with great honour and gave him great treasures, consisting of gold and silver; and then he sent him to England and there he was received by all good men and they all gave him treasures – and in Scotland also – and sent by him to Jerusalem great property entirely in gold and silver; and he summoned people to Jerusalem', *The Anglo-Saxon Chronicle*, D. Whitelock (tr.), London, 1961, pp. 194–195.

[92] *CT*, no. 22, p. 16 (c. January 1129).

[93] 'Willelmo de Baudemento, tunc Templi magistro', *ibid.*, no. 27, p. 19 (1129x1132). He appeared at Troyes simply among the unlettered witnesses: 'Ceterum vero de non litteratis idoneum nobis videtur ut testes amatores veritatis adducantur in medium: Comes Theobaudus, comesque Nivernensis, ac Andreas de Baudimento', *RTemp*, *Primitive Rule*, caps. 6–7, pp. 18–19.

Count Fulk V in 1129. The two arrived in Acre that summer,[94] and Brother Hugh took part in the action against Damascus at the end of 1129.[95] Although it appears from two acts that Hugh was still in Occitania in 1130, the references to him are stylized and symbolic in the same vein as those which referred to Brother Gerard of the Hospital.[96]

All of Brother Hugh's objectives were fulfilled, although the contingent of knights he had taken over for the Damascus assault were, according to the Anglo-Saxon chronicle, deeply disappointed.[97] Yet, by the time of his departure for Outremer, not only had the Order received prestigious donations, but Brother Hugh had established an administrative network. Brother Pagan of Montdidier was deputed 'master of France',[98] and Brothers Hugh Rigaud and Raymond Bernard were charged with overseeing developments in Occitania.[99]

Raymond Bernard was at work first. He was in Portugal in March 1128 when Queen Teresa of Castile presented the Temple with the castle of Soure, near Coïmbra. In the following two years she was instrumental in persuading others to give the Temple benefactions.[100] Her son by her marriage to Henry of Burgundy, Afonso Henriques, declared in an act confirming his mother's gift that he was already a *confrater* of the Order in 1129.[101] Meanwhile, Brother Hugh Rigaud was in the Aude valley, promoting the Order so that, within four years, it would receive the castle of Douzens which, along with the main bulk of the commandery, came in the early 1130s. This commandery initially encompassed Douzens and Carcassonne, but the latter gained its independence in 1153.[102] Yet, before Douzens was founded both brethren had been active on a broad geographical scale.

In 1129 Brothers Hugh Rigaud and Raymond Bernard received Peter

---

[94] J. Pryor, 'Transportation of Horses by Sea During the Era of the Crusades: Eighth Century to 1285 A.D.', *The Mariner's Mirror* 68(1982), p. 15; William of Tyre, *Chronicon*, I, book 13, ch. 24, pp. 618–619.

[95] *ibid.*, I, book 13, ch. 26, pp. 620–622.

[96] *CT*, no. 30, p. 23 (1130); Demurger, *Temple*, p. 57 has suggested that this act is a fake because of the reference to Brother Hugh. This does not follow. *Douzens(Temple)*, C no. 1, p. 263 (1130). See pp. 56–7.

[97] 'and then there went with him and after him so large a number of people as never had done since the first expedition in the days of Pope Urban – though it came to little. He said that a great war was afoot between the Christians and the heathens. Then when they arrived there it was nothing but lies – thus miserably were all the people afflicted.' *Anglo-Saxon Chronicle*, pp. 194–195.

[98] M. Melville, 'Les Débuts de l'ordre du Temple', *Die geistlichen Ritterorden Europas, Vorträge und Forschungen* 26(1980), p. 26.

[99] *Douzens(Temple)*, C no. 7, p. 266 (1133x1134).

[100] *CT*, no. 10, p. 7 (1128).

[101] *ibid.*, no. 24, p. 17 (1129); Barber, *Knighthood*, p. 32.

[102] *Douzens(Temple)*, A no. 17, pp. 29–30 (1153).

Bernard and his wife Borella into confraternity, granting them a corrody to be fed and clothed for the rest of their lives.[103] In 1131 Raymond Pelet, seigneur of Alès and veteran of Count Raymond IV's First Crusade host, gifted the Order land in the Vivarais which was to form the embryo of the commandery of Jalès.[104] In 1132 Brother Hugh Rigaud was twenty-five miles from Valence where he received a donation of lands and men from the counts of Albon.[105] Three months later he was at Carcassonne in the company of the Trencavel.[106] By the end of the year Brother Hugh had travelled east and was, together with Brother William Solomon, at Le Puy where they bought a property known as the 'caves (crotis)[107] of Aiguilhe' for the large sum of 800 sous of Melgueil, mentioned that same month as the 'house' of the caves of Aiguilhe at Le Puy.[108] The Order may have already had a fairly advanced organization, for present with Brother Hugh Rigaud was Brother Robert 'seneschal of the Temple'.[109]

The cycle of donations which was to trigger the creation of the commandery of Douzens was begun by a meeting between the Temple and the Trencavel in 1132. The meeting brought together almost all the Trencavel clan: Roger I of Béziers (d.1150), his brothers Raymond Trencavel I (d.1167), Bernard Atton V (d.1159), and their mother, the recently widowed Viscountess Cecily (d.1150).[110] They gave the Temple a man, Pons the Gascon, his family and mas under the walls of the city of Carcassonne, together with all the services owed by Pons and his family. This was one of the first gifts made to the Order which clearly demonstrated the Order's success both as a spiritual

---

[103] ibid., C no. 11, p. 269 (1129).

[104] 56H5245 (1131); D le Blévec, 'Les Templiers en Vivarais: Les Archives de la commanderie de Jalèz et l'implantation de l'ordre du Temple en Cévennes', Revue du Vivarais 84(1980), pp. 36–49.

[105] Douzens(Temple), C no. 3, pp. 266–267 (1132).

[106] ibid., A no. 171, pp. 152–154 (1132).

[107] This is not a Latin word, presumably a corruption of the Occitan 'crota' nf meaning crypt or cave, E. Levy, Petit dictionnaire Provençal-Français, Heidelberg, 1973, p. 102.

[108] Douzens(Temple), C no. 10, pp. 268–269 (c.1132); C no. 10, pp. 268–269 (c.1132) for a dispute which soon arose.

[109] ibid., C no. 10, pp. 268–269 (c.1132). The post of seneschal is not mentioned in the Primitive Rule of Troyes, and it is odd to find a bearer of this office in Europe in 1132. The seneschal in Outremer was the master's deputy. It is possible he was from Outremer if he was either the 'Robert, knight of the Temple' present in Outremer in 1125 when Bishop Bernard of Nazareth exempted the Hospital from paying tithes in his diocese, or 'Robert of Burgundy, knight of Saint Stephen of Jeusalem' present in Saumur in 1127. There is also the possibility that it was Robert of Craon, who was to be made master of the Order in 1139, CT, no. 3, p. 2 (1125); CH, I, no. 71, p. 68 (1125); J. Chartrou, L'Anjou de 1109 à 1151, Paris, 1928, no. 37, pp. 364–367; Barber, Knighthood, p. 8.

[110] Douzens(Temple) A no. 171, pp. 152–154 (1132).

Order whose prayers were effective, and as one whose military mission in the Holy Land appealed to European society. It was made:

> for the remission, absolution and health of the soul of our father, Bernard Atton, and for the remission of his sins, our sins and those of our issue, we are donors to God, and to the holy knighthood of the Temple of Solomon of Jerusalem, and to the brothers in the same place fighting for the defence of Christendom.[111]

A year later to the day the family made another gift, welcoming the Order inside the city walls, for along with property at Brucafel, they gave land in the Saint Michael quarter of Carcassonne upon which the Order might build.[112]

The core of the commandery of Douzens came from the local knightly families of Barbaira and Canet in 1133. Both of these families were to foster long-standing relationships with the Order. Together they ceded the castle of Douzens, various lands, men and rights.[113] At the same time, and to seal the family links with the Order, the brothers Aimeric of Barbaira and William Chatbert gave themselves as *confratres*. In the years to come three of the four Barbaira brothers affiliated themselves to the Order with one, Raymond Ermengard, professing as a brother. Twenty years later, when the family made a gift to the Order, they were able to give it to 'you, Raymond Ermengard, our brother in flesh, and our spiritual brother in the knighthood . . . of the Temple'.[114]

The next significant event was a contribution by the Benedictine monks of Saint Mary of Alet near Espéraza, who welcomed the Templars, gathering many of the local seigneurs (including the Barbaira and Canet) for the occasion. As a result of three donations received here, the Order acquired wide-

---

[111] 'propter remissionem et absolutionem atque remedium anime patris nostri Bernardi Atonis, et propter remissionem peccatorum ejus atque nostrorum et posteritati nostre, donatores sumus Deo et sancte militie Templi Jherosolimitane Salomonis et fratribus ibidem Deo in deffensione Christianitatis militantibus', *ibid.*, A no. 171, pp. 152–154 (1132).

[112] *ibid.*, A no. 115, pp 106–108 (1133).

[113] *ibid.*, A no. 1, p. 305 (1133).

[114] *ibid.*, A no. 87, pp. 83–84 (1153). Demurger, *Temple*, pp. 164–167 has conducted a prosopographical study of the Barbaira family and its links with the Temple. Another Arnold of Barbaira, not to be confused with the brother of Aimeric, William Chatbert and Raymond Ermengaud, had professed in 1143 and was, too, receiving gifts on behalf of the Order. Demurger, *Temple*, pp. 164–167, makes an error when he claims that the Arnold of Barbaira who became a brother of the Temple was the brother of Aimeric, William Chatbert and Raymond Ermengard, for Arnold was still a secular in 1153 when they all made the donation of the church of Saint John of Carrière, whereas Brother Arnold of Barbaira was a Templar by 1143, *Douzens(Temple)*, A no. 47, pp. 56–57 (1143).

spread possessions around Douzens.[115] At the same time a gift of land from which the Order might draw revenue was presented by Lauretta, who made plain the fact that the military role of the Order had seized her imagination:

> fearing the future Day of Judgement where my redeemer will be sitting in His seat of majesty, and repaying every individual as he deserves . . . to the knights of Jerusalem . . . who courageously fight for the faith against the menacing Saracens, who try to destroy the law of God, and [His] faithful servants.[116]

Douzens demonstrates well the difficulty of ascertaining when a commandery was created. Although the gift of the castle of Douzens in April 1133 is the most obvious date for its 'foundation', the quantity of acts from the Douzens cartularies drawn up before April of that year clearly shows the extent of the Templar activities.[117] It is likely that the Order had an embryonic commandery before 1133 given the nature of the corrody granted to Peter Bernard and his wife Borella, and the purchase of the 'caves' for 800 *sous*. These two events are indicative of a base where the two could come to eat, and from which revenue could be drawn to finance the purchase. This type of corrody, to feed and clothe, is one that is normally found, for obvious reasons of resources, in fully developed houses. A typical example of such provision was:

> and in return, we promise to provide food for you, as long as you shall live, as if you were one of the brethren,[118]

or that granted by the Hospitallers to an aspiring *consoror*, Williametta:

> I concede to you the habit of the house that you may assume it whensoever you wish, and meanwhile you may take your food in the refectory of the house of the Hospital.[119]

---

[115] *ibid.*, C no. 4, p. 264 (1133x1134) (A no. 38, similar (1134); C no. 5, p. 264; C no. 6, pp. 265–266 (1133x1134).

[116] 'timens futurum diem juditii ubi erit redemptor meus sedens in sede magestatis sue et retribuens unicuique prout gesserit . . . militibus Jherosolimitanis . . . contra inopinatos Sarracenos qui legem Dei et fidelos Deo servientes destruere conantur . . . viriliter bellantibus per fidem', *ibid.*, A no. 40, p. 50 (C no. 3, p. 263 identical) (1133x1134).

[117] *ibid.*, C no. 9, p. 269 (1129); C no. I, p. 263 (1130); C no. 3, pp. 266–267; A no. 171, pp. 152–154 (1132); C no. 9, pp. 267–268; C no. 10, pp. 268–269 (1132?); A no. 95, pp 106–108 (1133); C no. 7, p. 266; C no. 4, p. 264; C no. 5, p. 264; C no. 6, pp. 265–266; A no. 40, p. 50 (1133x1134).

[118] 'et pro stipulatione promittimus quod alimenta tibi quamdiu vixeris præstabimus sicut unius ex nostris fratribus', *Saint-Gilles(Temple)*, fol. 172rv (1190).

[119] 'concedo tibi habitum domus ut illud assumas quandocumque tibi placuerit et interim habeas cibum tuum in refectorio domus Hospitalis', *Saint-Gilles(Hospital)*, fols. 35v–36r (1191).

The further provision to the corrody of Peter Bernard and his wife regarding their children adds to the evidence. The couple declared that if they had any children, the Order could deal with them as if they were the Order's own.[120] However, that very year at Troyes the Order had been forbidden to receive children as oblates,[121] so this provision in the corrody either confirms that the Order had earlier accepted children, and that this contract was thus in contravention of the new ban or, more likely, that the Order already possessed the children of those who had given themselves to the Order as vassals. This latter is more than certainly the case, for if the contract had illicitly meant that the children would be trained in arms, then there is a glaring omission in that no distinction was made between male and female issue.

Douzens expanded as a commandery. It already encompassed Carcassonne, and further to this Mas-des-Cours was added. It began with a donation of land by locals in 1136, followed two years later by the gift from Bishop Raymond of Carcassonne of the tithe from the church of Saint Mary at Les Cours.[122] These donations were to be followed by a period of expansion and consolidation, especially throughout the following two decades.[123] The first commander of Mas-des-Cours, Brother Isarn of Molières, appeared in 1162.[124]

The other main constituent part of the commandery of Douzens, that of Carrière, was first acquired by the Templars when Aimeric, William Chatbert and Arnold of Barbaira gave the Order the church of Saint John of Carrière in 1153.[125] Two days later the Canet family made over their rights concerning the church of Saint John, and expressly willed that the Peace of God be observed within its lands bordered by crosses.[126] This too, became a major

---

[120] 'Et si infantes habemus, et ipsi voluntatem militum Templi Salomonis facere volunt, ipse milites faciant de eis sicut de propriis suis infantibus', *Douzens(Temple)*, C no. 11, p. 269 (1129).

[121] 'Ut pueri, quamdiu sunt parvi, non accipiantur inter fratres Templi', *RTemp.*, *Primitive Rule*, cap. 14, p. 25.

[122] *Douzens(Temple)*, B no. 1, pp. 185–186 (1136); B no. 9, p. 195 (1138).

[123] *ibid.*, B no. 11, pp. 197–198 (1139); B no. 14, p. 200 (1142); B no. 3, pp. 187–188; B no. 2, pp. 186–187; B no. 4, pp. 189–190; B no. 5, pp. 190–191; B no. 18, pp. 203–204 (1147); B no. 10, pp. 196–197 (1149); B no. 22, pp. 206–207; B no. 37, pp. 217–218 (1157); B no. 16, pp. 201–202; B no. 17, pp. 202–203 (1158); B no. 21, pp. 205–206 (1162); B no. 8, pp. 193–194 (1162?); B no. 12, p. 198 (1162x1163); B no. 47, pp. 225–226 (1163); B no. 19, p. 204; B no. 24, pp. 207–208; B no. 39, p. 219 (1164); A no. 122, p. 155; B no. 20, p. 205; B no. 6, pp. 191–192 (1167); B no. 27, pp. 209–210 (1168); B no. 59, p. 235 (1168x1169); B no. 30, pp. 211–212 (1182).

[124] *ibid.*, B no. 21, pp. 205–206 (1162).

[125] *ibid.*, A no. 87, pp. 83–84 (1153).

[126] *ibid.*, A no. 88, pp. 84–85 (1153).

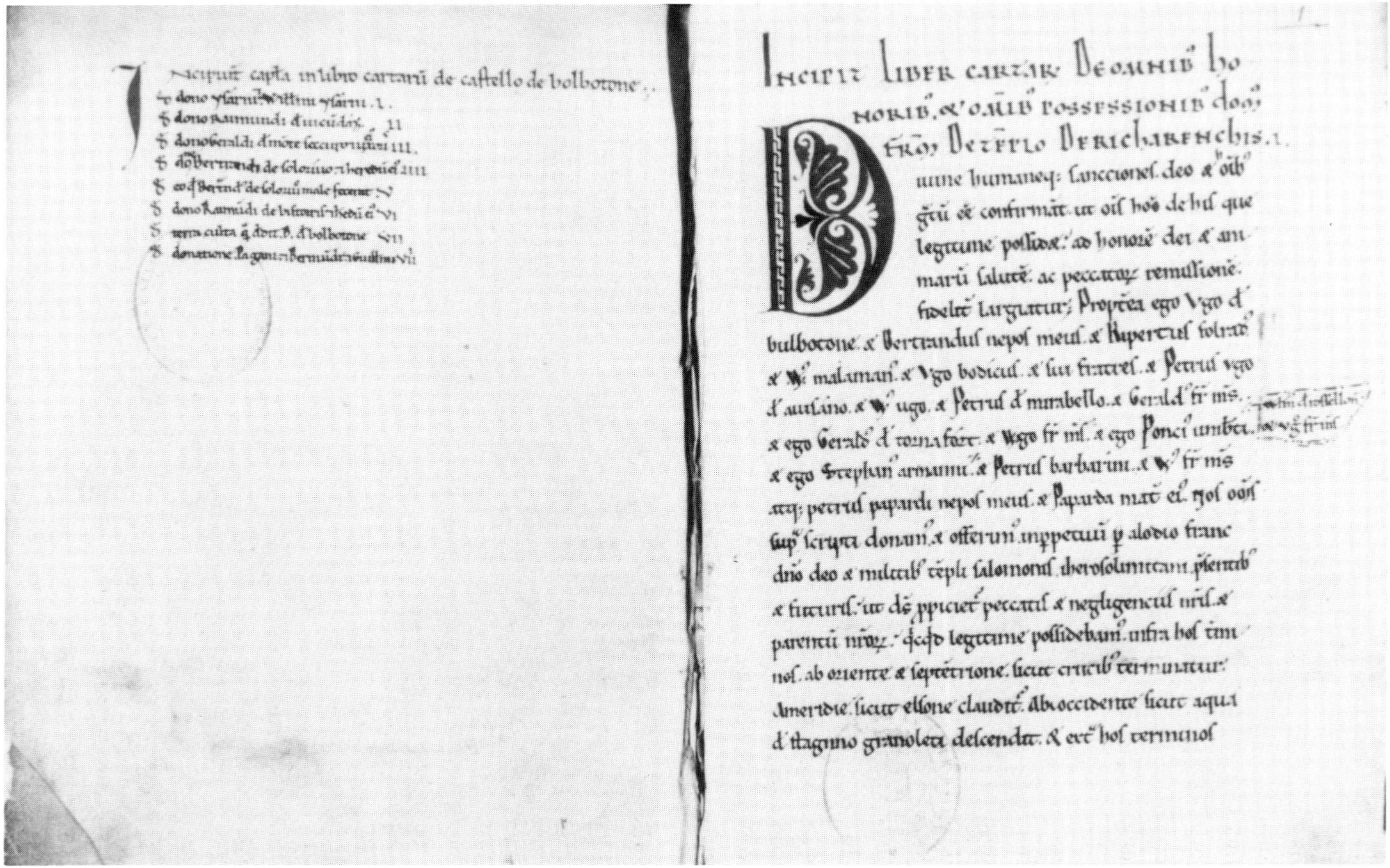

PLATE II: Copy of the 1136 charter of Hugh of Bourbouton. Title-page of the Templar cartulary of Richerenches.

dependency,[127] so much so that people gave themselves to be buried there as opposed to at Douzens.[128] Its first commander, Brother Peter of Padern, appeared in 1169.[129]

The next wave of activity was under Brother Arnold of Bedocio. Like Brother Hugh Rigaud, he appeared in documents from both Provence and Catalonia, but not Aragon or Navarre.[130] Brother Arnold was the successor of Brother Hugh Rigaud, and resided at Douzens. When summoned from the Iberian peninsula, he travelled first to Toulouse where he founded the commandery of La Villedieu with donations from the count of Foix and the bishop of Toulouse.[131] He journeyed on to Saint-Paul-Trois-Châteaux to found a commandery in the marquisate of Provence. On 19 March 1136, Maundy Thursday, he received two donations, one witnessed by Pons of Grillon, bishop of Saint-Paul-Trois-Châteaux, the other with the bishop as one of the principal donors.[132] In this latter Brother Arnold received the church of Saint John with its adjoining palace. This was the kernel of the commandery of Saint-Paul-Trois-Châteaux.

In December of that same year (1136), Brother Arnold received the lands that were to comprise one of the most important commanderies in Provence: Richerenches. It came from the local seigneur Hugh of Bourbouton. Clearly a devout man, Hugh's donation was prefaced by a pious arenga,[133] considerably more fulsome than the normal request for forgiveness of one's sins and those of one's relatives.[134] Together with his nephew, Bertrand, and others, he gave Brother Arnold land between Valréas and Saint-Paul-Trois-Châteaux in the seigneury of Bourbouton.[135] Two years later Hugh, his wife Marchesa, their

---

[127] *ibid.*, A no. 105, p. 99 (1167); A no. 74, pp. 75–76; A no. 93, pp. 90–91 (1168); A no. 113, p. 105 (1169).

[128] *ibid.*, A no. 74, pp. 75–76 (1168).

[129] *ibid.*, A no. 97, pp. 93–94 (1169).

[130] Forey, *Aragón*, p. 87.

[131] *Richerenches(Temple)*, p. cxlvii.

[132] *ibid.*, no. 27, pp. 28–29; no. 128, pp. 121–122 (1136). The charter is actually dated 1167, but in a lengthy explanation the Marquis of Ripert-Monclar explains his reasoning for the redating. It is more credible for the reasons he gives: (1) Bishop Pons of Grillon died in 1138 (2) the lunar dating is irreconcilable with 1167 (3) the other brethren mentioned were no longer active in 1167, and (4) there was a conflict in 1172, and the witnesses spoke of the founders as having been 'antecessores nostri', *ibid.*, no. 122, p. 117 (1172).

[133] An 'arenga' (or harangue) is an introduction to a charter, G. Constable, 'Papal, Imperial and Monastic Propaganda in the Eleventh and Twelfth Centuries', *Prédication et propagande au Moyen Age: Islam, Byzance, Occident. Penn-Paris-Dumbarton Oaks Colloquia (20–25 octobre 1980) III*, G. Makdisi (ed.), Paris, 1983, p. 182.

[134] 'Divine humaneque sancciones Deo et hominibus gratum esse confirmant ut omnis homo de his que legitime possidet, ad honorem Dei et animarum salutem ac peccatorum remissionem fideliter largiatur', *Richerenches(Temple)*, no. 1, pp. 3–4 (1136).

[135] *ibid.*, no. 1, pp. 3–4 (1136).

son Nicholas, his nephew Bertrand, and others made another donation of more adjoining land.[136] The following day Hugh professed as a Templar.[137] Brother Hugh had the great satisfaction of rising within seven years to command Richerenches;[138] a post he retained until his death in 1151.[139] The links with the family of Bourbouton were to remain strong. Six months after Brother Hugh became commander his son, Nicholas, also professed at Richerenches,[140] and Bertrand, Brother Hugh's nephew, who had been present for many of the early acts, became a *confrater* of the commandery the following year (1146),[141] witnessing just under sixty acts before his death in 1171x1175.[142]

The further expansion and implantation of the Temple in the twelfth century was more sustained than that of the Hospital, creating four or more commanderies every decade. In the 1140s the Order established themselves at Jalès (near where many Templars were to be imprisoned in the early fourteenth

---

[136] *ibid.*, no. 2, pp. 4–5 (1136).

[137] *ibid.*, no. 3, pp. 5–7 (1138); J. Durbec, 'Les Templiers en Provence. Formation des commanderies et répartition géographique de leurs biens', *PH* 9(1959), p. 15 believes this charter to be only one of confraternity. It is quite clear, however, that it is a profession. *A fortiori, Richerenches(Temple)*, no. 89, pp. 88–91, is another version of the act which enumerates all the lands he had given, and his act is quite clear, for he declared: 'relinquo seculum'. Moreover, by October of that year he spoke in an act quite clearly as a Templar when referring to 'domus nostre de Richarenchas', *ibid.*, no. 4, pp. 7–8 (1138).

[138] *ibid.*, no. 56, p. 57 (1145).

[139] *ibid.*, p. cliv.

[140] *ibid.*, no. 7, pp. 9–10 (1145).

[141] *ibid.*, no. 1, pp. 3–4; no. 38, pp. 40–41 (1136); no. 14, p. 18 (1136x1137); no. 2, pp. 4–5; no. 3, pp. 5–7; no. 4, pp. 7–8; no. 5, pp. 8–9; no. 47, pp. 48–49; no. 89, pp. 88–91 (1138); no. 48, pp. 49–50 (post 1138); no. 9, pp. 12–13; no. 11, pp. 14–15; no. 12, p. 16 (1144); no. 176, p. 155 (post 1145); no. 59, pp. 59–60 (1146).

[142] *ibid.*, no. 59, pp. 59–60 (1146); no. 31, pp. 33–34; no. 60, pp. 60–63 (1147); no. 32, pp. 34–36; no. 43, pp. 45–46; no. 57, p. 57 (1148); no. 50, p. 51 (1149); no. 61, pp. 63–65 (1150); no. 65, pp. 67–68; no. 67, p. 70; no. 71, pp. 72–73 (1151); no. 140, p. 130 (1151x1164); no. 72, pp. 73–74 (1152); no. 73, pp. 74–75 (1153); no. 75, p. 77; no. 187, pp. 162–166 (1155); no. 76, p. 78; no. 77, pp. 78–79; no. 129, pp. 123–124; no. 136, p. 128; no. 151, pp. 136–137; no. 152, p. 137; no. 159, pp. 142–143 (1156); no. 150, pp. 135–136 (1156–1158); no. 79, pp. 80–81; no. 80, p. 82; no. 92, p. 93 (1157); no. 132, p. 126; no. 134, pp. 127–128; no. 144, pp. 132–133; no. 188, pp. 166–168 (1158); no. 133, pp. 126–127; no. 84, pp. 84–85; no. 95, pp. 96–97; no. 137, pp. 128–129 (1159); no. 85, pp. 85–86; no. 161, pp. 143–144 (1160); no. 172, p. 152 (c.1160); no. 175, p. 154; no. 177, pp. 155–156; no. 190, pp. 169–170 (1161); no. 168, pp. 149–150; no. 209, p. 186 (1162); no. 164, pp. 146–147 (1162x1163); no. 189, pp. 168–169 (1163); no. 167, p. 149 (1163x1164); no. 100, pp. 101–102; no. 183, pp. 159–160; no. 191, pp. 170–171 (1164); no. 86, pp. 86–97; no. 88, pp. 87–88 (1167); no. 93, pp. 94–96 (1168); no. 96, pp. 97–100; no. 102, pp. 102–103 (1169); no. 81, p. 83 (1170); no. 103, pp. 103–104; no. 105, p. 106; no. 118, pp. 113–114 (1171). In this last act he was present, but by *ibid.*, no. 215, pp. 191–192 (1175), it was specifically stated that the act was 'post mortem Bertrandi de Borboto'.

century),[143] Montfrin,[144] Pézenas,[145] Saint Eulalia,[146] and Roaix;[147] whilst the 1150s brought Montsaunès and Boudrac,[148] Narbonne,[149] Nîmes,[150] Our Lady of Rué,[151] La Selve and La Villedieu.[152] The 1160s continued in like manner with the additions of Aix,[153] Drulhe,[154] Orange,[155] Saint-Emilien,[156] and Saint Maurice of Régusse.[157] The 1170s saw the foundation of a substantial number of commanderies, and heralded in a boom which was to decline sharply in the 1180s and 1190s. Before 1180 Bailles,[158] Aubais,[159] Avignon,[160] Barbentane,[161] Vaour and Montricoux[162] were founded, but up to the turn of the century only six more commanderies were to be added: Abeilhan,[163] Espalion,[164] Hyères and

---

[143] 56H5218 (1147). Attached to Jalès was Alès, where thirty-three knights (including the commanders of Saint-Gilles, Montpellier and Lunel) were imprisoned in the royal castle at the arrest, M Ménard, *Histoire civile, ecclésiastique et littéraire de la ville de Nismes*, Paris, 1750, doc. 136, pp. 166–219.

[144] 56H5247 (1147).

[145] E. Léonard, *Gallicarum militiae Templi domorum eorumque præceptorum seriem secundum Albonensia apographa in bibliotheca nationali Parisiensi asservata*, Paris, 1930, p. 53.

[146] Document in A. du Bourg, 'Etablissement des chevaliers du Temple et de Saint-Jean de Jérusalem en Rouergue', *Mémoires de la société des lettres* 13(1886), p. 179.

[147] D. Le Blévec and A. Venturini, 'Cartulaires des ordres militaires xiie–xiiie siècles', *Mémoires et documents de l'Ecole des Chartes* 39(1993), p. 462.

[148] Léonard, *Gallicarum*, p. 79.

[149] *ibid.*, p. 55.

[150] In 1151 Viscount Bernard Atton gave them permission to have a fire in the town, Ménard, *Histoire civile*, no. 20, pp. 32–33. Ménard thought this privilege to have been for Saint-Gilles. It was, in fact, for Nîmes, see Bonnet, 'Maisons', p. 522.

[151] It was sold to the Templars by the seigneurs of Flayosc, Salernes, Entrecasteaux and Tourtour. The donation was confirmed by Count Raymond Berenger, 56H5279 (1156).

[152] Léonard, *Gallicarum*, p. 65; C. Higounet, 'L'Occupation du sol du pays entre Tarn et Garonne au Moyen Age', *AM* 65(1953), p. 320.

[153] Before 1170 the Templars had installed themselves some 12km from Aix, and c.1185 they moved into the town, despite the protestations of the chapter, N. Coulet, 'Hôpitaux et œuvres d'assistance dans le diocèse et la ville d'Aix-en-Provence xiiie–mi-xive siècles', *CF* 13(1978), p. 221.

[154] du Bourg, *Grand-prieuré*, no. 94, p. lxv (1166).

[155] 56H5275 (1167).

[156] 56H5285 (1165).

[157] 56H4314 (1164).

[158] Léonard, *Gallicarum*, p. 44.

[159] *ibid.*, p. 35.

[160] 56H5198 (1174).

[161] Blancard, *Inventaire*, p. 20.

[162] Léonard, *Gallicarum militiæ*, p. 73.

[163] *ibid.*, p. 54.

[164] *ibid.*, p. 64.

Toulon,[165] Saliers,[166] and the influential Montpellier.[167] Despite the irregularity of these gifts, their large number and geographical diversity point to a concerted effort on behalf of the Temple to develop as many sites as possible over as broad an area of Occitania as they could practically distribute themselves.

Conclusion

In the process of settlement the Orders clearly were not able to choose the location of the land which was gifted to them. Nevertheless, some areas were of such strategic importance that both Orders came to have commanderies in them. Once the Hospitallers had founded Trinquetaille on the north bank of the river Rhône (1115x1126), the Templars built one of their most important commanderies, Saint Lucy of Arles, facing it on the south bank. It was built by 1142, for in that year the first provincial chapter of the Order was held there.[168] Likewise, by 1138 the Templars had begun building their commandery in the southern quarter of Saint-Gilles called Le Faraon, hard by the priory of the Hospitallers.[169] This was an important commandery, although not possessed of a status similar to that of the grand-priory of Saint-Gilles. It is likely that the Templars kept a central archive here for the province of Provence, for in 1256 Pope Alexander IV, still attempting to unravel the difficulties of the papal infeudation of the county of Melgueil into the bishopric of Nîmes, requested that the commander of Saint-Gilles supply the bishop of Maguelone with all acts he had concerning the county 'in the archives (*in deposito*) of your house'.[170]

There are a striking number of places where both Orders had commanderies: Aix, Arles Avignon, Barbentane, Espalion, Gap, Jalès, Marseille, Montpellier, Narbonne, Nice, Nîmes, Saint-Gilles, as well as granges and rights all over Occitania, the numbers of which are legion. Many have left insufficient records by which to gauge their importance. However, much can be interpreted

---

[165] *ibid.*, p. 46.
[166] Blancard, *Inventaire*, p. 33.
[167] 56H5263 (1196). This commandery was one of the most important in the Midi, A. Trudon des Ormes, *Liste des maisons et de quelques dignitaires de l'ordre du Temple en Syrie, en Chypre et en France d'après les pièces du procès*, Paris, 1900, pp. 252–253.
[168] Durbec, 'Templiers', p. 28.
[169] *ibid.*, p. 24; R. Jéolas, *Bulletin de l'association d'histoire et d'archéologie de Saint-Gilles, Exposition 1984, Les ordres militaires à Saint-Gilles au XIIe siècle*, 1984, p. 22. This quarter was where the modern day suspension bridge leads the road out from Saint-Gilles to Arles, some 2km from the town centre.
[170] *Bullaire de l'église de Maguelone (1030–1303)*, J. Rouquette and A. Villemagne (eds.), II, Montpellier, 1911, no. 458, p. 333 (1256).

by their locations. Unlike the Cistercians, the Military Orders did not seek to live in seclusion from the many urban centres which proliferated in Occitania. Rather, they cultivated towns and their inhabitants, both religious and secular. Thus, the early implantations at Douzens, Carcassonne, Trinquetaille and Saint Lucy show clear intentions to attract the favour of local magnates and the Empire. Additionally, they were episcopal cities of stature. But, unlike the mendicant Orders which were to come, the Military Orders did not seek to dwell exclusively in towns. They needed the agricultural revenue which only the countryside could provide, and thus they created large numbers of commanderies in areas where they might concentrate on working the land, and raising cattle. These two types of commandery were not differentiated one from the other by name or style, but demonstrate the Orders' will fully to exploit the possibilities of a religious community's potential. In this way they utilized to the maximum the substantial privileges exempting them from duties to be paid on lands, whilst simultaneously encouraging the support, financial donations, and advantages which close contact with the towns could bring. The rapidity of the implantation of the Military Orders, and the depth of the roots they put down in so large an area, brought them into direct contact and competition with the established religious communities in Occitania, and the following chapter will analyse these relationships.

CHAPTER III

The Church and the Military Orders

[the Templars] also became very troublesome to God's churches, for they
took the tithes and first fruits away from them, and unjustly disturbed their
possessions.[1]

[the Hospitallers] . . . never more displayed any reverence to the prelates of the
Church, and steadfastly refused to give up tithes from any of their estates, notwithstanding the covenants under which they had been granted the land.[2]

William of Tyre, *Chronicon*, I, book 7, ch. 7, p. 555 and
II, book 18, ch. 6, p. 817

THE Military Orders faced criticism during much of their existence.[3] But,
as with Juvenal's problem, 'sed quis custodiet ipsos custodes',[4] very few
criticized the critics of the Orders for their views. Save perhaps Walter Map,
who wrote:

Perhaps many lie when they tell those stories about the lords Templar; let us
ask them themselves, and believe what we hear. How they behave at Jerusalem I do not know; here with us they live harmlessly (*innocenter*) enough.[5]

Such critical 'stories' were often written by churchmen. There may be a temp-
tation to think the censorious writings of William of Tyre and John of Salis-
bury to be representative of the attitudes of the secular Church, and those of
Matthew Paris as exemplifying the views of the monastic. But, the criticism
was no more than that directed to other new Orders, or indeed to the Church

---

[1] 'sed et ecclesiis Dei, eis decimas et primicias subtrahentes et eorum indebite turbando
possessiones, facti sunt valde molesti'.
[2] 'nullam prorsus ecclesiarum prelatis deinceps exhibentes reverentiam, decimas sibi ex
quibuscumque prediis ad se quocumque iure devolutis, penitus negant'.
[3] H. Nicholson, *Templars, Hospitallers and Teutonic Knights, Images of the Military Orders
1128–1291*, Leicester, 1993, p. 129.
[4] Juvenal, *D. Iunii Iuvenalis saturæ*, A. Housman (ed.), Cambridge, 1931, 6, line 347,
p. 48.
[5] Walter Map, *De nugis curialium*, M. James (ed. and tr.), revised by C. Brooke and
R. Mynors, Oxford, 1983, pp. 68, 69.

as a whole.[6] The written accounts and complaints which refer to friction between the Orders and the Church must be of secondary importance when compared with the records of their daily relationships. These tell a markedly different story.

The attitudes of both the secular clergy and the monastic world were still undergoing change. In the aftermath of the Church reform movement the power of the Occitanian episcopacy dwindled, and the prestige and power of the monasteries rose. The great Benedictine abbey of Saint Victor of Marseille (dubbed 'the Pontifical state of Marseille')[7] had gained its independence from the bishop of Marseille in 1005, and had dependent priories as far afield as Catalonia by 1043.[8] But, by the twelfth century the Benedictine hegemony had been broken and diverse, new ways of religious life had become successful and popular. The most flourishing of these new observances, that of the Cistercian reformers, expanded into Occitania from their first foundation at Mazan (Ardèche),[9] but on a small scale.[10] Only twenty-nine Cistercian abbeys were built in the Languedoc in the twelfth century; twenty-four of these between 1135 and 1160.[11] A slightly older, new observance which was also becoming more popular was that of the Austin canons. Chapters of canons had been introduced into Avignon as early as 980, and they proliferated in Arles, Carpentras, Vaison and Apt before the turn of the millennium.[12] Regular canons came in the early eleventh century, and one of their most influential houses, Saint Ruf, was in the heart of the Rhône valley, two kilometres south of Avignon.[13]

Of other Orders, the first wave of Grandmontese settlement began in 1150, but resulted in the establishment of only thirteen houses,[14] whilst the impact of the Carthusians and Chalaisians was minimal. Later, in the thirteenth century,

---

[6] Nicholson, *Templars*, p. 129; generally, J. Dunbabin, *A Hound of God. Pierre de La Palud and the Fourteenth Century Church*, Oxford, 1991, p. 25.

[7] P. Schmid, 'Die Entstehung des Marseiller Kirchenstaates', *Archiv für Urkundenforschung* 10(1928), pp. 176–207.

[8] E. Baratier, 'Marquisat et comtés de Provence', *Histore de la Provence*, E. Baratier (ed.), Toulouse, 1969, p. 125.

[9] R. Saint-Jean, 'L'Abbaye cistercienne de Mazan (Ardèche) et ses filles provençales: Sénanque et Thoronet', *AM* 18(1968), pp. 77–100.

[10] Baratier, 'Marquisat', p. 131.

[11] *Les Cisterciens en Languedoc, CF* 21(1986), Introduction, p. 8.

[12] Baratier, 'Marquisat', p. 127.

[13] C. Lawrence, *Medieval Monasticism*, New York and London, 1992, p. 68; Baratier, 'Marquisat', p. 127; R. Hiestand, 'Saint-Ruf d'Avignon, Raymond de Saint-Gilles et l'Eglise Latine du comtée de Tripoli', *AM* 98(1986), pp. 327–336.

[14] G. Durand, 'L'Architecture grandmontaine dans le Midi Languedocien entre 1150 et 1250', *AM* 107(1995), pp. 5–34.

the numbers of convents of the mendicants were also on a small scale.[15] The major wave of Franciscan activity did not occur until the third quarter of the century.[16] Up until 1235 the Franciscans had only six houses in central-southern Occitania, and only around twenty-five by 1254.[17] The Dominicans operated on a smaller scale than the Franciscans, an example being that they received almost exactly half the value of the donations to the Franciscans in Narbonne in the period 1228–1281.[18]

Thus, the move of the Military Orders to Europe came at a time when they had to face not only the backlash for further disrupting the Benedictine empire, but also competition with the new observances of the twelfth century. This chapter will analyse the resultant relationships between the Church and the Military Orders, beginning with the Military Orders' substantial papal privileges, then examining the links between the Military Orders and first the secular clergy, then the monastic religious. This will demonstrate that William of Tyre's famous jeremiad against the Military Orders was neither true, nor justifiable.[19]

The Orders and the Secular Church

(i) Papal Privileges

From the earliest stages a problem posed by the Military Orders and addressed by Church authors was that of 'unfair competition'. Although the Temple and Hospital enjoyed the advantages of novelty and the appeal of the Crusades, the domain in which rival institutions were most handicapped was the arsenal of privileges the papacy accorded the Military Orders. These privileges gave them financial, spiritual and temporal advantages and, at times, these inevitably led to animosity and jealousy.[20]

The privileges accorded to the Military Orders were very similar to each

---

[15] R. Emery, *The Friars in Medieval France*, New York, 1962; C. Ribaucourt, 'Les Mendiants du Midi d'après la cartographie de "l'enquête" 146', *CF* 8(1973), pp. 25–33, maps, pp. 30–31.

[16] A. Guerreau, 'Observations statistiques sur les créations de couvents franciscains en France, XIIIe–XVe siècles', *Mouvements franciscains et société française XIIe–XXe siècles*, A. Vauchez (ed.), Paris, 1984, pp. 51, 55.

[17] *ibid.*, p. 55.

[18] R. Emery, *Heresy and Inquisition in Narbonne*, New York, 1941, p. 163; generally, M.-H. Vicaire, 'Le Développement de la province dominicaine de Provence', *CF* 8(1973), pp. 35–77.

[19] Two sections from these passages are quoted at the head of this chapter.

[20] J. Brundage, 'A Twelfth-Century Oxford Disputation Concerning the Privileges of the Knights Hospitalers', *Mediæval Studies* 24(1962), pp. 153–160.

other, yet a significant distinction was the chronology in which they were granted. The first to benefit in almost all cases was the Temple, and only subsequently was the Hospital accorded the equivalent privilege. For example, undoubtedly the most important privilege was that which Cluny had been granted in 1024, and which Cîteaux gradually acquired for all of its members: total freedom from episcopal control.[21] For the Military Orders, this was achieved by permission to retain their own priest-brothers. This right was granted to the Temple in 1139 by Pope Innocent II in the bull *Omne datum optimum*,[22] but not to the Hospital until Anastasius IV's repromulgation of *Christiane fidei religio* of 1154.[23] The relative length of time between the papal confirmations of the Orders and the granting of priest-brothers is striking. The Temple only had to wait nineteen years from the Council of Troyes (1129), whilst the Hospital was not to receive the privilege until forty-one years after its recognition in Pascal II's bull *Pie postulatio voluntatis* of 1113.[24]

The delay in this matter may be due to the fact that both of these privileges were recognitions of existing states of affairs. That is, the Orders were already accepting priest-brothers.[25] Yet, if these privileges were just papal ratifications of existing practices, then the length to which the papacy went to legitimate and facilitate this practice is startling, for it subjected the priest-brothers to the masters of the Orders, unordained laymen. More than this, it gave the masters power even over bishops. The privilege to the Templars stated:

> we also allow that you may be permitted to receive virtuous clerics and priests of God as you wish from wheresoever they may come to you. . . . You shall request these priests from their bishops, and thus they will be freed from all professional ties. If any bishop should not wish to grant you such priests, we empower you, by the authority of the Holy Roman Church, nevertheless to receive and retain them.[26]

---

[21] Lawrence, *Monasticism*, pp. 91, 136.

[22] *Papsturkunden für Templer und Johanniter*, R. Hiestand (ed.), Göttingen, 1972, no. 3, pp. 204–210 (1139).

[23] *CH*, I, no. 226, pp. 173–175 (1154).

[24] *ibid.*, I, no. 30, pp. 29–30 (1113).

[25] *RTemp.*, *Primitive Rule*, cap. 26, p. 36; 'capellanis vel aliis ad tempus manentibus', cap. 64, p. 64; Riley-Smith, *Knights*, pp. 49–50, 233–234; *CH*, I, no. 19, pp. 20–21 (1110); no. 22, pp. 23–24 (1111); no. 140 (deacon), pp. 114–115 (1141); no. 165, pp. 131–132 (1146x1157); no. 192, pp. 149–150 (1150); no. 202, pp. 155–157 (1151x1152); no. 220, p. 169 (1153).

[26] 'ut licent vobis honestos clericos et sacerdotes secundum Deum quantum ad vestram scientiam ordinatos undecumque ad nos venientes suscipere . . . eos a propriis episcopis expetatis idemque nulli alii professioni vel ordini teneantur obnoxii. Quod si episcopi eosdem vobis concedere forte noluerint, nichillominus tamen eos suscipiendi et retinendi auctoritate sancte Romane ecclesie licentiam habeatis', *Papsturkunden*, no. 3, pp. 204–210 (1139).

Priests of the Military Orders were used for preaching Crusade, at times at the command of the papacy. For example, Innocent III's encyclical *Post miserabile* stated that Bishops William of Nîmes and Arnulf of Orange were to be assisted by Templar and Hospitaller priests in their preaching.[27] To appease the episcopacy, a provision was included in *Omne datum optimum* that the Orders' priests were not permitted to preach for money, save, in the case of the Temple, if the master expressly licensed it.[28] The rise of priest-brothers to the episcopacy was envisaged in the Templar Rule, for those who had distinguished themselves by elevation to the episcopacy were permitted humbly to request from the master and convent the honour of wearing the white mantle of the knight.[29] Some of the priests the Orders recruited were very able, competent men, who did rise to the episcopacy. Amongst the Templars, Brother William of Saint John rose to be archbishop of Nazareth, and Brother Humbert became bishop of Banyas in the thirteenth century,[30] whilst the Hospitallers held the see of Valenia (near Margat) on and off, and at one stage the see of Tarsus was in their hands.[31]

Pope Innocent II made several other grants in *Omne datum optimum*. Notably, that the Temple could keep all spoils of war, that these and all the Order's houses and property were under the protection of the papacy, that the Order could build oratories, and that it could bury its brethren and 'family' there. Later promulgations of this privilege merely added the right to bury travellers.[32] The Order was freed from having to pay tithes, a privilege only possessed by Cîteaux at this date; and it was permitted to collect tithes if the local bishop was agreeable. The consent of the bishop was not a mere formality. It was a condition designed to minimize antagonism, and repromulgated many times in various guises, including at the Fourth Lateran Council, and in a decretal of Pope Gregory IX.[33] In some measure this was down to abuses of the privilege, for in 1188 Pope Clement III wrote to the three Orders in

---

[27] *Die Register Innocenz' III*, O. Hageneder *et al.* (eds.), I, Grasse and Cologne, 1964, no. 366, pp. 498–505 (1198); P. Cole, *The Preaching of the Crusades to the Holy Land, 1095–1270*, Cambridge (Mass.), 1991, pp. 83–84. A similar use of priests of the Military Orders was sanctioned by Innocent in a letter to the archbishop of York, *The Letters of Pope Innocent III (1198–1216) Concerning England and Wales: A Calender with an Appendix of Texts*, A and M. Cheney (eds. and trs.), Oxford, 1967, no. 38, p. 8 (1198).

[28] *Papsturkunden*, no. 3, p. 208 (1139).

[29] *R Temp., Ordinary Chapters*, cap. 434, pp. 235–236.

[30] B. Hamilton, *The Latin Church in the Crusader States, The Secular Church*, London, 1980, p. 279; M. Bulst-Thiele, *Sacræ domus militiæ Templi Hierosolymitani magistri: Untersuchungen zur Geschichte des Templerordens 1118/9–1314*, Göttingen, 1974, p. 254.

[31] Riley-Smith, *Knights*, p. 234.

[32] *Papsturkunden*, no. 3, pp. 204–210.

[33] H. Gilles, 'A Propos des dîmes monastiques', *CF* 19(1984), p. 295.

Provence which possessed the privilege (Templars, Hospitallers and Cistercians), and particularly the Cistercian abbey of Ulmet, to put a stop to their appropriation of tithes which rightfully belonged to the archbishop of Arles.[34]

In the bull *Milites Templi* of 1144 Pope Celestine II permitted Templar priests to enter areas under interdict and, once a year, open up the churches, celebrate mass, and take a collection. In such a region, where all churches were locked and no sacraments dispensed, the number of faithful attending a service would have given rise to a collection of considerable value. William of Tyre related that during an interdict in Outremer the Hospital, taking advantage of an identical privilege, would ring its bells more loudly than usual to attract the faithful to come and give donations.[35] Pope Celestine also granted an indulgence of a seventh of penance to all patrons who endowed the Order, and granted an annual gift, as well as exempting the brethren, vassals and tenants of the Order from episcopal excommunication.[36] One other important privilege was granted by Pope Urban IV in 1262 permitting the Temple to receive property which members of the Order would have inherited, except if held in fee.[37]

With regard to the Order of the Hospital, Pope Pascal II's bull *Pie postulatio voluntatis* (1113) marked a decisive step for the Order by placing it under the sole control of the Holy See.[38] Similar privileges as those granted to the Temple were to follow.[39] *Ad hoc nos disponente* of 1135 prevented any bishop from excommunicating a member of the Order or laying an interdict on their churches. It also granted the Hospital the right to celebrate the Divine Office in areas under interdict.[40] *Christiane fidei religio* of 1154 allowed the building of churches and cemeteries in wasteland, whilst elsewhere the Order could build and administer oratories and cemeteries.[41] In *Quam amabilis Deo* of 1139 all benefactors of the Hospital were granted remission of a seventh part of their penance.[42] Privileges to the Orders were often linguistically similar. For instance, the wording of the grants of priests was almost identical.[43]

These were not the only privileges which the Orders obtained. Many new

---

34 *GCN(Avignon)*, no. 304, col. 88 (1188).
35 William of Tyre, *Chronicon*, II, book 18, ch. 3, p. 812.
36 *Papsturkunden*, no. 8, pp. 214–215.
37 Forey, *Aragón*, p. 162.
38 *CH*, I, no. 30, pp. 29–30 (1113).
39 H. Prutz, *Die geistlichen Ritterorden. Ihre Stellung zur kirchlichen, politischen, gesellschaftlichen und wirtschaftlichen Entwicklung des Mittelalters*, Berlin, 1908, pp. 142–194 has a full discussion of the Hospitallers' privileges.
40 *CH*, I, no. 113, pp. 95–96 (1135).
41 *ibid.*, I, no. 226, pp. 173–175 (1154).
42 This bull dates from 1139, 1140 or 1143, *ibid.*, I, no. 130, pp. 107–108.
43 Compare *Omne datum optimum* in *Papsturkunden*, no. 3, pp. 207–208 (1139) and *Christiane fidei religio*, *CH*, I, no. 226, p. 174 (1154).

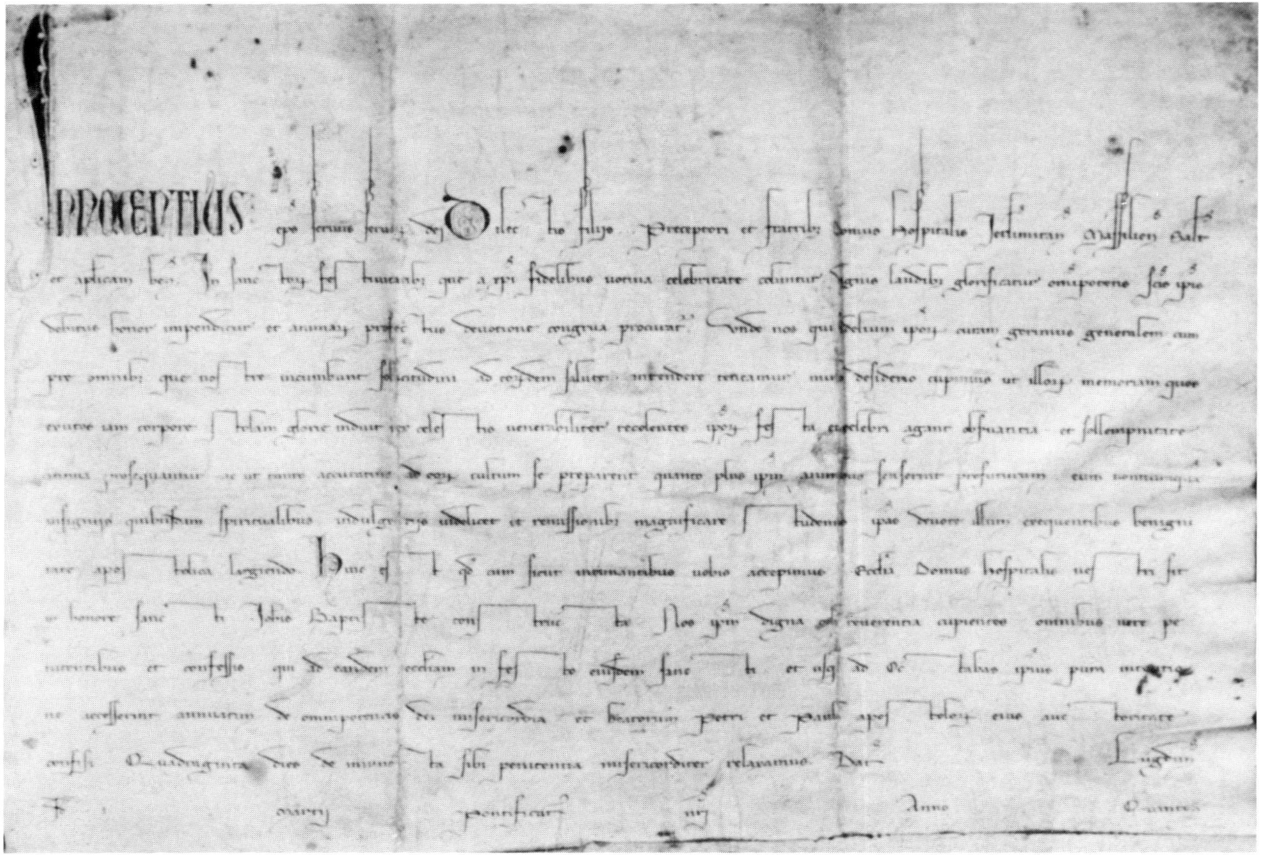

PLATE III: Bull of Pope Innocent IV granting an indulgence to all who visit the Hospital in Marseille

grants were given throughout the twelfth and thirteenth centuries, and the archives of the Orders are well endowed with papal bulls. By means of such letters the papacy could remind those ignoring the Orders' privileges of its support and approval of concessions it had formerly given. For instance, in 1250 Pope Innocent IV wrote to the archbishops of Provence instructing them to let the Hospitallers of Saint-Gilles make full use of the Apostolic letters which had been accorded them.[44] Many Popes had to repromulgate the salient parts of bulls to this end,[45] even imposing obligations on the clergy, such as the order to excommunicate anyone who attacked a brother of the Military Orders.[46]

New and particular privileges were promulgated as need arose. The Hospitaller commandery of Marseille was in papal favour in 1246 when Pope Innocent IV granted forty days indulgence to all who visited the Hospitaller's church in Marseille on the feast of Saint John and during the octave.[47] In 1292 the Pope granted forty years and forty periods of forty days indulgence to all who gave the Order alms and visited the Order's churches on Good Friday, the days of the Holy Cross in May and September, and the day of the patron of the church.[48]

When the Military Orders' financial privileges were threatened, they at times acted in unison. In 1269 the Temple and Hospital in Nice requested that the bishop of Nice petition the Holy See on their behalf against the demand from a visiting cardinal that they levy money from their churches and properties to defray his travelling costs.[49] This was not a unique attempt to contravene their privileges. In 1297 the commander of the Hospital of Avignon complained to the Pope of the demand by the papal legate, the archbishop of Otranto, that the commandery contribute to the legate's costs in journeying to Tarascon.[50] Good relationships with the Holy See can be seen by the presence at the Hospitaller grand-priory of Saint-Gilles in 1180 of Bishop Henry of Albano, Apostolic legate, who symbolically received a gift on their behalf.[51] Moreover, when the Apostolic Legate Roman Bonaventura excommunicated Count Raymond VI in 1216, he exempted the Military Orders, Cistercians and

---

[44] *GCN(Arles)*, no. 1150, col. 439 (1250).
[45] *inter alia, Si quando ab apostolica sede*, 56H5279 (1159x1181); *Dilecti filii nostri*, 56H5161 (1198); *Non absque dolore*, 56H5161 (1198); 56H4101 (1229).
[46] CH, I, no. 616, pp. 418–419 (after 1181).
[47] 56H4669 (1246).
[48] H30 (1292).
[49] 56H5266 (1269).
[50] 56H4219 (1297).
[51] *Trinquetaille(Hospital)*, no. 5, pp. 5–6 (1180).

Præmonstratensians from payment of the tithe to be levied on the Occitanian Church for the northern French campaigns against the heretic Cathars.[52]

These wide-ranging privileges served to facilitate the establishment of the Orders in Europe, and to make them attractive. In the East, the Military Orders were high profile enough to earn the support of the Latins, but in Europe they faced entrenched interests. By means of these privileges, they were given a head-start in the race for the attentions of the laity, as well as aided in their mission of raising the necessary materials to be shipped to Outremer.

(ii) Bishops

The relationship between the Military Orders and the episcopacy was necessarily one of frequent interaction, for the administration of the Orders' churches involved the bishop in whose dioceses they lay. As with other monastic Orders, the Military Orders controlled the temporal property of their churches along with the right of presentation to the benefice, and they could keep most of the *spiritualia* (moneys received from the exercise of spiritual duties). The bishop controlled the spiritual aspects of the church such as the consecration of the altar, the care of souls and visitation.[53] Once the Military Orders had the right to retain their own priest-brothers, this inevitably meant that they could present their own priests to benefices, and thereby avoid having to grant the living to a secular priest, a financially much more advantageous position.

Surprisingly, the Occitanian episcopacy did not resent the presence of the Military Orders; in fact, it took a keen interest in them. The archdiocese of Aix even kept a copy of the statutes of the Hospital.[54] This was perhaps owing to the inroads the Military Orders were making into large numbers of established monastic parishes, as evident in 1242 when the bishop of Viviers allowed the commander of the Hospital at Jalès to build a church at Bourg Saint-Andéol, sing the Office, and build a cemetery despite the protestations of the local prior.[55] Good personal relationships were naturally of import, and at least one example of episcopal interest was procured by high level flattery. In 1193 Pope Celestine III recommended the Order of the Temple to the archbishop

---

[52] *CH*, II, no. 1456, p. 182 (1216).
[53] G. Constable, 'Monasteries, Rural Churches and the Cura Animarum in the Early Middle Ages', *Settimane di studio del centro italiano de studi sull'altro medioevo,* XXVIII: *Cristainizzazione ad organizzazione ecclesiastica delle compagne nell'alto medioevo: espansione e resistenze,* II, Spoleto, 1982, pp. 349, 384.
[54] 1G426 (1182).
[55] 56H4585 (1242).

of Arles, apparently because the Order had been singing the praises of the arch-bishop in the papal curia.[56]

There were, of course, instances of friction between bishops and the Orders. At the commandery of Puimoisson a document had to be signed by which the Hospital agreed it would bear the financial burden of feeding the bishop's men when they came to the vicinity of the commandery collecting rents.[57] This hospitality was perhaps too easily abused. In 1234 Pope Gregory IX wrote to the bishops and clergy instructing them to stop indulging in the Order of the Temple's hospitality, for the Order could not demur, and the financial strain of such entertainment was detrimental to the Order.[58] However, the vast majority of acts bearing on the relationship between the Orders and the episcopacy show it to have been amicable. The principal areas of documented interaction are arbitrations, the receiving of gifts, the witnessing of acts, donations and confir-mations, and these will be examined in turn.

Bishops frequently conducted arbitrations between the Military Orders and other parties. From the litigants' point of view, a bishop was desirable for his disinterested opinion, legal authority, and high status. For the bishop, such work could procure a financial benefit as well as the re-establishment of concord. For instance, in June 1195 Bishop Bertrand of Saint-Gilles arbitrated in a dispute between Brother Gisbert of Costabella, preceptor of the Temple of Saint-Gilles, and Raymond and Bernard Ibelot.[59] Four months later the bishop claimed that as a result of the settlement reached, the Order would give him an eighth of the disputed property. The Temple duly complied, and the bishop received 3,000 sous.[60]

The other party in these arbitrations could be another ecclesiastical institu-tion, or even the other Military Order. For example, a land dispute concerning both Military Orders was presided over by Bishop Atton of Carcassonne in 1183.[61] Again concerning the two Military Orders, in 1198 Archbishop Imbert of Arles heard a land dispute between the Hospitallers of Trinquetaille and the Templar commander of Saint Lucy of Arles.[62] Judgement was given in favour of the Hospital. The Temple appealed, and the following year the archbishop welcomed some of the Orders' most senior local officials to his palace. Amongst the Hospitallers can be noted Brother Raymond of Acu, prior of

[56] 'Licet bone opinionis tue odorem noverimus, dilecti tamen filii nostri fratres militie Templi multa nobis de persona tua laudabilia retulerunt', GCN(Arles), no. 695, cols. 269–270 (1193).

[57] 56H4832 (undated).

[58] Evangelice doctrine, H103 (1234).

[59] Saint-Gilles(Temple), fols. 35v–36rv (1195).

[60] ibid., fols. 37v–39r (1195).

[61] Douzens(Temple), A no. 167, pp. 149–150 (1183).

[62] Trinquetaille(Hospital), no. 172, pp. 159–160 (1198).

Saint-Gilles, Brother Peter Elie, its commander, Brother Sanctioris of Lambese, the commander of Provence, and Brother William Raymond, the commander of Trinquetaille. The Templars were represented by Brother Fulk of Montpezat 'master of the knighthood of the Temple',[63] and Brother William of Le Soler, commander of Saint Lucy; but to no avail, for the Temple conceded, and judgement was again given in favour of the Hospital.[64]

A more involved relationship is evident with those bishops who agreed to receive and negotiate gifts designed for the Orders. In 1136 Bishop Raymond of Carcassonne was responsible for receiving gifts at Les Cours on behalf of the Temple.[65] In 1156 Peter of Bosc gave land to the Temple at Richerenches 'into the hands of' Bishop William Hugh of Saint-Paul-Trois-Châteaux in the presence of many brothers of the Order,[66] and in 1164 the same bishop again received a donation on behalf of the Order.[67]

The 1129 Primitive Latin Rule of the Temple stipulated that anyone wishing to become a brother of the Order should first go to his bishop, make known his intentions, receive absolution, and then present himself to the master of the Order.[68] Whether or not this happened as a matter of course is unverifiable, but there is a written account of such a procedure in Carcassonne in 1137 relating to an arrangement not of profession, but of confraternity. Arnold of Gaure gave lands at Gaure, and joined the commandery of Douzens as a *confrater* 'into the hands of, and by the authority of, lord Raymond, bishop of Carcassonne'.[69] He renewed his confraternity in 1150, again with the same formula, although this time his act was witnessed by a person of temporal influence, too: Viscount Raymond Trencavel I.[70] Such episcopal involvement was not particular to Templar professions. At Hospitaller Gap in the Provençal Alps Bishop William of Gers presided over the reception of a *confrater* in 1211.[71]

If bishops were likely to arbitrate, it was a sensible precaution to have an

---

63 His office in 1199 is not clear, but he soon rose to command Jalès (1201–1202, 1204, 1207–1214, 1218), Le Mas-Déu (1205–1207), Pézenas (1213, 1218–1219) and finally to become the 'master in Provence and Spain' (1224, 1228, 1234), E. Léonard, *Gallicarum militiæ Templi domorum eorumque praeceptorum seriem secundum Albonensia apographa in bibliotheca nationali Parisiensi asservata*, Paris, 1930, pp. 21, 25, 47, 53, 89.
64 *Trinquetaille(Hospital)*, no. 173, pp. 161–162 (1199).
65 *Douzens(Temple)*, B no. 1, pp. 185–186 (1136).
66 *Richerenches(Temple)*, no. 158, pp. 141–142 (1156).
67 *ibid.*, no. 186, p. 162 (1164).
68 *RTemp.*, Primitive Rule, cap. 12, pp. 23–24.
69 'Dono vobis et laudo me ipsum per confratrem vestrum in ipsa militia . . . in manu scilicet et auctoritate domni Raimundi, carcassensis episcopi', *Douzens(Temple)*, A no. 181, pp. 160–161 (1137).
70 *ibid.*, A no. 173, pp. 155–156 (1150).
71 *GCN(Gap)*, no. 20, cols. 284–285 (1211).

episcopal witness to charters. This would ensure that, in principle, the act was imbued with a degree of solemnity and trustworthiness. Such episcopal witnessing could lead to complex involvement, as in the case of Brocard, knight of Avignon. In 1189 Brocard informed Bishop Rostang II of Avignon that he had formerly given himself to the Hospital into the hands of Brother Otger, prior of Saint-Gilles. He had given the Order land, and in return had been presented with 100 marks of silver. He wished to be received again, and confirmed that the land in question now vested in the Hospital.[72] Ten years later Bishop Rostang III and William, his provost, gave permission to Brother Garcias of Liza, grand preceptor of the Hospital in Dèçamer, and Brother Raymond of Aiguille, prior of Saint-Gilles, to build a church and a cemetery on the land that they had received from Brocard (which the bishop had witnessed), or anywhere else they deemed fit.[73] By 1203 matters had been progressing, for a dispute had arisen and was being heard in the curia of Bishop Rostang III. The Hospitallers had gone ahead and built an oratory, an altar and a campanile on the land given by Brocard, and the bishop had consecrated the first stone of the buildings. The Order had been celebrating the Divine Office there for two years (the time taken to build the edifice was therefore two years), and they now wished to undertake alterations.

William, the provost of Avignon, challenged the Order's right to commission such work, and his grievances extended to many of their activities. The bishop decided that the Hospital could continue building its new oratory and cemetery away from Brocard's land, but that the one they had constructed on his land must either be demolished, or put to proper use. That is, that parishioners must not be admitted to the Divine Office, that the provost and canons were entitled to their canonical share of the gifts the Order received (except horses, arms and certain immoveables), that the Order was not to visit the sick in the hope of soliciting trade, that no-one, except their 'family', was to be admitted to the adorations of the Holy Cross on Good Friday, that there were to be no processions and blessings on Palm Sunday, that they were not to be seen publicly with crosses, incense, water or any other liturgical paraphernalia, that they were not to ring their bells unless strictly necessary, and even then not until the main bells of the city had been rung, as was the case for all the other churches.[74] Matters cannot have been helped by the Templars' construction of a cemetery in Avignon at this time, permission for which had been granted in 1198 by Bishop Rostang III.[75]

It is not surprising that resident clergy were apprehensive of the building of

[72] GCN(Avignon), no. 306, col. 88 (1189).
[73] ibid., no. 322, col. 93 (1199).
[74] ibid., no. 333, cols. 98–99 (1203).
[75] ibid., no. 315, col. 90 (1198).

a commandery, for the Orders, buoyed up with their privileges, sometimes acted with little sensitivity for the *status quo ante*. Accordingly, precautions were sometimes taken, as in April 1199 when Pope Innocent III wrote to the bishops of Saint-Paul-Trois-Châteaux and Avignon to intervene in a dispute between the provost and canons of Sisteron and the Temple. The Holy See permitted the canons to demand a security (*cautio*) from the Templars, who were about to begin work on an oratory.[76] This oratory was hotly disputed, the provost and canons being in strong opposition. The extent to which the papacy was prepared to protect the Orders can be seen in its actions in the face of this dispute: Innocent III simply laid an interdict on the provost and canons of Sisteron. The bishops of Avignon, Saint-Paul-Trois-Châteaux and Cavaillon were perhaps on the side of the provost in this matter, or maybe just lethargic, for in 1204 Innocent wrote to them commanding observation of the inter-dict.[77]

The presence of bishops can be noted mainly in acts which they witnessed. The earliest episcopal involvement is highly ambiguous, for it concerns the Hospitaller commandery of Gap, where Bishop Isoard (1090–1092, 1099 or 1104),[78] appeared three times, once with his mother.[79] At some commanderies episcopal involvement could be quite intense, at others negligible. For instance, both Templars and Hospitallers at Saint-Gilles rarely used bishops to witness their acts.[80] However, if the matter was of importance, such as the meeting between the prior of Saint-Gilles and Bertrand of Baux in Avignon when a papal legate was present, then the presence of the archbishops of Arles and Aix, and the bishop of Vaison was no doubt appreciated.[81]

Such episcopal involvement as witnesses was normally to mark a substantial transaction, as in 1142 when the Templars at Douzens paid 130 *sous* to William Roger of Aragon to be given to Viscount Roger Trencavel I of Béziers, an act witnessed by Bishop Pons of Carcassonne.[82] Bishop Pons again witnessed an act the following year by which the Temple was given land at Caumont, the water which crossed it, and the extant buildings.[83] The solem-nity of an episcopal curia helped to imbue an act with *gravitas*. In 1197 William

---

76 *GCN(Saint-Paul-Trois-Châteaux)*, no. 97, cols. 57–58 (1199); a similar document is dated the following day, *GCN(Avignon)*, no. 321, col. 93 (1199).

77 *ibid.*, no. 337, col. 103 (1204).

78 P. Gams, *Series episcoporum*, Ratisbon, 1873, p. 552; *GC* 1 (Paris, 1870), col. 461; *GC* (Paris, 1715), col. 462; *CH*, I, p. 6 suggests that Isoard was still Bishop in 1099.

79 *Gap(Hospital)*, no. 1, p. 15; no. 18, p. 21; no. 29, p. 25 (all undated).

80 Although one example is Bishop Bertrand of Saint-Gilles appearing as a witness in *Saint-Gilles(Temple)*, fol. 56r (1194).

81 *GCN(Arles)*, no. 645, col. 251 (1180).

82 *Douzens(Temple)*, A no. 121, pp. 114–115 (1142).

83 *ibid.*, A no. 140, pp. 128–129 (1148).

Porcellet gave Brother Bertrand of Beaucaire, commander of Saint-Gilles, a substantial gift of land, and William then went to the curia of Archbishop Imbert of Arles to repeat the terms of the gift in front of the curia, two consuls and the provost of Arles.[84]

A bishop's presence could also be desirable in matters of sensitivity, as in 1174 when Arnold of Villelaur had an admission to make to the Templars of Douzens. He had sold them land, but had fraudulently kept possession of the title deed. He wished to correct this oversight, and so presented the Temple with the document, swearing to respect them in the future. This restitution of the deed was witnessed by Bishop Atton of Carcassonne and his nephew Berenger the cantor.[85]

Bishops made gifts to the Military Orders in their own right. Amongst the more significant of these donations can be noted several made to the Orders whilst still establishing their networks in Occitania. The Hospitallers received the church of Saint Thomas, the kernel of the commandery of Trinquetaille, from Archbishop Atton of Arles in 1115x1126.[86] The first Templar possession in Europe, the church of Saint Bartholomew of La Motte-Palayson, was originally given to the Temple by Bishop Berenger of Fréjus (c.1090–1131),[87] and the gift of the church of Saint John the Baptist of Avignon was made by Bishop Laugier in 1130 soon after Brother Hugh's return to the Holy Land.[88] The first Templar commandery in what is now Provence, that of Saint-Paul-Trois-Châteaux, was founded principally by Bishop Pons of Saint-Paul-Trois-Châteaux on 19 March 1136,[89] and this same bishop was present again that year for the founding of the commandery of Richerenches by Hugh of Bourbouton; and for many other acts concerning the commandery,[90] as when Hugh's son joined the Orders in 1145 after seeking the bishop's advice.[91]

Confirmations of gifts by predecessors comprise a significant proportion of episcopal acts, and they sometimes even entailed another gift. In 1153 Bishop Peter of Sisteron confirmed to the Hospital five churches which his predeces-

---

84 *Saint-Gilles(Temple)*, fols. 86r–87v (1197).
85 'sed quia retinui tunc male cartam hereditariam meam de illo honore', *Douzens(Temple)*, B no. 77, p. 249 (probably 1174).
86 *Trinquetaille(Hospital)*, no. 257, p. 272 (1115x1126); *GCN(Arles)*, no. 487, col. 196 (1119); *CH*, I, no. 42, p. 36 (1118x1126). This was confirmed by Archbishop Raymond of Montredon of Arles, *GCN(Arles)*, no. 289, pp. 291–292 (1144).
87 *CT*, no. 2, pp. 1–2 (1124); *Saint Victor*, no. 1102, pp. 574–575 (1124); *GCN(Marseille)*, no. 141, col. 65 (1124).
88 *CT*, no. 30, p. 23 (1130).
89 *Richerenches(Temple)*, no. 128, pp. 121–122 (1136).
90 *ibid.*, no. 1, pp. 3–4 (1136) and *passim.*; *GCN(Saint-Paul-Trois-Châteaux) inter alia*, no. 58, cols. 47–48 (1136); no. 59, col. 48 (1136); no. 64, col. 49 (1138).
91 *Richerenches(Temple)*, no. 7, pp. 9–10 (1145).

sors Bishops Gerald and Raimbald had given the Order, and for goodwill he gave another church to mark the occasion.[92] Bishops did not always act alone. Sometimes secular powers were brought in, too. In Arles the archbishop and the consuls joined forces to sell the Templars a road which would connect the commandery of Arles with that of Bonpas. In this case the payment, 2,500 *sous*, went to the consuls.[93]

Amongst bishops who entertained a good relationship with the Orders, Bishop Berenger of Vaison is prominent for his long-standing relationship of thirty-nine years with the Temple, which he considered to be a spiritually rich institution. In 1137 he gave Brother Arnold of Bedocio land as a pious donation 'for the redemption of my soul'.[94] He appeared frequently in charters of the commandery of Roaix, notably in 1137, 1139 and 1153.[95] He took an interest, too, in the commandery of Richerenches, staying at the commandery, and being involved in its affairs in 1147–1148, 1157, 1161, 1169 and 1174.[96] He declared in 1141 that the commandery of Roaix had been built 'by the grace of God in our episcopacy', and gave the Temple an island on which they later built a mill.[97] He settled disputes for the Order,[98] and was still witnessing charters in 1176.[99] After his departure from the see of Vaison, the relationship between the see and the Temple remained cordial. In 1203 the then incumbent, Bishop Raimbald, was present at the commandery of Roaix; and in 1211 he used his seal to authenticate a Templar act.[100]

A cordial relationship could either be with the bishop at a personal level, or with the see as an institution. A relationship of this latter kind can be seen between the Templars and the see of Carcassonne. Bishop Raymond II was evidently on good terms with the Order, for in 1138 he and his canons of Saint Nazarius gave the Temple the tithes of Les Cours, the products of its gardens, and its animals. Aware that this might provoke hostility from the local clergy at Les Cours, he expressed his sincere wish that the Temple and its successors would be 'upright and faithful friends to the aforementioned church of Saint

---

[92] *GCN(Sisteron)*, no. 13, col. 450 (1155).

[93] *GCN(Arles)*, no. 675, cols. 261–262 (1190).

[94] 'pro redemptione animæ meæ', *Roaix(Temple)*, no. 103, pp. 61–62 (1137).

[95] *ibid.*, no. 104, pp. 62–63 (1137); no. 112, pp. 69–70 (1139); no. 118, pp. 74–75 (1153).

[96] *Richerenches(Temple)*, no. 60, pp. 60–63 (1147); no. 92, p. 93 (1157); no. 190, pp. 169–170 (1161); no. 98, pp. 97–99; no. 207, pp. 184–185 (1169); no. 201, pp. 178–179 (1174); *Roaix(Temple)*, no. 110, p. 68 (1148).

[97] 'domui de Roais quae in nostro episcopatu gratia Deo est et hedificatur', *Roaix(Temple)*, no. 115, pp. 71–73 (1141); no. 116, p. 73; no. 118, pp. 74–75 (1153).

[98] *ibid.*, no. 159, pp. 164–165 (1158).

[99] *ibid.*, no. 165, pp. 110–112 (1176).

[100] *ibid.*, no. 153, p. 100 (1203); no. 178, pp. 126–7 (1211).

Mary, and to its clerks and those of Saint Stephen's'.[101] All went well initially, but twenty-four years later problems arose. The desired relationship between the Order and the local religious had not been an easy matter. Bishop Raymond's successor, Pons I of Carcassonne, was summoned to arbitrate between the Temple and the provost of Saint Stephen of Le Mas concerning the tithes at Les Cours.[102] The Temple had clearly been lax in restraining the grazing of its animals, and had claimed some pretence to present to the benefice of the church. To ensure no repetition, when in 1164 Isalguier and his family exchanged certain lands at Les Cours for property possessed by the Temple at the same place (all of which was held in fief from the prior of Saint Stephen of Le Mas), the exchange was effected into the hands of Bishop Pons.[103] And it was he who sealed the acts by which the local clans of Barbaira and Canet founded the Templar commandery of Saint John of Carrière, an offshoot of Douzens, in 1153.[104]

Thus, although there is evidence of isolated incidents of conflict, the overall tenor of the relationship between the Orders and the episcopacy was that of the latter's support and aid. When speaking of the hostility and aggression surrounding the Orders' relationships with the Church, detractors of the Orders were referring to the attitude of some of the monastic religious. This will be examined next.

The Orders and the Monastic World

(i) Abbots

As landholders, the Orders inevitably had extensive relations with monastic houses, and from an early date. In the early 1130s a Templar promotion was held at the Benedictine monastery of Saint Mary of Alet near Carcassonne.[105] The abbot of the monastery provided a scribe and the location for the gifting of three donations to Brother Hugh Rigaud and the Holy Sepulchre.[106] One of these donations holds the reason for the occasion. A local, Arnold of Corneille,

---

[101] 'et ut vos et successores vestri sitis recti et fideles amici predicte Sancte Marie et clericis ibidem manentibus et clericis predicti Sancti Stephani', *Douzens(Temple)*, B no. 9, p. 195 (1138).

[102] *ibid.*, B no. 8, pp. 193–194 (1162).

[103] *ibid.*, B no. 7, pp. 192–193 (1164).

[104] *ibid.*, A no. 87, pp. 83–84; A no. 88, pp. 84–85 (1153).

[105] Although the editors of the cartulary suggest 26 March 1133 x 18 March 1134 for all three acts, it is most likely, judging by the similarities in the wording of the charters, and the witnesses present, that they were all drawn up contemporaneously.

[106] 'Sancto Sepulchro et ad ipsam cavalleriam Templi Salomonis', *Douzens(Temple)*, C no. 4, p. 264; C no. 5, p. 264; C no. 6, p. 264 (1133x1134).

had given the Temple a man with his children and *casal*. The abbot contested this gift, claiming the man to belong to the monastery. A council of *prud'hommes* advised the abbot to renounce this claim; which he duly did. The Templar promotion may well have been meant to re-establish good relations, for the Temple was a newcomer to the area. However, this was not the first involvement between the Templars and Occitanian monasteries. Some years earlier, when the commandery of Douzens was in its very infancy, Abbot Armand of Séguret had relinquished his rights over the 'caves' of Aiguille near Le Puy, although problems soon arose over a service to be paid on the property.[107] Sometimes friendly abbots were entrusted with helping the Orders, as in 1207 when Pope Innocent III intervened to put a stop to abuses of Templar privileges in Béziers by turning to the abbot of Saint Aphrodisius to ensure non-violation of papal privileges.[108]

In acts relating to the Military Orders the worlds of the cloister and the cathedral were kept separate. Rarely were a bishop and an abbot requested to intervene in a matter concerning the Orders at the same time. At Montpellier in 1187 an agreement was drawn up between a local person and two Hospitallers from the grand-priory of Saint-Gilles, with the mediation of the bishop of Maguelone and the Benedictine abbot of Aniane, but this was an uncommon combination.[109] As with the episcopacy, there are sporadic gifts from abbots and priors to both Military Orders throughout the twelfth and thirteenth centuries, but these monastic gifts do not evince a discernible pattern. Rather, they were mutually beneficial exchanges, as when the Cistercians of Franquevaux received a dwelling in 1191 from one Raymunda and her husband.[110] In 1214 the monastery decided to liquidate the asset, and accordingly Bertrand, the subprior, sold it to the Hospitallers of Avignon for 3,000 *sous*.[111]

As part of the Military Orders' expansion and consolidation of holdings, they approached monasteries requesting purchases, as in 1211 when the prior of the Benedictine abbey of Bonpas sold the Templars of Arles a house adjoining the Temple's property.[112] Such sales and exchanges took place not only in southern Provence, but also in the more isolated areas such as Vaour in the Toulousain, where the Templars had dealings with the Benedictines of Vailhourles and the Augustinians of Chancelade.[113] Exchanges of realty were

---

107 *ibid.*, C no. 9, pp. 267–268; C no. 10, p. 268–269 (probably 1132).
108 *Et si quibuslibet*, H102 (1207).
109 *Saint-Gilles(Hospital)*, fols. 155r–157r (1187).
110 *Avignon(Hospital)*, fols. 99r–100r (1191).
111 *ibid.*, fol. 100rv (1214).
112 56H5170 (1211).
113 *Vaour(Temple)*, no. 20, pp. 15–16 (1173); no. 13, pp. 10–11 (1175).

inevitable, for landholders such as the Orders and the monasteries frequently had abutting territory.

It has already been mentioned that in Saint-Gilles the Orders rarely used the services of the local bishop for validating, authenticating, and witnessing acts. However, this is easily explained by the proximity of the prestigious Cluniac abbey of Saint-Gilles, whose abbots were used instead. Abbot Bertrand was present for Templar acts in 1156, 1158 and 1163,[114] and Abbot Ermengard in 1183, 1185, 1190 and 1194.[115] Gifts from the monastery to the Temple had begun within a few years of the Order's settling in Saint-Gilles. In 1139 Abbot Peter, with the consent of Prior Raymond and the whole chapter, gave the Templars and Brother Robert of Craon, the master of the Order, the measure (*sextarialaticus*) due on all wheat and flour sold in the town, along with the privilege that all the Order's own wheat and flour could be sold with no due payable.[116] And in 1155 Abbot Bertrand rented the Order a garden for 2 *sous* a year to be paid at the feast of Saint Michael on the condition that they built no church, oratory or cemetery there.[117] Abbot Ermengard too, made gifts to the Order,[118] as did Abbot Peter.[119]

Relationships between the abbey and the Hospital were on a slightly less cordial footing. It is even possible that the abbey welcomed the Temple as a pretext to curb the power of the Hospital. Abbot Bertrand approved two acts in 1164 and 1168,[120] Abbot Raymond confirmed a predecessor's gift lifting the building restriction on the land,[121] and Abbot Ermengard witnessed an act in 1179.[122] That same year the abbey was short of funds, for land at Brujacans was sold to the Hospital with the consent of the bishop of Nîmes 'on account of the monastery's need'.[123]

The Cistercians and the Templars are often deemed to have shared a bond.[124] There is little evidence that this was particularly strong in Occitania, no more so than with the Benedictines, or between the Hospital and the

---

[114] *Saint-Gilles(Temple)*, fols. 14v–15r (1156); 25r–26r (1158); 24rv (1163).

[115] *ibid.*, fols. 9rv (1183); 4rv; 16v–17v (1185); 22v–24r (1190); 20r (1194).

[116] *ibid.*, fol. 2rv (1139).

[117] *ibid.*, fols. 7r–8r (1185).

[118] *ibid.*, fols. 7r–8r (1185); 43v–44v (1188).

[119] *ibid.*, fol. 43r (1195).

[120] *Saint-Gilles(Hospital)*, fols. 145rv (1164); 137v (1168).

[121] *ibid.*, fol. 182rv (1173).

[122] *ibid.*, fol. 130rv (1179).

[123] 'propter necessitatis monasterii', *ibid.*, fols. 16v–18r (1179).

[124] But see D. Selwood, '*Quidem autem dubitaverunt*: The Saint, the Sinner, the Temple and a Possible Chronology', *Autour de la première croisade, Actes du colloque de la Society for the Study of the Crusades and the Latin East (Clermont-Ferrand, 22–25 juin 1995)*, M. Balard (ed.), Paris, 1996, pp. 221–230.

Cistercians. For instance, a gift to the Hospital of Saint-Paul-les-Romans was made in the presence of the Benedictine abbot of Montmajour and a monk from Clairvaux.[125] The Cistercians were in fact reprimanded by the Holy See for their hostility. In 1288 Pope Nicholas IV had to write to the bishop of Albi, his provost, and to the prior of Saint-Affrique asking them to put an end to the activities of the Cistercians of La Bénisson-Dieu against the property of the Templars.[126]

One of the Orders' many privileges was that they need not contribute to ordinary ecclesiastical taxation. However, on land which was not the Orders' demesne, complications could arise. Although in most cases such problems were dealt with by legal process, sometimes a word in the right ear, or a display of strength, would suffice. In 1203 the bishop of Saint-Paul-Trois-Châteaux summoned the Templars of Saint-Vincent to a confrontation with his chapter in the episcopal chamber. The chapter openly debated whether or not legal proceedings should be brought against the Templars for non payment of tithes, oblations, and moneys due from burials. Ripert the dean, Jordan the archdeacon, Isnard the sacristan and Raymond the precentor voted against legal action, and so the Templars were persuaded by threats and cajolement instead.[127] Yet, the papacy was willing to defend the Orders' privileges, as can be seen by a letter from Pope Clement IV in 1267 to the Benedictine prior of Saint-Amant (diocese of Rodez) requesting that he put an end, under pain of excommunication, to the habit of consuls and secular ecclesiastics extorting taxes from the Hospitallers.[128]

Although relations were generally much less warm between the Military Orders and the religious than they were with the episcopacy, there was one area which excited quite notable hostility: the Military Orders' burial of members of the laity in their cemeteries.

(ii) Burial

Pope Innocent II had decreed in the bull *Omne datum optimum* (1139) that the Order of the Temple could build houses, churches and cemeteries for the use of the inhabitants on any wasteland on the condition that this did not interfere with the neighbouring abbeys or religious societies. On any other land, however legitimately acquired, they might build churches and burial places for their 'family'.[129] The Hospital received an identical privilege in *Christiane fidei religio*

---

125 *Saint-Paul(Hospital)*, no. 12, pp. 10–11 (undated).
126 *Conquesti sunt nobis*, H112 (1288).
127 *GCN(Saint-Paul-Trois-Châteaux)*, no. 100, col. 64 (1203).
128 *Quereta dilectorum filiorum*, H24 (1267).
129 *Papsturkunden*, no. 3, pp. 204–210.

(1154).[130] If an individual chose burial in a cemetery of a Military Order, this entailed a financial loss for the parochial clergy, who would be deprived of the gifts and oblations associated with the building up of a relationship and subsequent burial services. Accordingly, whenever and wherever possible, the clergy, and especially local monastic houses to which parishes were appropriated, attempted to prevent the Military Orders from building cemeteries, the most direct way of obviating effective burial. At times seculars were also co-opted to help, as when Count Alfonso II of Barcelona intervened to block the Hospital from building a cemetery at Milhau in 1190.[131]

This hostility sometimes drove the Military Orders to take matters up with the highest authority, as in the instance of the appeal from the Hospitaller commander of Nice to the Holy See against the decision of the bishop of Nice prohibiting the Hospitallers from burying the dead in their own church.[132] The Military Orders did occasionally overstep the mark with regard to burials. At least, the Holy See was worried about rumours, for in 1202 Pope Innocent III wrote to the Hospitallers in Marseille:

> it has reached our ears that you presume to bury the bodies of the dead in unconsecrated ground. Such abuses bring opprobrium to the whole of Christianity, contempt for your Order, and cause the Holy See to be insulted by all.[133]

Some abuses the papacy was not prepared to condone. Aside from possible flagrant breaches of ethics such as this, conflicts were normally matters which concerned only the local bishop, as for instance the arbitration conducted by Bishop Rainer of Marseille between Abbess Ermeline of Saint Saviour and the Hospitallers in 1205.[134]

The restrictions imposed on the Military Orders normally sought to limit ever more precisely the categories of those who could qualify for burial in their cemeteries. The battery of papal privileges promulgated and repromulgated outlining the categories of those whom the Orders might bury were fine-tuned at a local level. Taking the example of Saint-Gilles, the Hospital had a presence there since the first decade of the twelfth century, and the Temple had

---

[130] *CH*, I, no. 226, pp. 173–175 (1154).

[131] *ibid.*, I, no. 892, p. 566 (1190).

[132] 56H4784 (undated).

[133] 'nostris auribus intimavit, vos in terra non benedicta presumitis mortuorum corpora sepelire, quasdam abusiones alias exercentes in totius Christianitatis opprobrium, et religionis vestrum contemptum, unde apostolice sedi ab omnibus insultatur', *GCN(Marseille)*, no. 1123, cols. 704–705 (1202).

[134] *ibid.*, no. 193, col. 97 (1205).

PLATE IV: Plaster-cast of a seal of the Hospitaller grand-priory of Saint-Gilles depicting an *Agnus Dei*.

been there since the mid-1130s.[135] In 1157 Abbot Bertrand of Saint-Gilles conceded the right to Brother Raymond of Le Puy, master of the Order, to develop the priory by adding a commandery. The Order could build an 'oratory of twelve cubits in length, four in width, and the same in height, that is four [cubits] up to the rafters'.[136] That is, 19.5 metres long by 7 wide and high.[137] This is instructive, for it demonstrates a very grand self image on the part of the abbey. The Hospitaller oratory was uncompromisingly dwarfed by the abbey church whose dimensions were 98 metres in length, 25 in width, and 24 in height,[138] roughly five times as large as the Hospitaller oratory. Nevertheless, it may be that the oratory was of a graceful beauty, for other churches built at the time in Saint-Gilles, not least the abbey, have exceptionally delicate and sensitive carvings.[139]

The Hospitallers were only permitted a campanile of 1 cubit in height (approximately 1.66m), compared to the abbey's bell tower of 35 metres. However, the Hospitallers were permitted two bells, each weighing no more than a quintal (100 pounds), to be rung at Matins, in honour of their dead, and at Mass, but only after the monastery had rung their own bells. The question of bells was an important one, for whilst their proper purpose was serious,[140] abuses, such as the Hospital's drowning out of the patriarch's sermons in Jerusalem, were not unknown.[141] As we have seen, this concern was widely held, for although the bishop of Viviers had given permission to the Hospital at Jalès to build a church and cemetery at Bourg Saint-Andéol in the face of opposition from the prior, in deference to the latter the Hospital was not to be allowed bells.[142]

The permitted devotions in the Hospitallers' oratory at Saint-Gilles were strictly limited. No sacraments were to be administered except those of the

---

135 J. Durbec, 'Les Templiers en Provence. Formation des commanderies et répartitions géographique de leurs biens', *PH* 8(1959), p. 24.

136 'oratorium longitudinis duodecim brachiatarum, amplitudinis quatuor et totidem altitudinis, scilicet quatuor usque ad trabes', 56H4101 (1157). It has been published by M. Ménard, *Histoire civile, ecclesiastique, et litteraire de la ville de Nismes avec les preuves*, Paris, 1744, pp. 35–36.

137 The meaning of a *brachiata* is not clear. Clearly it comes from *bracchium*, an arm. 'Cubit' might then be a sensible translation. However, a cubit is not a set measurement. The estimation comes from R. Jéolas, *Bulletin de l'association d'histoire et d'archeologie de Saint-Gilles, exposition 1984, les ordres religieux militaires à Saint-Gilles au XIIe siècle*, p. 8.

138 *ibid.*, p. 8.

139 M. Gouron, 'Découverte du tympan de l'église Saint-Martin à Saint-Gilles', *AM* 62(1950), pp. 115–120. This was constructed c.1183.

140 For bells at Mass, see M. Rubin, *Corpus Christi, The Eucharist in Late Medieval Culture*, Cambridge, 1991, pp. 58–60.

141 William of Tyre, *Chronicon*, II, book 18, ch. 3, pp. 812–813.

142 56H4585 (1242).

Holy Eucharist and penance, and these only for the brothers and 'family' of the Order. All vigils and oblations were prohibited except on the eve and feast of Saint John. The Order was allowed to build a new, larger cemetery measuring no more than 20 square cubits (approximately 55.5m²), but use of this cemetery was tightly restricted:

> only for brothers who have promised chastity, who have relinquished prop-erty, and who have received your habit in perpetuity: we also permit you to bury your dead 'family' here, too, as long as they are not of our parish.[143]

In return for these privileges, the Order would present one pound of Arabic incense to the abbot at the feast of Saint-Gilles. The oratory was duly con-structed, and consecrated by Peter of Sabran, bishop of Sisteron and Bishop Aldebert of Nîmes in whose diocese Saint-Gilles lay.[144] In 1185 the abbot of Saint-Gilles relaxed the conditions and gave the Hospitallers permission to construct an altar to Saint Stephen beside that dedicated to Saint John the Baptist, to bury strangers who wished to be buried with the Order, and to receive all the oblations made to the altar on the eve and feast of Saint Stephen.[145]

Twelve years later in 1169 the Temple obtained an identical concession at Saint-Gilles: that is, an oratory and a cemetery of identical dimensions, with the same restrictions upon usage of both, except for one significant variation. Members of the 'family' of the Order did not automatically qualify for burial in the cemetery. Evidently, the abbot was not satisfied with the development of the Hospitaller's burial service, and he thus instructed the Templars that those who wished to be buried in the Order's cemetery had to be capable of getting to the commandery unassisted.[146] This was designed to exclude those so ill that they had been received *ad succurrendum* on their death beds in their own homes. It was not particular to Occitania, for a similar provision was enacted by the bishop of Tortosa concerning the Templar commandery of Zuda.[147]

Problems simmered between the Hospitallers and the abbot in Saint-Gilles, and by 1222 flashpoint had been reached. The Holy See took charge of the dispute, and sent commissioners to broker peace. The abbot was sentenced to repay the Hospital 100 Raymondine pounds, which he had illegitimately taken from legacies gifted to the Hospital. To much protestation from the abbot, the

---

[143] 'et hoc solum fratribus qui castitatem promiserint, et proprium reliquerint, et habitum vestrum susceperint perpetuo: hoc etiam de familia vestra qui hic defuncti fuerint permitti-mus ibi sepeliri, nisi sit noster parrochianus', 56H4101 (1157).

[144] Ménard, *Histoire*, p. 220.

[145] 56H4101 (1185).

[146] 56H5289 (1169).

[147] J. Villanueva, *Viage literario á las iglesias de España*, v, Madrid, 1806, p. 277.

Hospitallers were allowed to keep their bells, church and cemetery as they were.[148] Evidently they were enjoying quite some success with the local laity.

There were problems in Arles, too. After the initial gift of the church of Saint Thomas of Trinquetaille in 1115x1126 by Archbishop Atton,[149] the gift was confirmed in 1129, but further proscriptions were imposed. Archbishop Atton had placed restrictions on burial in the church and on the Order receiving tithes. In 1129 Archbishop Bernard Guérin confirmed the gift and the ban on tithes, but tightened up the burial conditions, permitting that only *confratres* and members of the Orders' 'family' might be buried without the express permission of the archbishop and his canons. Clearly, the Hospital was already attracting lay attention, for the archbishop also held that if the Order wished to enlarge its cemetery, it would first have to obtain his permission.[150] Matters were coming to a head towards the turn of the century, for Pope Celestine III wrote to the Hospitallers of Trinquetaille instructing them to respect the interdicts of the archbishop of Arles and the burial privileges of other churches.[151] In 1210 disputes over land added to the problems.[152] In 1229 the canons and clerks behaved abominably towards the Hospitallers, breaking into the church of Saint Thomas of Trinquetaille, desecrating the Host and ransacking the building.[153] As part of the ensuing proceedings the archbishop was forced to have the body of Mary, wife of Bertrand Senaquier, disinterred from the cemetery of Saint Trophimus, and buried in the Hospitaller cemetery at Trinquetaille as she had requested. Furthermore, Hospitaller autonomy was re-stressed, for it was underlined that the Hospitallers could bury whomsoever elected burial in their cemetery, with the cross of the Order, in a service conducted by Hospitaller priests.[154]

The Templars also had an early success with the laity in Arles. In 1153 Archbishop Raymond of Arles gave permission for the Templars to build a cemetery by their oratory, but for the use of the congregation, and no-one else.[155] The archbishop gave no definition of 'congregation', but this implies

---

[148] 56H4102 (1222).

[149] *CH*, I, no. 42, p. 36 (1118x1126); *Trinquetaille(Hospital)*, no. 257, p. 272 (1115x1126); *GCN(Arles)*, no. 487, col. 196 (1118).

[150] *ibid.*, no. 516, col. 201 (1129); *Trinquetaille(Hospital)*, no. 258, pp. 272–273 (1129). The act was reconfirmed in 1144, *ibid.*, no. 289, pp. 291–292 (1144).

[151] *GCN(Arles)*, no. 697 col. 721 (1194).

[152] *ibid.*, no. 3248, cols. 1244–1245 (1210).

[153] 'quod canonici et alii clerici arelatensis ecclesie invaserunt dictam domum hospitalis sancti Thome fragendo ostia dicte domus et unam percusserunt de campanis ecclesie dicte domus cum baculis et clavis volentes eam frangere et aliam fregerunt et quasdam res de dicta domo exportaverunt', 56H5021 (1229).

[154] 56H5021 (1229).

[155] *GCN(Arles)*, no. 564, col. 220 (1152).

only the Order and its 'family'. By 1201 problems had arisen between the Templars and the local abbey, for there were negotiations between Brother Deudat, master of the Temple in Provence, and the prior of Saint Martin in whose parish the Templar chapel lay.[156]

There were troubles in Montpellier, too. The provost of Maguelone disputed the Temple's oblations from vigils, burials and tithes, the Order's proposal to construct a new church, and sought redress for various cases of damage and trespass. Brother Deudat of Breisaco, the master of Narbonne, Arles and Provence, represented the Temple, and the agreement reached was formally submitted to Pope Celestine III for approval. By this agreement the Order agreed to give the prior of Saint Firmin a third of all oblations, money, candles, bread and wine, whether they had been given to a brother-chaplain or offered to an altar. The prior was also to receive a third of all moveables and immoveables (except arms, armour and horses) gained from legacies given for burial, even if the property was given in lieu of horses, arms or armour. Further, restrictions similar to those at Saint-Gilles and at Zuda were imposed on those who could be buried in the cemetery with the sign of the Temple: they had to be capable of transporting themselves to the commandery on foot, or on horseback, without assistance.[157] This arrangement may not have been properly implemented, for two years later it was re-confirmed by Pope Innocent III.[158]

Such problems were, in fact, endemic. At Bras in 1220 the local Benedictine prior needed to agree in writing with the commander of the Temple that oblations, excepting arms, from the Templar oratory would be split between himself and the Temple.[159] In 1250 the Templar commander and the prior of Alais went to arbitration over many issues including tithes, first fruits and the like, but mainly over burial of the dead. The prior would only be permitted to receive one quarter of the legacies given to the Order by those choosing burial in the Hospitaller's cemetery, except if they comprised horses, arms or ornaments for their church. Pope Honorius III had stated in 1216 that clerics were to be content with one quarter of the Hospital's burial gifts, and he justified the Orders' retention of all arms and horses for their work in the Holy Land.[160] The handing over of dead bodies was also to be properly regulated. The prioral clergy would lead the funeral cortège, 'with a cross and a thurible as it should

---

156 *GCN(Marseille)*, no. 1122, cols. 702–704 (1201).
157 *Bullaire de l'eglise de Maguelone (1030–1303)*, J. Rouquette and A. Villemagne (eds.), I, Montpellier, 1911, no. 135, pp. 222–226 (1196).
158 *ibid.*, I, no. 150, pp. 253–256 (1198).
159 56H5203 (1220). Bras was a dependency of Saint Victor of Marseille.
160 *Si diligenter attenditis*, H20 (1216).

be done', to the gates of the town, where the Hospitaller clergy would meet the procession, and lead it up to the commandery 'with a cross and a censer'.[161]

The process of preparation for burial leaves few documents, but an interesting example was that of Count Charles of Anjou's first wife, Beatrix of Provence. Charles required prompting from Pope Clement IV in 1268 to fulfil his late wife's wishes and organize her burial in the Hospitaller chapel at Aix.[162] It took four years before he requested permission from the provost and chapter of Aix to undertake the necessary building work at the Hospital which would permit the addition of an extra three altars, and the creation of an appropriate resting place for her body near that of Count Raymond Berenger of Provence.[163] Perhaps in recompense for the inconvenience, that same year Count Charles sent the Hospitallers at Aix an impressive quantity of relics, vestments, ecclesiastical ornaments and precious metals.[164]

Thus, although there are instances of disputes with the secular clergy over burials, the numerically greater, and seemingly more acrimonious, disagreements over burial and its associated oblations rent the relationship between the Military Orders and the monastic world more than the relationship between the Orders and the secular clergy. Yet, it ought to be highlighted that the monastic religious in Occitania originally supported the Military Orders. It was only as a result of their success that the relationship degenerated. The Military Orders were depriving the monastic establishment of a large part of their traditional income, and the monasteries' attempts to block, or at the very least prevent, this change was a natural reflex of self-defence.

Conclusion

It is clear that, wherever they settled, the Military Orders affected the livelihoods of the pre-existing Orders and the secular clergy to some extent. The Military Orders developed deep relationships with episcopal friends, and were most troubled by antagonism with one group: the local monastic houses, who perceived a threat to income from established *spiritualia*, especially in the domain of burial and its associated oblations to churches held and served by them. The widespread exploitation of parishes by the Benedictines had been a

---

[161] 'usque ad portale ville ducere cum cruce et turibulo sicut decet . . . cum cruce et incensario', 56H4992 (1250). The use of both thurible and censer is curious, for there is no liturgical distinction between the two in terms of solemnity. My thanks to the Rev. Dr David Forrester (Old Palace, Oxford) for his comments on liturgical instruments.

[162] *CH*, III, no. 3319, p. 181 (1268).

[163] *ibid.*, III, no. 478, pp. 277–278 (1272).

[164] *ibid.*, III, no. 3657, pp. 360–362 (1278).

relatively recent venture, developing since the eighth century, and exploding in the eleventh. It caused problems with the episcopacy among whom the notion that the monastic and the clerical life were to be kept distinct still had support.[165] Perhaps the episcopacy appreciated the Orders breaking up the Benedictine domination of parishes not directly under secular clerical control. However, William of Tyre's assertions that the Templars 'became very troublesome' to the Church, and that the Hospitallers 'never showed any reverence to the prelates' are an exaggeration of the state of affairs as seen in Occitania.[166]

A mention should also be made of the mendicants. As would be expected, as Orders which 'owned' no property at all, there was little scope for land transactions with the Military Orders. Moreover, mendicants do not appear as witnesses to the Military Orders' charters. Some of the few references that do occur concern not the Dominicans and Franciscans, but the Pied Friars and the Friars of the Sack, Provençal Orders founded in the mid-thirteenth century in Hyères and Marseille respectively.[167] The latter even had a house in Acre.[168] When they were suppressed by the Council of Lyons (1274), some of their 'property' (at Marseilles, Tarascon and Brignolles) was vested in the Temple and Hospital.[169]

The Occitanian Church is often accused of being lax. Examples such as the Spanish Archbishop Berenger of Narbonne (1190–1212), who did not visit his diocese in ten years, are frequently cited.[170] But, the claim of an eminent historian that Occitania was a 'sort of religious backwater' is too harsh.[171] The evidence of the relationship between the Orders and the Church shows the Church to have been, in the main, a dynamic, well-connected institution at pains to preserve its links with the laity (to assume that the motivation was always financial would be to assume that which we can never know). That the Cathar heresy penetrated into this area is a phenomenon as much to do with

---

[165] Constable, 'Monasteries', *passim*.

[166] William of Tyre, *Chronicon*, I, book 12, ch. 7, p. 555; II, book 18, ch. 6, p. 817.

[167] R. Emery, 'The Friars of the Blessed Virgin Mary and the Pied Friars', *Speculum* 24(1949), p. 288; *idem*, 'The Friars of the Sack', *Speculum* 18(1943), p. 325. Generally, and for a detailed historiographical introduction, see K. Elm, 'Ausbreitung, Wirksamkeit und Ende des provençal-ischen Sackbrüder (*Fratres de poenitentia Jesu Christi*) in Deutschland und den Niederlanden. Ein Beitrag zur kurialen und konziliaren Ordenspolitik des 13. Jahrhunderts', *Francia. Forschungen zur Westeuropäischen Geschichte* 1(1973), pp. 257–324.

[168] Emery, 'The Friars of the Sack', p. 328.

[169] M. de Fontette, 'Les Mendiants supprimés au 2e concile de Lyon (1274). Frères sachets et frères pies', *CF* 8(1973), pp. 203, 217; Elm, 'Ausbreitung', pp. 313–323.

[170] J. Strayer, *The Albigensian Crusades*, Ann Arbor, 1992, p. 19; *cf.* Emery, *Heresy*, pp. 56–57.

[171] Strayer, *Albigensian*, p. 25.

the location of Occitania, the Mediterranean, trade routes, contact with Eastern Europe, and the people's religious tolerance, as with the resident Church. For after all, the same historian admitted

> we shall never know the exact figures [of numbers of heretics], but it is probable that even at the peak of their success the heretics, avowed or concealed, were only a minority of the population.[172]

Occitania was by no means a religious wasteland. The success of local pilgrimages, and the sheer size of the Orders' activities, which almost all involved the laity, testify to the fertility of the religious soil.

Reflective of this, certain aspects of popular piety were well developed. The practice of making *ex voto* donations was commonplace,[173] and the veneration of relics was widespread. In 1286 Brother William of Villaret, grand-prior of Saint-Gilles, gave the Hospitallers at Aix a finger of Saint Mary Magdalene encased in silver, and an image of Saint Veronica which he had brought from Rome. Four years earlier the Order had translated an arm of Saint John the Pilgrim and relics of Saint George the Martyr to the grand-priory of Auvergne, presumably to exhibit them.[174] This was not peculiar to the European commanderies. In the Crusader states the Templars possessed a substantial number of major relics, and exhibited them.[175] In the late thirteenth century Pope Nicholas IV even recorded that miracles had been reported at the Templar church of the Blessed Virgin Mary at Silva in the diocese of Rodez.[176] When the Orders encountered problems from the Church in Occitania, it was not as a result of a lack of faith amongst the people, nor a question of the other religious institutions obstructing the Orders as lay-Orders, but rather an attempt by the established religious communities to minimize the impact the advent of the Orders was having on their livings.

One of the main methods of securing the allegiance and support of locals, and indeed a measure of the Orders' integration, was recruitment into the Orders by the various mechanisms whereby the laity could affiliate themselves. These will be examined in the following chapter.

---

[172] *ibid.*, p. 21.
[173] P.-A. Sigal, 'L'Ex-voto au Moyen Age dans les régions Nord-Ouest de la Méditeranée (xiie–xve siècles)', *PH* 33(1983), pp. 13–31.
[174] 56H4175 (1286); 4049 (1282).
[175] Barber, *Knighthood*, pp. 199–200.
[176] The Pope granted an indulgence of a year and eleven days to all who visited, on the feast of the Assumption of the Blessed Virgin Mary, the 'capellam ejusdem domus, in honorem beatæ Mariæ virginis dedicatem, in qua fiunt multa miracula', Nicholas IV, *Loca sanctorum omnium*, in *Registres de Nicholas IV, Recueil des bulles de ce pape*, E. Langlois (ed.), Paris, 1886, nos. 897–898, p. 197 (1289).

CHAPTER IV

The Laity and the Military Orders

A new knighthood has been born – the whole world will hear of it – in that region where once present in the flesh *the day dawned from on high*. . . . Thus He accomplishes, still today, *the redemption of His people, raising for us the horn of salvation in the house of David, His servant*. . . .

This is what is occurring in Jerusalem, and the whole world is roused. *The islands hear, and far off peoples take notice*, and from East to West they are stirred up, *like the overflowing torrent of the glory of nations*, like *the impetuous course of the river which gladdens the city of God*.[1]

Saint Bernard, *Liber ad milites Templi de laude novæ militiæ*,
in *Sources Chrétiennes* 367, P.-Y. Emery (ed.),
Paris, 1990, ch. 1, p. 50, ch. 5, p. 76

BOTH Military Orders had been founded to aid a specific group of lay people: pilgrims. Yet, pilgrims were not the only group to come into close, often prolonged, contact with the Orders. There were two other principal ways for non-members to share in the Orders' lives, participate in their activities, and reap the spiritual benefits with which the Orders were endowed. The first was to enter into relations with the Order by a gift of property. The second was to give the most valuable property one possessed: oneself. Whilst these two categories were not mutually exclusive, for all gifts to a religious Order were deemed spiritually meritorious, this chapter will analyse these two types of pious donations separately under sections treating economic relations with the laity, and recruitment and confraternity.

---

[1] 'Novum militiæ genus ortum nuper auditur in terris, et in illa regione, quam olim in carne præsens *visitavit Oriens ex alto*, . . . *faciens* etiam nunc *redemptionem plebis suæ, et rursum erigens cornu salutis nobis in domo David pueri sui*. . . . Hæc Ierosolymis actitantur, et orbis excitatur. *Audiunt insulæ, et attendunt populi de longe*, et ebulliunt ab Oriente et Occidente, tamquam *torrens inundans gloriæ gentium*, et tamquam *fluminis impetus lætificans civitatem Dei*.'

Economic Relations with the Laity

(i) Imperial and Comital Privileges

It has been suggested that the Military Orders appealed to the minor nobility, whilst the most influential families patronized the Cistercians.[2] The evidence from Occitania does not support this. Rather, it can be seen that the most influential families took their patronage of the Orders seriously. This section will detail some of the more significant privileges.

The senior power east of the Rhône was the Roman Empire. Relations between the emperor and the Orders date from the mid-twelfth century. In 1156, after having visited the Hospital in Jerusalem, Emperor Frederick I Barbarossa took all of the Hospital's possessions in imperial lands under his protection, and exempted the Order from payment of imperial taxes and levies.[3] This protection was re-confirmed by Emperors Otto IV, Frederick II and Charles IV.[4] Likewise, Frederick granted the Templars a similar privilege in 1184.[5] This privilege was confirmed by Frederick II,[6] who at some unspecified date also made a generous donation of land to the Hospital in Occitania.[7] The relationship between Frederick II and the Orders was complex, especially in the Italian peninsula and Sicily where alliances shifted. Whilst he was persuaded by the Pope to re-enter into a good relationship with the Hospital, his general animosity towards the Temple lasted until his death.[8]

The Empire was a shadowy institution in Occitanian life, and a much more intense relationship is evident between local comital families and the Orders. The counts of Toulouse were on close terms with the Hospital. Count Bertrand (1105–1112) witnessed a gift in 1101,[9] and his son, Pons of Tripoli, confirmed all his father's gifts to the Order in 1126 and 1128.[10] Count Alfonso Jordan made only one gift,[11] but his successor, Raymond V (1148–1195), was the count of Toulouse to feature most frequently in Hospitaller documents. Together with his wife, Queen Constance, he gave the Hospital at Saint-

---

2 E. Delaruelle, 'Templiers et Hospitaliers en Languedoc pendant la croisade des Albigeois', *CF* 4(1969), p. 328; P. Ourliac, cited by Delaruelle, gave an unpublished paper on the subject, *ibid.*, p. 328.
3 56H4040 (1156); similar privilege in *Saint-Gilles(Hospital)*, fol. 170v (1158).
4 56H4040 (1211); (1221); (1365).
5 56H5168 (1184).
6 56H5168 (1216); (1223).
7 56H5065 (undated).
8 Demurger, *Temple*, p. 248.
9 *CH*, I, no. 6, pp. 9–11 (1101).
10 *ibid.*, I, no. 79, pp. 74–75 (1126); no. 82, pp. 76–78 (1128).
11 *ibid.*, I, no. 169, pp. 133–134 (1146).

Gilles considerable interests at Saint-Pierre-de-Camp-Public in return for lands which the Order held at Valabrègue in 1158.[12] That same year, once again with his wife, he gave forty measures of land to the Hospital of Saint-Gilles.[13] In 1164 he gave more land,[14] and in 1175 he permitted them the right to have fires for the making of bread.[15] The arenga to this charter is fulsome testimony to the count's piety:

> Since it is the frailness of man to slide into sinning, and the days of man are short, as the Prophet said 'Man is as hay, and his days as flowers of the field (variant of Isaiah XL, 6)', and the Apostle James asked 'what is our life on earth, if not steam appearing but briefly'; therefore Our Lord exhorted us, saying 'Sell and give that which you possess, and ensure that your treasure-house in heaven is not wanting (variant of Saints Matthew XIX, 21; Mark X, 20 and Luke XVIII, 22).'[16]

In 1177 he granted the Order exemption from all taxes in his domains,[17] and the following year saw the Order exempted from payments on pasturing.[18] In 1182 he circulated a bull of Pope Alexander III guaranteeing the lawfulness of wills made out to the Order in the presence of only two or three witnesses.[19] In 1184 he gave the Order the town of Saint-Martin of Jonquières, a donation which was formally received in chapter,[20] and in 1186 he was in Saint-Gilles where he used the opportunity to re-confirm all Hospitallers possessions in his lands.[21] As shall be demonstrated, this count was also involved in dealings which led to the foundation of the commandery of Saint Maurice of Aix.

Of the other counts of Toulouse, Count Raymond VI was also on very close terms with the Hospital. His use of the Order during the Albigensian campaigns has been described in chapter one, as has his reception into the Order whilst excommunicate. In 1190, before becoming count, he took the Hospital under his protection as his father had done.[22] In 1202 he was present in Saint-

---

[12] *Saint-Gilles(Hospital)*, fol. 118rv (1158); *CH*, I, no. 220, p. 169 (1158).

[13] *Saint-Gilles(Hospital)*, fols. 118v–119r (1158); *CH*, I, no. 269, p. 202 (1158).

[14] *ibid.*, I, no. 333, pp. 234–235 (1164).

[15] *ibid.*, I, no. 484, pp. 333–334 (1175).

[16] 'Quum humana fragilitas labilis est ad peccandum et dies hominis breves sunt, Propheta testante, "Homo sic fenum et dies ejus sicut flos agri"; et Jacobus apostolus, "quod est vita nostra super terram, nisi vapor ad modicum parens"; ob hoc Dominus nos hortatur, dicens, "Vendite et date quæ possedetis et facite vobis thesauros in cælo non deficientes." '

[17] *Saint-Gilles(Hospital)*, fols. 157v–158r (1177); *CH*, I, no. 520, pp. 345–5; no. 525, p. 359 (1177).

[18] *Saint-Gilles(Hospital)*, fol. 158v (1178).

[19] *ibid.*, fol. 159r (1182); *CH*, I, no. 624, pp. 423–424 (1182).

[20] *Saint-Gilles(Hospital)*, fol. 158r (1164); *CH*, I, no. 684, pp. 455–456 (1184).

[21] *Saint-Gilles(Hospital)*, fol. 182r (1186); *CH*, I, no. 781, p. 490 (1186).

[22] *ibid.*, I, no. 884, p. 562 (1190).

Gilles where he witnessed a Hospitaller act.[23] The following year he invested the Order with some property,[24] and the year after that he used his seal to authenticate a Hospitaller act.[25] Although a *confrater* of the Hospital, he included both Military Orders in a will he had drawn up in 1209 when setting out for Rome, and again in his final testament of 1218.[26] The last count of Toulouse of Saint-Gilles, Raymond VII, passed no new acts himself, but confirmed and ratified the privileges accorded by Raymond V, and took the Hospitallers of Narbonne under his special protection.[27] Additionally, there are occasional mentions of the deputies of the counts. For instance, in 1206 a chancellor of Count Raymond VI was present at Saint-Gilles.[28]

In the Holy Land, the Order supported the cadet branch of the Toulouse family: the counts of Tripoli. In return, in 1174 Count Raymond III of Tripoli thanked the Order for their strenuous efforts to secure his ransom.[29] Based on this relationship the dramatic build-up to the battle of Ḥiṭṭīn saw the Hospital firmly in the Tripolitanian camp.

The counts of Toulouse of Saint-Gilles appear somewhat less frequently in Templar documentation, and their gifts were not as generous as those which they presented to the Hospital. Yet, as early as 1134 Count Alfonso Jordan made a substantial donation to the Templars of Saint-Gilles in the presence of his rivals, Count Raymond Berenger III of Barcelona and Viscount Roger Trencavel of Béziers.[30] In the East Alfonso Jordan entrusted the care of his son Raymond to the Order. But, on his father's death the young Raymond V sailed swiftly for Occitania.[31] As count he gave little to the Templars. He witnessed an act at Richerenches in 1141,[32] was present in 1153 when Brother Peter of Rovira of the Temple gave the Hospitallers one fifth of Amposta and Candela,[33] and he again witnessed a Templar act in Saint-Gilles in 1175.[34] Donations aside, the Templars were in high favour with the counts, and listed at the commandery of Toulouse was a sacerdotal vestment embroidered with

---

23 *Saint-Gilles(Hospital)*, fols. 1r–2v (1202); *CH*, ii, no. 1163, p. 17 (1202).

24 *ibid.*, ii, no. 1179, p. 25 (1203).

25 *ibid.*, ii, no. 1190, p. 30 (1204).

26 *ibid.*, ii, no. 1334, p. 110 (1209); no. 1612, pp. 243–244 (1218).

27 *ibid.*, ii, no. 1759, pp. 307–308 (1222); no. 2289, p. 600 (1242).

28 *Saint-Gilles(Hospital)* fols. 41r–42r (1201).

29 *CH*, i, no. 467, pp. 319–320 (1174).

30 *CT*, no. 87, p. 66 (1134).

31 Rorgo Fretellus, *Rorgo Fretellus de Nazareth et sa description de la Terre Sainte. Histoire et édition du texte*, P. Boeren (ed.), Amsterdam, 1980, pp. 54, 72–77.

32 *Richerenches(Temple)*, no. 3, pp. 31–32 (1141).

33 *CH*, i, no. 220, p. 169 (1153).

34 *Saint-Gilles(Temple)*, fols. 20v–21v (1175).

the arms of the house of Toulouse,[35] an unambiguous visual statement that the Order was under the protection of the counts.[36]

Deputies of the counts of Toulouse appeared more frequently in Templar than in Hospitaller acts. In 1201 three judges were chosen to arbitrate in a matter concerning the Temple, one of whom was Peter John, bailiff to Count Raymond VI.[37] In 1206 the commander of Roaix sought to collect depositions demonstrating that a certain individual had left the Order various goods. The depositions were sworn in front of Count Raymond VI's *viguier*, and his judge and chancellor in the Venaissin and beyond the Rhône, both of whom were all present at the commandery of Roaix.[38] At Roaix in 1191 Peter Humbert settled his dispute with the Temple in front of Dragonet, bailiff of Count Raymond V.[39] After this, all concerned repaired to the commandery of Roaix where they announced this to all the brethren. They then removed to Roque-brune, and swore their reconciliation a third time in front of Peter's family.[40] Comital scribes could also work for the Orders, as when Bertrand, notary to Count Raymond V, drew up an act for the Temple in 1158.[41]

The counts of Barcelona were equally as generous to the Hospital. Count Raymond Berenger III and his wife's privileges for the transport of the Order's goods from Gap to Saint-Gilles in 1114 have been discussed in chapter two.[42] The most generous count of Barcelona was Raymond Berenger IV, king of Aragon. He received the Hospitallers' third of Aragon from Master Raymond of Le Puy in 1140, but did not begin making gifts to the Order until 1148.[43] In 1150 he was together with his nephew, Count Raymond Berenger II of Provence, when they gave the Order the town of Saint Michael of Puimoisson, where the Order built a commandery. In addition, they granted the Order lodging rights in any town in Provence, the right to collect dead wood in the pine forest of the Camargue, and an exemption from various taxes and levies.[44] This gift was made not only for the spiritual health of the donors, but also for

35 A. du Bourg, *Histoire du grand-prieuré de Toulouse*, Toulouse, 1883, no. 23, p. xvii.
36 See R. Macalister, *Ecclesiastical Vestments*, London, 1896, pp. 155–162.
37 *Roaix(Temple)*, no. 147, p. 94 (1201).
38 *ibid.*, no. 162, p. 107–108 (1206).
39 *ibid.*, no. 143, pp. 98–90 (1191).
40 *ibid.*, no. 143, pp. 98–90 (1191).
41 *Saint-Gilles(Temple)*, fols. 4v–6r (1158).
42 *Trinquetaille(Hospital)*, no. 261, p. 276 (1114); *CH*, ɪ, no. 33, pp. 31–32 (1114); *Trinquetaille(Hospital)*, no. 260, pp. 274–275 (1114x1150); *CH*, ɪ, no. 24, pp. 24–25 (1112x1128); 56H4050 (1114). Earlier, an unknown count of Provence made a gift to Gap, but he was not of the house of Barcelona.
43 *CH*, ɪ, no. 136, pp. 111–112 (1140); no. 178, p. 139 (1148).
44 *Saint-Gilles(Hospital)*, fols. 172v–173r (1150); *Trinquetaille(Hospital)*, no. 206, pp. 203–204 (1150); 56H4825 (1150); *CH*, ɪ, no. 194, pp. 150–151 (1150).

that of the late Count Berenger Raymond of Provence (father of Raymond Berenger II), whose remains had been interred in the Hospitaller church at Trinquetaille in 1144.[45] This configuration of the senior and cadet branches of the family of Barcelona making a gift together was to happen again thirty years later when Alfonso II, king of Aragon and count of Barcelona, and Sancho, count of Provence, granted the Hospital substantial privileges over livestock.[46] In 1190 the 1150 privilege to collect wood was evidently still being exercised, for Count Alfonso's *viguier* delimited the areas within the pine forest from which the Order might collect the wood.[47]

This count Alfonso, 'the Wise', son of Count Raymond Berenger IV, was more concerned with the Iberian peninsula than with Provence. This is reflected in his patronage. The vast majority of his substantial donations to the Hospital were to the west of the Pyrenees.[48] However, he did draw up various charters concerning the Occitanian Hospital,[49] notably a confirmation of his father's privileges to the Order,[50] an exemption on all taxes in his lands in 1170,[51] the protection of the Peace and Truce of God to both Military Orders in Catalonia in 1173,[52] further exemption from all taxes in his lands,[53] and another declaration of his protection of the Order in 1189.[54] In his will of 1194 he left legacies to both Military Orders: land, his horse and arms to the Temple, and a considerable amount of land and rights to the Hospital.[55]

Gifts to the Temple from the house of Barcelona were not so numerous, yet equally as significant. In 1134 Count Raymond Berenger IV of Barcelona headed twenty men who gave themselves to the Temple for a year,[56] and he also gave the Order a large part of the patrimony of the commandery of Saint Eulalia in 1159.[57] In 1202 the Order was granted a confirmation of all their

[45] *ibid.*
[46] *Trinquetaille(Hospital)*, no. 186, p. 180 (1182); 56H4050 (1182).
[47] *Saint-Gilles(Hospital)*, fol. 171v (1190).
[48] *CH*, I, no. 380, p. 260 (1167); no. 426, pp. 295–296 (1171); no. 461, p. 316 (1174); no. 523, pp. 357–358 (1177); no. 541, pp. 368–369 (1178); no. 586, pp. 397–398; no. 587, pp. 389–390; no. 588, pp. 399–400 (1180); no. 597, pp. 407–408; no. 598, pp. 408–409 (1181x1182); no. 619, pp. 420–421; no. 625, p. 424 (1182); no. 820, pp. 511–512 (1186); no. 834, pp. 519–520 (1187); no. 901, pp. 571–572 (1190).
[49] *ibid.*, I, no. 306, p. 221 (1162); no. 436, p. 302 (1172); no. 615, p. 418 (1181x1184).
[50] *ibid.*, I, no. 410, p. 284 (1169).
[51] *ibid.*, I, no. 415, pp. 287–288 (1170).
[52] *ibid.*, I, no. 445, p. 309 (1173).
[53] *ibid.*, I, no. 539, pp. 367–368 (1178); no. 647, pp. 435–436 (1182).
[54] *ibid.*, I, no. 866, p. 551 (1189).
[55] *ibid.*, I, no. 968, p. 614 (1194).
[56] *CT*, no. 72, p. 55 (1134).
[57] A. du Bourg, 'Etablissement des chevaliers du Temple et de Saint-Jean de Jérusalem en Rouergue', *Mémoires de la société des lettres* 13(1886), p. 180.

goods and privileges by letters patent of Count Alfonso II of Provence.[58] This was re-issued by Count Raymond Berenger V of Provence in 1235;[59] and in 1244 he gave the Templars at Arles permission to build an aqueduct to bring water from the Durance to Arles.[60] There was, more generally, involvement by the counts of Barcelona in the confirmation of large land transfers. For instance, Rué, a future commandery, had been gifted to the Order by the seigneurs of Salernes, Flayosc and Entrecasteux, and the formalization of this was provided by the count of Barcelona in 1156.[61] Albeit that there is a low survival rate of Templar charters from the house of Barcelona, this should not be read as indifference. The most famous son of this house, Count Raymond Berenger III 'the Great' of Barcelona, professed as a brother of the Temple in 1130 despite the fact that he had given considerable privileges to the Hospital some fifteen years earlier.[62] Count Raymond Berenger IV's donation of the village of Saint-Eulalie was specifically:

> for the remission of my sins, and the health of the soul of my father, who was a knight and brother of the holy knighthood of the Temple of Solomon.[63]

Of the cadet branch of Barcelona, Count Raymond Berenger IV of Provence and Forcalquier gave generously to the Hospital.[64] His favourite city was Aix. He made special provision for the lighting of the commandery by a generous subsidy,[65] and gave 20,000 *sous* in revenues from Nice and Grasse for two chaplains to be maintained at Aix, and three at Vinon, to offer daily masses for his family.[66] He was buried in the commandery of Aix beside Count Alfonso II.[67] His widow, Beatrix of Savoy, continued to give to the Hospital after her husband's death,[68] and one of these donations attested to the continuing perception of the Order as one whose primary aim was charitable and hospitaller. She gifted land at Echelles (diocese of Grenoble), to Brother Ferald of Barras, grand-preceptor, stipulating that a hospital for the poor be built there,

---

58 56H5168 (1202).

59 56H5168 (1235).

60 56H5170 (1244).

61 56H5279 (1156).

62 *CT*, no. 33, p. 25 (1130).

63 'pro remissione peccatorum meorum et salute anime patris mei qui fuit miles ac frater sancte milicie Templi Salomonis', du Bourg, *Histoire*, no. 110, p. lxxii (1159).

64 *CH*, II, no. 2016, pp. 430–431; no. 2018, pp. 435–436; no. 2023, p. 435 (1232); no. 2066, pp. 461–462 (1233).

65 *ibid.*, II, no. 2112, pp. 484–485 (1235).

66 *ibid.*, II, no. 2278, pp. 592–593 (1241).

67 *ibid.*, II, no. 2022, pp. 531–532 (1238).

68 *ibid.*, II, no. 2392, pp. 639–640 (1246).

with the religious Offices to be provided by thirteen priests, two deacons, and three clerks.[69] This was accordingly constructed, and became a commandery.

The county of Provence was taken over by the able administrator Count Charles of Anjou in 1246. In 1262 he passed a number of acts in favour of the Hospital, and granted it wide-ranging privileges.[70] Notably, that the Order would be exempt from all payments on grain and animals in Provence, that the Order could graze its flocks on any imperial land, that the Order would be exempt from all taxes on salt and salt-works destined for use in their own houses, that the count could not acquire jurisdiction over land belonging to the Order without the express permission of the grand-prior of Saint-Gilles, and that he could not exact revenues from any such places. In return, the Order agreed that the commanders of Gap and Manosque would be bound to contribute annually to the cavalcade,[71] would provide the count with ten knights and one hundred foot-soldiers for forty days,[72] that in the case of war in Provence the count could take over any Hospitaller castle provided he returned it after the hostilities, that members of the Order would not be subject to imperial jurisdiction except in actions concerning realty, and that the count could exact no homage or recognition from the Order's vassals.[73] Some of the benefits he gave the Orders were practical, as when in 1278 he gave Brother William of Villaret, grand-prior of Saint-Gilles, letters of safe conduct for a journey to Rome.[74] The inhabitants of Arles certainly perceived the Hospitallers as having been overly familiar with Charles and his *franciots* and, when Charles was absent on the Seventh Crusade (1248–1249), they stormed the commandery of Trinquetaille, killing several brethren.[75]

---

[69] 56H3875 (suppl.) (1260, vidimus 1265); 56H5125 (1260); *CH*, II, no. 2965, pp. 892–894 (1260).

[70] 56H4418; 56H4799; 56H4051 (1262) of which there are five copies; *CH*, III, no. 3003, p. 19; no. 3035, pp. 35–42 (1262). This latter was twice confirmed by his son, no. 4207, pp. 615–616 (1293); IV, no. 4759, p. 152 (1307).

[71] The *majus dominium* of the large comital houses comprised (1) the *quista*, a royal tax (2) the high justice (3) the cavalcade and (4) the *albergum*, a cash payment descended from the old duty of hospitality, E. Baratier, *La Démographie provençale du XIIe au XVIe siècle*, Paris, 1961, pp. 13–22.

[72] These would not have been Hospitallers, but rather, raised from the tenants of the Order. A similar practice was to be found in many Benedictine houses although not those of the Cluniac congregation, C. Lawrence, *Medieval Monasticism*, London and New York, 1989, pp. 130–131.

[73] 56H4051 (1262).

[74] *CH*, III, no. 3686, p. 379 (1278).

[75] M. Chailan, *L'Ordre de Malte dans la ville d'Arles*, Marseille, 1974, p. 5. Avignon, too, revolted, as did Marseille, L. Stouff, 'La Commune d'Arles au XIIIe siècle', *PH* 11(1961), pp. 314–315.

The relationship between Charles and the Temple was warm.[76] They financed much of his Sicilian venture,[77] and when he staked his claim for the crown of Jerusalem in 1268, the Temple was prominent in its support, even lodging him at the Acre Temple.[78] The Hospital had initially supported Charles' rival for the throne, King Hugh III of Cyprus. But, once Charles had secured the crown, they welcomed and supported his representative, Roger of San Severino.[79] Perhaps in revenge for their earlier indifference his son, Charles II, began blocking the Hospitaller's Occitanian responsions (whilst encouraging the Templar traffic flowing through Apulia),[80] and in 1291 Pope Nicholas IV exhorted him to permit the Hospitallers in Provence to send a thousand charges of wheat to help Christians in the Holy Land.[81]

Of the other great families in Occitania, the Catalan counts of Urgel gave the Templars a castle as early as 1132.[82] As vassals of Barcelona the Trencavel supported primarily the Templars, and to a lesser extent the Hospital. Between 1132 and 1150 they made gifts to the Temple at Douzens and Carcassonne, and witnessed acts concerning the Temple.[83] In 1133 Viscount Roger I of Béziers (d.1150) requested burial with the Templars.[84] In 1151 Viscount Bernard Atton Trencavel of Nîmes forbade the building of any ovens, public or private, licensing the Templars to destroy any built contrary to this order.[85] However, the 1153 will of Viscount Raymond Trencavel I of Béziers made clear that the 1,000 *sous* he left to each Order, as well as his horse and arms to the Temple, were in reparation for the 'evil I have done to the houses of the Temple and Hospital in Roussillon with my cavalcades'.[86]

Conversely, the counts of Forcalquier supported the Hospital to the exclusion of the Temple. Over a period of many years they slowly granted the Hospitallers the whole of Manosque, and more besides.[87] The first donation

[76] E. Léonard, *Les Angevins de Naples*, Paris, 1954, p. 130; Barber, *Knighthood*, pp. 169–172, 239–240, 274–275.

[77] Demurger, *Temple*, p. 257.

[78] Barber, *Knighthood*, p. 172; H. Mayer, *The Crusades*, J. Gillingham (tr.), Oxford, 1972, p. 271.

[79] Riley-Smith, *Knights*, pp. 188–189.

[80] Barber, *Knighthood*, p. 291.

[81] 56H4023 (1291).

[82] *CT*, no. 47, p. 13 (1132).

[83] *Douzens(Temple)*, A no. 171, pp. 152–154 (1132); A no. 115, pp. 106–108 (1133); A no. 172, p. 154 (1134); D no. 4, pp. 275–277 (1148); A no. 173, pp. 155–156 (1150).

[84] C. Devic and J. Vaissete, *Histoire générale de Languedoc*, III, Toulouse, 1872, p. 780.

[85] *Saint-Gilles(Temple)*, fol. 188r (1151).

[86] 'Mala que ego feci cum mea cavalgada in Rossilono domibus Templi et domibus Hospitalis', *CH*, I, no. 218, p. 168 (1153).

[87] 56H4626 (1149) (1150) (undated) (1153x1154) (undated) (1162); 56H4627 (1168); 56H4628 (1208) (1211) (1206); 56H4670 (1168) (1175). Some of these appear in *Saint-*

came in 1129 when Countess Adalaïs and her son, Count William, gave the Hospital all their rights over boats which navigated the river Durance to Sisteron.[88] The transfer of Manosque began twenty years later, and included neighbouring castles. Count Bertrand left the Order the castles of Manosque, Toutes-Aures, Châteauneuf-de-Bénévent, Grambois, Limans, Beaumont, Richecuberte, Saint-Tulle, two named Pierrevert, Saint-Marme, Châteaudauphin, Laroche, Voix and Montaigu.[89] All the initial acts of transfer of Manosque were confirmed by Emperor Frederick I.[90] Once Charles of Anjou had become count of Forcalquier, he recognized in 1262 that the Order paid him homage for all they possessed around Manosque, and that the Order would provide him with forty knights and one hundred foot-soldiers in time of war to be fed at his expense, for which he renounced various claims in the area.[91]

Of other, lesser, comital families, the numbers of those who made gifts is large. For instance, the family of the viscounts of Marseille gave generously to both Orders,[92] as well as to many others.[93] The counts of Comminges gave generously to the Templars at Montsaunès.[94] The counts of Albon gave to Templar Douzens and Hospitaller Gap.[95] Viscount Dragonet of Embrun, with the consent of the count of Forcalquier, gave the Hospital mills on the Durance in 1203,[96] and Count Bertrand of Melgueil made a donation to the Hospital in 1171.[97]

Although the quantity and largesse of the comital and imperial privileges is

---

Gilles(Hospital), fols. 159v–160r (1149); 164v; 164rv (1168); 163v–164r (1175); 167rv; 166v–167r (1206).

[88] *ibid.*, fols. 161v–162v (1129).

[89] *ibid.*, fols. 160v–161v (1168).

[90] *ibid.*, fols. 168r–169r (1162).

[91] 56H4631 (1262).

[92] *Inventaire chronologique et analytique des chartes de la maison de Baux*, L. Barthélemy (ed.), Marseille, 1882. To the Temple: no. 172, p. 47 (1215); no. 254, p. 72; no. 258, p. 74 (1234); no. 284, p. 81 (1240); no. 309, p. 87 (1243); no. 145, p. 125 (1258). To the Hospital: no. 35, p. 8 (1137); no. 58, p. 15 (1160); no. 68, p. 18 (1173); no. 73, p. 19 (1180); no. 55, p. 22 (1186); no. 89, pp. 23–24 (1192); no. 94, p. 25 (1193); no. 98, p. 26 (1199); no. 131, p. 36 (1208); no. 134, p. 37 (1209); no. 177, p. 48 (1215); no. 168, p. 46 (1216); no. 216, p. 60 (1225); no. 285, p. 81 (1240); no. 319, p. 91 (1246); no. 390, p. 112 (1255); no. 422, pp. 121–122 (1257); no. 569, p. 163 (1272); no. 223, p. 62 (1277); no. 619, pp. 178–179 (1281).

[93] *ibid.*, *passim*: gifts to Saint Victor of Marseille, Saint Cæsarius of Arles, Saint Trophimus, Sénanque, and so on; 1G1 (thirteenth century) cartulary, *passim*.

[94] *Montsaunès(Temple)*, no. 3, p. 227 (before 1176); no. 1, pp. 223–226 (1176); no. 24, pp. 238–239; no. 29, pp. 241–242 (1178); no. 2, p. 226 (1182); no. 5, pp. 227–228 (1184).

[95] *Douzens(Temple)*, C no. 3, pp. 266–267 (1132); *Gap(Hospital)*, no. 25, p. 25 (1112).

[96] 56H4415 (1203).

[97] 56H4922 (1171).

indicative of a developed relationship with the Military Orders, there were instances of friction, too. In 1241 the Hospitaller prior of Bonpas complained to the Holy See that although the Hospital had bought the bridge of Bonpas in the past for 78,000 *sous*, Count Raymond VII of Toulouse was still mounting a guard on the bridge, taxing travellers and pilgrims. Moreover, a group of brigands and 'servants of the Devil' led by Nicholas, bailiff of Châteauneuf, was robbing the travellers, committing all sorts of excesses, and ravaging the land belonging to the priory. The prior wished this to be drawn particularly to the attention of the bishop of Avignon, in whose name Nicholas claimed to be acting.[98] However, this is the exception in what was an almost exclusively mutually beneficial relationship between the Hospital and the counts of Toulouse.

Imperial and comital privileges guaranteed the Orders special status in the management of their patrimonies. Free from obligations to pay levies and taxes for farming, travelling, transporting and selling goods, they were able to expand and develop with relative freedom. For the donors and grantors there were spiritual advantages. Count Raymond Berenger III thought the Hospital to be a spiritually rich institution when he declared on giving a privilege to the Hospital in 1114 'As water extinguishes fire, so alms extinguish sin',[99] clear in his mind that the Order was a repository of grace. Indeed, the number of gifts made for the forgiveness of the sins of the donor and of his or her ancestors testifies to the perception of the Orders as effective intercessors. The powerful could also hope to make allies of the Orders, a benefit which was used to the full by the excommunicate Count Raymond VI of Toulouse when he sent the prior of the Hospital to Rome as his ambassador during the Albigensian Crusade.[100] These special relationships could, of course, put the Orders into difficult positions if called upon to act against a patron, as for instance when the *infante* Alfonso of Aragon requested help from both the Templars of Aragon and the Hospitallers of the castellany of Amposta against the king of France and Charles of Anjou in 1283.[101] But in the main, the fact that the Orders refrained from fighting in Occitania ensured that such conflicts of patrons' interests did not intrude into their lives as religious communities. The most important feature of the patterns of patronage is that, unlike in England where the two Orders had entirely separate networks of patrons,[102] in Occitania they

---

98   56H4265 (1241).
99   'Sicut aqua extinguit ignem, ita elemosina extinguit peccatum', *Trinquetaille(Hospital)*, no. 260, pp. 274–275 (1114x1150); *CH*, I, no. 24, pp. 24–25 (1112x1128).
100 William of Tudela, *La Chanson de la croisade albigeoise*, H. Gougaud (ed.), Paris, 1989, verse 10, lines 11–13, p. 50.
101 *CH*, III, no. 3826, p. 442 (1283).
102 M. Gervers, *'Pro defensionis Terre Sancte*: the Development and Exploitation of the

shared the favours of donors, albeit with some of the patrons showing preferences.

(ii) Pilgrims

Aside from protecting and housing pilgrims in the Holy Land, the Orders were involved with pilgrims in many ways elsewhere. One of the more unusual stemmed from a letter of Pope Innocent III, which ruled that to prevent pseudo-Crusaders from claiming that they had fulfilled their vow by producing palm-fronds, verificatory letters would be required, signed by the king or the patriarch of Jerusalem, or the masters of the Temple and Hospital, or an Apostolic legate.[103] Although this related to those who had been given the finance for Crusade from the faithful's offerings, it is likely that similar proof was required of those who undertook penitential Crusades.[104]

Inevitably, the Military Orders in Europe were involved in aiding pilgrims. Some commanderies were not designed to accommodate pilgrims, being purely agricultural complexes, but of those commanderies that accommodated travellers, many were enticingly situated along the *via Egidiana* and the *via Tolosa*, from which pilgrims could go on to Santiago, Rome, and the ports from which ships sailed to Outremer. That pilgrims stayed at these commanderies is also visible from architectural remains. At Templar Montsaunès there is a lintel carved with representations of the scallop-shell of the Santiago pilgrim.[105] Such commanderies along pilgrimage routes were not only in the large towns. The twelfth century pilgrim's guide to Santiago, contained in the *Codex Calixtinus*, specifically recommended a detour:

> There is a suburb near Arles, between two branches of the Rhône, called Trinquetaille, where there is a magnificent, very tall, marble column, built on land behind the church of this Saint. It is there, so it is said, that the wicked people tied the Blessed Genès before decapitating him,[106]

Hospitallers' Landed Estate in Essex', in *The Military Orders. Fighting for the Faith and Caring for the Sick*, M. Barber (ed.), Aldershot, 1994, p. 5.

[103] Innocent III, *Opera omnia*, in *PL* 214, letter 260, col. 831.

[104] J. Brundage, *Medieval Canon Law and the Crusader*, Madison, Milwaukee and London, 1969, pp. 125–126.

[105] H. Treuille, 'Autour d'une variante du chemin de Saint Jacques de Toulouse vers le haut Comminges', *CF* 15(1980), p. 114.

[106] 'Est igitur vicus juxta Arelatem, inter duo Rodani brachia, qui dicitur Trenquetalla, in quo est columna quedam marmorea, obtima, valde excelsa, super terram erecta, scilicet retro ejus ecclesiam, ad quam perfidi populi beatum Genesium ut fertur alligantes decollarunt', *Le Guide du pèlerin de Saint-Jacques de Compostella*, J. Vielliard (ed.), Macon, 1950, cap. 8, p. 36.

and it was here, the headquarters of the viscomital family of Baux, that the Hospitallers had one of their most important Occitanian commanderies: Saint Thomas of Trinquetaille.

The average Crusader needed to liquidate four to five times his annual income to finance the Jerusalem pilgrimage.[107] Although it is the Temple which has the reputation for money-lending, both Orders were involved in such contracts. Toward the end of the twelfth century Hugh of Aix wished to raise money to go on Crusade. Accordingly, he granted the Hospital the usufruct of his lands at Tort d'Enseric, for which he was given a loan of 2,000 *sous*. If this were not redeemed in three years, or if he died, the property would then become the Hospital's.[108] It is clear from other sources that a period of three years in which to fulfil a Crusade vow was standard.[109]

The Orders could also benefit from pilgrims giving them property to guard and keep whilst they were away. This benefitted the Orders, which could retain the usufruct, and ensured the safety of the land and family for the pilgrim. The duration of such contracts could be relatively long term. In 1160 Pons Lautiers gave the Temple his lands on the understanding that the Order might have full possession if he did not return within fifteen years.[110] Pons continued by stating that he made the donation 'on the day I began my journey to Jerusalem, which the aforesaid brothers prepared for me'.[111] This may well have entailed advice, a passage to Outremer, contacts, and possibly letters of introduction. Goods were sometimes liquidated to fund pilgrimage without recourse being had to pledges. For example, Conreda and her son William sold the Templars at Roaix some land to fund a journey to the Holy Sepulchre.[112]

Such charters were drawn up as part of the final actions of the pilgrim before departing, often on the very day, as was also the case with William of Visan, who made a donation to the Order of the Temple at Richerenches on the day he set out for Jerusalem in 1159.[113] At Agde some 20 kilometres east of

[107] J. Riley-Smith, *The First Crusade and the Idea of Crusading*, London, 1986, p. 43.

[108] 'pro duobus millibus sol. nove melgoriensis monete quibus, bona voluntate et bono animo, predicte possessionis usum fructum quamdiu eis obligata fuerit dono et concedo. Hec autem obligatio tali tenere est facta quod a principio mei itineris penes Iherosolimam transactis iiibus annis potestate redimendi predictum pignus habeam, Set si interea descenderem, prefatam possessionem, pro Dei amore, eisdem relinquo', *Trinquetaille(Hospital)*, no. 142, pp. 125–126 (1170x1200).

[109] G. Constable, 'Medieval Charters as a Source for the History of the Crusades', *Crusade and Settlement: Papers read at the First Conference of the Society for the Study of the Crusades and the Latins East and presented to R. C. Smail*, P. Edbury (ed.), Cardiff, 1985, p. 77.

[110] *Richerenches(Temple)*, no. 163, pp. 145–146 (1160).

[111] 'in die qua apuz Iherosolimam iter incepi quem fratres suprascripti mihi preparaverunt,' *ibid.*, no. 163, p. 146 (1160).

[112] *Roaix(Temple)*, no. 121, p. 77 (undated).

[113] *Richerenches(Temple)*, no. 84, pp. 84–85 (1159).

Béziers, Count Roger I of Carcassonne made a donation to the Temple of Douzens on embarking for Outremer in 1147. The gift was substantial, and was drawn up on the quayside 'at the port of La Tourette at Agde'.[114] Donations on the day of departure were also normal for the Santiago pilgrimage. In 1157 Armand of Bordeaux made a donation to the Templars when setting out for the Pyrenees,[115] and in 1175 Pons Davis made a gift to the Templars, confirmed on the day his son, Rigaud, set out for Santiago.[116]

As somewhat ritualized acts, motivations for pilgrimage were sometimes solemnly expressed in these documents. In 1148 two brothers stated their reasons for joining the Second Crusade:

> By divine and human precept it is law that donations, sales, or any transaction, be notified to posterity by writing. Therefore notice is made to all men ... [that] we two brothers, Raymond and William of La Baume, wishing to go to Jerusalem for the remittance of our sins, and desiring to renounce all bad ways ...[117]

This demonstrates the penitential nature of their Crusade motivation, and was the norm for most pilgrimage donations. At Roaix in 1142 Pons Calvaira stated that he longed to go to the Holy Sepulchre so that God would forgive him his sins.[118] He either returned safely, or had a son of the same name, for he appeared at Richerenches thirty years later in 1174 and 1175.[119] Others who returned from Crusades, inspired by the Military Orders, sensed that their futures lay with the Orders. For example, the troubadour Cadenet participated in the Fourth Crusade, and subsequently joined the Hospital.[120]

Of a more general nature, and evidence of sensitivity in Occitania to the vicissitudes of the Holy Land, the Temple was attuned to European activities relating to crusading. At Richerenches in September 1147 charters were drawn up and dated specifically with regard to the Second Crusade:

---

[114] 'aput Agaten, ad portum scilicet de Turreta', *Douzens(Temple)*, D no. 4, pp. 275–277 (1147).

[115] *Richerenches(Temple)*, no. 92, p. 93 (1157).

[116] *ibid.*, no. 204, pp. 181–182 (1175).

[117] 'Divinis et humanis precentum est legibus, ut donaciones, vendiciones, sive quelibet transacciones, scriptura posteris notificentur. Notum itaque fiat omnibus hominibus . . . nos duos fratres, Raimundus, et Wilelmus de Balmis, Ierosolimam propter peccatorum nostrorum indulgentiam ire volontes, et omnem maliciam deponere desiderantes,' *ibid.*, no. 43, pp. 46–46 (1148).

[118] *ibid.*, Roaix, no. 6, p. 233 (1142).

[119] *ibid.*, no. 206, pp. 183–184 (1174); no. 113, p. 110 (1175).

[120] R. Nelli, 'Le Vicomte de Béziers (1185–1209) vu par les Troubadours', *CF* 4(1969), p. 312.

when Louis, glorious king of the French, was striking out to repress the enemies of the Cross of Christ,[121]

for the king had passed through Orange that month, and emphasis was laid on the numbers that went with him.[122]

Sometimes the Orders benefitted from pilgrims without an obvious return. In 1134 William Peter divided up his goods before departing for Jerusalem. If he remained in Outremer 'through death or any other reason',[123] he granted the Templars of Douzens seven sheep, lands, vines and agricultural revenues.[124] Despite the fact that the Orders had exceptionally good links between Europe and Syria-Palestine, they did not agree to bring the bodies back of those who fell overseas, an arrangement which can be seen between the monks of Saint Andrew of Clermont and William of Auvergne in 1149, and the monks of the Cambridgeshire priory of Barnwell and Gilbert of Pecche's father.[125] However, there was probably an understanding that the pilgrim-Crusader could be buried with the Order in Outremer. Such arrangements were not solely linked to the Jerusalem pilgrimage, for Raymond Bertrand of Saint-Gilles, on setting out for Santiago de Compostela in 1170, became a *confrater* of the Temple. He stipulated that if he died on the way he wished to be buried at the Temple in Saint-Gilles or any other Templar commandery.[126]

Thus, the Military Orders utilized both aspects of their natures to attract the laity to give to them. They promoted both their religious and their military facets, and conjointly or separately these appealed to benefactors. As would be expected, both Orders aided pilgrimage in the West and to the East. In a society where voyage was known to be desperately dangerous,[127] it is natural

---

[121] 'quando videlicet Lodovicus, rex Francorum gloriosus, Ierosolimam tendens ad confutandos crucis Christi inimicos', *Richerenches(Temple)*, no. 60, pp. 60–63 (1147).

[122] 'innumeram secum duxit exercitum,' *ibid.*, no. 17, pp. 20–21 (1147); 'innumeros peregre proficiscendo commodovit populos', *ibid.*, no. 60, pp. 60–63 (1147); 'Hoc autem donum factum est tempore et anno quo rex Francorum cum exercitu suo, et alii plures, apud Iherosolimam perrexerunt', *ibid.*, no. 31, pp. 33–34 (1147).

[123] 'morte vel aliquo modo', *Douzens(Temple)*, A no. 45, p. 55 (1134).

[124] *ibid.*, A no. 45, p. 55 (1134).

[125] C.-L. Hugo, *Sacri et canonici ordinis Præmonstratensis annales*, in G. Constable, 'The Financing of the Crusades in the Twelfth Century', *Outremer – Studies in the History of the Crusading Kingdom of Jerusalem presented to Joshua Prawer*, B. Kedar *et al.* (eds.), Jerusalem, 1982, p. 81; *Liber memorandorum ecclesie de Bernewell*, J. Clark (ed.), Cambridge, 1907, cap. 23, p. 48.

[126] *Saint-Gilles(Temple)*, fol. 97v (1170).

[127] The twelfth century bestial epic *Ysengrinus* colourfully stressed the need for pilgrims to be protected). 'Orandi studio loca visere sacra volebat/ Caprea cum sociis Bertiliana suis . . ./ Rearidus cervus, suspectum ductor in agmen/ Horrida ramosi verticis arma gerit;/ Berfridus caper et vervecum satrapa Joseph/ Presidium armata fronte tuentur idem', *Ysengrinus*, J.

that pilgrims should have turned to the Temple and Hospital for advice and assistance.

Recruitment and Confraternity

In order for a monastery to function properly it required the services of certain lay-people: servants, craftsmen, cooks, stable-lads, shepherds, goatherds, cattlehers, labourers and the like. These formed part of what is termed the 'family' (*familia*, or *la familha*) of a monastery,[128] whilst the professed brethren constituted the *societas*.[129] The members of the 'family' were dependents of the Order, and some became more broadly affiliated to it. This section will analyse recruitment to both the 'family' and the *societas*.

A recent study of contact between the monastic world and the laity in south-western France at the time of the First Crusade has laid emphasis on child oblation as a central vehicle for fostering deep links between the cloister and local families.[130] In the early Middle Ages it had been thought that the placing of children, particularly as Cluniac *nutriti*, was a spiritually rewarding gift, as it was a contribution to the monastery's future.[131] However, prevailing thought in twelfth century reforming circles such as those of Cîteaux and Grandmont was questioning the validity of oblation.[132] Even some Benedictines were not wholly satisfied with the system.[133] Reflective of this trend, and also of the practicalities, the Council of Troyes (1129) deemed it unsuitable for the Temple to receive children, and so proscribed oblation in the Order.[134] In practice, the majority of Templars were between twenty and twenty-nine years of age on profession.[135] Likewise, despite their Benedictine inheritance, the

---

Mann (ed.), Mittellateinische Studien und Texte 12, Leiden, 1987, book 4, lines 1–8, p. 364.

[128] See Chapter 5, pp. 155–157.

[129] U. Berlière, 'La Familia dans les monastères bénédictins du moyen âge', *Mémoires de l'Académie royale de Belgique* 29(1931), pp. 3–123.

[130] M. Bull, *Knightly Piety and the Lay Response to the First Crusade*, Oxford, 1993, pp. 116–125.

[131] Lawrence, *Monasticism*, p. 99.

[132] In 1157 the Cistercians forbade the reception of novices under the age of eighteen, *Statuta capitulorum generalium ordinis Cisterciensis*, J. Canivez (ed.), I, Louvain, 1933, p. 62; generally J. Lynch, *Simoniacal Entry into Religious Life from 1000 to 1260*, Columbia, 1976, pp. 37–39.

[133] Bull, *Knightly*, p. 117.

[134] *RTemp., Primitive Rule*, cap. 14, pp. 25–26.

[135] A. Forey, 'Recruitment to the Military Orders (Twelfth to mid-Fourteenth centuries)', *Viator* 17(1986), table, p. 150.

Hospitallers also rejected oblation; although they did take in orphans.[136] Although both Orders at times made exceptions, for example at Richerenches the Templars accepted two oblates in 1138,[137] the general trend was for adult entry.[138]

To foster links with the laity, the Military Orders offered bonds of confraternity, an established method for laymen to attach themselves to a monastery, and to benefit from its spiritual grace.[139] In a culture in which heavy penance could be enjoined on believers, and thoughts of purgation in the hereafter abounded,[140] participation in the fruits of the prayers of the religious allayed fears of the Day of Judgement. Benefit was gained by the monastery, for it received an annual gift from the *confrater*,[141] and it could also put any skill he might possess to the community's use. Peter, *confrater* of the monastery of Saint Victor of Marseille, undertook the building of Notre-Dame de la Garde, the modern counterpart of which still dominates the skyline for miles around Marseille.[142] Whilst the Cistercians did not generally have *confratres*, they did have affiliates. At Silvacane in 1294 Bertrand of Pierrevert gave three charges of corn for the foundation of an anniversary to be celebrated in his memory,[143] and three similar arrangements were made that year.[144]

Anniversaries entailed liturgical celebration. Typical components of such celebrations can be gleaned from Cistercian Silvacane, where a roll of prayers to be said for the repose of the soul of Bertrand of Beaux (d.1181) included penitential psalms, masses, and the *Pater noster*.[145] In total, one priest would celebrate twenty masses, a clerk would sing ten complete psalters and 1,500 recitations of the *Pater noster*. Added to this were prayers of the style:

---

136 *CH*, I, *Statutes of Brother Roger of Les Moulins* (1182), no. 627, p. 428. There is no specific ban on oblation, but a statute with regard to sisters prohibits the profession of those 'in juvenili aut suspecta etate', *ibid., Statutes of Brother Hugh Revel* (1262), III, no. 3039, cap. 22, p. 48.

137 *Richerenches(Temple)*, no. 25, pp. 27–28 (1138).

138 Forey, 'Recruitment', pp. 148–150. There are instances where boys were taken, and the assumption was that they would eventually profess, *Prov*, II, no. 372, pp. 18–19 (1164).

139 L. Gougaud, *Dévotions et pratiques ascétiques du moyen âge*, Paris, 1925, p. 133; Lawrence, *Monasticism*, p. 99.

140 Generally, J. Le Goff, *La Naissance du purgatoire*, Paris, 1981.

141 Unlike the French *confrère*, in English (as in German), there is no suitable translation for *confrater*.

142 *Saint Victor*, no. 1028, pp. 488–489 (1214); F. Hildesheimer, *Notre-Dame de la Garde, la bonne mère de Marseille*, Marseille, 1985, p. 15.

143 3H33 (1274).

144 *ibid.*

145 3H67 (post 1181).

We concede participation in our benefits to lord Bertrand; may his soul and the souls of all the defunct faithful rest in peace. Amen. We have prayed for you, pray for us . . . [we] concede to Bertrand of Beaux offices and masses . . . May the soul of lord Bertrand and the souls of all the departed rest, by the Lord's mercy, in peace. Amen. We have prayed for you that you might pray for us.[146]

These package arrangements offered by the Cistercians for Bertrand provide an example of the competition the Military Orders faced in vying for the attentions of the laity.

For the Military Orders *confratres* originated in the laity and the priesthood alike. Unlike the Franciscans a century later, the Orders did not have difficulty in allowing priests and the laity, professed and affiliated, to share in confraternity together. More importantly, unlike the mendicant Third Orders, the *confratres* of the Military Orders did not have to follow an ordered religious life. The earliest Rule of a Franciscan Third Order (Brescia, late thirteenth century) stipulated that the tertiaries had regularly to go to Mass, recite a simplified version of the canonical Hours, confess twice a year, and observe the Church fasts.[147] Habitually, confraternity with the Military Orders involved only a vow of obedience, and a promise that if the individual wished to abandon the secular life and enter a religious Order, he or she would first offer themselves to the Military Order of which they were a *confrater* or *consoror*.[148]

(i) Provisions in the Rules

From the evidence provided by the Rules of the Military Orders, a certain ambiguity is evident in the treatment of confraternity. In the Rule of the Hospitallers, the first mention of confraternity appears only c.1239, long after the Order was in fact receiving *confratres*. This is a section of the *Usances* dedicated specifically to reception into confraternity.[149] The layman had first to present himself to whoever was to conduct the reception ceremony. The brethren were

[146] 'Concedimus participationem beneficiorum nostrorum domno Bertranno; anima ejus et anime omnium fidelium defunctorum requiescant in pace amen. Oravimus pro vestris, orate pro nostris . . . concedo B[ertranno] de Bauciaco officia et missæ . . . Anima dompni B[ertranni] et anime omnium fidelium defunctorum per misericordia domini requiescant in pace. Amen. Oravimus pro vestris ut oretis pro nostris.'
[147] J. Moorman, *A History of the Franciscan Order*, Oxford, 1968, p. 219.
[148] E. Magnou, 'Oblature, classe chevaleresque et servage dans les maisons méridionales du Temple au XIIe siècle', *AM* 73(1961), pp. 377–397 studies Templar houses in the Rouergue. The rigid classification system adopted (spiritual, remunerated and servile confraternity) imposes order onto what was, by its nature, flexible, and obscures the individual nature of the arrangements. See also Demurger, *Temple*, pp. 92–98.
[149] *CH*, II, *Usances*, no. 2213, cap. 122, pp. 557–559.

then assembled, and the ceremony could proceed. The officiator would hold up the missal, inviting the layman to place his hands on it. He had to promise that thenceforward he would, to the best of his ability, cleave to the Hospital and its brethren in all things, and would defend them and the goods of the house to his utmost against all malefactors. Furthermore, if he should wish to abandon the secular life and enter an Order, it must be that of the Hospital. On his death, if he had not entered the Order, he would be deemed to have done so, and accorded burial in the Order's cemetery. Additionally, in gratitude for the confraternity, every year on the feast of Saint John he had to make a gift to the Hospital. This completed, the officiator would then pronounce:

> By your promise to God, Our Lady, Saint John the Baptist, and to our lords the sick we include you, and the souls of your father, mother, and relatives in the masses, matins, vespers and all the prayers which are offered, and will be offered in the houses of the Hospital throughout the world until the Day of Judgement. May Our Lord grant you as good a reward as each of us hopes to receive.[150]

The officiator, followed by all the brethren, would then give the new *confrater* the kiss of peace, as for a normal gift.[151] As in Cluniac monasteries,[152] his name would be inscribed into the book of the *confratres* along with the gift he promised to present each year. Thus were the formalities completed.

Although the ceremony was not too dissimilar from that by which a brother was received, some important differences can be noted. Brothers were received only on Sundays, when a vote would be held in chapter after Mass. Their verdict, a simple majority system, was final. The postulant was asked detailed personal questions about his ties to the secular or religious world and, the responses being satisfactory, the three monastic vows would be exacted from him. Finally, as with the *confrater*, his family would be welcomed into the spiritual benefits of the house.[153] Family and friends were aware of receptions into

---

[150] 'Par la promession que vos avés faite à Dyeu et à Nostre-Dame, et à monseignor saint Johan Baptiste, et à nos seignors de malades, nos retenons vos, e l'arme de vostre peire et de vostre meire et de tous vos parens en las messas, en matines, en vespres et en toutes les oresions, que se fant et chascun jour se faront et fuerent fais en la maison del Hospital par tout le monde, ni seront fais jusques au jour dou juyse; que Nostre-Seignor vos en done si bone part quant chascuns de nous a esperence d'avoer', *ibid.*, cap. 122, p. 558.

[151] 'dedit preterea et per oris osculum Rotberto Tilio domus videlicet de Roais preceptori', *Roaix(Temple)*, no. 147, p. 94 (1201).

[152] A Cluniac *Liber vitæ* from Lausanne contains some ten thousand names, J. Wollasch, 'A Cluniac Necrology from the Time of Abbot Hugh', *Cluniac Monasticism in the central Middle Ages*, N. Hunt (ed.), London and Basingstoke, 1971, pp. 143–190.

[153] *CH*, II, *Usances*, no. 2213, cap. 121, p. 556; III, *Statutes of Brother Hugh Revel* (1262), no. 3039, cap. 26, p. 49.

confraternity. At Montaren in 1248 a dispute as to exactly when a *consoror* had become affiliated brought out many witnesses who said that they had heard of the lady's reception.[154]

The only other mention of a *confrater* in the Rule of the Hospital related to his relationship with the commandery and its brethren. He was bound to attend the burials of all deceased brothers, unless he had been ordered elsewhere. The sanction for non-attendance was the severe *septaine*, a punishment requiring seven days' fast, the penitent being allowed only bread and water on Wednesdays and Fridays, taking these meals seated not at table, but on his mantle on the floor. On these days he was also submitted to flogging in front of all the brethren in church whilst the psalm *Deus misereatur nostris* was sung.[155]

The Hospitallers had another category of *confrater*: the donat, distinguishable from the *confrater* by his noble birth. There are six provisions in the Rule relating to the conduct of these noble laymen, the earliest dating from 1262. One of these sections dealt with how a donat was not to be received. It ordered that on his return from the baths the donat should not be paraded around the town with trumpets and tabors, but should be brought immediately back to the house. These banned activities perhaps comprised part of the customary reception of normal brethren, but a privilege to which the donats were not entitled.[156] In 1262 it was decreed that no brother or donat should be ordered to Outremer without the express permission of the master.[157] If this permission were given then the donat, wishing to become a combatant brother, was to come to Outremer carrying 2,000 *deniers* of Tours with which to purchase equipment.[158]

Some donats lived in the commanderies, for that same year (1262) they were forbidden to distribute allowances to those sick in the Hospital.[159] Thirty years later the Order's houses in Europe were overcrowded with laymen. The master, Brother John of Villaret, decreed at the chapter-general of 1292 that no new donats could be received without the permission of the grand-commander of Deçàmer, except in Spain where there was a frontier with Islam.[160] At the beginning of the century the Cluniacs had similar problems, and many monasteries had implemented a *numerus clausus*, ensuring that no

---

[154] 56H4959 (1248).

[155] *CH*, III, *Statutes of Brother Hugh Revel* (1265), no. 3180, cap. 5, p. 119. For the *septaine* see *The Rule, Statutes and Customs of the Hospitallers*, E. King (ed.), London, 1934, p. 142.

[156] *CH*, III, *Statutes of Brother Hugh Revel* (1270), no. 3396, cap. 19, p. 229.

[157] *ibid.*, III, *Statutes of Brother Hugh Revel* (1262), no. 3039, cap. 14, p. 46.

[158] *ibid.*, cap. 26 *bis*, p. 49.

[159] *ibid.*, cap. 33, p. 51. For monastic allowances, see F. Gasquet, *English Monastic Life*, London, 1904, p. 105.

[160] *CH*, III, *Statutes of Brother John of Villiers* (1292), no. 4194, cap. 2, p. 609.

new brothers could be received.[161] By 1303 the Hospitaller statute of 1262 requesting that the donat bring 2,000 *deniers* of Tours with him to Outremer was modified bringing the amount down to 1,000 *deniers*.[162]

The Order of the Temple made mention of *confratres* in the Rule, but the provisions were not as well defined as in the Hospital. In the Temple a distinction must be made between *confratres* and those serving for a term. The *miles ad terminum* was a knight of the Order. He did not rank as a full knight-brother, not having taken the seven vows of a Templar, but he was a knight-brother.[163] His lesser status can be seen by the fact that on his death the other brothers of the house were to recite the *Pater noster* thirty times, whereas on the death of a full brother each Templar, including those serving for a term, was to say one hundred.[164] Married men were permitted to affiliate themselves to the Order solely as *confratres*.[165] From the references to confraternity, his living in his own home, and the lack of reference to any combat possibilities, it is reasonable to conclude that the *frater conjugatus* was more precisely a *confrater conjugatus*.

The specific provisions in the Rule regarding *confratres* stress the privileged position of these friends of the Order. Knights-commander of houses and the commanders of Tripoli and Antioch were not allowed to disburse money or large gifts to lay persons, except to *confratres*.[166] If any worthy man or a *confrater* reported to the master the behaviour of a brother who had brought shame upon the Order, the master was to give him credence, and take further action.[167]

Confraternity was not exclusively limited to men. Both Orders had *consorores*. At the close of a Templar chapter, the officiator was to pray specifically for peace, for the Church, for the holy kingdom of Jerusalem, for the house of the Temple, for all religious houses, for all religious men, and for the *confratres* and *consorores* of the Temple.[168] On an individual basis, the brethren were also to pray for them daily, for when the brethren heard matins rung, if there were no priest present they were to recite the *Pater noster* twenty-six times (thirteen for Our Lady and thirteen for the day) followed by thirty for the dead and

---

161 Lawrence, *Monasticism*, p. 274.

162 *CH*, IV, *Statutes of Brother William of Villaret* (1303), no. 4612, cap. 7, p. 58.

163 'Sunt namque milites in domo Dei Templique Salomonis ad terminum misericorditer vobiscum degentes', *RTemp.*, *Primitive Rule*, cap. 65, pp. 64–65.

164 *ibid.*, *Primitive Rule*, caps. 62, 65, pp. 62–62, 65.

165 *ibid.*, cap. 69, p. 68.

166 'se n'est a aucun confrere, ou a aucun amis de la maison privéement', *ibid.*, *Hierarchical Statutes*, cap. 133, pp. 107–108; 'se n'est a aucuns amis [ou] confreres de la maison', *ibid.*, cap. 128, p. 104.

167 *ibid.*, *Ordinary Chapters*, cap. 411, pp. 225–226.

168 *ibid.*, cap. 541, p. 283.

thirty for the living, this latter category being specifically designed to include the *confratres* and *consorores*.[169] Although the Templar Rule banned the admission of women as sisters, there was no restriction on their being affiliated to the Order as *consorores*.[170] In the main they lived away from the commanderies, but there is an example of a *consoror* living within a commandery. In Zaragoza in 1248 the *consoror* Dominica of Sieste was given a lodging hard by the Templars' church within the commandery.[171] The Temple also made an exception for widows, whom it agreed to protect.[172]

Not to be confused with confraternity was death-bed reception *ad succurrendum*. This was a widespread monastic practice for receiving the laity as monks when *in extremis*.[173] Not to be undertaken lightly, the Cistercian Cæsarius of Heisterbach (c.1180–c.1240) wrote of the importance of internal conversion when having the habit laid over the dying body.[174] The Rule of the Temple stipulated how it was to be performed. Normally the consent of the whole chapter was required to admit a new brother, but an exception was that if the master was somewhere where there was no chapter, and a worthy man wished to become a brother on account of illness and the proximity of death, he could be made a brother with the consent of any brothers present (four brothers were normally required to form a quorate chapter).[175] This was innovative. Monasteries required the consent of the chapter, as did the Dominicans in the thirteenth century. Thomas of Cantimpré wrote (1256–1261) that on one occasion all brothers of the friary were summoned in the middle of the night to discuss such a reception.[176] In the Temple, if the newly received recovered, he was then to make his profession, and learn how to be a brother.[177] Yet, if the man sinned, presumably before professing, the habit could be taken back from him.[178] This is different from monastic practice, where a person received *ad*

---

[169] *ibid., Reception*, cap. 683, p. 349.

[170] *ibid., Primitive Rule*, cap. 70, p. 69.

[171] A. Forey, 'Women and the Military Orders in the Twelfth and Thirteenth Centuries', *Studia Monastica* 29(1987), p. 65.

[172] *RTemp, Primitive Rule*, cap. 2, pp. 12–13; Forey, *Aragón*, piece no. 10, p. 375.

[173] For normal monastic profession *ad succurrendum*, see Gougaud, *Dévotions*, pp. 129–142; J. Leclercq, 'La Vêture "ad succurrendum" d'après le moine Raoul', *Analecta monastica, Studia Anselmiana* 37(1955), pp. 158–168.

[174] Cæsarius of Heisterbach, *Dialogus miraculorum*, J. Strange (ed.), II, Cologne, Bonn, Brussels, 1851, distinctio 12, ch. 2, pp. 316–317.

[175] *RTemp., Conventual Life*, cap. 385, p. 215.

[176] Thomas of Cantimpré, *Bonum universale de apibus*, G. Colverinus (ed.), Douai, 1627, book 2, ch. 51, pp. 474–475.

[177] *RTemp., Hierarchical Statutes*, cap. 87, p. 85.

[178] *ibid., Further Penances*, cap. 632, p. 325.

succurrendum was to be counted a full brother, for to decide otherwise was an affront to the mercy of God.[179]

An article from the Barcelona Rule of the Temple demonstrates the practicalities of profession *ad succurrendum*.[180] It relates that Brother Pons of Gusans was travelling to Outremer in a ship:

> and fell ill, and requested the house; a mantle was laid over him as for the dead, and he made neither vow nor promise, but the truth is that he became a brother.[181]

He recovered, rising to be the Turcopolier (a senior military official) in Jerusalem before leaving the Order to marry. On his wife's death he wished to be received into the Order anew, and pleaded that as he had never taken any vows, he need not do heavy penance for having left the Order. The chapter ruled that Church law recognized that a year and a day in an Order was sufficient to constitute a vow, and that accordingly he would have to do a year and a day's penance. He did, and was re-admitted.[182]

(ii) In Occitania

The reality of confraternity shifts the emphasis from the clarity and rigidity of the Rules to more vague, individual arrangements. It is often hard to know whether a given charter concerns a full profession or a contract of confraternity.[183] A preliminary point is that professions and affiliations were not normally recorded in charters. At the Trial of the Templars brothers were incapable of demonstrating when they had joined the Order, claiming that they had been brothers for five or seven years, twenty or twenty-five.[184] Also, the brethren were unable to remember the witnesses and officials present, often only being able to inform their inquisitors of the person who conducted their

---

[179] Bull, *Knightly*, p. 144.

[180] Excerpts from this Rule have been published in 'Un Nouveau manuscrit de la règle du Temple', J. Delaville le Roulx (ed.), *Annuaire-bulletin de la société de l'histoire de France* 26(1889), cap. 51, p. 212. A full transcript exists in Paris, BN, nouv. acq. lat. 68, fols. 55–142.

[181] 'e fo malade en la nave, e requist la maiso, e hom gita li lo manteu desus com a la mort, e no fist vot ni promesio; mais ver es que el usa coma frere', in 'Nouveau manuscrit', Delaville le Roulx (ed.), cap. 51, p. 212.

[182] *ibid.*, p. 212.

[183] The citation of Saint Matthew xvi, 24 ('Tunc Iesus dixit discipulis suis si quis vult post me venire abneget semet ipsum et tollat crucem suam et sequatur me') is a good indicator of a full profession. It was so common at Richerenches that it was often abbreviated to 'si quis vult post me venire a. s. e. t. c. s. e. s. m', or 'Si quis vult post me venire, a. s. et t. c. s. et s. q. t. me'. *Richerenbces(Temple)*, no. 33, pp. 36–37 (c.1138); no. 146, pp. 134–135 (1157).

[184] See *Procès des Templiers*, J. Michelet (ed.), 2 vols., Paris, 1861, *passim*.

reception. Additionally, the charters of profession copied into cartularies do not represent the totality of professions and receptions into confraternity. The majority of brethren appearing regularly in documents have left no trace of their entries into the Orders.

The criterion for the drawing up of a charter of profession or reception into confraternity was that it brought a gift which the Order wished to record. As in other religious institutions, it was normal, indeed expected, that all who professed would make a gift, despite the fact that this procedure was beginning to be questioned by canonists in the eleventh century, and was proscribed by canon law by the 1160s.[185] Disputes over land were commonplace, and controversies form a large part of the material in cartularies. But this does not explain why in the charters kept by the Orders there are none which witness the profession or reception into confraternity of an individual with few private means. An answer can be found in the Rule of the Hospital, which alludes to the inscription of the *confrater*'s name in the Book of *confratres*. This was the full extent of the written formalities. Although not mentioned in the Rule, the Templars, too, had books of *confratres*.[186] Charters which have survived and refer to confraternity or profession do so either because the individual gifted a substantial piece of land or property, or the disposition relating to confraternity or consorority was a provision in a will.

This emphasis on property can be reinforced if one considers the unfree. In the Templar cartulary of Montsaunès there are only four recorded professions into the Order,[187] but if the emphasis is shifted to people as property, there are eighteen charters relating to the Temple's acquisition of serfs.[188] Lordship over unfree people was permitted to the Order from its very inception.[189] Those who gave themselves to the Orders as vassals should also be classed in this way. For example, in 1210 Peter Boniza and his wife, Garsinda, gave themselves and their posterity as liege-men and vassals to the Hospital at Saint Felix of Campagnolles. This was accompanied by an annual gift to the Order of a

---

185 Lynch, *Simoniacal*, pp. xvii, 61 and *passim*.

186 Demurger, *Temple*, p. 94; Forey, *Aragón*, p. 36.

187 *Montsaunès(Temple)*, no. 8, p. 230 (1134); no. 1, pp. 223–226 (1136); no. 62, p. 256 (1168); no. 58, pp. 254–255 (1179).

188 *ibid.*, no. 4, p. 227; no. 20, p. 236; no. 47, p. 251 (undated); no. 76, pp. 266–267 (1164x1168); no. 61, pp. 258–259 (1165); no. 32, pp. 243–244 (1166); no. 94, pp. 276–277 (1168); no. 36, pp. 245–246 (1170); no. 35, p. 245 (1175); no. 60, p. 256 (1175x1176); no. 69, p. 263; no. 71, pp. 264–265; no. 72, p. 265; no. 73, p. 265 (after 1180); no. 74, pp. 265–266 (1180x1185); no. 82, p. 270 (1182); no. 75, p. 266 (after 1185); no. 43, pp. 249–250 (1192).

189 The Latin version reads 'terram et homines habere et agricolas possidere'. The French version adds the word villeins 'et poés avoir terres et homes et vilains', *RTemp., Primitive Rule*, cap 57, pp. 58–59.

pound of pepper to be paid at the feast of Saint Andrew, along with certain agricultural services.[190]

A record of these possessions was desirable in case any dispute were to arise, and this was the motive for the retention of charters, indeed, for the very existence of cartularies. Charters, in conjunction with witnesses, were adduced in evidence at proceedings to establish rights. This can be seen when Brother Bernard the Catalan, Templar commander of Saint-Gilles, was involved in a dispute with Peter Pons. Once the complainant had put his case, it was recorded that 'against this the said Bernard the Catalan introduced many witnesses, and many written instruments'.[191]

Gifts by affiliates were expected, and even papally approved.[192] Although *confratres* might later enter the Order, these gifts were not simoniacal. The charge of simony was levelled against the Templars by Pope Innocent III, but this in no way singled the Order out from the mainstream world of the cloister. Innocent warned the Templars about their practice of receiving gifts when brethren professed, but believed this was more a result of the Templar's *'simplicitas'* than any direct attempt to contravene canon law.[193] Nevertheless, he stressed that no money was to change hands, not even if it was disguised as aid. The Temple had, in fact, begun to legislate against simony c.1165,[194] but the provisions were carefully worded, and the key phrase that it was simony if the gift 'helped [the simoniac] to enter the religion of the Temple',[195] had no doubt been carefully drafted to allow the interpretation that gifts on profession were pious, and distinct from the individual's entry into the Order. There was at least one case of simony within the Temple in 1231x1244,[196] but the

---

[190] 56H4966 (1210).

[191] 'contra hoc predictus Bernardus Catalanus plures testes et plura instrumenta induxit', *Saint-Gilles(Temple)*, fols. 162v–163r (1167).

[192] Celestine II, *Milites Templi*, in *Papsturkunden für Templer und Johanniter*, R. Hiestand (ed.), Göttingen, 1972, no. 8, pp. 214–215 (1144).

[193] *Vitiam pravitatis*, in *Regesta pontificum romanorum inde ab anno 1198 ad annum 1304*, A. Potthast (ed.), I, Berlin, 1874, no. 4783, pp. 416–417 (1213); generally, Lynch, *Simoniacal*, pp. 190–192.

[194] *RTemp., Penances*, cap. 224, p. 152; cap. 246, pp. 158–159; cap. 272, p. 166; cap. 273, p. 166; *Ordinary Chapters*, cap. 417, p. 228; cap. 431, p. 234; *Further Penance*, cap. 544, p. 285; cap. 598, pp. 310–311; *Reception*, cap. 673, p. 343. Lynch, *Simoniacal*, p. 214 is wrong to date the first of these statutes to c.1229. The section on *Penances* is deemed to be contemporaneous with that entitled *Hierarchical Statutes* which dates from 1165, *The Rule of the Templars*, J. Upton-Ward (ed. and tr.), Woodbridge, 1992, pp. 13–14.

[195] 'Et symonie se fait par don ou par proumesse a frere dou Temple ou a autre qui li puisse aider a entrer en la relegion dou Temple', *RTemp., Penances*, cap. 224, p. 153.

[196] *ibid., Further Penances*, caps 545–548, pp. 285–287.

brothers were permitted to rejoin the Temple 'as if they had never before been brethren'.[197]

Turning to the substance of the Occitanian charters of confraternity, because their aim was not to give evidence of the *confrater* and his status, but rather of the accompanying gift, the terminology is often vague. Beginning with the Hospitallers, the cartulary of the grand-priory of Saint-Gilles contains numerous acts of profession and confraternity. Only infrequently is the charter unambiguous, and can it be clearly seen as either an act of confraternity, or of profession. An explicit act of profession was that of Peter Trucus:

> In the name of the Holy and indivisible Trinity. Let all men, present and future, know that in the year of the incarnation of the Divine Word M°C°LXX°VIIII° in the month of January (January 1180, new style). I, Peter Trucus give and offer myself as a brother to Lord God, Saint Mary, Saint John of Jerusalem, the holy house of the poor of Christ of the Hospital of Jerusalem, and to the brothers of the Hospital, both present and future, into the hands of Robert the prior of the clerics, who gave me the habit of the Hospital, and made me a brother. I promise the three (vows) to him, that is, chastity, obedience, and to live without property.[198]

All elements present define this as a full profession: the giving of oneself *per fratrem*, the receiving of the habit, and the taking of the three monastic vows. By contrast, a more ambiguous act was that of Peter Garcin. It was a profession, and demonstrates that sometimes only one of the classic vows might be mentioned. In 1146 he gave himself body and soul to God, Saint Mary, Saint John, the Hospital of Saint-Gilles, and to the holy poor of the Hospital of Jerusalem. He also gave his property to the Order, and promised obedience into the hands of Brother Arnold, prior of Saint-Gilles.[199] It was a profession with a simple promise of obedience, a formula common also with the Cistercians.[200]

---

[197] 'Et il les firent freres de novel, tout aussi come se il n'eussent onques esté freres,' *ibid.*, cap. 548, p. 287. Such a re-profession was permitted under canon 64 of the Fourth Lateran Council, *Conciliorum œcumenicorum decreta*, J. Alberigo *et al.* (eds.), Freiburg im Breisgau, 1962, pp. 240–241.

[198] 'In nomine Sancte et individue Trinitatis. Notum sit omnibus hominibus tam presentibus quam futuris quod anno incarnati Verbi M°C°LXX°VIIII° mense Januario. Ego Petrus Trucus dono et offero me per fratrem domino Deo et Beate Marie et Beato Johanni Jherosolimitani et sancte domui Hospitalis Jherusalem pauperum Christi et fratribus Hospitalis presentibus et futuris inter manibus fratris Rotberti priorii clericorum qui habitum Hospitalis mihi dedit et fratrem de me fecit. Promitto sibi tria scilicet obedientiam et castitem ac sine proprio vivere', *Saint-Gilles(Hospital)*, fols. 180v–181r (1170).

[199] *ibid.*, fols. 128v–129r (1146).

[200] 3H18 (1215).

Profession was flexible. An *exemplum* by James of Vitry laid emphasis on this:

> It happened that a certain noble knight from France, who had set out to the Holy Land to go on a pilgrimage, was captured with some brothers of the knighthood of the Temple. Seeing he was bald but bearded, the Saracens thought him a Templar, and fit to be killed with the Templars whilst all the others, who were secular knights, were not killed, but led off into captivity. The Saracens said to him,
> 'Are you a Templar?'
> and he replied, because it was the truth,
> 'I am a secular knight, and a pilgrim.'
> They responded,
> 'On the contrary, you are a Templar!'
> Struck by the zeal of faith he drew himself up, and pronounced,
> 'In the name of the Lord, I am a Templar.'
> Having said this, he was put to the sword with the other brothers of the Temple, and a new Templar flew to the Lord, joyfully crowned with the martyrs.[201]

The issue at stake in this *exemplum*, as in the remarks of Cæsarius of Hiester-bach mentioned above, is the internal state of the person when making profession: a simple declaration of belonging to a Military Order could accordingly suffice.

An example of a *confrater* was Raymond Hair-lip, who gave himself explicitly *per confratrem* in 1167.[202] Sometimes matters were made even more clear. Not only did the individual give himself as a *confrater*, but the Hospitaller into whose hands he professed confirmed this. Such was the case with William of Valfleur, who gave himself in 1201. The grand-prior of Saint-Gilles concluded the act by announcing:

---

[201] 'Accidit quod quidam miles nobilis, qui de partibus Franciæ causa peregrinationis ultra mare perrexerat, captus fuit cum quibusdam fratribus militiæ Templi, et quia calvus erat et barbatus, credebant Sarraceni quod esset Templarius, et cum Templariis occidendus. Alii autem qui seculares erant milites, non occidebantur, sed captivi ducebantur. Quumque dicerent ei: Tu Templarius es? Et ille sicut verum erat, diceret: Miles sum secularis et peregrinus, respondentibus: Immo Templarius es! ille zelo fidei succensus, extento collo dixit: In nomine Domini sum Templarius. Quo dicto, gladio percussus cum fratribus Templi, novus Templarius ad Dominum migravit, martyrio feliciter coronatus', James of Vitry, *Sermo XXXVII ad fratres ordinis militaris*, in *Analecta novissima: Spicilegii Solesmensis altera continuatio*, J. Pitra (ed.), II, Paris, 1888, pp. 412–413.

[202] *Saint-Gilles(Hospital)*, fol. 120r (1167).

in return I receive you as a *confrater*, and include you, and all your family, in all the (spiritual) benefits of the house.[203]

The Hospital received not only *consorores*, but also fully professed sisters, and there is an analogous problem as with brothers in establishing whether the act relates to a profession or an arrangement of consorority. For instance, in 1191 Brother John Francon, commander of Saint-Gilles, gave Williametta, a married woman, a habit she could assume whenever she wished.[204] This was an act of consorority, and illustrates well the category of affiliation which was undertaken when the individual had the intention of professing into the Order in the future.

Unlike in neighbouring Catalonia where Count Alfonso II of Barcelona endowed a Hospitaller nunnery in 1177,[205] there were no houses for sisters in Occitania, and the sisters lived and worked in the commanderies alongside the brothers. For instance, Galburge became a Hospitaller sister at Saint-Gilles.[206] There were also sisters and *consorores* elsewhere. At Trinquetaille in 1197 was a Mabel, *hospitaleria*.[207] Agnes was received into consorority in the graveyard of Trinquetaille in 1210, being promised food, water, and a humble habit when she chose to take them 'as it is our custom to promise to the brothers of the Hospital';[208] and at Saint-Paul-les-Romans a woman was promised that if she died before her husband she would be buried 'as a sister with a cross'.[209] A noble woman, Adelaïde, wife of Bertrand of La Vérune, professed at Trinquetaille in 1146, giving the Order her land, houses in Arles and revenue from various marine taxes. She was moved to Outremer, and finished her days in the Hospital in Jerusalem.[210]

The Hospitaller Rule stipulated that on death the *confratres* were to be deemed full brothers of the Order, and buried accordingly. This appeared rarely in charters, but an example which confirms this is a charter of the viscount of Marseille, Hugh of Baux, who became a *confrater* of the Hospitaller commandery at Trinquetaille. He promised the Order a charge of wheat each year, and in return was told 'I receive you, Hugh of Baux, as a *confrater*, and on

---

[203] 'propterea te confratrem recipio et te et omnes parentes tuos in omni beneficio domus nos participes instituo,' *ibid.*, fols. 65v–66r (1201).

[204] 'ut illud assumas quandocumque tibi placuerit', *Saint-Gilles(Hospital)*, fols. 35v–36r (1191).

[205] *CH*, I, no. 523, pp. 357–358 (1177).

[206] *Saint-Gilles(Hospital)*, fol. 132rv (1186).

[207] *Trinquetaille(Hospital)*, no. 311, p. 316 (1197).

[208] 'sicut consuetum est promittere fratribus Hospitalis,' *ibid.*, no. 210, pp. 209–210 (1210).

[209] 'si prius moreretur quam maritus ejus sepeliretur sicut soror cum cruce', *Saint-Paul(Hospital)*, no. 81, p. 44 (early thirteenth century).

[210] *Trinquetaille(Hospital)*, no. 110, pp. 95–96 (after 1146).

your death a brother.'[211] Part of such arrangements was the stipulation that the *confrater*, if he wished to enter the religious life, had to profess into the Order, and no other. This can be seen in the case of the brothers Counts William and Bertrand of Forcalquier, who became *confratres* of the bailiwick of Manosque. They gave themselves as brothers to Lord God and to the Hospital of Jerusalem at their deaths with their horses and arms. If, during their lives, they wished to submit themselves to the religious life, they would only enter the Hospital, and would only be buried in the Hospitallers' cemetery.[212] This right of first refusal was sometimes worded more strongly, placing an obligation on the Hospital. In 1191 Richard of Grèzes gave himself as a *confrater*, and insisted that the Hospital accept him as a brother when he so desired.[213]

The Rule also mentioned that the Hospitaller conducting the ceremony should summon all the brethren who would give the kiss of peace after the reception. Normally the charters relate that a *confrater* professed 'into the hands of' the person officiating, but sometimes the entire community was involved. Raynald Autard was made a *confrater* at Trinquetaille in 1182, and gave himself 'in the presence of William Alvernicus, said master of the house of Saint Thomas, and into the hands of all the brothers'.[214] This sometimes happened with the Templars, and on one occasion at Saint-Gilles in 1182 the brethren were asked to consider whether a man was worthy of confraternity.[215] The kiss of peace, mentioned in the Hospitaller article on profession, was used in the Temple, too. At La Selve one *confrater* recorded that 'the commander and all the other brothers of the house corporally received and welcomed me into the spiritual benefits of the house'.[216]

Confratres were accorded the privilege of burial in a cemetery of the Order. As discussed in chapter three, this posed problems for the clergy and those responsible for local parishes. If an individual chose to be buried with a Military Order, his or her parish church would lose the offerings given on death, and the subsequent interest of the deceased's family, who frequently in turn requested to be buried with the Order, as in 1260 when Bertrand Rainoard chose to be buried in a Templar cemetery as his father had done.[217] The Holy See had been advised of the problems these arrangements were causing, and in

---

[211] *Trinquetaille(Hospital)*, no. 6, p. 7 (1192).

[212] 56H4670 (1168).

[213] 'Propter hanc autem donationem et concessionem iamdictum ospitale (sic) debet me suscipere quandocumque ego vellem', 56H4813 (1191).

[214] 'in presencia Willelmi Aluernici dicti magistris domus S. Tome et in manibus aliorum fratrum', *Trinquetaille(Hospital)*, no. 38, pp. 32–33 (1182).

[215] *Saint-Gilles(Temple)*, fol. 119rv (1182).

[216] 'El comandaire e tuih li autre fraire de la maio au me receubut et acollit en totz los bes de la maio corporalment', *La Selve(Temple)*, no. 84, pp. 177–178 (1233).

[217] 56H5177 (1260).

1184x1185 Pope Lucius III promulgated a bull which reconfirmed the Hospitallers' right to bury *confratres* in their cemeteries, and to offer masses for the repose of their souls.[218] By 1216 the need for money had become more pressing on account of the loss of the majority of the Holy Land, and accordingly Pope Honorius III issued a bull restressing that *confratres* were to be buried in Hospitaller cemeteries, also that the priests of the Order be allowed to carry the Viaticum to all those who chose burial with the Order.[219] Such burials were often part of a broader disposition of property. In 1201 William Bonit gave his body to the Hospitallers at Trinquetaille, along with his hut, horse, arms, and decorated bed of cloth. For the rest he wished 'those who redeem captives' (the Trinitarian Order)[220] to have 10 *sous*, whilst his brother was to have his green cloak, scarlet tunic, and coat of rabbit fur.[221]

Just as the prayers for *confratres* included them in the benefits of not just the commandery, but the whole Order, there was also flexibility about burial arrangements. In 1157 a *confrater* of Jalès, possibly recognizing that his life was not a sedentary one, requested burial at Jalès, or in any other Templar cemetery.[222] This burial arrangement demonstrates that although confraternity was linked to a specific commandery, it did, in fact, entail a more general affiliation to the Order. This is borne out by a charter from La Selve in which a *confrater* was received into the benefits of the commandery, and the Templars welcomed the souls of his father, mother, and relations into the spiritual benefits 'of the whole Order'.[223]

Templar *confratres* were to be trusted with informing the master of any shameful behaviour by the brethren, and similarly Hospitaller *confratres* were also given positions of trust. In 1144 Raymond of Montredon, archbishop of Arles, confirmed to the commandery of Trinquetaille the gift of the church of Saint Thomas by his predecessor, Archbishop Atton of Bruniquel, and representing the Hospital were numerous *confratres*.[224] They could also put their expertise and secular knowledge to the use of the Order and were sometimes consulted before a major transaction was undertaken.[225]

The degree of affiliation was a matter to be defined by the individuals depending on their motivations for seeking confraternity. Sometimes they simply wished for a purer life. In 1183 a married couple, Joanna and William

---

[218] 56H4008 (1184x1185).

[219] 56H4013 (1216). This was repromulgated the following year, 56H4013 (1217).

[220] See F. de Saint-Paul, *Jean de Matha, un fondateur d'avant-garde*, Paris, Montreal, 1960.

[221] *Trinquetaille(Hospital)*, no. 68, pp. 59–60 (1201).

[222] 56H5218 (1157).

[223] 'de tot l'orde', *La Selve(Temple)*, no. 84, pp. 177–178 (1233).

[224] *Trinquetaille(Hospital)*, no. 289, pp. 291–292 (1144).

[225] *ibid.*, no. 22, p. 21 (1181).

Porcelli, gave themselves in life and death wishing to be buried in the cemetery at Saint-Gilles. They undertook vows of chastity and obedience. The commander, Brother Bernard the Catalan, reciprocated by welcoming them into the spiritual benefits of the house.[226] These benefits could comprise more elaborate celebrations than the prayers outlined in the Rule. The widow Sacrosancta was received by the commander, Brother Gisbert of Costabella, into consorority with the commandery of Saint-Gilles in 1194. She was told exactly what spiritual benefits she would receive:

> Therefore I, Gisbert, receiving the said property from you, Lady Sacrosancta, receive you, all your relatives, your (late) husband Bertrand Raimbald, and all your friends into the benefits of our house. And for you, and for them, a priest of our house will daily sing a special prayer to God, and after your death on the day of your anniversary each year I will ensure that a priest of our house sings a mass for your soul.[227]

Another example was Brocard, who wished to be buried in the Hospitaller cemetery at Avignon. He gave the Order property, and wished for five thousand masses to be said for him in a period of four years.[228] Spiritual benefits are mentioned in charters drafted in Occitan, too. Azalaïs gave herself to the Templar commandery of La Selve, and was reported as having been 'received into the house and the spiritual benefits'.[229] In another instance at La Selve the *confrater* reported that he, his father and his mother had been received into the spiritual benefits.[230]

Some *confratres* sought more than just a vehicle for the leading of a purer life: they affiliated as a precursor to a full profession. In 1188 Bernard Radulph became a *confrater* of the Temple at Saint-Gilles. He was promised by the commander that he would be accepted as a brother whenever he wished.[231] At La Selve Hugh of Moussac insisted that he be corporally received as a donat or a brother.[232] The use of the word 'donat' is rare in Templar charters, although

---

[226] *Saint-Gilles(Temple)*, fol. 142v (1183).

[227] 'Ad hec ego Gisbertus predicta omnia a te domina Sacrosancta accipiens recipio te in beneficiis domus nostre et alias parentum tuorum et mariti tui B(ertrandi) Raimbaldi et omnium amicorum tuorum et pro te et illis specialem orationem sacerdotem domus nostre Deo cotidie cantare faciant et post obitum tuum die aniversarii tui singulis annis pro anima tua sacerdotes domus nostre missas cantare curabo,' *ibid.*, fols. 88r–89r (1195).

[228] *GCN(Avignon)*, no. 5137, col. 876 (1178).

[229] 'receubutz e la maio e los bes esperitals', *La Selve(Temple)*, no. 36, p. 145 (1229).

[230] *ibid.*, no. 81, p. 175 (1232).

[231] *Saint-Gilles(Temple)*, fol. 171r (1188).

[232] 'e devo m'en recebre corporalmen comas ou donat ou fraire', *La Selve(Temple)*, no. 81, p. 175 (1232).

it does occur elsewhere,[233] for there was no distinction between noble and non-noble *confratres* as there was with the Hospital. It is simply an Occitan word for *confrater*.[234]

The ban on entering other Orders was sometimes reinforced.[235] A particularly precise charter was that of Richard and his brother Raymond, who became *confratres* of the Templar commandery at Roaix in 1217. The charter demonstrates well the efforts made by the Order to free prospective brethren from secular ties:

> I, Richard of Boissione, and my brother Raymond give ourselves to God, and to the house of Roaix in the following way: that whensoever we wish to receive the habit of that house, we shall be allowed to do it with no hindrance. However, we may not take wives in marriage or accede to any other Order without the will and consent of the commander of the aforesaid house. . . . Again, we recognize that we have had and received 250 *sous Raimondine* from the benefits of the aforesaid house, out of which we must marry our sister, Azalaïs.[236]

The same can be seen at Richerenches where Bertrand of Bourbouton offered himself anew as a *confrater* in 1151, promising this time never to accept a wife.[237]

The Hospitaller Rule made mention of the vow to be extracted from the *confrater* that he would defend the Order. This was also the case in the Temple. In 1160 Bertrand of Avisano confirmed to the Temple the large number of gifts his family had presented over the years. He continued:

> Moreover I promise and affirm over the Holy Gospels that from this day, as before, I shall be a faithful defender, in word and deed, of the house of Richerenches, and of the brothers there serving God.[238]

---

[233] *Vaour(Temple)*, no. 42, pp. 28–29 (1180).

[234] It has been argued by Demurger, *Temple*, p. 93 that donats were a separate category within the 'family' of the Temple, distinguished on the basis that they wished eventually to become brothers, whereas *confratres* did not. There is no evidence to support this.

[235] *Saint-Gilles(Temple)*, fols. 146v–147r (1195); *Richerenches(Temple)*, no. 241, pp. 214–215 (1179).

[236] 'Ego Ricavus de Boissone et frater meus Raimundus Deo et domui de Roais nosmetipsos donamus in hunc modum, quod quandocumque habitum ejusdem domus voluerimus recipere, sine ulla contradicione poterimus hoc facere: tamen uxores ducere vel ad alium ordinem accedere non possumus, sine voluntate et concessu preceptoris ejusdem domus . . . Iterum recongnoscimus (sic) nos habuisse et percepisse de beneficio supradicte domus ducentos et quinquaginta sol. Raimundin., de quibus sororem nostram Alaziam debemus maritare', *Roaix(Temple)*, no. 186, pp. 135–136 (1217).

[237] *Richerenches(Temple)*, no. 72, pp. 73–74 (1151).

[238] 'Promitto insuper quod ab hac die in antea, et super sancta Euvangelia affirmo, quod

At around the same time Rostang Carrella and his brother Bertrand gave themselves as *confratres*, and promised to be good friends and defenders of the commandery of Richerenches.[239]

The Orders sometimes gave the *confrater* money or a gift to seal the bargain, often a corrody to feed and clothe the *confrater*. Amongst the first ever Templar acts to be recorded in Europe (1129) was just such an arrangement between Peter Bernard, his wife Borrella and the Temple at Douzens.[240] These corrodies were common to both the Temple and the Hospital; on one occasion it even comprised a pair of slippers (*sotulares*).[241]

The Orders kept copies of acts which formed part of large and often complex enterprises. The case of Brother Peter of the landholding family of Vezenobre is one such. Beginning with a separate incident in August 1186, the family of Caylar gave the Hospital their rights over the castle of Saint Maurice.[242] In October of the same year, Peter of Vezenobre was received into the Hospital as a brother, ceding to the Order all his goods with the consent of his father, also called Peter.[243] That same month his father, perhaps to ease his son's career in the Order, gifted to Brother Ermengard of Aspa, grand-prior of Saint-Gilles, the remaining rights over the castle of Saint Maurice.[244] Yet, his motives were not quite what they seemed. The previous month, on 11 September, Peter of Vezenobre senior had written to Count Raymond of Toulouse giving him one sixth of his rights over the castle of Montbrand, and much else besides, on the condition that the count approved the donation of the castle of Saint Maurice to the Hospital. More importantly, he requested that the count intervene in a case pending before the bishop of Nîmes to which he, Peter of Vezenobre senior, was a party. If the count felt he was unable to procure a satisfactory outcome to the case, he was to return the gifted property within a period of eight days.[245] Matters progressed far enough for the forty-one men of the castle of Saint Maurice to swear fealty to the Hospital soon after the reception of Peter junior.[246] Count Raymond formalized matters by officially infeudating the Order with the castle, and promising to intervene and

---

fidelis amicus et defensor, dicto et facto, domui de Ricarensis, et fratribus ibi Deo servienti-bus, ero', *ibid.*, no. 161, pp. 143–144 (1160).

[239] *ibid.*, no. 206, p. 187 (1161x1162).

[240] The Marquis d'Albon (*CT*, no. 18, p. 12 (1128)) has this act wrongly dated. It was in fact in 1129. *Douzens(Temple)*, C no. 11, p. 249 (1129).

[241] *Richerenches(Temple)*, no. 242, p. 215 (1180).

[242] *Saint-Gilles(Hospital)*, fols. 151v–152r (1186).

[243] *ibid.*, fol. 152v (1186).

[244] *ibid.*, fols. 150v–151rv (1186).

[245] *ibid.*, fol. 153rv (1186).

[246] *ibid.*, fol. 152rv (1186).

render justice in the case that was troubling Peter of Vezenobre senior.[247] Thus, by some astute management, Peter of Vezenobre managed, ostensibly to thank the Order for taking his son, to give the Order the remaining rights it needed over a castle, to gain the goodwill of the count of Toulouse, to procure a presumably happy outcome to a case that was weighing on his mind, and almost certainly to earn his son some preferment within the Order. This castle was no insignificant gift, for it was to become an important house for the Order, a matter which had no doubt been in their minds all along, for it soon became the commandery of Saint Maurice of Aix.[248]

Confraternity could be bound up in even more complex familial situations, the substance of which it is sometimes difficult to discern. An anomalous example of this is presented by the case of Peter Reboul of Villeneuve who, in 1200, recognized that he had been given to the Hospital. He remained a tenant owing an annual rent of 5 *sous*, and his sons, were he to have any, would be bound by the same obligation. The dowries for any daughters he might have were not to come from the allodial land, and they could not marry without the consent of the Hospital. The Hospital would only allow marriage if, within a period of forty days after the marriage, the daughters agreed to the same conditions. Peter swore homage to the Hospital, and was given an extraordinary right in return:

> Moreover, we concede to you that in place of us you may receive *confratres* of the Hospital in life, or brothers in death, . . . we grant you, and all your family, and their successors the right to wear the sign of the Hospital.[249]

Although it was normal for those under the protection of an Order to paint its cross on their door,[250] and to display the Orders' cross openly, it is unclear what the right 'to receive' constituted in this case. Whilst it may mean that Peter and his family were to provide hospitality to *confratres*, this cannot be applicable to *fratres in morte* unless they were expected to prepare the bodies for burial. The act remains both anomalous and ambiguous.

For the Templars too, there is evidence of familial involvement. In 1261 William of Fors became a *confrater* of the commandery of Saint Maurice. One

---

[247] *CH*, I, no. 818, pp. 509–510 (1186); *Saint-Gilles(Hospital)*, fols. 153v–154r (1187); 56H4892; *CH*, I, no. 829, pp. 515–516 (1187).

[248] 56H4892–4964.

[249] 'Preterea concedimus tibi ut in locum nostrum confratres Hospitales in vita, et fratres in morte recipere possis . . . damus ut tu et omnia tua familia successoresque tui et eorum familia signum Hospitalis super se portent', *Trinquetaille(Hospital)*, no. 75, pp. 67–68 (1200).

[250] For example, Statute of Westminster (1285), *Parliament Acts, The Statutes of the Realm*, I, London, 1810, p. 87.

of his conditions was 'I wish and instruct that my son, Agachatus, be [made a member of] the Order of the Temple.' The reward for the Order was that the Temple would be made the sole heir of William's estate.[251] In 1224 the records of the Templars of Saint Lucy in Arles again show the power a gift could produce. Jacina, a married woman, saw a way of fulfilling what may have been a long-held ambition of one of her employees. She first requested that on her death she be buried as a nun at the monastery of Saint Cæsarius, but one of the dispositions in her will left property to the Templars. She asked in return that the Order take Helisarius, her bailiff, give him a horse and arms, ship him to Outremer, and make him a brother of the Temple, if he still so wished.[252] The extent to which these examples may have been simoniacal will forever remain unclear with no more knowledge of the context which gave rise to them. Whatever verdict a canonist may have reached, it is clear that such practices were widespread, and involved the laity of all social strata.

The Templar Rule outlined that widows of married-brethren were to be cared for financially out of the brothers' estates.[253] This could sometimes result in her profession, as in the case of Maria of Valréas who, feeling the approach of her death, gave the Temple her half of the estate, and herself in consorority.[254] The Hospital took this one stage further, by allowing the laity to buy annuities. Thus, in 1131 Francon Artaud agreed to give the Order his houses and two vineyards at Colonnes as well as his patrimony at Port Arnaud on his death, on the condition that if his wife survived him, she could continue to occupy the buildings, and receive half of the yield of the gifted lands until her death.[255] Yet, the most important part of the deal is not mentioned in the charter. He was securing her welfare after his death. For, as a tenant of the Order, and one under their protection, she was guaranteed the physical security and stability to live out her days free from the possibility of attack and dispossession of her home and income.

The language of the charters could be martial, reminiscent of the early Christian usage of *militare* meaning spiritually to fight for the faith (there are seventy-one uses of the word in the Bible, of which the best known is Job VII, 1 '*militia est vita hominis super terram*'). For example, in 1146 Bertrand of Bourbouton became a *confrater* of the commandery at Richerenches. He gave

---

[251] 'et volo et mando quod Agachatus filius meus sit ordinis domus Templi', 56H5315 (1261).

[252] 'et dare ei equum et arma et alios apparatus milicie et ipsum Helisiarium ducere ultra mare et de eo facere fratrem Templi si tamen dictus Helisiarius frater esse voluerit', 56H5175 (1224).

[253] *RTemp., Primitive Rule*, cap. 69, p. 68.

[254] *Richerenches(Temple)*, no. 259, pp. 226–227 (1207x1208).

[255] *Trinquetaille(Hospital)*, no. 29, pp. 26–27 (1131); no. 279, pp. 286–7 is identical.

himself of his free will, with purity of heart, and offered his body and soul 'in the service and defence of the Christian faith to the society of knights and of *confratres* of the Temple of Solomon'.[256] Another example was Pons of Meynes, who professed to the Temple in 1146, and expressed his wish by the words:

> I give and offer myself to God Omnipotent, and to the knighthood of the Temple of Solomon of Jerusalem, promising to serve and to fight for God under obedience to the master for the rest of the days of my life.[257]

Normally however, the gift was a simple one of body and soul to the commandery. This was not solely a Latin formula; in the charters which survive in Occitan, it was also employed.[258]

Finally, the social characteristics of those who gave themselves as *confratres* to the Orders is a subject which deserves attention, for it demonstrates the integration of the Orders into the area, and the groups of society which were drawn to them. With regard to full profession, in the twelfth and thirteenth centuries the only real criterion was that the postulant be a free man. In practice the majority were drawn from the local knighthood. In the thirteenth century the requirement for noble birth was phased into the Hospital's policy,[259] whilst the Temple required that the entrant already be knighted, or at least from a knightly family.[260] Conversely, amongst the *confratres* were to be found a range of individuals from kings to peasants. In the Holy Land, Count Fulk V of Anjou lodged with the Templars, and became a *confrater* in 1120x1121, only one year after the foundation of the Order. He presented them with an annual gift of thirty Angevin pounds, probably a payment for his confraternity. Orderic Vitalis recounted that many other French nobles 'undertook a similar obligation'.[261] The attention of the magnate, later to become king of Jerusalem, puts into perspective the importance that the Temple had already attained, and sheds further doubts on the trustworthiness of William of

---

[256] 'ad servicium et defensionem Christiane fidei in societatem militum et confratrum Templi Salomonis', *Richerenches(Temple)*, no. 59, pp. 59–60 (1146).

[257] 'dono et offero memetipsum omnipotenti Deo et milicie Templi Salomonis Jerosolimitani promittens me serviturum et militaturum ibidem Deo sub obedientia magistri diebus omnibus vite mee', 56H5247 (1146).

[258] 'do e ab aquesta present carta liura mo cors e ma arma a Deu e a sancta Maria e a la mayso del Temple', *La Selve(Temple)*, no. 20, p. 135 (c.1180). There are many other examples, *inter alia*, no. 52, pp. 153–154 (1227); no. 82, pp. 175–176 (1228); no. 53, pp. 154–155 (1256).

[259] Forey, 'Recruitment', pp. 139–171.

[260] *RTemp.*, *Further Penances*, cap. 637, p. 343; *Conventual Life*, cap. 337, p. 194.

[261] Orderic Vitalis, *The Ecclesiastical History of Orderic Vitalis*, M. Chibnall (ed. and tr.), VI, Oxford, 1978, book 12, ch. 29, p. 310.

Tyre's assertions that the Temple remained insignificant until 1129.[262] The Hospital, too, had its successes amongst the potentates in Outremer. Prince Bohemond of Antioch became a *confrater*, as did Count Raymond III of Tripoli.[263] Also in Outremer, Countess Constance of Saint-Gilles (widow of Eustace of Blois, unhappily married to Count Raymond V in 1154) became a consoror of the Hospital in 1178x1179, gifting the Order land in the East, and requesting burial with the Order, and an anniversary.[264]

In western Occitania the Temple achieved a major coup with the full profession into the Order's commandery at Barcelona of Count Raymond Berenger III of Barcelona in 1130. At the same time he gifted the Order the manned Catalan castle of Grañena in the border lands facing Muslim territory.[265] The count had given numerous privileges to the Hospitallers some sixteen years previously, but evidently had switched his loyalties once the Order of the Temple appeared in Europe. Perhaps he hoped to encourage the Templars to participate in the *Reconquista*, a hope which was not realized until years later (see Chapter 1). Also of this family, Count Berenger Raymond (d.1144) was killed by Genoese in the pay of Toulouse in naval combat at Melgueil, and buried in the Hospitaller church of Trinquetaille.[266] In 1129 Count Afonso Henriques, later king of Portugal, son of Queen Teresa of Castile, confirmed his status as a *confrater*.[267] In 1196 Count Sancho, brother of the late King Alfonso of Aragon, then regent of the kingdom, gave himself as a *confrater* to the Hospitaller commandery of Cavaillon promising not to enter any other Order.[268] Count Raymond of Barcelona and his nephew Raymond Berenger III, count of Provence, gave the Hospital at Trinquetaille the village of Puimoisson in 1150, and wished that the gift would benefit the souls of their ancestors, and particularly Count Berenger Raymond of Provence, who had been buried at Trinquetaille in 1144.[269] Counts William and Bertrand of

---

262 William of Tyre, *Chronicon*, I, book 12, ch. 7, pp. 553–555.

263 Riley-Smith, *Knights*, pp. 242, 243.

264 L. Sery, 'Constance, fille de France, "Reine d'Angleterre", Comtesse de Toulouse', *AM* 63(1951), p. 205; *CH*, I, no. 551, pp. 373–374 (1178x1179).

265 *CT*, no. 33, p. 25 (1130). The information that he professed into the commandery of Barcelona comes from the *Gesta comitum Barchionensium*, L. Barrau Dihigo and J. Massó Torrents (eds.), Barcelona, 1925, p. 38. There is some uncertainty as to this date, for the charter of profession might have been drawn up in 1131 after he had made his will, *CT*, no. 38, pp. 28–29; J. Miret y Sans, *Les Cases de Templers y Hospitalers en Catalunya*, Barcelona, 1910, p. 16 located a manuscript of the charter of profession dated 1131. It is, however, a late copy; Forey, *Aragón*, pp. 8–9 discusses the matter fully, reaching no firm conclusion.

266 Chailan, *L'Ordre*, pp. 3–4; Baratier, 'Marquisat', p. 138.

267 *CT*, no. 24, p. 17 (1129); see Barber, *Knighthood*, p. 32.

268 *Trinquetaille(Hospital)*, no. 185, p. 179 (1196).

269 *ibid.*, no. 206, pp. 203–204 (1150); 56H4825 (1150).

Forcalquier gave themselves as *confratres* to the Hospital of Manosque in 1168.[270] Count William IV of Forcalquier (son of Bertrand) gave himself to the Hospital in 1206.[271] Although not an arrangement of consorority, Beatrix of Savoy, countess of Provence (widow of Count Raymond Berenger V) gave the Hospital of Aix-en-Provence land in return for the establishment of three priests to sing masses for her soul.[272]

Amongst the lesser, but nevertheless influential families of Occitania there were professions, too. In 1176 the count of Comminges professed as a Templar at Montsaunès.[273] His family was deeply ecclesiastically motivated, for his brothers held the sees of Comminges and Le Couserans.[274] In 1192 the viscount of Marseille, Hugh of Baux (son of Tiburge of Orange) became a *confrater* of the Hospitaller commandery of Trinquetaille.[275] Another local magnate, Rostang Porcellet, also affiliated himself to the Hospital at Trinquetaille shortly before his death,[276] whilst in the second quarter of the twelfth century, the seigneur of Nefin, Pons of Meynes, became a brother of the Temple.[277]

Of the non-noble *confratres* little can be said. Jobs or professions are not mentioned in the charters, but it is apparent that the vast majority were able to cede to the Orders land of some significance. The one notable exception to this is the category that gave themselves *per hominem*. This was a feudal arrangement of protection, created by the oath of homage given by an individual as he became a vassal of the Order. This was an attractive option for poorer folk, as it brought with it the security provided by the Order, and the spiritual advantages of its prayers. An 1180 example from Douzens was the recognition by Peter Novelli that he and his family were vassals of the Order. In recognition of their homage they owed the Temple 2 *sous* of Melgueil annually, for which they were granted the Order's protection.[278]

It is difficult to know the social standings of the brethren, but a survey of the Hospitaller house at Trinquetaille is indicative of the composition of an urban commandery. Of around 180 brethren mentioned, some 65 came from the region of Arles itself, 15 from noble families, 8 from consular families, 4 were canons, and 2 were from the notariat.[279] The high percentage of non-

---

[270] *Saint-Gilles(Hospital)*, fol. 164rv (1168); 56H4670 (1168).

[271] *Saint-Gilles(Hospital)*, fol. 167rv (1206); 56H4628 (1206).

[272] 56H4180 (1256).

[273] *Montsaunès(Temple)*, no. 1, pp. 223–226 (1176).

[274] E. Delaruelle, 'Templiers et Hospitaliers en Languedoc pendant la croisade des Albigeois', *CF* 4(1969), p. 327.

[275] *Trinquetaille(Hospital)*, no. 6, p. 7 (1192).

[276] *ibid.*, no. 63, pp. 53–54 (1185).

[277] J. Richard, 'Les Saint-Gilles et le comté de Tripoli', *CF* 18(1983), p. 73.

[278] *Douzens(Temple)*, A no. 168, pp. 150–151 (1180).

[279] G. Giordanengo, 'Les Hôpitaux arlésiens du XIIe au XIVe siècle', *CF* 13(1976), p. 199.

noble brethren is in stark contrast to the monastic norms of the time. Additionally, attention should be drawn to the six noble donats and one non-noble in 1338.[280] The commandery was, in this respect, the mirror image of a monastic house, for it provided a vehicle for socially advantaged families to share in the religious benefits of an institution made up of largely socially inferior religious.

A demonstration of the manner in which a family could forge links with a commandery can be seen by a small prosopographical study of the Pelicers or Pelliparius (Tanner) family and its relations with the Templars. As is evident from that which precedes, those received as brethren were frequently known to the Orders, and such close contact may well be one explanation for the Orders' rejection of periods of novitiate.[281] Four members of the family became brethren of the Order of the Temple at Richerenches: Brothers Stephen (1146–1159),[282] Gerald (priest-brother, 1173),[283] Radulph (1179),[284] and Ismido (1176–1182).[285] Other members of the family joined the commandery of Roaix, notably Brother Pons, who rose to be its commander in the first half of the thirteenth century.[286] Additionally, G. Pellicer commanded Bras in the Var in 1221.[287] On the side of the family which were associated with Richerenches, none became *confratres*, although fourteen members of the family

280 *Visites*, Beaucage (ed.), p. 588.
281 Generally, A. Forey, 'Novitiate and Instruction in the Military Orders in the Twelfth and Thirteenth Centuries', *Speculum* 61(1986), pp. 1–17. The Templars had a period of novitiate, but it was soon phased out: 'Legatur igitur regula in ejus presencia, et si ipse preceptis exposite regulæ diligenter obtemperaverit tunc, si magistro et fratribus ejus recipere placuerit, convocatis fratribus, desiderium et peticionem suam cunctis animi putitate patefaciat', *R Temp., Primitive Rule*, cap. 11, pp. 22–23.
282 *Richerenches(Temple)*, no. 59, pp. 59–60 (1146); no. 31, pp. 33–34; no. 60, pp. 60–63 (1147); no. 32, pp. 34–36; no. 43, pp. 45–46 (1148); no. 49, pp. 50–51; no. 50, p. 51 (1149); no. 61, pp. 63–65; no. 66 (1 and 2), pp. 68–69 (1150); no. 64, pp. 66–67; no. 67, p. 70; no. 195, p. 174 (1151); no. 73, pp. 74–75 (1153); no. 76, p. 78; no. 77, pp. 78–79; no. 136, p. 128; no. 151, pp. 136–137; no. 152, p. 137; no. 153, p. 138; no. 154, p. 139 (1156); no. 139, pp. 129–130; no. 142, pp. 131–132; no. 144, pp. 132–133; no. 155, pp. 139–140; no. 188, pp. 166–168 (1158); no. 84, pp. 84–85 (1159).
283 *ibid.*, no. 199, pp. 176–178 (1173).
284 *ibid.*, no. 237, pp. 211–212 (1179).
285 *ibid.*, no. 218, p. 195 (1176); no. 245, pp. 217–218 (1181); no. 240, pp. 213–214 (1182). The Marquis de Ripert-Monclar, editor of the cartulary, makes an error when he states in the Introduction (p. clxii) that Ismido was a brother between 1182 and 1183. In general, the information he has gathered together in his introduction and indices is not exhaustive and, therefore, unreliable.
286 *ibid.*, appendix 2, pp. 237–241 (commander, 1244) and *Roaix(Temple)* no. 144, pp. 91–92 (1200); no. 148, p. 96; no. 162, pp. 107–108 (1206); no. 180, p. 129 (commander, 1219).
287 Léonard, *Gallicarum*, p. 44.

regularly appeared as witnesses from 1146–1182. In total, members of the family appeared in charters from Richerenches ninety-six times.[288] Oddly, no member ever made a donation to the Order (apart, presumably, from gifts on entry) contenting themselves with acting as witnesses to charters. The family was large and disparate. Only two genealogical links can be made: the brothers Peter and Hugh appeared together in 1155,[289] as did the brothers Bertrand and Ismido on twelve occasions between 1175 and 1181.[290] Unusually, no females of the family appear at all.

Conclusion

Although it seems that the Hospital tempted more of the high aristocracy to join in confraternity than did the Temple, it must be remembered, here more than anywhere else, that lack of evidence is not evidence of a lack, particularly when bearing in mind the much lower survival rate of Templar documents compared with those of the Hospital. Many instances of confraternity are known through related documentation. For example, the murderers of Saint Thomas Becket were ordered by Pope Alexander III to fight as military *confratres* of the Temple, a category which only existed in the Holy Land and Iberian

[288] *Richerenches(Temple)* no. 59, pp. 59–60 (1146); no. 31, pp. 33–34; no. 60, pp. 60–63 (1147); no. 32, pp. 34–35; no. 43, pp. 45–46 (1148); no. 49, pp. 50–51; no. 50, p. 51 (1149); no. 61, pp. 63–65; no. 66 (1 and 2), pp. 68–69 (1150); no. 64, pp. 66–67; no. 67, p. 70; no. 195, p. 174 (1151); no. 73, pp. 74–75 (1153); no. 74, pp. 76–77 (1155); no. 76, p. 78; no. 77, pp. 78–79; no. 136, p. 128; no. 151, pp. 136–137; no. 152, p. 137; no. 153, pp. 138–139; no. 154, p. 139 (1156); no. 79, pp. 80–81 (1157); no. 132, p. 126; no. 139, pp. 129–130; no. 142, pp. 131–132; no. 144, pp. 132–133; no. 155, pp. 139–140; no. 188, pp. 166–168 (1158); no. 84, pp. 84–85; no. 137, pp. 128–129 (1159); no. 85, pp. 85–86 (1160); no. 174, pp. 153–154 (1160x1161); no. 177, pp. 155–156 (1161); no. 171, pp. 151–152 (1162); no. 100, pp. 101–102 (1164); no. 112, pp. 109–110 (1166); no. 111, pp. 108–109 (1167); no. 93, pp. 94–96 (1168); no. 119, pp. 114–115 (1168x1169); no. 97, pp. 99–100; no. 98, p. 100 (1169); no. 81, p. 83; no. 106, pp. 106–107; no. 116, pp. 112–113 (1170); no. 118, pp. 113–114; no. 103, pp. 103–105; no. 105, p. 106; no. 124, pp. 118–119 (1171); no. 126, pp. 119–120; no. 120, p. 116 (1172); no. 199, pp. 176–178 (1173); no. 216, pp. 192–193; no. 210, p. 187; no. 211, p. 188; no. 225, pp. 200–201; no. 226, pp. 201–202 (1175); no. 214, pp. 190–191; no. 217, pp. 193–194; no. 218, pp. 194–195 (1176); no. 220, pp. 196–197 (1177); no. 237, pp. 211–212 (1179); no. 227, pp. 202–203; no. 243, p. 216 (1180); no. 245, pp. 217–218; no. 233, pp. 208–209; no. 235, p. 210; no. 238, pp. 212–213 (1181); no. 240, pp. 213–214 (1182).

[289] *ibid.*, no. 74, p. 76 (1155).

[290] *ibid.*, no. 210, p. 187; no. 211, p. 188; no. 216, pp. 192–193; no. 225, pp. 200–20; no. 226, pp. 201–202 (1175); no. 214, pp. 190–191; no. 217, pp. 193–194 (1176); no. 220, pp. 196–197 (1177); no. 227, pp. 202–203; no. 243, p. 216 (1180); no. 233, pp. 208–209; no. 238, pp. 212–213 (1181).

peninsula.[291] This aspect of the Temple was well known. It even surfaced in romances of the period such as the thirteenth century courtly tale, *The Chastelaine of Vergy*, in which the duke of Burgundy, after killing his wife for betraying the secret love between his favourite knight and niece,

> was so angered by events that no one ever heard any more of it. He soon took the Cross to the Holy Land; he arrived with no delay, and became a Templar.[292]

This popular image of the Templars supported the notion of a haven for men for whom the world held no more pleasure. Significantly, it was not a local commandery which the duke joined, but rather, the battle outposts of Syria-Palestine, whose image still prompted troubadours to delight in 'glorious songs'.[293] The Hospital, too, had something of this allure, for one man expressly joined it so that he could have the opportunity to travel.[294] The loss of the central archives of the Temple means, of course, that it is impossible to comment upon professions of pilgrims once in Outremer. For this reason alone, our knowledge of confraternity is necessarily one based almost entirely on European sources. But in itself that is testimony to the flexibility of the Orders. Born in Jerusalem, their integration into the West was not only economic, agricultural and maritime, but involved the active participation of members of local communities at all levels, and of both sexes.

By way of an overview, the Benedictines recruited principally amongst the educated groups and the high ranking military aristocracy, although there were *conversi* at Cluny.[295] The Cistercians had admitted the peasant and artisans on an unprecedented scale, but still recruited essentially from amongst the intelligentsia,[296] as did the mendicants in the thirteenth century.[297] Indeed, both Orders of friars, as remarked by the Franciscan Salimbene de Adam, drew on

---

[291] D. Knowles, *Thomas Beckett*, London, 1970, pp. 139–140.

[292] 'mais de l'aventure ot tele ire/ c'onques puis ne l'oÿ on rire./ Errant se croisa d'outremer,/ u il ala sans demourer,/ et devint illoeques Templier', *La Chastelaine de Vergy*, R. Stuip (ed.), Saint-Amand-Montrond, 1985, lines 929–932, p. 46.

[293] 'Seigneur, soies en pais, laisés la noise ester,/ Sé vous volés chançon gloriose escouter/ Jà de nule millor ne vous dira jongler;/ C'est de la Sainte ville qui tant fait à luer,/ Où Diex laisa son cors et plaier et navrer,/ Et ferir de la lance et en la crois poser', Richard the Pilgrim, *La Chanson d'Antioche*, P. Paulin (ed.), i, Paris, 1848, chant premier, ch. 1, p. 1.

[294] 'terram Ierosolimitanam et alias videre desiderans', *Die Register Innocenz III*, O. Hageneder *et al.* (eds.), ii, Rome and Vienna, 1979, no. 54, pp. 100–101 (1199).

[295] Lawrence, *Monasticism*, p. 178.

[296] *ibid.*, pp. 37, 183.

[297] J. Paul, 'La Signification sociale du Franciscanisme', in *Mouvements franciscains et société française XIIe–XXe siècles*, A. Vauchez (ed.), Paris, 1984, pp. 9–25; C. Lawrence, *The Friars*, London, 1994, pp. 34–35, 49, 72–73.

the same classes as those who had always risen to positions of prestige in the Church.[298] Yet the Military and Religious Orders were much more radical in attracting all ranks of society.

The Hospital and Temple were highly innovative with their systems of confraternity. They opened up this method of affiliation to an unprecedented extent. It was not a precursor of the systems that were to be adopted by the mendicants. For, when the friars turned the penitential confraternities under their tutelage into Third Orders, they created ascetic and penitential groups centred on instruction and devotion, supervised by elected members of the laity.[299] Moreover, these were a late creation. It is a myth that Saint Francis founded a Third Order; for this Order was not approved until the publication of the bull *Supra montem Catholicæ* of Pope Nicholas IV in 1289.[300] Conversely, the Military Orders' systems of confraternity were much wider in scope than established monastic fraternity or the mendicant Third Orders, for they were general mechanisms for affiliation to the spiritual benefits of the Orders.

Moreover, the Military Orders recruited locally. This can be contrasted with the Cistercians, an example of whose recruitment can be seen at the abbey of Bonnefont in Comminges, where the first two generations came exclusively from Lorraine, Champagne and Burgundy.[301] By contrast, amongst the Templars Hugh of Bourbouton rose to command the commandery he had founded at Richerenches,[302] and Bertrand of Cobrac founded the Hospitaller commandery of Le Burgaud in the Haute-Garonne during the Albigensian Crusade and, after professing, commanded this house as well as becoming prior of Toulouse, commander of Castelsarrasin, and then of Verdun-sur-Garonne.[303]

In order to achieve the deep relationships with both laity and clergy discussed in this and the previous chapter, the Orders needed efficient systems of administration as well as structures which facilitated their operations. The next chapter will discuss exactly how these were constituted, with a particular emphasis on the hierarchies in Occitania.

[298] Salimbene de Adam, *Cronica*, G. Scalia (ed.), ii, Bari, 1966, p. 606.

[299] Lawrence, *Friars*, pp. 112–116.

[300] *Bullarium Franciscanum*, J. Sbaraglia (ed.), iv, Rome, 1768, pp. 94–97.

[301] C. Higounet in discussion following P. Ourliac, 'Le Pays de La Selve à la fin du xiie siècle', *AM* 80(1968), p. 593.

[302] See Chapter 2, pp. 67–68.

[303] C. Higounet, 'Les Origines d'une commanderie de l'ordre de Malte: le Burgaud (Haute-Garonne)', *AM* 44(1932), pp. 134, 136.

CHAPTER V

Administrative Structures

> But the habits of regularity, order, and prompt obedience to command, can be
> acquired only by troops which are exercised in great bodies . . . The soldiers
> who are bound to obey their officers only once a week or once a month, and
> who are at all other times at liberty to manage their own affairs their own way,
> without being in any respect accountable to him, can never be under the same
> awe in his presence, can never have the same disposition to ready obedience,
> with those whose whole life and conduct are every day directed by him.
>
> A. Smith, *An Enquiry into the Wealth of Nations*,
> Edinburgh, 1850, book 5, ch. 1, p. 315

THE aim of this chapter is to examine the structures of the Military
Orders' Occitanian commanderies, and to discuss the details of their
operations. The emphasis is on the composition of the Occitanian commanderies, as opposed to the Orders' combat-personnel, a topic excellently analysed
in other works.[1] This will be achieved by an analysis of the officials and their
geographic competence, the brethren and 'family' who lived in the commanderies, and the feudal jurisdictions of the Courts of the Commanders.

The structures which the Military Orders employed were innovative. Initially, personal contact was sufficient for the management of properties in
Outremer. But, when the Military Orders moved to Europe a model was
needed upon which to base systems of international administration, and this
needed to guarantee two things. First, that the satellites could be responsive to
Jerusalem. Second, that officials were available to manage them.

The Military Orders required administrative systems which could accommodate geographical distance without losing the ability to respond to their
needs in Outremer. No monastic Order had yet devised such an ambitious
network. Benedictine abbeys were traditionally independent, notwithstanding
responsibility for their dependent priories. The Cluniac congregation did, in
principal, look to Cluny as spiritual leader of the congregation. But, the

---

[1] Riley-Smith, *Knights*, pp. 227–373; Barber, *Knighthood*, pp. 179–280; Demurger,
Temple, pp. 89–117.

systems of affiliation devised were of great complexity, and could not have fur-
nished a model tight enough for the requirements of a Military Order.[2]

The Cistercians created a radical new organization with a strong chain of
command, fine-tuned by Abbot Stephen Harding in the *Carta caritatis* of
1114.[3] Whilst it might appear that this system could have proved useful to the
Military Orders, it was not adopted. To think that it was is a misunderstanding stemming from the belief that the Order of the Temple was intrinsically
linked to Saint Bernard and the Cistercians.[4] This is a fallacy, doubly wrong
because not only were their administrations different, but the Templars emulated the Hospitallers,[5] who have never been deemed to have had close links
with Cîteaux. It was the Hospital which first needed a model for its European
operations, and the Cistercian system had a big failing. The Military Orders
required their houses to be grouped regionally, but the Cistercian model of
affiliation could not accommodate this, for their mother and daughter houses
were often separated by great distances, denying effective regional control.[6]

Authority

(i) Geographical Competence

When the Hospital moved to Europe it was faced with the task of creating
responsive, manageable European satellites. The solution it devised was
unprecedented. It created the 'priory', an area in which individual commanderies were responsible to a main house: the grand-priory. There was thus a
three-tiered command structure. In the thirteenth century the priories them-

---

[2] Barber, *Knighthood*, p. 19; G. Duby, *Le Moyen Age*, Paris, 1987, p. 31; *Cluniac Monasteries in the central Middle Ages*, N. Hunt (ed.), London and Basingstoke, 1971, *passim; Cf.*
M. Pacaut, 'Structures monastiques, société et l'Eglise en Occident aux xie et xiie siècles',
*Cahiers d'histoire 20, Aspects de la vie conventuelle aux xie et xiie siècles. Actes du ve congrès de la
société des historiens médiévistes (St-Etienne, 1974)*, Lyons, 1975, p. 123; C. Lawrence, *Medi-
eval Monasticism*, New York, 1989, pp. 95–96.
[3] *Carta caritatis*, in *Documenta pro Cisterciensis ordinis historiæ ac juris studio*, J.-B. Van
Damme (ed.), Westmalle, 1959, pp. 15–21; generally, R. Southern, *Western Society and the
Church in the Middle Ages*, Harmondsworth, 1990, pp. 255–259.
[4] This is rejected in D. Selwood, '*Quidam autem dubitaverunt*: The Saint, the Sinner, the
Temple and a Possible Chronology', *Autour de la première croisade, Actes du colloque de la
Society for the Study of the Crusades and the Latin East (Clermont-Ferrand, 22–25 juin 1995)*,
M. Balard (ed.), Paris, 1996, pp. 221–230.
[5] This was first noted by James of Vitry, *Historia Hierosolymitana*, in *Gesta Dei per
Francos*, J. Bongars (ed.), Hanover, 1611, book 65, p. 1084.
[6] Lawrence, *Monasticism*, p. 188.

PLATE V: Seal of the Hospitaller preceptory of Provence depicting
a dove clenching an olive-branch in its beak.

selves were grouped into larger units: Tongues,[7] Areas, as the name implies, defined by linguistic practice.

The Hospital had originally envisaged the priory of Italy as its European mainstay. In 1113 the Order had six houses in the Italian peninsula compared to the lone Provençal houses of Saint-Gilles and Gap.[8] But this plan was abandoned, for it was in central-southern Occitania that most subsequent growth took place. Although in medieval parlance 'Provence' meant the Midi,[9] the Hospitaller priory of Provence was initially far larger than geographical Provence, larger even than greater Occitania. It covered Provence, the Languedoc, Catalonia, Aragon, France, Belgium and probably England.[10] All this was administered from Saint-Gilles. In time this was recognized as unworkable, so various areas seceded from the control of Saint-Gilles. The priory of England was formed in the 1140s,[11] the castellany of Amposta was created in the Iberian peninsula c.1154,[12] the priory of France became autonomous in 1178x1179,[13] and the priory of Auvergne was recognized in 1229x1245.[14]

The Hospital's properties and estates in Occitania swelled in the wake of Clement V's bull *Ad providam* of 1312, which vested much Templar property in the Hospital,[15] a process not completed in Provence until 1319 when King Robert of Naples complied with regard to his dynastic lands in Provence.[16] Accordingly, even this reduced Tongue of Provence became too complex to be effectively controlled from Saint-Gilles. Thus, in 1315 the Tongue was split into two zones: the eastern half managed from the grand-priory of Saint-Gilles, the western half from a newly created grand-priory of Toulouse.[17]

The fundamental aspects of the Hospitaller's tripartite system of administration were emulated by the Order of the Temple when it came to Europe,[18] although there was a difference in terminology. Where the Hospital had 'priories', the Temple created 'provinces'. In Occitania there were two further

7 Riley-Smith, *Knights*, p. 230.
8 *CH*, I, no. 30, pp. 29–30 (1113), See Chapter 2, pp. 53–54.
9 E. Baratier, 'Marquisat et comtés en Provence', *Histoire de la Provence*, E. Baratier (ed.), Toulouse. 1969, pp. 134–135.
10 *CH*, I, Introduction, p. xxviii; Riley-Smith, *Knights*, p. 353.
11 *ibid.*, pp. 357–358.
12 *ibid.*, pp. 356–357.
13 *ibid.*, pp. 353–354.
14 *ibid.*, p. 354.
15 A copy of *Ad providam* is at 56H5166 (1312). Not all Occitanian Templar property went to the Hospital; for example, Montsaunès passed into secular hands, A. du Mège, 'Notes sur quelque monuments de l'ordre de la milice du Temple et sur l'église de Montsaunès', *Mémoires de la société archéologique du Midi de la France* 5(1842), p. 193.
16 M. Barber, *The Trial of the Templars*, Cambridge, 1993, p. 238.
17 *CH*, I, Introduction, p. xxviii.
18 Barber, *Knighthood*, p. 20; Riley-Smith, *Knights*, pp. 40–41, 353.

differences. First, the Temple did not have a commandery to which all others in Occitania were responsible, although all were, of course, subject to the control of the senior Templar official in Provence. Second, the geographical area covered by the Templars' Occitanian administration was smaller, for Templar 'Provence' was parallel to Occitania in its largest sense, that is, from the Alps across to the Pyrenees, and over into the Iberian peninsula.

In time this Templar province was reflected by the fact that the senior Templar official in Occitania took the title of the 'master of the houses of the Temple in Provence and parts of Spain'.[19] Whilst the date of the appearance of this title is well known (Brother Peter of Rovira in 1143),[20] its implications have not been fully examined. Brother Peter had been exercising the function, although simply as a brother, since 1139.[21] Something decisive must have happened in the fourth year of his unofficial magistracy which prompted him to take the title. One significant event readily presents itself as the explanation. Whilst the Hospitallers and the Order of the Holy Sepulchre had renounced their claims to the kingdoms of King Alfonso I 'the Battler' of Aragon and Navarre in 1140, the Temple did not do so until 1143, the year which marked the conclusion of their negotiations with the count of Barcelona, and their entry into the *Reconquista* as a military force.[22] Accordingly, the creation of a 'master in Provence and parts of Spain' was part of a formalization and consolidation of their properties. Henceforward Templars were to be combatants in the Iberian peninsula. The words *'et in partibus Ispanie'* were devised to reflect the fact that the Templars would be active wherever the *Reconquista* took them, for negotiations with the count of Barcelona had ensured that the Templars were to be able to acquire one fifth of all lands reconquered from the Moors.[23] The relationship between the peninsula and Occitania can be seen by the presence of the 'master in Provence', Brother Hugh of Montlaur, at the siege of Valencia in 1238.[24]

(ii) Officials

The competence of regional officials can best be traced by an examination of the officials and their titles. This is an inexact exercise because both titles and responsibilities are often unclear. In the monastic world an abbot was the head

---

[19] 'Magister domorum Templi in Provincia et partibus Ispanie'.
[20] Forey, *Orders*, p. 149.
[21] E. Léonard, *Gallicarum militiæ Templi domorum eorumque præceptorum seriem secundum Albonensia apographa in bibliotheca nationali Parisiensi asservata*, Paris, 1930, p. 23.
[22] *CT*, no. 314, pp. 204–205 (1143). See Chapter 1, pp. 37–39.
[23] *CT*, no. 314, pp. 204–205 (1143).
[24] Demurger, *Temple*, p. 250, believes that Brother Hugh was not yet 'master of Provence'. He was. He had held the office since 1234, Forey, *Aragón*, p. 420.

of a house, and his authority was second only to that of God.[25] Resistance to his authority was therefore akin to resistance to God.[26] But for the Military Orders, to know over whom an official had authority, and to compile lists of such officials with their dates, is no simple matter. It is often considered impossible.[27]

The reason is easily demonstrated. Brother Hugh Rigaud, the Templar most responsible for overseeing the Order's early activities on both sides of the Pyrenees at Le Mas-Déu, Douzens, Uzès, and generally in Catalonia and the Dauphiné,[28] appeared in the documentation of Douzens alone as *servus*,[29] *miles et frater*,[30] *confrater*,[31] *dom[i]nus*[32] and *procurator*.[33] Coupled with this, on three occasions in 1133x1134 he received gifts as an official of the Holy Sepulchre.[34] His successor, Brother Arnold of Bedocio (1136–1139), also appeared with no definite styling.[35] His successor, Brother Peter of Rovira, took the styling 'master of Provence and parts of Spain' in 1143; but even this was not fixed, for in 1202 Brother Pons of Rigaud varied the title to 'master of Italy, Provence and Spain'.[36] Similar inconsistencies are to be found in the titles of officials of the Hospital.[37]

Just as the Hospital faced problems over the size of the Tongue of Provence, the Temple was aware that to have one man holding overall

---

[25] 'Christi enim agere vices in monasterio creditur, quando ipsius vocatur pronomine', *RB*, cap. 2, line 2, p. 172.

[26] 'Omnis anima potestatibus sublimioribus subdita sit non est enim potestas nisi a Deo quæ autem sunt a Deo ordinatæ sunt, itaque qui resistit potestati Dei ordinationi resistit qui autem resistunt ipsi sibi damnationem adquirunt (Romans XIII, 1–2.)'; see G. Constable, 'The Authority of Superiors in Religious Communities', *La Notion d'autorité au moyen age: Islam, Byzance, Occident. Colloques internationaux de la Napoule*, G. Makdisi *et al.* (eds.), Paris, 1982, p. 190.

[27] *La Selve(Temple)*, p. 74.

[28] Léonard, *Gallicarum*, p. 23.

[29] *Douzens(Temple)*, A no. 199, pp. 171–172 (1151); A no. 127, pp. 119–120; A no. 131, p. 122 (1156); A no. 133, pp. 123–124 (1163); B no. 19, p. 204 (1164).

[30] *ibid.*, C no. 1, p. 263 (1130).

[31] *ibid.*, C no. 3, pp. 266–267 (1132); A no. 95, pp. 106–108; A no. 1, pp. 3–5 (1133).

[32] *ibid.*, C no. 11, p. 269 (1129); C no. 3, pp. 266–267; A no. 171, pp. 152–154 (1132); C no. 4, p. 264; C no. 5, p. 264; C no. 6, pp. 265–266 (1133x1134); A no. 95, pp. 106–108 (1135).

[33] *ibid.*, A no. 40, p. 50 (1133x1134). C no. 3, p. 263 is identical but (1132).

[34] 'dono domino Deo et sancto Sepulchro Jherusalem et ad ipsam cavalleriam Templi Salomonis . . . et in manu domni Hugonis Rigauldi', *ibid.*, C no. 4, p. 264; C no. 5, p. 264; C no. 6, pp. 265–266 (1133x1134).

[35] Léonard, *Gallicarum*, p. 23.

[36] 'fratri Poncio de Rigaldo ejusdem domus in Ytalia Provincia et Yspania honorabili magistro', 56H5168 (1202).

[37] Riley-Smith, *Knights*, p. 341.

responsibility for these ever growing lands was burdensome, and impractical. Thus, to cope effectively with the province, the 'master of Provence and parts of Spain' had lieutenants responsible for the east and the west of the Pyrenees. A 'master of Provence' was in office in the mid-twelfth century,[38] and there was a 'master of Spain' in 1219.[39] There were also masters of smaller regional groupings. For example, lieutenants had been exercising power in Catalonia and Aragon since 1151.[40] A 'master of Carcassonne and the Razès', a 'master of Roussillon', and a 'master of the Narbonnais' all appeared for the first time around the mid-twelfth century.[41] Whilst a 'master of Toulouse' appeared before the turn of the thirteenth century.[42] When Templar Spain was granted its independence from Provence remains unclear. It has been suggested that it was in 1240, for in 1239 Brother Stephen of Belmonte was 'master of Provence and parts of Spain', but in 1240 Brother Raymond of Serra succeeded him, but as 'master in Catalonia and Aragon'. This province also covered Roussillon, Navarre, Mallorca, and Valencia, the same boundaries which were later to be followed by the Dominican province of Aragon.[43]

The Templar 'master in Provence and parts of Spain' was not only a link between Outremer and Occitania, but he could actively intervene in the daily running of commanderies under his control. Brother Bernard the Catalan, commander of Saint-Gilles, sold a vineyard in 1160 with the advice of three brethren, but also 'by order of our [regional] master, Hugh of Barcelonne'.[44] There was one official more senior even than the provincial master: the 'master of Deçàmer'. This title was changed to 'the visitor' c.1250.[45] Significantly, the first two holders of this office, Brothers Peter and Berenger of Rovira, were both from Provence.[46]

The principal Hospitaller official in Occitania was the grand-prior of Saint-Gilles. He first appears with such a styling in 1142,[47] although the priory

38 Léonard, *Gallicarum*, pp. 25–26.
39 *Roaix(Temple)*, no. 180, p. 107 (1219).
40 Forey, *Aragón*, p. 421.
41 Léonard, *Gallicarum*, pp. 56–57, 60; *Douzens(Temple)*, A no. 20, pp. 22–23 (1167).
42 Léonard, *Gallicarum*, p. 76.
43 F. Diago, *Historia de la provincia de Aragón de la orden de Predicadores*, Barcelona, 1599, fols. 2–3.
44 'et mandato magistri nostri Hugonis de Barcilona', *Saint-Gilles(Temple)*, fols. 30v–31r (1160). Barcelonne is not to be confused with Barcelona, it is a town in the Drôme.
45 Forey, *Aragón*, pp. 328–329 suggests that the switch from master in Deçàmer to visitor(s) was the result of two districts being formed: France, England and Germany, and the Iberian peninsula.
46 *CT*, no. 408, pp. 256–257; no. 409, p. 257 (1146).
47 P. Santoni, 'Les Deux premiers siècles du prieuré de Saint-Gilles de l'ordre de l'Hôpital de Saint-Jean de Jérusalem', *Actes du colloque de Barroux, Des hospitaliers de Saint-Jean de Jérusalem, de Chypre et de Rhodes hier aux chevaliers de Malte aujourd'hui*, Paris, 1983, p. 121.

had been formed c.1120.[48] This is not to be confused with the appearance in 1158 of a commander of Saint-Gilles, a post created to alleviate the grand-prior's burden of administering the commandery of Saint-Gilles as well as the grand-priory.[49] Commanding the grand-priory carried enormous prestige. Thirteen grand-priors of Saint-Gilles had previously commanded key houses such as Saint-Gilles, Trinquetaille, and the bailiwick of Manosque. Three had previously been castellans of Amposta, and one, Brother Ximen de Lavata (1205–1206), had been grand-prior of Lombardy and Venice.[50] Four had considerable careers in Outremer before coming to Saint-Gilles. Brother Guirald of Saint-André (grand-prior in 1170) had been treasurer of the Hospital in Jerusalem. Brother Odin Rollant (grand-prior in 1177) had been a commander and castellan in the Holy Land. Brother Ferald of Barras (grand-prior in 1245–1269) had been castellan of Armenia, commander of Antioch, and marshal of the Order. And Brother William of Villaret (grand-prior from 1270–1296) had been the Order's draper.[51] Not only were the previous careers of some grand-priors of Saint-Gilles high profile, but three went on to become masters of the Order: Brothers Ermengard of Aspa (grand-prior from 1182–1187), Bertrand of Comps (grand-prior 1231–1243) and William of Villaret (*supra*).[52]

As with the Templars, the Hospitallers had a 'grand-commander of Deçàmer', the master's representative for the whole of Europe.[53] He is a shadowy figure, but significantly, as in the case of the Temple, his residence was in Provence.[54] His first appearance was to preside over a chapter at Saint-Gilles in 1164,[55] eighteen years after the Templar official of the same styling first appeared.[56] Yet, the Hospitaller post did not appear in the Rule until 1204x1206, when it was recorded that the office was not a permanent position, but one that had from time to time existed.[57] In Occitanian documents this officer subsequently appeared in Avignon in the company of the grand-prior of

---

[48] Forey, *Orders*, p. 149.

[49] *Saint-Gilles(Hospital)*, fols. 118v–119r (1158).

[50] Santoni, 'Deux premiers', p. 149.

[51] *ibid.*, p. 149.

[52] *ibid.*, p. 151; Riley-Smith, *Knights*, p. 353.

[53] Riley-Smith, *Knights*, pp. 366–367 discusses the remit of this commander. At times he was limited to the priories of Saint-Gilles, Auvergne, France, England and Ireland, whilst at others his remit was all inclusive.

[54] E. King, *Knights Hospitallers in the Holy Land*, London, 1931, p. 80; Riley-Smith, *Knights*, p. 366.

[55] Santoni, 'Deux premiers', p. 157.

[56] *CT*, no. 408, pp. 256–257; no. 409, p. 257 (1146).

[57] *CH*, II, *Statutes of Brother Alfonso of Portugal (1204x1206)*, no. 1193, p. 39. There is some ambiguity as to whether this statute refers to the grand-commander of Outremer; Riley-Smith, *Knights*, pp. 367–368 does not reach a firm conclusion.

Saint-Gilles in 1199,[58] and in 1262 Charles of Anjou signed two treaties with Brother Ferald of Barres, the then grand-commander of Deçàmer, confirming all the Order's acquisitions in Provence.[59]

Beneath these high-ranking officials came a limited number of regional commanders,[60] followed by the commanders of houses. In the Order of the Hospital the possibility of a plurality of commands was banned until the early fourteenth century,[61] and so the compilation of lists of twelfth and thirteenth century Hospitaller commanders is not problematic.[62] However, plurality was the norm in the Temple, as was rotation. Thus, to take the example of Vaour, the following list emerges:[63]

1173	Brother Fort Sens	1191	Brother Peter the Chaplain,
c.1177–1179	Brother Guiral Bada		Brother Arnold of Bosc.
1179	Brother Fort Sans,	1192	Brother Fort Sans
	Brother John of Nougairols	1192	Brother Doat Dahas,
1181	Brother Fort Sans,		Brother Bertrand Bonafous
	Brother Durand Oeiller	1193	Brother Bertrand Bonafous
1184	Brother Fort Sans,	1195	Brother Peter the Chaplain
	Brother Peter of Tudela	1199	Brother Daide of Sainte-
1185	Brother Fort Sans		Croix
1186	Brother Fort Sans,	1202	Brother Peter del Castel
	Brother Peter of Tudela,		
	Brother William Atton		

However, this table presents only a partial picture, for Brother John of Nougairols commanded the Toulouse Temple in 1170, Larramet in 1172–1173, Vaour in 1179, and Larramet again in 1189 and 1194–1197.[64] Clearly, a system of rotation was being enforced.

A list of commanders from Richerenches demonstrates the same pattern of multiple commands. Brother Deudat of l'Etang appeared sporadically as commander of Richerenches from 1151 until 1175, but shared the magistracy with, among others, Brother Peter of Rovira (1151 and 1156–1157), and Brother Hugh of Barcelonne (1156–1160 and 1163). An explanation is possible.

---

[58] GCN(Avignon), no. 322, col. 93 (1199).

[59] 56H4418; 56H4799 (1262). In this text he is called the grand-commander of Outremer, but the two terms were interchangeable depending on which side of the sea the emphasis was being laid.

[60] For example, a 'magers comandaire que so en tot Rozergue', in A. Soutou, 'Trois chartes occitanes du XIIIe siècle concernant les Hospitaliers de la Bastide-Pradines (Aveyron)', AM 79(1967), no. 1, pp. 122–124 (1233); no. 2, pp. 125–129 (1256).

[61] Riley-Smith, Knights, p. 349.

[62] For example, Trinquetaille(Hospital), p. iv.

[63] Vaour(Temple), p. xvi.

[64] ibid., p. xiv.

Brother Deudat was commander for this entire period. On all three occasions when Brother Peter of Rovira seemed to be commander, Brother Deudat was present, but shorn of his title. Brother Peter was referred to as 'master', 'master in Provence', and 'master of the house of Richerenches', which he patently was not,[65] because for all of this period he was the 'master in Provence and parts of Spain'.[66]

The most plausible explanation for the phenomenon of Brother Peter's repeated interruptions of the command of Brother Deudat is that Brother Peter was not the commander, and Brother Deudat was. But, when Brother Peter was present, Brother Deudat ceded to him temporary and symbolic command of the house as a sign of respect for his office. A similar situation occurred with Brother Hugh of Barcelonne. He was 'master in Provence' in 1155, and probably remained so until he succeeded Brother Peter of Rovira as 'master in Provence and parts of Spain' in 1158. He held this post until 1162, after which he appeared periodically (1163, 1165 and 1171–1178) as 'master in Provence' once again.[67] In all three of these periods he was recorded present at Richerenches during the command of Brother Deudat. When 'master in Provence' for the first time he was at Richerenches on six occasions,[68] and unfailingly took precedence over Brother Deudat in the charters, once even being styled 'master of the house of Richerenches'. On only one of these occasions was Brother Deudat accorded his title.[69] In 1158 Brother Hugh became 'master of Provence and parts of Spain', and on his first two appearances in this office he was called the 'master of the house of Richerenches' and the 'master and bailiff of the house of Richerenches'. On both occasions Brother Deudat appeared as a simple brother.[70] In his other five appearances during this period he was again always styled 'master', and preceded Brother Deudat in the charters.[71] Once he had resumed the magistracy of Provence, as deputy to first Brother Hugh Geoffrey, and then Brother Arnold of Torroja, he appeared

---

[65] *Richerenches(Temple)*, no. 72, pp. 73–74 (1151); no. 129, pp. 123–124 (1156); no. 130, pp. 124–125 (1157); no. 150, pp. 136–137 (1156x1158).

[66] Forey, *Aragón*, has 1143–1158; Léonard, *Gallicarum*, p. 23 has 1139–1158.

[67] *ibid.*, p. 25.

[68] *Richerenches(Temple)*, no. 153, pp. 138–139; no. 158, pp. 141–142 (1156); no. 150, pp. 135–136 (1156x1158); no. 79, pp. 80–81; no. 92, p. 93; no. 146, pp. 134–135 (1157).

[69] *ibid.*, no. 153, pp. 138–139 (1156).

[70] *ibid.*, no. 188, pp. 166–168; no. 155, pp. 139–140 (1158).

[71] *ibid.*, no. 132, p. 126 (1158); no. 4, pp. 84–85; no. 133, pp. 126–127 (1159); no. 5, pp. 85–86 (1160); no. 90, pp. 169–170 (1161). In this latter, Brother Deudat is styled 'master of Richerenches', but comes after Brother Hugh, and Brother W. of Bais 'magistro militum Templi'. This person only appears once in the cartulary, and does not appear in Léonard.

another seven times, always in precedence over Brother Deudat (save the two occasions of his absence),[72] but never with the title of 'master'.[73]

What emerges is that a commander permitted a visiting dignitary to act *in loco magistri*, and to receive gifts on behalf of the house, even permitting the official to take the styling 'master' of the house. The other interruptions of Brother Deudat's magistracy can likewise be explained by the presence of officials of superior rank.[74] Broadening the examination a little, another factor becomes apparent in the material from the Templar cartulary from Saint-Gilles whose list of commanders should be the following:[75]

1154–1182	Brother Bernard the Catalan[76]	1191–1192	Brother Bernard the Catalan,
1183	Brother Bernard the Catalan,		Brother Bernard Bedocio[77]
	Brother John Aiguilhe[78]	1193–1195	Brother Bernard the Catalan,
1184–1185	Brother Bernard the Catalan[79]		Brother Gisbert of Costabella[80]
1186	Brother Bernard the Catalan,	1196	Brother Bernard the Catalan,

---

[72] *ibid.*, no. 179, p. 157; no. 180, pp. 157–158 (1163).

[73] *ibid.*, no. 100, pp. 101–102 (1164); no. 149, p. 135 (1168); no. 116, pp. 112–113 (1170); no. 120, p. 116; no. 126, pp. 119–120 (1172). No. 164, pp. 146–147 (1162x1163) possibly belongs to this period.

[74] *ibid.*, no. 74, pp. 76–77 (1155); no. 90, pp. 169–170 (1161); no. 103, pp. 101–102 (1164); no. 116, pp. 112–113 (1170); no. 104, p. 104; no. 105, p. 106; no. 118, pp. 113–114 (1171); see also pp. clv–clvi notes.

[75] Léonard, *Gallicarum*, pp. 30–31 provides a list of dates which are defective.

[76] *Saint-Gilles(Temple)*, fols. 3v–4r (1154); 4v–6r (1158); 26v–27r (1161); 154rv (1162); 153v–154r (1165); 155rv; 188v–189r (1166); 162v–163r (1167); 158rv; 106v; 106v-107r; 107rv (1168); 97v; 70v–71r (1170); 52rv (1171); 31rv–32r; 150v (1172); 24v–25r; 46v–47r; 199v–200r; 142v–143r; 201rv; 205rv; 93rv (1173); 26rv; 47v–48r; 195v–196r (1174); 58rv; 58v; 196rv; 196v–197r; 194v; 202v (1175); 55rv; 65v (1176); 14rv; 39r; 194rv; 57r; 199v; 66rv; 94v–95r; 96rv; 96v (1177); 191v–192v (1178); 30rv; 65v–66r (1179); 62v–63r; 152v–153r; 156rv; 195r (1180); 54v–55r; 57rv; 57v–58r; 100rv (1181); 66v–67r; 69rv; 128rv (1182).

[77] *ibid.*, fols. 22rv; 59v–60r; 84rv; 116rv; 206rv; 98rv; 54rv; 180v–181r (1191); 40rv; 52v–53r; 101rv; 89r–91r; 82rv; 167v–168r; 98v–99r; 134r (1192). Brother Bernard Bedocio was commander once in 1191, fols. 172v–173r (1191) and twice in 1192, fols. 180rv; 174r–175v (1192).

[78] *ibid.*, fols. 8r–9r; 48rv; 142v; 109r–110r; 208rv; 9rv; 85rv (1183). Brother John was commander once, fols. 130v–131r (1183).

[79] *ibid.*, fols. 55v–56r; 197v–198v; 58v–59r; 97rv (1184); 16v–17v; 44v–45v; 68rv; 137v–138r; 68v–69r; 72v; 139v–140r; 7r–8r (1185).

[80] *ibid.*; fols. 49rv; 53rv; 169v; 82v–83r; 183r–184r (1193); 56r; 53v–54r; 200v–201r; 71rv; 93v–94r (1194); 45v–46v; 15r–16v; 32r–33v; 10rv; 50v–51r; 51rv; 198v–199v; 121v–122r; 129v–130r (1195); Brother Gisbert was commander, fols. 42v–43r (1193); 205v–206r (1194); 41v; 6r–7r; 103r–104r; 35v–36v; 43r; 37v–39r; 51v–52r; 45v; 49v–50v; 51v–52r (1195). The two appeared as co-commanders on one occasion, fol. 122r (1195).

	Brother Peter of Sancto Tiberio[81]		Brother Gisbert of Costabella,
1187	Brother Bernard the Catalan[82]		Brother Bertrand of Beaucaire[83]
1188	Brother Bernard the Catalan,	1197	Brother Bertrand of Beaucaire,
	Brother Bertrand Hugh[84]		Brother Peter Raymond[85]
1189	Brother Bernard the Catalan[86]	1198	Brother Bertrand of Beaucaire[87]
1190	Brother Bernard the Catalan,	1199	Brother Bernard of Casa[88]
	Brother Bertrand of Beaucaire[89]	1200	Brother Bernard the Catalan[90]
		1201–1203	Brother William Cadel[91]

It seems, at first glance, that Brother Bernard the Catalan had a patchy career. But, a list of sub-commanders explains why:

1185	Brother John of Aiguna[92]	1188	Brother Bertrand Hugh[93]
1186	Brother Bertrand of Beaucaire,	1193	Brother Gisbert of Costabella[94]
	Brother Peter of Sancto Tiberio[95]	1197	Brother P. Raymond[96]
1187	Brother Bertrand,		
	Brother Bertrand Hugh[97]		

It becomes evident that most of the interruptions before 1191 were by the sub-commanders, either standing in for the commander, or being trained. Sub-commanders first appeared in Occitania, not arriving in the Iberian

---

[81] *ibid.*, fols. 67v–68r; 171v–172r; 81rv; 180r (1186). Brother Peter was commander once, fols. 138v–139r (1186).

[82] *ibid.*, fols. 10v–11r; 19rv; 63r–64r; 131rv; 197rv; 143rv; 176rv; 168v–171r; 184r–185r (1187).

[83] Brothers Bernard the Catalan and Gisbert of Costabella appeared as co-commanders on one occasion, fol. 138r (1196). Brother Bertrand of Beaucaire was commander for the others, fols. 60v–61r; 64r–65r; 203r; 83r; 99rv; 165v–167r; 178r (1196).

[84] *ibid.*, fols. 75r–76v; 157r; 171r; 173rv; 78r; 171rv; 100v–101r; 192v–193v; 179v–180r (1188). Brother Bernard Hugh was commander once, fols. 43v–44v (1188).

[85] *ibid.*, fols. 72v–73v; 86r–87v; 95r–96r; 12rv; 12v–13r; 13v–14r; 73v–74v; 74v–75r (1198). Brother Peter Raymond appeared as commander once, fols. 161v–162r (1197).

[86] *ibid.*, fols. 21v; 34v–35r; 35rv; 36v–37r; 39v; 40rv; 67rv (1189).

[87] *ibid.*, fols. 12rv; 12v–13r; 13v–14r; 73v–74v; 74v–75r (1198).

[88] *ibid.*, fols. 102v–103r; 104v; 208v–209v; 213r–214r (1199).

[89] *ibid.*, fols. 17v–19r; 22v–24r; 61r–62r; 62rv; 79v–81v; 84r; 91r–92r; 159rv; 150r; 179rv; 181v–182r; 185rv; 172rv (1190). Bertrand of Beaucaire was commander once, fols. 33r–34v (1190).

[90] *ibid.*, fols. 71v–72v (1200).

[91] *ibid.*, fols. 216rv; 216v–217v (1201); 211rv; 217r–216v; 212r–213r; 214rv; 211v–212r; 214v–215v (1202); 209v–211r; 215v–216r (1203).

[92] *ibid.*, fol. 134v (1185).

[93] *ibid.*, fols. 75r–76v; 175v–176r (1188).

[94] *ibid.*, fol. 169v (1193).

[95] *ibid.*, fols. 81rv; 173v–174r; 178v–179r (1186).

[96] *ibid.*, fols. 86r–87v (1197).

[97] *ibid.*, fols. 182rv; 203v–204r; 193v–194r (1187).

peninsula until the thirteenth century.[98] Their role was to assist the commander, and to be trained as career administrators.

After 1191 matters became confused at Saint-Gilles. This is unsurprising, owing to the fact that the commander, Brother Bernard the Catalan, was at a conservative estimate in his sixtieth year. The Order decided to let a younger man help him, thereby also gaining experience for himself. Accordingly, Brother Bernard Bedocio helped relieve Brother Bernard the Catalan in 1191–1192, and from 1193 Brother Gisbert of Costabella, the sub-commander, was his assistant. On two occasions in 1195 and 1196 the charters are clear that the two were co-commanders.[99] Brother Bernard retired in 1196, although not completely. His last appearance as commander was in January 1200, probably a celebration of both the turn of the century and his outstanding service to the Order.

Individual careers are difficult to trace, but an interesting example is Brother Arnold of Torroja.[100] He hailed from an Aragonese family with ecclesiastical links, for Brother Arnold's brother was William of Torroja, bishop of Barcelona.[101] Brother Arnold initially appeared as a benefactor to the commandery of Gardeny in Catalonia in the middle years of the twelfth century.[102] Presumably he professed as a Templar in Catalonia, but he never commanded a house west of the Pyrenees. He rose rapidly to become 'master in Provence and parts of Spain' (1166–1181), and then in Outremer to the mastership of the Order (1181–1184).

During his time in Occitania he appeared at Saint-Gilles for the first time in 1170, and the scribe of the cartulary was at somewhat of a loss to know how to style him.[103] He first wrote 'master', then crossed it out, and replaced it with 'master of the lands of Spain and Provence'.[104] In an act the following year he was called 'master of the house of Saint-Gilles', despite the presence of its proper commander, Brother Bernard the Catalan, who appeared with his title,[105] showing that a similar practice of substitution to that at Richerenches was also in operation at Saint-Gilles.

---

[98] Forey, *Aragón*, pp. 268–269.
[99] 'Bernardi Catalani et Gisberti de Costabella eisdem domus preceptores', *Saint-Gilles(Temple)*, fol. 122r (1195); *ibid.*, fol. 138r (1196) where they are both given the title 'preceptor'.
[100] see M. Bulst-Thiele, *Sacræ domus militiæ Templi Hierosolymitani magistri*, Göttingen, 1974, pp. 99–105; Forey, *Aragón*, pp. 55–56.
[101] S. Puig y Puig, *Episcopologio de la sede Barcinonense*, Barcelona, 1929, p. 157.
[102] Forey, *Aragón*, pp. 55, 83.
[103] Whether the scribe was copying what was on the original charter, or was confused by his own knowledge of Brother Arnold, it is impossible to say.
[104] *Saint-Gilles(Temple)*, fol. 97v (1170).
[105] *ibid.*, fols. 31r–32r (1172).

The styling given such visiting dignitaries at Saint-Gilles, as at Richer-enches, was 'master', to avoid confusion with the commander. Further exami-nation of the cartulary reveals that in each and every of the twenty-four other mentions of Brother Arnold, although he was the 'master of Provence and parts of Spain', he was only ever titled 'master'.[106] This title could sometimes be given to a commander,[107] but it is most common when the vernacular was being used: *lo maistre*.[108] Amongst the titles habitually used by commanders when being styled in Latin were *preceptor, regens, procurator, administrator, con-servator, commendator* and *rector*.[109] However, it is unwise to fix these titles, since the most striking feature to emerge from the documents, for both Orders, is that the use and assumption of the varying titles was fluid and inconsistent.

Thus, it is clear that both Orders had a similar structure in that they based their European operations about a tripartite chain of command, although a fundamental difference was that the Hospital had a senior commandery in the priory with an associated official. This does not imply that the Hospital was more bureaucratic, for the Templars had more regional officials. Accordingly, it developed a system of protocol whereby visiting dignitaries were accorded the honorary command of a house. Moreover, far from having a horror of 'administrative specialists', as a leading historian has claimed,[110] the system of rotation in the Temple positively encouraged the accumulation of administra-tive experience by its high ranking brethren.

The Familia *and the* Societas

In addition to the members of the Orders, commanders exercised power over labourers, artisans, cattle-men, and others employed to ensure the smooth running of the Orders' houses and land. Some of the necessary manual tasks were performed by sergeant-brothers, who brought their trades from their secular life,[111] but the Orders retained large numbers of additional, skilled workers.

---

[106] *ibid.*, fols. 52rv (1171); 31r–32r (1172); 26rv; 46v–47r; 24v–25r; 93rv; 201rv; 205rv (1173); 47v–48r; 195v–196r (1174); 196rv; 202v; 196v–197r; 200rv (1175); 55rv; 202rv (1176); 14rv; 39r; 65rv; 66rv (1177); 28rv; 191v–192v (1178); 30rv (1179); 62v–63r (1180).

[107] *ibid.*, fols. 199v–200r (1173).

[108] *inter alia: Prov*, no. 201, pp. 189–190 (1182); *Vaour(Temple)*, no. 13, pp. 10–11 (1175).

[109] To take just the example of *Saint-Gilles(Temple)*, *inter alia*, fols. 3v–4r (1154); 26v–27r (1161); 154rv (1162); 153v–154r (1165); 155rv; 188v–189r (1166); 150v (1172); 142v–143r (1173).

[110] Demurger, *Temple*, p. 193.

[111] 'quilibet fratrum, intrans religionem Hospitalis, servitio quod ipse in seculo exercebat in

There are no sources upon which to base an examination of the 'family' of the Order in Occitania in the twelfth and thirteenth centuries.[112] Yet a source from 1338 provides valuable information. Although of the fourteenth century, this document may reflect longstanding practice in the field of the management of an agricultural patrimony, where few significant changes in the techniques and tools used had been effected since the twelfth century.[113]

The document is the Hospitaller 'Visitation' of the priory of Saint-Gilles.[114] Similar visitations for all priories were commissioned contemporaneously by Pope Benedict XII in Avignon with a view to reforming the Order, that it might be returned to a fit condition to re-engage in Outremer.[115] The Hospitallers' lands had swollen by their assumption of the Templars' property in Occitania, and one regret is that the visitation does not highlight those properties which had formerly been Templar. However, it does brush on the fate of a few Templars who had survived the suppression of the Order. In Provence two ex-Templars were being sheltered in Hospitaller commanderies, and they were still given the respect of their Templar origin. Brother Raymond of Aurayata lived in the Hospitaller commandery at Ruou, and was noted as *Templarius*;[116] whilst at Valence, Brother John of Morazas,

> former brother of the Temple, had [all provided for him], in the said house or bailiwick, just as a brother of the Hospital.[117]

The expense lists of the visitation deal in detail with those employed or bound to the Order. Many of them ate in the commanderies, and were clothed, shod and paid by the Order. At Trinquetaille, listed amongst others were servants, millers, carpenters, gardeners, pigmen, the three pages of the

domo Hospitalis utatur, vel alio si extiterit ei commissum', *CH*, II, *Statutes of Brother Alfonso of Portugal* (1204x1206), no. 1193, pp. 31–40.

[112] The situation is different for England, where the twelfth century *inquisitio*, written in 1185x1195, is preserved amongst the books of the Exchequer (Public Record Office, King's Remembrancer, Miscellaneous Books, Series I [E. 164], Number 16). This is the source used by B. Lees, *Records of the Templars in England in the Twelfth Century*, London, 1935.

[113] The greatest change and slow down did not occur until the second and third decades of the fourteenth century, G. Hodgett, *A Social and Economic History of Medieval Europe*, London, 1972, p. 201; Carcenac, pp. 85, 129.

[114] 56H123 (1338). It has been integrally transcribed, *Visites générales des commanderies de l'ordre des Hospitaliers dépendantes du grand prieuré de Saint-Gilles (1338)*, B. Beaucage (ed.), Aix-en-Provence, 1982.

[115] The visitation from England also survives: *The Knights Hospitallers in England; the Report of Prior Philip de Thames to the Great Master Elyan de Villanova for* A.D. 1338, L. Larking and J. Kemble (eds.), London, 1856.

[116] *Visites*, p. 264.

[117] 'olim frater Templi, habet in dicta domo seu baiulia sicut unus frater Hospitalis', *ibid.*, p. 75.

commander, the page of the sub-commander, cowherds, butchers, farmers, carters, grooms, launderers, swineherds and bakers. As well as this permanent staff, professionals were also on the pay roll. At Trinquetaille and other houses such as Marseille, advocates were charged with taking care of the houses' legal interests, and a *procurator* was kept to ensure the smooth running of dispute-resolution. Physicians were also paid retainers, such as a doctor and a surgeon at Trinquetaille.[118]

Amongst the officials who managed aspects of the life of a commandery, a few can be noted. By the fourteenth century the Templars had moved to employing laymen to administer their lands: bailiffs in Catalonia, and bailiffs and justiciars in Aragon.[119] Similar practices were almost certainly in operation in twelfth and thirteenth century Occitania, but there is no evidence. In the Iberian peninsula the Templar commander was usually assisted by a chamberlain (*camerarius*),[120] the thirteenth century Occitanian equivalent of whom was the *cambrerius/cambrier*,[121] not the cellarer (*claviger/clavier*).[122] In the Order of the Hospital the equivalent was the steward (*dapifer*).[123] An additional post in rural commanderies was the commander of animals, and one such can be found at Saint Eulalia, others at Montsaunès.[124]

Of the brethren, the *societas*, there is ample evidence of the presence of knights, sergeants and priest-brothers. The average Templar chapel could accommodate around twenty-five people,[125] but in both Orders numbers varied enormously. In 1338 only three Hospitallers lived at each of Venterol, La Croix and Malemort, whilst there were twenty-one at Valence, and twenty-

[118] 'Item, pro pensione medici phisici, libras tres, solidos quindecim. Item, pro pensione medici surgici, libras unam, solidos duodecim', *ibid.*, p. 614.

[119] Forey, *Aragón*, p. 190.

[120] *ibid.*, p. 270.

[121] 56H5171 (1303). The chamberlain was 'Officium monasticum, quod describitur in libro Ordinis S. Victoris Parisiensis MS cap. 10: *Ad officium Camerarii pertinent omnes census et reditus monasterii*', whereas a *cambrerius* was a draper, 'Officium monasticum a *Camerario* distinctum, cui pannorum cura præcipue erat; unde *Draperius* in quibusdam monasteriis nuncupabatur', C. du Cange, *Glossarium mediæ et infimæ latinitatis*, II, Paris, 1842, pp. 43, 49; 'Charte de la communauté de Montsaunès', A. du Mège (ed.), *Mémoires de la société archéologique du Midi de la France* 5(1842), p. 210.

[122] 'Bertrandus de Boazono, qui claviger et bajulus inerat domus supradicte', *Richerenches(Temple)*, no. 29, pp. 30–31 (1142); no. 146, pp. 134–135 (1157); *Roaix(Temple)*, no. 131, p. 83 (undated); 'Charte', p. 210; *cf.* Demurger, *Temple*, p. 193.

[123] *Saint-Gilles(Hospital)*, fols. 136v–137r; 63r; 58v–59r (1195); 60v–61r (1198); 67rv; 66v–67r (1204).

[124] 'præceptor bestiarii', Carcenac, *Larzac*, p. 98; 'las gardas del bestial', 'Charte', p. 221.

[125] Delaruelle, 'Templiers', p. 325.

nine at Manosque.[126] Not all of these brethren lived in the commandery itself. Some resided at the granges, occupying themselves with agriculture and livestock. Their existence was not necessarily any less religious than that of those living around the community chapel in the main commandery, for provision was made for them, as at the grange of Castillione, dependent from Trinquetaille, where there lived permanently a priest and a clerk.[127]

The Hospitaller visitation records a total of 72 knights, 144 sergeants, and 119 priests, making a sum total of 335 brethren in the priory of Saint-Gilles. The ratio of knights to sergeants to priests is therefore in the order of 7:14:12, more than one priest for every two lay-brothers. Numbers of priests in the Orders were high. In 1179 Master Roger of Les Moulins of the Hospital claimed that in return for alms he could organize masses to be celebrated by 14,139 priests worldwide.[128]

By contrast, information from the Trial of the Templars demonstrates a much heavier preponderance of sergeants to knights in general. Of the 193 lay-brothers brought before the papal commissioners in Paris (1310–1311) whose ranks are specified, 177 were sergeants, and only 16 were knights.[129] A ratio of slightly greater than 9:1. Trial information regarding priest-brothers of the Temple evinces a low number of priests as compared with the Hospital. Out of the 213 brethren of known rank who testified at Paris, only 20 were priests,[130] giving a ratio of 1:10, priests to lay-brothers. By contrast, in Cistercian houses the ratios fell somewhere in between those of the Temple and the Hospital. In 1167 at Rievaulx the ratio of choir-monks to *conversi* was 3:10. At Pontigny at around the same time it was 1:3, and at Himmerod in 1224 it was also 3:10.[131]

The large number of Hospitaller priests in the priory of Saint-Gilles gave rise to a special post: the *prior clericorum/ecclesie*, a senior priest put over the others. He was principally resident at Saint-Gilles,[132] and at times acted as the

---

[126] *Visites*, p. 24 (Venterol); p. 200 (La Croix); p. 564 (Malemort); p. 75 (Valence); p. 333 (Manosque).

[127] *ibid.*, p. 596.

[128] Riley-Smith, *Knights*, p. 235.

[129] Forey, 'Recruitment', p. 144. Only a dozen brothers are given no rank, so the maximum number of knights could only have been just under thirty.

[130] *ibid.*, p. 158.

[131] Walter Daniel, *Vita Ailredi abbatis Rievall'*, F. Powicke (ed.), London, 1950, p. 38; M. Toepfer, *Die Konversen der Zisterzienser. Untersuchungen über Ihren Beitrag zur mittelalterlichen Blüte des Ordens*, Berlin, 1983, pp. 53–54.

[132] *Saint-Gilles(Hospital)*, fols. 180v–181r (1171); 140rv (1180); 14v–15r (1185); 59rv (1192); 55v; 55rv (1194); 56rv; 63r (1195); 60v–61r (1198); 38rv; 37v–38r (1202); 133rv (1205).

grand-prior's deputy.[133] The Templars did not adopt a similar command structure for their priests. This cannot be explained by the numerical inferiority of Templar priests as suggested by the unsafe Trial information alone. There was certainly a lower incidence of Templar priest-brothers on witness lists, but this proves little. For example, the 1306 Hospitaller inventory of Aix listed all the brethren, but included no priests. Yet, it can be confirmed that in 1338 there were fifteen priests resident at Aix.[134] The inventory of the Templar commandery of Saint Eulalia certainly implies that numbers of Templar priests were similar to those in the Hospital. That is, around four priests per commandery, for their chapel inventory contained five sets of robes for feast days, and four priest's robes with gold trimmings.[135] Although Saint Eulalia was a major commandery, similar numbers of vestments were also recorded at the much smaller La Cavalerie.[136] The lack of any hierarchy of Templar priests means only that the Order took the strictures of the bull *Omne datum optimum* seriously, and kept the priests in direct subordination to the master.

As to the non-brethren attached to the various commanderies, the statistics regarding affiliates are surprising, for their number was low. The term *confrater* does not appear in the visitation. All affiliates were termed '*donati*', and classified as noble, or not. The low number of *confratres* is explicable, for only those living in the commandery or on the Order's land were included. Nevertheless, 224 were recorded, of whom the vast majority, 159, were noble. In addition, there were 27 ordained *confratres*, and 5 women, making a total of 259, giving a ratio of almost 3:2, brethren to donats.

As with their secular counterparts, knights of the Military Orders required squires.[137] Each Templar knight was permitted one squire, each Hospitaller two.[138] As in northern French society, Occitania knew two kinds of squire (*escudier*): the paid commoner, and the young aspirant knight, who could take

---

[133] 'preterea ego frater Raimundus de Alignano prior ecclesie in hoc locum preceptoris tenens', *ibid.*, fol. 133rv (1205).

[134] *CH*, iv, no. 4708, p. 124 (1306); *Visites*, p. 450.

[135] *Saint Eulalia(1308)*, p. 258.

[136] *ibid.*, p. 260.

[137] *RTemp.*, *Primitive Rule*, caps. 19, 26, 31, 51, 66, 67, 68, pp. 30, 35, 39, 54, 65–66, 66, 67–68; *Hierarchical Statutes*, caps. 77, 94, 99, 101, 110, 120, 130, 132, 138, 140, 132, 143, 144, 149, 157, 158, 162, 175, 176, 177, 178, 179, 180, 181, 183, pp. 75, 83–84, 86–87, 88–89, 94, 100, 105–106, 106–107, 109–111, 111–112, 113, 113, 113–114, 116–117, 121–122, 122, 124, 130–131, 131–132, 132, 132–133, 133, 134, 134, 135; *Conventual Life*, caps. 286, 305, 323, 326, pp. 172–173, 179–180, 188, 189; *CH*, ii, *Statutes of Brother Alfonso of Portugal* (1204x1206), no. 1193, pp. 38–39.

[138] *RTemp.*, *Primitive Rule*, cap. 51, pp. 54; *CH*, iii, *Statutes of Brother William of Villaret* (1302), no. 4574, cap. 14, p. 39.

up service as a *donzel*, or attendant.[139] In both Orders squires were paid commoners.[140] They appear rarely as witnesses, but some held positions of prestige: Squire Armand of the Hospital of Avignon styled himself 'squire of the commander'.[141] On an occasion when squires Durand and Gerald of Saint-Gilles were listed as witnesses, the former was in precedence over the latter, owing to their ranks: squires to the prior and commander of Saint-Gilles respectively.[142] Simple squires to knights of the Orders also appeared, such as Squires Pons, Rostang and William at Trinquetaille.[143] In the Temple the squires preferred to use the name of their lord. In 1171 Squire Bernard styled himself 'squire of Hugh of Barcelonne', the current master of Provence. As with the Hospitallers, simple squires to knights of the Temple appeared under their own names, such as Squire Stephen, who was recorded three times at Saint-Gilles.[144]

The Hospitaller visitation provides evidence not only of personnel, but also of materials, and gives an idea of the heavy incidental expenses. Money was disbursed on food, clothes, tallow candles for the illumination of commanderies, white wax candles for the chapel, sustenance for the animals, food for the dogs which guarded the horses, raw materials such as wood and metal for repairs and shoeing horses, expenses related to the annual visitation of the prior of Saint-Gilles, and the commanders' costs whilst travelling to chapters and on other business.[145]

To summarize, the responsibilities of a commander covered the well-being of a broad range of people, as well as the maintenance of buildings, and general leadership as head of the house. Another function not yet mentioned was that of local seigneur. This made him responsible for legal matters affecting the commandery's tenants and lands. It is an important area which has received no treatment in any work on the Orders, and which will be examined next.

---

[139] For a full discussion of the distinctions between the two see L. Paterson, 'The Occitan Squire in the Twelfth and Thirteenth Centuries', *The Ideals and Practice of Medieval Knighthood, Papers from the First and Second Strawberry Hill Conferences*, C. Harper-Bill and R. Harvey (eds.), Woodbridge, 1986, pp. 133–152.

[140] Barber, *Knighthood*, p. 190; Riley-Smith, *Knights*, pp. 240, 322; *The Rule, Statutes and Customs of the Hospitallers*, E. King (ed. and tr.), London, 1934, p. 48 n. 2.

[141] *Avignon(Hospital)*, fols. 75r–76v (1227).

[142] *Saint-Gilles(Hospital)*, fol. 77v (undated), but Peter of Ista Villa was commander.

[143] *Trinquetaille(Hospital)*, no. 166, p. 151 (1178); no. 177, pp. 169–170 (1187); no. 165, pp. 150–151 (1188); no. 196, pp. 190–191 (1191).

[144] *Saint-Gilles(Temple)*, fols. 48v–49r (1191); 82rv; 180rv (1192).

[145] *Visites*, pp. 595, 612 (Trinquetaille), p. 583 (Saliers).

The Courts of the Commanders

A commander was responsible for members of the *familia* and tenants on the commandery's lands. To this end he presided over a seigneurial court, known as the Court of the Commander. The Court enforced tenurial obligations, and also tried offenders among its tenants. Thus, in 1295 John Durand could stand accused in the Templar commandery of Montfrin of having:

> maliciously wished to deflower and have carnal knowledge of a certain young virgin named Michaela.[146]

Offences were proclaimed by a crier, and a list of such proclamations read annually at Saint-Christol and Montfrin by order of Brother Gaspard of Barras included formulations such as the following:

> Item. It is prohibited and forbidden to all persons of whatever estate or condition to swear, blaspheme or deny the name of God, the glorious Virgin Mary or the saints of Paradise on pain of a fine of 100 *sous*, payable to the commander, for the first offence; for the second, to have their tongue pierced, or other lawful punishment.[147]

These cries fulfilled the same role as the civic penal statutes to be found in major towns such as Marseille, Aix, Grasse and others.[148] Clearly, the sanctions available to a commander with which to punish members of the Order were unsuitable for punishing the laity.[149] Rather, the seigneurial sanctions of the high and low justice were enforced. The distinction between high and low

---

[146] 'quandam puellam virginem nomine Michælis maline eam voluit deflorare et carnaliter cognoscere', 56H5252 (1295).

[147] 'Item est prohibé et deffendu à toutte personne de quelque estast ou condition qu'ilz soient jurer, blasphemer ny renier le nom de Dieu, de la glorieuse Vierge Marie, saintz et saintes de paradis, sur peyne de cent soulz d'esmande pour la permiere fois, aplicable au s'commandeur; pour la seconde, d'avoir la langue percée, et autres de droict', 56H4872 (undated).

[148] R. Lavoie, 'Les Statistiques criminelles et le visage du justicier: Justice royale et justice seigneuriale en Provence au Moyen Age', *PH* 28(1979), p. 8.

[149] In the Hospital: (1) the permanent loss of the habit (2) the loss of the habit (3) the quarantaine, (4) the septaine and (5) the deprivation of wine and food, *CH*, II, *Esgarts*, no. 2213, cap. 58, p. 544 and *passim; ibid.*, I, *Rule of Brother Raymond of Le Puy*, no. 70, cap. 10, p. 65; III, *Statutes of Brother Hugh Revel* (1262), no. 3039, cap. 6., p. 45. In the Temple: (1) expulsion from the House (2) loss of the habit (3) retention of the habit for the love of God (4) two or three days punishment per week (5) two days punishment per week (6) one day punishment per week (7) punishment on Fridays and corporal punishment (8) referral to others, and (9) being sent to the chaplain brother. *RTemp., Penances* and *Further Penances*, caps. 224–272, pp. 153–166; caps. 544–656, pp. 285–336.

justice is important. High justice corresponded to the ancient jurisdiction of the Carolingian counts: competence in all criminal matters with the death penalty as a sanction, and the exterior sign of this jurisdiction was the right to erect gibbets. Low justice, on the other hand, comprised competence in all criminal matters not carrying the death penalty, along with civil matters of lesser importance.[150]

Jurisdiction was tied to the land, and is often mentioned as having passed with title in a deed of sale. In 1263 Berenger Guillen, seigneur of Clermont, sold Liausson to the Hospital at Nébian for 5,000 *sous*, and he specifically mentioned the transfer of jurisdiction.[151] Such transfers occurred not only in sales, but also in gifts. In 1185 Count Raymond of Mauguis donated the jurisdiction of Berrias, a future commandery, to the Temple at Jalès.[152] The property subsequently became disputed, and in 1267 the seneschal of Nîmes ruled that the entire jurisdiction now belonged to the Temple.[153] Possession of certain jurisdictions could lead to extra responsibilities. In Aix in 1218 a document was drawn up between the city, the archbishop and all Orders stipulating that the financial burden of the upkeep of the city's fountains, bridges, and roads would be defrayed by all of them.[154] Such responsibilities could also lead to participation in consulates. In 1329 the Hospitaller commander of Jalès was recognized to be a co-seigneur of Saint-Marcel, owing to the Order's interests there, and he was permitted to become a consul of Saint-Marcel in recognition of this.[155] A graphic example of the Order's total control of an area is the overturning by the legate to the Holy See, on the advice of the archbishop of Aix and the bishops of Riez, Fréjus, Cavaillon and Sisteron, of acts passed by the consuls of Manosque, because the entire jurisdiction of Manosque belonged solely to the Hospitaller bailiff.[156] Such jurisdiction did not only pass with the land, people could also bring themselves under the jurisdiction of the courts by vassalage to the Orders.[157]

Wherever possible the Military Orders shared jurisdiction with local seigneurs in order to divest themselves of the high justice and its ensuing sanctions of death and mutilation. In 1253 a judge of Béziers made a ruling on the jurisdiction of the seigneury of the Mas de Jonquière, contested between the Hospital at Nébian and the seigneur of Clermont. The hearing had been prompted by a catalogue of cases justiciable under the high justice. The judge ruled that

---

[150] M. Mourre, *Dictionnaire encyclopédique d'histoire*, Paris, 1978, p. 2448.
[151] 56H4361 (1263).
[152] 56H5236 (1185).
[153] 56H5236 (1267).
[154] 1G407 (1218).
[155] 56H4578 (1329).
[156] 56H4652 (1211).
[157] 56H4643 (1275x1282).

the seigneur of Clermont should have the competence in the pending cases of homicide, larceny and adultery, for they could entail sanctions requiring the death penalty and the mutilation of limbs, but that all remaining jurisdiction belonged to the Hospital.[158] Likewise, in 1263 the Hospitaller commander of Gap-Françès agreed with the local seigneurs of Randon and Fornel that with regard to the villages which the Order possessed on the river Dozère, all jurisdiction except blood justice would belong to the commander.[159] In 1322 a judge made a similar ruling on this point regarding the high justice of the Mas de Malavieille, La Frayasse and Crussines. It would belong to the seigneur of Fornel in the cases which entailed the death penalty or mutilation, but all the rest would be within the purview of the commander of the Hospital of Gap-Françès.[160]

The Templars also had disputes over jurisdiction. In 1287 the Templar commander of Bras appealed to the judge of appeals of Provence claiming that the judge of Hyères had taken control of a case of theft which rightly belonged to the Temple. The appellate judge ruled that the Temple possessed all jurisdiction in the area except the high.[161] Affairs did not remain settled for, in 1298, the commander of Bras had once again to petition the judge of appeals, claiming that this time the judges of Brignolles and Saint-Maximin had interfered in his jurisdiction.[162]

This sharing of jurisdiction was a matter of preference, politics, and resources. The fact that the Orders were religious bodies did not present a bar to the possession of high justice, for other religious institutions were prepared to exercise it. Benedictine monasteries had long possessed this jurisdiction, normally delegating it to a secular advocate, who presided over their manorial and feudal courts.[163] Local abbeys were sometimes prepared to shoulder this responsibility for the Military Orders. In 1265 the Hospitaller commander of Saint-Christol agreed with the abbot of Sendras, seigneur of Saint-Hilaire, that he would only retain the low justice, whilst the abbot would enforce the high justice.[164] Inevitably, sometimes the Orders did retain the high justice, and made this public. In 1299 the Hospitaller commander of Gap, Brother Raymond Osasèche, declared his jurisdiction of Peschière to be high by flying the standard of the Order from the battlements of the castle of Peschière for twenty-four hours.[165] This right was sometimes delegated. At the command-

---

158 'de quo penam corporalem . . . et membrorum mutilatione', 56H4361 (1253).
159 56H4496 (1263).
160 56H4460 (1322).
161 56H5204 (1287).
162 56H5204 (1298).
163 Lawrence, *Monasticism*, p. 132.
164 56H4929 (1265).
165 56H4394 (1299).

ery of Le Poëtlaval, Dragonnet and her husband agreed with the Hospital that they would continue to maintain the castles which her father had kept for the Order. As a sign of this, the Hospital granted her the right to fly the standard of the Order over the castles to show suzerainty.[166]

Unlawful display of the gibbet was an offence, for it suggested possession of the high justice. In 1311 John Bonfils, liege-man of the Hospitaller commander of Gap, unlawfully planted gibbets on the Order's land at Chassagnes, and was accordingly sentenced to a fine of 100 silver marks.[167] The gibbet was as much a deterrent as a symbol of justice. In 1274 the seneschal of Beaucaire conducted an enquiry into the dismantling of the Hospital's gibbets in the castle of Pillon by the *viguier* of Anduse, who had been protesting at the Hospital's assertion of its jurisdiction. After hearing the witnesses, the Hospital was adjudged in this case to be entitled to the public display of its gibbets.[168]

The Orders did have to use their gibbets. In 1324 John Leautaud was hanged by the Hospitallers for crimes of homicide, murder, theft and arson.[169] In 1280 the Templars of Saint Eulalia were instructed by the seneschal of Rouergue to proceed with trying a case of homicide, a case in which the penalty for a guilty verdict would have been death.[170] Hangings were public, as were mutilations.[171] The deterrent aspect of the gibbet was highlighted in 1283 when the Templars re-erected their gibbet at Jalès by command of the royal *viguier*. It bore a grim reminder: the body of a murderer recently hanged by the Order.[172]

Problems at Anduse continued, and its secular officials may have harboured a grudge against the Hospital. The commander of Gap-Françès appealed to the judge of Anduse over a matter he deemed to be within the competence of the Hospital. He had begun questioning witnesses concerning the whipping of women by a local bailiff, but the judge once again denied the Hospital competence to continue with its enquiry.[173] Whipping appears to have been not uncommon at Gap-Françès, for some five years later the Court of the Commander punished a group of locals for whipping girls.[174] Indeed, the Court of

---

[166] 56H4822 (1283).
[167] 56H4422 (1311).
[168] 56H4444 (1274).
[169] 56H4956 (1324).
[170] 56H5286 (1280).
[171] R. Grand, 'Justice criminelle, procèdure et peines dans les villes aux xiiie et xive siècles', *Bibliothèque de l'Ecole des Chartes* 102(1941), p. 85.
[172] 'quasdam furchas erectas seu plantatas pro domo Templi predicta cum uno suspensso qui ibi extitaverat et erat suspenssus pro dicta domo Templi de Jalezio pro homicidio quod perpetraverat in eodem loco', 56H5223 (1283).
[173] 56H4444 (undated).
[174] 56H4444 (1279).

the Commander at Gap-Françès was busy with a number of assault cases, one particular trouble-spot being the dependency of Pierrefiche. Here in 1275 Vitalis Florensac was fined 50 *sous* for having inflicted a head injury on another inhabitant. At the same time the judge dealt with another two cases of assault. One concerned an assault to the head of another inhabitant for which the guilty party was fined 40 *sous*, and the other a woman who was fined for having assaulted another woman.[175]

Minor corporal punishment was dispensed to the laity in these feudal courts. In 1266 the officers of the grand-prior of Saint-Gilles had a shepherd flogged for stealing one of the Order's lambs grazing at Canavère.[176] Such flogging was a standard penalty for theft. In 1271 the judge of the Hospitaller commandery at Gap-Françès sentenced a thief to a flogging, also for stealing from the Order's land.[177] Other possibilities included banishment, a punishment meted out by the Templars of Montfrin to a thief in 1308.[178]

As in all medieval courts, fines were the preferred sanction, for they brought substantial revenue.[179] In the eleven year period from 1289–1300 at Hospitaller Manosque, the judges of the court commuted nine sentences of corporal punishment to fines which would only revert to blood justice if the individual defaulted on the payments.[180] Moreover, the judges were careful to give these decisions weight by insisting on mitigation, such as the criminal's contrition.[181] Banishment was common, either temporary or perpetual, for it triggered the confiscation of the criminal's property, and the destruction of his abode.[182] Most theft and minor violence would be sanctioned by a fine and/or banishment, and mutilation was normally meted out to thieves to brand them.[183] The death penalty was reserved for the dangerous, the notorious and the destitute.[184]

Cases were begun by a 'crier' who summonsed the accused, as at Aix in 1306 when Matthew Frinier was publicly summonsed for having illegally minted money.[185] Cries were a formal part of the legal process. Non-compliance with the formalities vitiated the legality of an arrest, as can be seen by the Hospitaller commander of Puimoisson's application to the judge of Moustiers to have

---

[175] 56H4482 (1275).
[176] 56H4110 (1266).
[177] 56H4444 (1271).
[178] 56H5252 (1308).
[179] Grand, 'Justice', pp. 91–92.
[180] 56H831–1106 and 56H1106–4697.
[181] Lavoie, 'Statistiques', p. 15.
[182] Grand, 'Justice', p. 93.
[183] *ibid.*, p. 94.
[184] Lavoie, 'Statistiques', p. 16.
[185] 56H4204 (1306).

returned to his custody one Arnoux, who had been improperly arrested.[186] Nor were arrests legal if performed by unauthorized agents, as highlighted by the commander of Puimoisson in a complaint about the cries which the judge of Moustiers had pronounced in Puimoisson.[187] The Orders had their own prisons in the commanderies, and accused people were kept there. When jurisdiction was shared, mistakes were made, and it is clear that prisoners were transferred from secular prisons to those of the Orders, and *vice versa*.[188]

The process in seigneurial courts in the twelfth and thirteenth centuries was generally adversarial. Although there were areas where the inquisitorial system was supplanting it, owing to the ever increasing remit of canon law.[189] The exact composition of the courts of the Orders cannot be deduced from the documents. There is no indication that the Military Orders, like the Benedictines, used *advocati* to preside over their feudal courts,[190] but it is clear that legally trained personnel were sometimes employed to assist and give counsel. Up until c.1270 Occitanian lawyers (doctors and licentiates) were trained in Italy, but in the late thirteenth century *studia* of lawyers began to operate locally,[191] principally as arbitrators.[192] It has been claimed that the Hospitallers embraced the growing legalism of the later thirteenth century by employing and training lawyers, whilst the Templars neglected to adapt.[193] This is not borne out by the Occitanian evidence.

In a case concerning land rights, the Templars of Saint Maurice of Régusse employed Master Andrew of L'Isle and Andrew Diagre, a Doctor of Laws, to give opinions concerning a fault in the formalities of an infeudation.[194] The Hospitallers sometimes did the same, as at Saint-Christol where a Doctor of Laws was requested to help adjudicate a case.[195] Some brethren of the Orders even had legal training. A commander of Templar Le Bastit, Gerald of Causse,

---

[186] 56H4837 (1298x1300).

[187] *ibid.*

[188] 56H5204 (1298).

[189] Grand, 'Justice', pp. 51, 70–71, 91; A. Thomas and F. Olivier-Martin, 'Un Document inédit sur la procédure accusatoire dans la châtellenie de Bellac au XIVe siècle', *Revue historique de droit français et etranger* 14(1935), p. 710.

[190] Lawrence, *Monasticism*, p. 132.

[191] A. Gouron, 'The Training of Southern French Lawyers during the Thirteenth and Fourteenth Centuries', *La Société du droit dans le Midi de la France au Moyen Age*, Variorum (ed.), London, 1984, pp. 220, 222.

[192] A. Gouron, 'Le Rôle social des juristes dans les villes méridionales au Moyen Age', *Annales de la Faculté des Lettres et Sciences humaines de Nice* 9–10(1969), p. 56.

[193] J. Brundage, 'The Lawyers of the Military Orders', in *The Military Orders. Fighting for the Faith and Caring for the Sick*, M. Barber (ed.), Aldershot, 1994, p. 356.

[194] 56H5315 (thirteenth century).

[195] 56H4892, reclassed to 56H5315 (thirteenth century).

ADMINISTRATIVE STRUCTURES

was noted for being 'literate, and skilled in law'.[196] However, whereas members of the Military Orders were tried by chapter, over one hundred at a Templar hearing at La Fève in Outremer in 1180x1184,[197] the Courts of the Commanders could not have comprised more than select senior brethren, witnesses and attendant scribes. Information is scarce, for there is no mention of such courts in the Rules of the Orders, and the records that survive are not detailed. Consequently, the degree of involvement of brethren of the Orders in such cases is not clear, although the judges of the Templar courts could be permanent members of the commanderies.[198]

Thus, the responsibility of running seigneurial courts was another task ascribed to the Military Orders in Europe. This was inevitably a function ancillary to landholding. It is somewhat of a surprise that Military Orders should have made such strenuous attempts to avoid possession of the high justice and its attendant sanctions, yet this reinforces the distinction between the battle outposts of the Military Orders and their support commanderies. These latter made real efforts to be simple religious houses, unburdened even by the demands of a normal monastic seigneurial administration.

Conclusion

The structures developed by the Orders and put in place in Occitania were flexible. Not only did the titles of officials undergo periodic revision, but so, too, did the responsibilities that accompanied them. Whilst it is not possible to formulate lists of commanders and their dates to any degree of exactitude for all commanderies, hypotheses can be formulated which seek to explain why the lists are as fragmentary as they appear. The mechanisms whereby men could act *in loco magistri*, could be trained by means of a sub-commandership, or a less formal method, and circulated from one commandery to another (not necessarily always in the same province), demonstrate the Orders' growing awareness for the need to train and establish a class of administrators, a necessary adjunct to the effective supply of their outposts in Outremer. These men gained not only intimate working knowledge of the Order and its needs, but also experience of high level negotiation with the politically and ecclesiastically

---

[196] 'qui litteratus est et in jure peritus', *Procès des Templiers*, J. Michelet (ed.), Paris, 1861, I, p. 379.

[197] 'et fuerunt ibi bene .c. milites', in 'Lettre d'un Templier trouvée récemment à Jérusalem', F. Abel (ed.), *Revue biblique* 35(1926), p. 288.

[198] For example at Montfrin, there was listed a 'judex curie domus Templi apud Montemfrinum', E. Bonnet, 'Les Maisons de l'ordre du Temple dans le Languedoc méditerranéen', *Cahiers d'histoire et d'archéologie* 7(1934), p. 519.

influential; skills that were useful not only in Europe, but also in Outremer. The combined responsibilities of ensuring the upkeep of the fabric of commanderies, the welfare of the brethren and its 'family', the exercise of justice to brethren and those within the Orders' jurisdiction, and the role of mediating at all levels was in many senses a fast track administrative programme for men to rise within the Order.

The reason for the existence of these structures was to act as a support mechanism for the brethren in the Holy Land. The following chapter will analyse the resources they collected and dispatched: the international operation at the heart of the function of the Military Orders' activities in Europe.

CHAPTER VI

The Eastern Horizon

La rezenson e'l sepulcre breumen
als pagas fals convenra a laissar,
per que n'an fag mans homs de say crozar:
coms, dicx, marques e d'autres eyssamens;
per qu'ien prec sel qu'es visibles trinitz,
ver deu, vers homs e vers sans esperitz,
ques er lur sia esrel'e caramida
e'ls guit e'ls gart e'ls perdon lor falhida.

Olivier del Temple,[1] 'Estat aurai', in *Das
Altprovenzalische Kreuzlied*, K. Lewent (ed.),
Geneva, 1976, pp. 439–441

THE fundamental obligation of all European commanderies was to supply the Military Orders in the Holy Land with the resources required to maintain them as battle-ready, armed and provisioned fighting forces.[2] This chapter analyses the associated activities of the commanderies under four headings: the provisions in the Rules, the resources to be sent east, the Orders' sources of income, and shipping between the West and the East.

Provisions in the Rules

Throughout the twelfth and thirteenth centuries regular shipments to Outremer were undertaken by the Military Orders with no specific regulation. Yet, once Acre had fallen in 1291 the Hospital found it difficult to lure combatants overseas, and accordingly in 1302 the chapter-general stipulated how many

---

[1] Also known as the Chevalier du Temple, *Choix des poésies originales des troubadours*, M. Renouard (ed.), v, Paris, 1820, p. 272.

[2] D. Metcalf, 'The Templars as Bankers and Monetary Transfers between West and East in the Twelfth Century', *Coinage in the Latin East: the Fourth Oxford Symposium on Coinage and Monetary History*, P. Edbury and D. Metcalf (eds.), Oxford, 1980, pp. 1–17 suggests that the Temple financed itself solely from good management of its property in the Holy Land. This is a mistaken view.

brethren-at-arms were to be supplied by each Tongue. For Provence it was fifteen, a number rivalled only by France,[3] with the total from all Tongues giving a minimum garrison of eighty. It is difficult to calculate the size of the contingents prior to this. But, a great number of men were shipped in the preceding centuries to replace losses, and to take on responsibilities from conquest, acquisition and donation. Before the battle of Ḥiṭṭīn (1187) the Templars' strength in the Holy Land may have been in the order of six hundred knights, two thousand sergeants and fifty priests,[4] and in addition to these figures ought to be added in excess of a thousand paid servants: squires, cooks, pack-handlers and other retainers.

The Hospitaller Rule of Brother Raymond of Le Puy made allusion to what was later to become the responson (*responsio*): the third of each commanderies' bread, wine and food to be sent to Jerusalem.[5] This was to evolve into one third of the net income of each commandery.[6] In 1182 Brother Roger of Les Moulins provided a breakdown of the specific items to be included in the responsions from each Tongue. The grand-priors of Saint-Gilles and France were both to dispatch one hundred sheets of dyed cotton to replace the coverlets of the sick.[7] John of Würzburg related in the 1170s that fifty died in the Jerusalem Hospital every night, and their places were immediately taken by more,[8] an expensive undertaking in bed-linen alone. For ease of administration, the supply of materials was allocated by Tongue, although this practice left the Hospital vulnerable to failure of supply in the event of a local problem.[9] The receipt of responsions was also regulated. In 1206 it was ruled that if the master was not able to receive the responsions in person, they should be received by the commander, paraded before the sick, and deposited in the treasury.[10] Unconvinced that all that was due from Europe was being dispatched, Brother Hugh Revel tightened up the system in 1262 by insisting

[3] For Spain it was fourteen, Italy thirteen, Auvergne eleven, Germany seven, England five, *CH*, III, *Statutes of Brother William of Villaret* (1302), no. 4574, cap. 14, p. 39.
[4] M. Barber, 'Supplying the Crusader States: The Role of the Templars', *The Horns of Ḥaṭṭīn*, B. Kedar (ed.), London, 1992, p. 318.
[5] *CH*, I, *Rule of Brother Raymond of Le Puy* (1125–1153), no. 70, cap. 6, p. 64.
[6] W. Porter, *A History of the Knights of Malta*, II, London, 1858, p. 214; Riley-Smith, *Knights*, pp. 51, 344.
[7] *CH*, I, *Statutes of Brother Roger of Les Moulins* (1182), no. 627, p. 427.
[8] John of Würzburg, *Descriptio Terræ Sanctæ*, in *Descriptiones Terræ Sanctæ ex sæc. VIII. IX. XII. et XV.*, T. Tobler (ed.), Leipzig, 1874, p. 159.
[9] Italy, Venice and Pisa were to send two thousand ells (an ell is about 45 inches) of fustian of varied colours, Constantinople was to send two hundred felts, Antioch was to send two thousand ells of cotton cloth, whilst Tripoli and Tiberias were to send two quintals each of sugar for the syrups, medicines and electuaries to be fed to the sick, *CH*, I, *Statutes of Brother Roger of Les Moulins* (1182), no. 627, pp. 426, 427.
[10] *ibid.*, II, *Statutes of Brother Alfonso of Portugal* (1206), no. 1193, cap. 11, p. 37.

that all commanders and priors beyond the sea (in Europe) fix a responsion for their dependencies, and attach a report of these when shipping responsions to the East.[11]

Somewhat glibly, Matthew Paris claimed that the Military Orders squandered their resources by pouring them into an abyss.[12] But, as early as 1154 Pope Hadrian IV had thought the resources of the Hospital in Europe insufficient even to support the poor and pilgrims lodged in Jerusalem.[13] The problem of the paucity of resources in the Holy Land surfaced again in 1301, for the loss of the Holy Land and its accompanying revenue was of prime financial concern to the Order. Emergency measures were instituted so that all responsions were sent without fail. If this was not possible, the defaulting commander was to take the next passage to Outremer to explain the failure to the master in person.[14] Dispatching commanders to Outremer with their attendants was an expensive measure, and this statute was repealed the following year, replacing it with a mandatory written explanation.[15]

The Templars had no such provisions in their Rule. It referred simply to assets, horses, robes and grain from overseas.[16] Yet, it is clear that the Order did move large quantities of materials from West to East on an organized basis.[17] For example, a document from the Parisian Temple lists collected responsions from thirty-eight commanderies for the year 1295/1296.[18] These Templar responsions were fixed,[19] although emergency measures could be ordered, as when Master James of Molay triggered an increase in 1290 to help the Cypriot headquarters maintain the island garrison of Ruad, and sustain the pressure of the Order's naval activities against the Mamlūks in Egypt.[20]

Thus, although the Rules of the Orders make few provisions with regard to the responsions, it is clear that they had detailed working practices which ensured a proper supply of resources. Latin commentators in Outremer such as

[11] ibid., III, Statutes of Brother Hugh Revel (1262), no. 3039, cap. 20, pp. 47–48.
[12] 'et quasi in voraginem baratri demergunt', Matthew Paris, Chronica majora, Rolls Series 57, H. Luard (ed.), III, London, 1876, p. 178.
[13] E. Delaruelle, 'Templiers et Hospitaliers en Languedoc pendant la croisade des Albigeois', CF 4(1969), p. 318.
[14] CH, III, Statutes of Brother William of Villaret (1301), no. 4549, cap. 23, pp. 19–20.
[15] ibid. (1302), no. 4574, cap. 17, p. 40.
[16] RTemp., Hierarchical Statutes, cap. 83, p. 78 (avoirs); cap. 84, pp. 78–79 (bestes); cap. 107, pp. 92–93 (bestes); cap. 130 (robes); Further Penances, cap. 609, pp. 314–315 (forment).
[17] Barber, Knighthood, p. 243.
[18] ibid., p. 243.
[19] Demurger, Temple, p. 174.
[20] Forey, Aragón, p. 324.

James of Vitry were well aware that the shipment of such materials was the prime obligation of the support commanderies.[21]

Resources Sent to the East

First and most important among resources moved from Europe to the Holy Land were the regular shipments of men. There were high losses in battle, and both Orders' policy was, in principle, not to pay ransoms for brothers who fell into captivity, save for a token sword-belt and knife.[22] In addition, the policy of entrusting large castles to the Orders was dependent on substantial levels of manpower. Templar Safet housed and fed 1,700 people.[23] Of Hospitaller castles, Count Raymond II of Tripoli gave the Order the formerly Kurdish castle, Hiṣn al-Akrād (corrupted to 'Krak' of the Knights) in 1144, and forty-two years later Count Raymond III gave it the equally formidable Margat.[24] In the early years of the century Krak kept a garrison of two thousand, but by 1268 these two castles together, the only remaining inland castles which had not fallen to Sultan al-Malik Baybars, could only boast a combined contingent of three hundred knights.[25] However, manpower was needed throughout the twelfth and thirteenth centuries, for the Hospital possessed fifty-six castles,[26] and the Temple fifty-three.[27] In the twelfth century this represented 35 per cent of the lordships in Outremer.[28]

The vast majority of the Orders' brethren came from all over Europe, and the Temple and the Hospital were the only Military Orders to recruit so

---

[21] James of Vitry, *Historia Hierosolymitana*, in *Gesta Dei per Francos*, J. Bongars (ed.), Hanover, 1611, book 65, p. 1084.

[22] This was even the case for a master of the Order. Brother Odo of Saint-Amand (c.1171–1179) died in captivity as a result of this policy, Robert of Torigny, *Chronica*, Rolls Series 82, R. Howlett (ed.), IV, London, 1889, p. 288. Matthew Paris, *Chronica majora*, p. 525 spoke of a similar policy in force in the Hospital. A. Forey, 'The Military Orders and the Ransoming of Captives from Islam (Twelfth to Early Fourteenth Centuries)', *Studia monastica* 33(1991), p. 264 questions whether this was, in fact, the case, and gives demonstrations of negotiations and exchanges of captives. Nevertheless, it was certainly a wide spread belief that the Orders behaved in this way.

[23] 'Un Nouveau texte du traité "De constructione castri Safet"', R. Huygens (ed.), *Studi medievali* 6(1965), pp. 355–387.

[24] Riley-Smith, *Knights*, pp. 55, 68.

[25] R. Fedden and J. Thomson, *Crusader Castles*, London, 1957, p. 86.

[26] Forey, *Orders*, p. 59.

[27] Barber, 'Supplying', p. 315.

[28] Barber, *Knighthood*, p. 89.

extensively across national borders.[29] Of the seventy-six Templars questioned at the battle headquarters in Cyprus during the Trial (1310), only five had professed in the East. The rest came from Europe,[30] and forty of these from France and Provence.[31] Brother Stephen of Troyes spoke at the Trial of a shipment in 1297 of three hundred Templars, and other sources confirm that such shipments were the normal method for the Temple and Hospital to replace lost men.[32] The Occitanian brethren were sensitive to the needs of the Holy Land; witness the aching *sirventés* by the Occitanian Templar Richard Bonomel, who wrote his poem 'Ir'e dolors s'es mon cor asseza' ('Anger and grief have filled my heart') in 1265 following the fall of Arsuf and Cæsarea.[33] Calls for extra manpower could come for a particular engagement, as in 1291 when the Military Orders required combatants for their climactic stance against al-Ashraf Khalīl at Acre (1291).[34]

Coupled with the men, one of the most valuable resources was that which differentiated the knight and sergeant from others: his horses. Although one of the seals of the Order of the Temple depicted two knights astride one horse, this was not a realistic representation of the distribution of mounts within the Order (as Matthew Paris claimed),[35] but a symbolic representation of unity and fraternity. The Rule of the Temple allowed each knight three horses, with a fourth at the discretion of the master.[36] Hospitaller knights were initially also permitted three, but by 1302 the number had dropped to two.[37] The Templars certainly had large facilities for stabling their horses in Jerusalem, as attested to by the descriptions of their stables by John of Würzburg and Theodoric.[38]

A knight had various horses, the main battle horse being the destrier. This

---

[29] A. Forey, 'Recruitment to the Military Orders (Twelfth to mid-Fourteenth Centuries)', *Viator* 17(1986), p. 140.

[30] Barber, 'Supplying', pp. 320–321; Forey, 'Recruitment', p. 140 puts the number at seventy-five.

[31] *ibid.*, p. 140.

[32] *Papsttum und Untergang der Templerordens*, H. Finke (ed.), II, Münster, 1907, pp. 334–335; *Flores historiarum*, H. Luard (ed.), Rolls Series 95, II, London, 1890, p. 287; generally, Forey, 'Recruitment', pp. 157–162.

[33] Richard Bonomel, 'Ir'e dolors s'es mon cor asseza', in *Choix des poésies originales des troubadours*, M. Renouard (ed.), IV, 1819, no. 22, pp. 131–133.

[34] H. Mayer, *The Crusades*, J. Gillingham (tr.), Oxford, 1972, p. 273.

[35] Matthew Paris, *Historia Anglorum*, Rolls Series 44, F. Madden (ed.), I, London, 1866, p. 223.

[36] *RTemp., Primitive Rule*, cap. 51, p. 54.

[37] *CH*, III, *Statutes of Brother John of Villaret* (1293), no. 4234, cap. 5, p. 639; *Statutes of Brother William of Villaret* (1302), no. 4574, cap. 14, p. 39.

[38] They had a capacity of 2,000 horses or 1,500 camels according to John of Würzburg, *Descriptio*, pp. 129–130; Theodoric, *Libellus de locis sanctis*, M.–L. and W. Bulst (eds.), Heidelberg, 1976, pp. 26–27.

was always a stallion, around 14 hands high, weighing around 1,300 pounds.[39] The destrier was a specialized beast, and was unsuited for general transport. Accordingly, the knight would also have in his string a palfrey for normal riding, and a rouncy for his squire and armour. The loss of horses through disease and injury was high, and a constant stream of mounts was needed from Europe,[40] although there is evidence for limited breeding in Outremer.[41] Elite destriers, turcomans, were kept in the Holy Land, and these were reserved for the very high officials of the Temple.[42] The preferred source of horses for the knights was the Iberian peninsula, owing to the heavy mix of Arabic bloodlines.[43] However, raising horses was not an Iberian monopoly. Large scale stud farming was undertaken in Occitania by the Military Orders.

It was not uncommon for religious Orders to breed horses; the monks of the Cantabrian mountains in the Iberian peninsula had made a speciality of it.[44] Operating a stud farm required detailed economic planning, the main concern being the provision of winter fodder. This was crucial, as a horse spends up to twenty-two hours a day grazing. Stocks of fodder were thus essential, and the distribution had to be carefully regulated, especially as stud farming was a seasonal practice, the majority of foals being born between April and June, more than half of them in May.[45] Breeding practices had not evolved much since the time of Charlemagne: stallions were separated at the age of two, before which they ran with the dam, each stallion then being given a harem of mares.[46]

There are no specific documents of the Orders' shipments of horses from Occitania. But, the frequency with which some Occitanian commanderies used horses as payment in charity (caritative)[47] in return for valuable gifts is a good indicator of the stocks at their disposal. The Templars' main stud farm in Occitania was at Richerenches, where there may well have also been a saddlery.[48] As early as 1143, six years after the foundation of the commandery, a

---

[39] R. Davis, 'The Warhorses of the Normans', Anglo-Norman Studies 10, Proceedings of the Battle Conference, R. Allen Brown (ed.), Woodbridge, 1987, pp. 79–80.

[40] A. Hyland, The Medieval Warhorse from Byzantium to the Crusades, Stroud, 1994, p. 168.

[41] RTemp., Hierarchical Statutes, cap. 114, p. 96 refers to foals in Outremer.

[42] ibid., cap. 77, p. 75 (for the master); cap. 101, p. 88 (for the marshal); cap. 120, p. 100 (for the commander of the city of Jerusalem); cap. 169, p. 128 (for the turcopolier). The Hospitallers used the term 'turqueman/turqmanum', but it is not certain that this was an elite horse, CH, II, Statutes of Brother Alfonso of Portugal (1206), no. 1193, p. 37.

[43] Davis, 'Warhorses', p. 73.

[44] ibid., p. 73.

[45] ibid., pp. 71–72.

[46] ibid., p. 71.

[47] In Occitan it is called caritat, be e caritat, do, or be e amor, Carcenac, Larzac, p. 33. It was not an economic gift, but a spiritual one, La Selve(Temple), p. 100.

[48] Richerenches(Temple), no. 176, p. 155 (after 1145); no. 149, p. 135 (1158).

two year old foal was presented to a benefactor.[49] In the next four decades at least another twenty-four horses of all three kinds were recorded as having been given: four foals,[50] eighteen destriers,[51] one rouncy and a palfrey.[52] The charters also provide approximate prices for these mounts, the average price of a destrier during the twelfth century being 200 *sous*. It is clear that Richerenches specialized in some fine horses, for three destriers were worth 300 *sous*,[53] one 400,[54] and three as much as 500 *sous*.[55] The foals were worth from 40 to 100 *sous*, and the palfrey 60.[56] Destriers of quality were also raised at nearby Roaix;[57] one was quoted at 300 *sous*.[58] Amongst horses of lesser quality, two rouncies were given away.[59] Further towards the Toulousain, horses were also given in charity at La Selve.[60]

The lower incidence of Hospitaller gifts of horses might be indicative of smaller scale stud farming, but more probably suggests that the Hospital shipped a greater percentage of its horses to Outremer. This in turn may be linked to the evidence that the Hospital took great pride in the quality of its horses.[61] Nevertheless, some horses were donated 'in charity'. At Trinquetaille the Order gave away a horse worth 60 *sous*,[62] and a mare foal was given at Barbentane.[63] But, on the whole there is little evidence. As is to be expected,

[49] *ibid.*, no. 8, p. 11 (1143).
[50] *ibid.*, no. 11, pp. 14–15 (1144); no. 167, p. 149 (1163x1164); no. 170, pp. 150–151 (1163); no. 199, pp. 176–178 (1173).
[51] *ibid.*, no. 12, p. 16 (1144); no. 59, pp. 59–60 (1146); no. 32, pp. 34–35; no. 43, pp. 45–46 (1148); no. 75, p. 77 (1155); no. 130, pp. 124–125 (1157); no. 168, pp. 149–150 (1162); no. 100, pp. 101–102 (1164); no. 111, pp. 108–109 (1167); no. 93, pp. 94–95 (1168); no. 96, pp. 97–99 (1169); no. 104, p. 105 (1171); no. 199, pp. 176–178 (1173); no. 211, p. 188 (1175); no. 214, pp. 190–191 (1175x1176); no. 227, pp. 202–203 (1180); no. 245, pp. 217–218; no. 248, pp. 219–22) (1181).
[52] *ibid.*, no. 130, pp. 124–125 (1157); no. 189, pp. 168–189 (1163).
[53] *ibid.*, no. 130, pp. 124–125 (1157); no. 227, pp. 202–203 (1180).
[54] *ibid.*, no. 245, pp. 217–218 (1181).
[55] *ibid.*, no. 93, pp. 94–95 (1168); no. 96, pp. 97–99 (1169); no. 211, p. 188 (1175).
[56] *ibid.*, no. 11, pp. 14–15 (1144); no. 130, pp. 124–125 (1157); no. 170, pp. 150–151 (1163).
[57] *Roaix(Temple)*, no. 122, pp. 77–78 (undated); no. 125, pp. 79–80 (undated); no. 124, pp. 78–79 (1157); no. 133, p. 84 (1165); no. 139, p. 87 (1178); no. 185, pp. 133–134 (1182); no. 146, pp. 93–94 (1185); no. 163, pp. 108–109 (1207).
[58] *ibid.*, no. 163, pp. 108–109 (1207).
[59] *ibid.*, no. 105, pp. 64–65 (undated); no. 115, pp. 71–73 (1141).
[60] *La Selve(Temple)*, for example, no. 139, p. 220 (c.1160); no. 142, p. 222 (c.1170).
[61] H. Nicholson, *Templars, Hospitallers and Teutonic Knights, Images of the Military Orders 1128–1291*, Leicester, 1993, p. 131.
[62] *Trinquetaille(Hospital)*, no. 56, p. 48 (1160–1167).
[63] 56H4324 (1176).

neither Orders had many animals to give in charity in the large urban centres such as Saint-Gilles, although the Hospitallers had a 'master of pack-animals' (*magister jumentorum*) there in 1179.[64]

Along with the animals bred by the Orders, horses given to them as pious gifts were also shipped east. An example is the permission given to Brother Aymeric of Petrucia of the Temple to ship the horses and arms of a deceased knight for the use of the Order in Outremer.[65] Normally from knights, such horses would have been destriers. It comes as somewhat of a paradox then, that the Hospital was receiving considerable gifts of horses and arms at a date prior to its emergence as a Military Order c.1130.[66] For example, the cartulary from Gap contains eleven donations of horses and arms before 1121.[67] Clearly these were not part of any *traditio cum equis et armis* (a type of profession), for the majority of these gifts were to be effective only on the deaths of the donors. More importantly, the 'tradition of arms and horses' could only be contracted, for obvious reasons, with a Military Order, which the Hospital was not.[68] Two explanations seem plausible. Either the horses and arms were sold to raise money, or they were shipped to Outremer. This latter is certainly what was expected once the Order had been militarized, for in 1216 Pope Honorius III stated that horses and arms received in Europe were expressly for use in the Holy Land.[69] If this was true before the Hospital had become a Military Order, then it may have been employing mercenaries to protect its hospices, and the appearance of Constable Durand in Outremer in 1126 is suggestive.[70] The Order certainly had numerous horses in Outremer at an early date, for

---

[64] *Saint-Gilles(Temple)*, fols. 54rv (1191); 76v–77v (1192); *Saint-Gilles(Hospital)*, fols. 10v–11r (1179); 21rv (1194); 61v–62r (1197).

[65] J. Pryor, 'Transportation of Horses by Sea During the Era of the Crusades: Eighth Century to 1285 A.D.', *The Mariner's Mirror* 68(1982), p. 110.

[66] The most recent study of the militarization is A. Forey, 'The Militarisation of the Hospital of Saint John', *Studia monastica* 26(1984), pp. 75–89.

[67] *Gap(Hospital)*, no. 31, p. 25; no. 32, p. 25; no. 33, p. 25; no. 34, p. 26; no. 35, p. 26; no. 37, p. 26 (just horse); no. 47, p. 27; no. 49, p. 27; no. 57, p. 29; no. 58, p. 29; no. 61, p. 29. The editor deems all these acts to be probably pre-1121.

[68] '[La] *traditio cum equis et armis* . . . ne peut être consentie que par ceux qui pratiquent le dur métier des armes, et en faveur d'un ordre qui en fait lui-même usage', E. Magnou, 'Oblature, classe chevaleresque et servage dans les maisons méridionales du Temple au xiie siècle', *AM* 73(1961), p. 384.

[69] *Si diligenter attenditis*, H20 (1216); *Cart Hosp.*, iii, no. 1496, p. 197 (1216).

[70] Constable Durand appears in two charters, *ibid.*, i, no. 74, p. 71; no. 77, pp. 72–73 (1126); the argument for early retention of mercenaries is from Riley-Smith, *Knights*, p. 53; H. Prütz, *Die geistlichen Ritterorden. Ihre Stellung zur kirchlichen, politischen, gesellschaftlichen Entwicklung des Mittelalters*, Berlin, 1908, p. 38.

sometime during the patriarchate of Bernard of Antioch (1100–1134), the Antiochene Hospital was granted the right to build stables.[71]

However, there is also strong evidence that throughout the twelfth and thirteenth centuries gifts of horses to the Orders were seen primarily as financial, and only secondarily as of military value. There is a consistently high number of charters in which a sum of money was vowed in lieu of the horse and arms if, by the time of the donor's death, the horse and arms were in an unfit condition to be donated.[72] This can be reinforced by the incidence of substitute gifts mentioned in the charters. For example, Berenger made a gift to the Temple at Saint Eulalia c.1160 in which he wished the Order to have his horse and arms on his death, but if he had no horse, then the Order was to have his 'mellor bestia'.[73] This makes plain that the gift was ostensibly for its monetary value, for pack-animals were also shipped to Outremer. Master James of Molay of the Temple made references to these practices in a memorandum to the Holy See in 1306x1307. He phrased it to demonstrate that the competition between the Orders was a healthy rivalry, whose end result was detrimental to the Saracens:

> Item, when the Templars undertake a large shipment of men, horses, and other animals, the Hospitallers have no rest until they have equalled or bettered the quantities.[74]

The emphasis on the economic value of the horse and arms, and the inclusion of a default-gift either in money or in kind, shifts the tenor of such gifts to a financial context. This is further reinforced by the fact that knights did not always give their battle-horses. At Trinquetaille Cap Saur gave the Hospital his arms, and not his prized destrier, but his rouncy. Likewise, Raymond Laugier gave his rouncy, arms and hauberk.[75] Whilst knights could and did give the tools of knighthood to the Orders as a symbolic renunciation of the chivalric world when professing as brethren, this must not be confused with the principally economic gifts of horses and arms designed to aid the Orders in Outremer.

Another commodity of prime concern to the Orders were arms, and these

[71] *CH*, I, no. 5, p. 9 (1100–1134).
[72] For example, *Douzens(Temple)*, A no. 1, pp. 3–5 (1133); C no. 2, p. 263 is identical.
[73] *Prov*, no. 369, p. 16 (c.1160).
[74] 'Item, si Templarii faciebant magnum passagium fratrum, equorum et aliarum bestiarum, Hospitalarii non cessabant donec similem fecissent vel plus', James of Molay, *De unione Templi et Hospitalis ordinum*, in *Le Dossier de l'affaire des Templiers*, G. Lizerand (ed.), Paris, 1923, p. 8.
[75] *Trinquetaille(Hospital)*, no. 187, pp. 181–182 (1194); no. 188, pp. 183 (c.1300).

were to be found in the commanderies in the West. The Rule of the Templars related an incident that occurred in Occitania:

> It happened that a brother tried out a sword at Montpellier, and the sword broke. The brother came this side of the sea, and pleaded mercy for this matter, and the brothers condemned him to lose the habit, then permitted him to keep it for the love of God.[76]

This demonstrates not only the presence of weapons, but also the high value attached to them. Loss of the habit and subsequent retention of it for the love of God was one of the severest penalties meted out by the chapter.

Not all arms were amassed in cities from which ships might carry them to Outremer. Some were kept in commanderies as part of their permanent arsenals.[77] Many arms may have been shipped in bulk, but it is possible that knights of the Orders were expected to use their arms from before their professions (all had to be of arms bearing age),[78] albeit that their weapons had become communal property. However, this does not account for the arms of the sergeants. These were essentially identical to those of the knight, and they were distributed 'according to the means of the house'.[79]

The Orders certainly had forges in Outremer. The Rule of the Temple told of a brother working at the forge at Safet who went absent without leave,[80] and at the Trial there was a brother-blacksmith who had been at Chastel-Blanc.[81] It also mentioned twice that if a brother was working at the forge with the furnace heated, he was excused attendance in chapel.[82] There was undoubtedly a forge at each battle commandery for the inevitable repairs to weapons and mail, but that does not imply that the more complex and specialized items were manufactured there. As most metal was imported into the Holy Land,[83] this would have increased the cost of manufacture considerably. Rather, the Orders' communal arms were procured in four ways: by express

---

[76] 'Il avint que un frere essaia une espée a Monpeillier, et l'espée brisa; et le frere vint deça mer et cria merci de ceste chose et li frere li regarderent l'abit, puis li laissierent por Dieu', *RTemp.*, *Further Penances*, cap. 607, p. 314.

[77] For example at Manosque, 56H4364 (1299).

[78] *RTemp.*, *Primitive Rule*, cap. 14, p. 25.

[79] 'selonc l'aise de la maison', *ibid.*, *Hierarchical Statutes*, cap. 141, pp. 112–113.

[80] *ibid.*, *Further Penances*, cap. 570, p. 297.

[81] Barber, *Knighthood*, p. 192.

[82] *RTemp.*, *Hierarchical Statutes*, cap. 146, p. 115; *Conventual Life*, cap. 300, p. 178 ('le frere de la grosse forge').

[83] J. Pryor, 'In subsidiam Terræ Sanctæ: Exports of Foodstuffs and War Materials from the Kingdom of Sicily to the Kingdom of Jerusalem, 1285–1284', *Asian and African Studies* 22(1988), pp. 127–146.

manufacture, by donation, as spoils of war,[84] and by recycling, for it was in the Templar under-marshal's power to gift an old sword to any brother.[85]

The responsion was only one third of the income of the commandery, and this demonstrates that even given the more expensive lifestyle of the brethren in Outremer, who also increased their income by raiding, ransoming and protection money,[86] the greater part of the money raised in Europe remained in Europe. This was simply because more members of the Orders resided in Europe than in Outremer. Donors were aware of this, and that their gifts might end up on either side of the Mediterranean, as testified to by a gift to Templar Jalès in 1244:

> to the Blessed Mary, and all the brothers in the holy religion of the house of the Temple serving the Lord this side and beyond the sea.[87]

There was a realization among donors that the European houses of the Orders were part of an organization with a broader aim, as illustrated by a gift made:

> to the house of Richerenches, which is built for the edification and sustenance of the militia which is constituted in the Temple of Jerusalem.[88]

These European commanderies had to create wealth for their own survival as much as for provisioning the Holy Land. Accounts remain which testify to the price of building and maintenance work from the Temple at Saint-Gilles. For 'building and rebuilding', and for the price of five vases and two wine pitchers, Brother Bernard the Catalan dispensed 1,000 *sous* in 1208.[89] Some of the commanderies knew periods of great prosperity. In 1286 Brother William of Villaret, later to become master of the Order, then prior of Saint-Gilles, made a presentation to the church of the Hospitallers of Aix, comprising a silver cross of twenty-two marks garnished with emeralds and other precious stones, a finger of Saint Mary Magdalene encased in silver, an image of Saint Veronica which he had brought from Rome, two silver bowls (one embellished with a cross, the other with his arms), a missal with gold clasps, a cushion with gold

---

[84] Usāmah ibn Munqidh, *Kitāb al l'tibār*, in D. Nicolle, 'Arms and Armor Illustrated in the Art of the Latin East', *The Horns of Ḥaṭṭīn*, B. Kedar (ed.), Jerusalem and London, 1992, p. 327.

[85] *RTemp., Hierarchical Statutes*, cap. 173, pp. 129–130.

[86] For example, the Temple received 2,000 dinars each year from the Assassins in the early 1170s, Forey, *Orders*, p. 99.

[87] 'et beate Marie et omnibus fratribus in sancta religione domus Templi domino servientibus citra et ultra mare', 56H5220 (1244).

[88] 'domus de Richarensis, que edificatur ad edificacionem et sustentationem milicie quę est in Templo Ierosolimitani constituta', *Richerenches(Temple)*, no. 19, pp. 22–23 (1143).

[89] 56H5175 (1208).

tassels, and a cloth of gold.[90] The Orders were affluent, and the next section will discuss their principle sources of revenue.

Income

The primary source of income for both Military Orders was rent payable on lands which they owned. Their proprietary interests were diverse, being landlords both in cities and over large swathes of farm-land. In Arles a list of rents owed to the Hospitaller commandery at Trinquetaille (pre-1212) attests to the Orders holdings in the city itself. Their most expensive properties cost the tenants 150 *sous* per year, whilst at the lower end of the market small dwellings could cost as little as 3 *deniers*, although the average was somewhat higher.[91] Vested interests in some towns sometimes placed restrictive covenants on alienations of land to prevent the Orders from acquiring more property. In Avignon in 1184 the provost rented a house on the market-place near the butcher's-shop to a citizen, with a restrictive covenant excluding the tenant from alienating the property to a Templar or Hospitaller.[92] A similar condition was imposed at some time before 1201 when the same provost rented out land near the church of Saint Michael.[93] In the 1220s similar restrictions were also enforced in Arles.[94]

The rents which the Orders exacted from agricultural holdings were habitually a mixture of monetary payment and payment in kind. At Trinquetaille payments involved a mixture of wheat and barley as well as money. For example, a certain piece of land owed:

> ten sextaries of wheat, and another ten sextaries of barley, which the [tenant] must bring to the house of Saint Thomas at the harvest at his own expense.[95]

---

[90] 56H4175 (1278).

[91] The full list is, *domi*: 150 *sous*, 100 *sous*, 25 *sous*, 20 *sous*, 12 *sous; estares*: 10 *sous*, 10 *sous*, 7 *sous*, 6 *sous*, 5 *sous*, 5 *sous*, 5 *sous*, 5 *sous*, 4 *sous*, 2 *sous*, 2 *deniers*, 2 *sous*, 2 *sous*, 12 *deniers*, 12 *deniers*, 12 *deniers*, 6 *deniers*, 6 *deniers*, 3 *deniers*, 3 *deniers*, 3 *deniers*. One *stare* cost £6 per year, *Trinquetaille(Hospital), censier*, pp. 317–318.

[92] The other proscribed future purchasers were counts, bailiffs, or any other religious, except the church of Our Lady of Avignon. *GCN(Avignon)*, no. 5140, col. 877 (1184).

[93] This time the proscribed parties were counts, Templars, Hospitallers or any church. *GCN(Avignon)*, no. 5154, col. 882 (before 1201).

[94] L. Stouff, 'La Commune d'Arles au XIIIe siècle', *PH* 11(1961), p. 308.

[95] 'x sextarios frumenti et alios x sextarios ordei quos debet oportare suis propriis expensis in messibus in domo S. Thome', *Trinquetaille(Hospital), censier*, pp. 318–319.

The standard rent for a simple vine was two sextaries of wheat and two of barley, as well as 12 *deniers*, whilst for small vines these amounts were halved. In some instances capons (castrated cocks, fattened for the table) were accepted, too. Once again, all of these had to be taken to the commandery, or to the quayside if for shipping,[96] at the expense of the tenant,[97] Templar rents were made in a similar way. At Roaix, rent on a vine was payable as a mixture of money and payment in kind, an example being a sextary of corn and a cut of salted pig.[98]

Both Orders had expertise in the cultivation of crops,[99] and they leased land for cultivation. For example, in 1146 Hugh Botin rented the Hospital some land in Corrège for 1,000 *sous* of Melgueil, and the land would only revert to Hugh once the Hospital had completed five harvests on it. Moreover, the Hospital could use the land to recoup any losses occasioned to the harvest in the eventuality of a flood of the Rhône.[100] At other times, these arrangements could be wrapped up in mortgage and pledge agreements.[101]

Another primary source of income was cattle. In Provence these were kept and grazed locally, the large scale transhumance to the summer pastures in the Alps did not begin until the early fourteenth century.[102] Herd and flock sizes were large. In 1308 the Templar commanderies of Saint Eulalia, La Cavalerie and Fraissinette together possessed an impressive 2,098 head of livestock.[103] An instance of cattle theft from Saint Eulalia gives an intimation of numbers of animals the previous century, for the Order claimed that in 1257 Arnold of Roquefeuil stole over one thousand sheep, eighty pigs and twenty-four oxen.[104] Animals needed protection, and in 1160 Pope Alexander III wrote to the clergy of Comminges instructing them to respect the Order of the Temple's cows, which were marked with a cross showing them to be under papal protection, as were the cowherds.[105]

The Orders' privileges over cattle were as fiercely guarded as those over land. In 1182 Pope Lucius II wrote to the clergy of Roazon reproaching them for having taken tithes, at times with violence, cattle and land which the Temple

---

96 *ibid.*, no. 22, p. 21 (1181).
97 *ibid., censier*, pp. 318–319.
98 'e i. sester d'anona, e una peza doe baco', *Roaix(Temple)*, no. 137, p. 86 (undated).
99 L. Daillez, *Les Templiers et l'agriculture ou les composts Templiers*, Nice, 1981.
100 *Trinquetaille(Hospital)*, no. 259, pp. 273–274 (1146).
101 *ibid.*, no. 288, p. 291 (c.1121).
102 R.-H. Bautier, *The Economic Development of Medieval Europe*, H. Karolyi (ed.), London, 1971, p. 204.
103 *Saint Eulalia(1308)*, pp. 258–260.
104 published in A. Soutou, *La Couvertoirade*, Millau, 1973, p. 8.
105 *Audivimus et audientes*, H99 (1160).

raised and cultivated itself.[106] In 1155 it took papal intervention to establish the freedoms of the Order of the Temple in the diocese of Narbonne. Acting on a suggestion from Archbishop Arnold of Lévezon, the Holy See confirmed that all the Orders' men, beasts of burden and ploughing implements would be granted perpetual security when used in the fields, that all those who assured the execution of this would be granted remission of their sins, whilst all violators would be excommunicated. An interdict would be laid on a place to which any of the above goods had been carried until restoration was made, although such an interdict would not be effective in the cases of baptism of children and the confession of the dying. A collector was to be appointed in each area to assemble, with the help of the bishops, revenue destined for the Order, and finally that the protection of the Truce of God was to be applicable.[107] There must have been cases of quite substantial abuse to merit such strict guidelines, and such problems seem to have been endemic. Another example comes from the Toulousain, where the Holy See was forced to raise a complaint against the prior of Saint Antony of Toulouse for having fraudulently taken goods belonging to the Temple.[108]

In an agricultural society the wherewithal to sustain and maintain livestock was a commodity to be valued. Accordingly, there are many documents which testify to the management of grazing rights,[109] for stray flocks grazing on the land of another were likely to excite reprisals, as in 1269 when the bishop of Fréjus unlawfully seized Templar animals he deemed to be trespassing on his land at Flayosc.[110]

The grape naturally played its part in the Orders' economy in Occitania.[111] Wine was a part of the medieval Mediterranean diet, drunk at meal times, in infirmaries and at the Mass. For Hospitallers undergoing discipline, it could be withdrawn.[112] It was made for sale by the Orders, testified to by the frequent mentions of vineyards in their land transactions. Unlike in northern Europe where wine was of a poor quality, Mediterranean wine could be laid down, and vintage wines were appreciated as commodities for sale.[113] An example of the

---

[106] *Cum dilecti fili*, H45 (1182).

[107] *Sicut sacra evangelii*, H98 (1155); *Papsturkunden für Templer und Johanniter*, R. Hiestand (ed.), Göttingen, 1972, no. 27, pp. 233–235.

[108] *Dilectorum filiorum preceptoris*, H110 (1281).

[109] One example is Notre Dame de Rué where the commander had the right to graze his flocks at Flayosc, Castellane, Sallègues, Lorgues, Astros, Rué, Salerne, Peyrolles and Aiguiner, 56H5289 (1225–1277).

[110] 56H5289 (1269).

[111] G. Caster, 'Le Vignoble suburbain de Toulouse au XIIe siècle', *AM* 78(1966), pp. 201–207.

[112] *CH*, III, *Statutes of Brother Hugh Revel* (1262), no. 3039, cap. 5, p. 45.

[113] Y. Renouard, 'Le Vin vieux au Moyen Age', *AM* 76(1964), pp. 448–455.

value Hospitallers placed on their sales of wine can be seen in 1270 when the chapter at Saint-Gilles passed a resolution concerning the commandery of Puimoisson. The Order granted the locals substantial rights regarding testamentary dispositions of property, and in return the inhabitants agreed that the commandery might have a total monopoly on the sale of wine for thirty consecutive days before the inhabitants could put theirs on the market.[114] This was a considerable concession, for the Orders' produce was normally sold through markets and fairs; where, once again, the Orders had substantial privileges, like that of 1222 from the count of Toulouse which released the Hospitallers from paying the taxes normally levied at fairs and markets.[115] The Templars were also involved in viticulture. In the commandery of Saint Eulalia in 1308 the storehouse contained sixteen barrels and twelve casks, whilst at Millau there were twelve barrels, and a further six at La Cavalerie. This equates to a capacity, at Saint Eulalia alone, to store some 20,000 litres of wine.[116]

One of the Orders' most intensive activities in Occitania (and elsewhere in Europe) was milling;[117] primarily grain, but also cloth. Milling was widespread on the larger rivers such as the Rhône and the Durance,[118] as well as in the marshy lands of the Camargue. Mills were normally owned either by secular proprietors, who often delegated management to specialist millers, or by religious communities. They were frequently the objects of donation to religious Orders. For example, the Cistercians at Silvacane had considerable milling interests at Gontard gifted to them in 1168,[119] and the Cistercian abbey of Franquevaux had mills in the Camargue at a very early date.[120]

Occitan mills were principally water mills, either stretched across the rivers (boat-mills) or built onto the banks (land mills), depending on the strength of the current. On the fast flowing Garonne boat-mills were preferable, whereas smaller rivers such as the Aude were more conducive to the erection of land-mills. The essential principle required a mill race to take the water to a system of sluice gates which controlled the reservoir across which the mill, often many mills in series, was built. The mill wheel turned a horizontal pole attached to a large spoked wheel with small protruding teeth. This engaged a ribbed drum, which transmitted the turn down a horizontal pole to the mill stone.[121] A

---

[114] 56H4836 (1270).

[115] H216 (1222).

[116] *Saint Eulalia(1308)*, pp. 256–257.

[117] In England the first fulling mills were Templar, R. Holt, *The Mills of Medieval England*, Oxford, 1988, p. 153.

[118] Generally, S. Gagnière, 'Les Moulins à bateaux sur le Rhône à Avignon et dans les environs', *PH* 1(1950), pp. 75–87.

[119] 3H11 (1168).

[120] J. Cabot, *Anciens ports et moulins de petite Camargue*, Montpellier, 1991, p. 81.

[121] *ibid.*, pp. 86–87.

lucrative off-shoot from the design of these mills was a sealable basin of water, the *paxeria*, a rich source of fish. Such mill reservoirs were a major source of fish for the Orders, although permission to fish lakes and stocked waters was also traded, as in 1247 when Florence sold fishing rights in Bodel and Lauger to the Hospitaller commander of Saint-Gilles for 1,800 *sous*.[122]

The Temple was heavily involved in milling. In 1141 the seneschal of Beaucaire permitted the Temple at Saint-Gilles to build mills on the river Gardon.[123] Exactly one hundred years later further permission was given to build new mills wherever the Order wished on territory at Montfrin.[124] In 1148 the Order acquired the right to build cloth mills at Caumont on the river Orbiel, on the understanding that if the mills were built, the vendors could have cloth made up for them at no charge.[125] In 1188 Ermengard, abbot of Saint-Gilles, gave the Temple a mill at Pelamorgues,[126] and at the commandery of Saint-Maurice of Régusse in the Var the Order acquired the right to build a mill reservoir on the river Verdon.[127] These gifts sometimes came from the clergy, as in Arles when a representative of the archbishop gave the commander of Saint Lucy permission to build mills at Trébon.[128] The Hospital was no less involved in milling. In 1171 Count Bertrand of Melgueil gave the commander of Saint-Christol all rights over a mill called Salvan and another called New Mill.[129] As part of the steady flow of grants of the whole of Manosque to the Hospitallers, Count William of Forcalquier gave the Order milling rights there as early as 1175,[130] and in 1203 Viscount Dragonet of Embrun, with the consent of the count of Forcalquier, gave the Hospital mills in Vachères north of the Durance.[131]

As with any property, rights over the mills, and especially the *paxeriæ*, were often given, bought and sold,[132] processes which frequently led to disputes. A particularly protracted case arose over Templar mills called Dominical and

---

[122] 56H4875 (1247).
[123] 56H5297 (1141).
[124] 56H5297 (1241).
[125] *Douzens(Temple)*, A no. 140, pp. 128–129 (1148).
[126] *Saint-Gilles(Temple)*, fols. 43v–44v (1189).
[127] 56H5315 (1236).
[128] 56H5177 (1244).
[129] 56H4922 (1171).
[130] *GCN(Aix)*, no. 15, col. 281 (1175).
[131] 56H4415 (1203).
[132] To take just the example of Douzens: *Douzens(Temple)*, A no. 202, pp. 174–175 (1138x1139); A no. 100; pp. 95–96 (1139); A no. 61, pp. 67; A no. 13, pp. 25–26 (1141); A no. 70, pp. 72–73; A no. 52, pp. 52–53 (1142); A no. 142, pp. 130–131; A no. 144, p. 132; A no. 145, p 133; A no. 60, pp 66–67 (1147); A no. 140, pp. 128–129 (1148); A no. 54, pp. 62–63; A no. 2, pp. 6–8; A no. 50, p 59 (1152); A no. 17, pp. 29–30 (1153); A no. 141, pp. 129–130; A no. 26, p. 38 (1160); A no. 118, pp. 111–112 (1166).

New Mill. These were built at Bras, and were finally confirmed to the Order by the judge of Saint-Maximin after the verdict of the judge of Bras had been appealed by the seigneurs of Bras, who contested the ownership.[133]

An example of a developed mill complex was built by the Templars on the Aude at Brucafel. It comprised six mills in a row on the same channel, with planning permission to build as many as desired. The Order rented it out to Arnold of Carcassonne and others on the conditions that they were paid twenty sextaries of wheat and twenty of barley each year, and that they could mill, at no charge, four sextaries of wheat per week along with an entitlement to half of all the fish caught in the *paxeria*. A benefit of renting from the Temple was that the Order, protecting their own interest as much as anything else, agreed to provide guards for the complex.[134]

Free use of a mill was often an integral part of a rent agreement. In 1148 Peter Aymeric of Conques and his family gave the Temple land at Caumont near the river Orbiel. The land was suitable for the erection of mills, and Peter stipulated that if the Order were to build mills there, he wished to have his cloth milled for free.[135] It was no accident that the Order had acquired this land from Peter Aymeric, for the previous year they had bought up four other sets of rights over the area.[136] Evidently, they had a milling development in mind and unsurprisingly, after so concerted an effort to acquire the property, there is mention in 1160 of Templar milling activity at Caumont.[137]

Further sources of income included banking and money lending.[138] Not only were commanderies strong houses in which valuables could be kept safely, and money could be deposited (a speciality of the Paris and London Temples), but it was possible to raise money from the Orders. As demonstrated in chapter four, individuals raised money for pilgrimage by pledging land to the Orders as security. This reciprocal loan circumvented the laws of usury.[139] In the case of the Temple it was also possible to have an international 'current account'. Money deposited in Europe could be withdrawn in the East, and *vice versa*. An example of this can be seen in the case of the Catalan knight William of Pujolt, who deposited 2,600 *livres* in the East, and withdrew it back in Catalonia from the commandery of Saint Mary of Palau-Solita.[140] This has long been accepted

---

133 56H5203 (1283).
134 *Douzens(Temple)*, A no. 118, pp. 111–112 (1166).
135 ibid., A no. 140, pp. 128–129 (1148).
136 ibid., A no. 139, pp. 127–128; A no. 142, pp. 130–131; A no. 144, p. 132; A no. 145, pp. 133 (1147).
137 ibid., A no. 41, pp. 129–139 (1160).
138 For an excellent survey of these activities, see Barber, *Knighthood*, pp. 266–279.
139 Metcalf, 'Templars', p. 12.
140 M. Vilar Bonet, 'Actividades financieras de la orden del Templo en la Corona de Aragón', *VIIᵉ Congreso de historia de la Corona de Aragón*, Barcelona, 1962, p. 577.

as a service the Temple provided,[141] but there are very few such examples. The loss of the Templar central archive precludes verification of many of these transactions, but such information may well have been lost in any event. The customs of Toulouse of 1288 relate that loan contracts, once discharged, were stamped or destroyed.[142]

It is more likely that the system operated by the Templars was a hybrid of the pledge and letters of credit. The pledgor made over land to the Order in the West, and the loan from the Order was advanced upon the pledgor's arrival in the East. The benefit of this system would be that the Order made a large profit from the disparity between the usufruct and the loan, whilst the pledgor did not have to be concerned with the security risk of transporting money through port towns. Moreover, the welfare of his lands and family would be assured, for the Order would see to both, perhaps even improving the yield from the land with their superior agricultural expertise. The Hospital also provided money against pledges. Count Raymond Berenger IV of Barcelona gave his lands as security for a loan from the Order of 1,500 *morabotins*;[143] and both Counts Raymond Berenger IV and Alfonso I borrowed extensively from the Military Orders in the furtherance of their dynastic ambitions in Occitania.[144]

Additionally, the Templars acted as straightforward money-lenders. The amount of money dispensed from the treasury of the Temple during Saint Louis' Egypt Crusade is testimony enough to this.[145] Another example was the loan granted by the Order to the needy King Baldwin III after the death of Prince Raymond of Antioch in 1149.[146] With regard to 'interest rates' (*lucra*), the Templars charged between 16 to 33%, rates typical of the period.[147] Also, both Orders had a reputation as secure couriers for money. Abbot Suger and King Louis VII used the Templars for this purpose in 1148, and Suger was contemplating using the Order again the following year to transport money raised from his abbey's estates.[148] More complex, the levy of 1185, a precursor

---

[141] For example, J. Richard, *The Latin Kingdom of Jerusalem*, J. Shirley (tr.), Amsterdam, 1979, p. 116.

[142] P. Amblard Larolphie, 'Le Crédit à Toulouse et dans le Toulousain (1140–1208)', *AM* 10(1944), p. 7.

[143] *CH*, I, no. 266, pp. 200–201 (1158).

[144] S. P. Bensch, *Barcelona and its Rulers, 1096–1291*, Cambridge, 1995, pp. 206–207.

[145] John of Joinville, *Histoire de Saint-Louis*, N. de Wailly (ed.), Paris, 1868, ch. 75, pp. 134–136.

[146] *Epistola a. dapiferi militiæ Templi*, in *Recueil des historiens des Gaules et de la Frence* 15, M. Bouquet *et al.* (eds.), Paris, p. 540; J. Phillips, *Defenders of the Holy Land, Relations between the Latin East and the West 1119–1187*, Oxford, 1996, p. 9.

[147] Amblard Larolphie, 'Le Crédit', p. 11.

[148] Phillips, *Defenders*, p. 111.

of the 'Saladin tithe', was to be collected in each parish by a priest, two parishioners, and a Templar and a Hospitaller.[149]

Of higher profile, both Orders were used for the collection of vow redemption monies, papal census monies and money for the papal camera.[150] Innocent III's encyclical *Post miserabile* of 1198 ushered in a climate where financial contribution to Crusade was wholeheartedly encouraged, and so the presence of Templars and Hospitallers on preaching tours may also signal that they were being used as guards for the money collected.[151] A transaction encompassing all these elements was an arrangement between Viscount Hugh of Baux of Marseille and the Templars of Saint Lucy of Arles. Hugh pledged the Order the castles of Trinquetaille (his head-quarters), Villeneuve and Méjanes, against a loan of 100,000 new *sous Raymondines*. But, the money was not to be advanced to Hugh; he wished it to be distributed, by the Templars, to a number of his creditors.[152]

Money was, of course, something which the Orders were granted by various arrangements, and it was sometimes specifically earmarked for use in the Holy Land. Amongst the richer donors of money can be noted kings. King Henry II of England (1154–1189) consecrated the very first article of his will to giving the two Military Orders in Outremer 5,000 silver marks each;[153] and King Philip Augustus of France (1180–1223), prompted to make his will by the appearance of a 'horrible comet in the west', gave 2,000 silver marks to each Order, to be shipped without fail in the passage that March.[154]

When income became scarce, special measures were taken by the Orders. A fundamental precept of canon law was that Church property was inalienable.[155] Accordingly, papal permission was required for any major sale. This can be seen during the period of inflation in the late thirteenth century. In January 1253 Pope Innocent IV allowed the Order of the Temple to liquidate assets in Provence by selling and leasing property up to a value of 2,000 silver marks.[156]

---

[149] F. Cazel, 'The Tax of 1185 in Aid of the Holy Land', *Speculum* 30(1955), p. 385.

[150] W. Lunt, *Papal Revenue in the Middle Ages*, Baltimore, 1934, I, pp. 51, 39, 118, 120, 184, 306, II, p. 492; Ralph of Diceto, *Opera historica*, Rolls Series 68, W. Stubbs (ed.), II, London, 1876, pp. 168–169; Matthew Paris, *Chronica majora*, III, pp. 373–374.

[151] See Chapter 3, p. 76.

[152] *Inventaire chronologique et analytique des chartes de la maison de Baux*, L. Barthélemy (ed.), Marseille, 1882, no. 258, p. 74 (1234).

[153] Gervase of Dover, *Chronico de regibus Angliæ*, in *Recueil des Historiens des Gaules* 17, M.-J.-J. Brial (ed.), Paris, 1818, p. 662.

[154] William Armoricus, *Gesta Philippi Augusti Francorum regis*, in *Recueil des Historiens des Gaules* 17, M.-J.-J. Brial (ed.), Paris, 1818, pp. 114–115.

[155] J. Brundage, *Medieval Canon Law*, London, 1995, p. 27.

[156] In England this was permitted up to 4,000 marks sterling, in Poitou up to 3,000 silver marks, and in France up to 6,000 marks, A. Spicciani, 'Papa Innocenzo IV e i Templari', *I*.

The papacy periodically chastised the Military Orders for selling their land, even to other Church institutions.[157] Popes Gregory X, John XXI, Nicholas III, Martin IV and Nicholas IV all promulgated the bull *Ad audienciam* to the ecclesiastics of Riez, Sisteron, Béziers, Saint-Castor (diocese of Apt), Foix, Saint-Affrique and Lescar respectively.[158] It instructed them to ensure the return of property to the Order of the Hospital which had been given by priors and brothers of the Order to the laity and ecclesiastics, either as life tenancies, temporarily, or in perpetuity. In 1304 Pope Benedict IX addressed the bull to the precentor of the church in Agde in favour of the Templars. Benedict recognized that such Templar alienations had even, at times, been effected with the consent of the Holy See, but they were, nevertheless, illicit. The precentor was to catalogue all such alienations his researches might uncover, and any resistance was punishable by excommunication.[159]

The 1338 inventory of the Hospitaller grand-priory of Saint-Gilles provides detailed information of the total revenue of the Hospitaller property.[160] A surprising feature is that the projected expenses mean the Order was running at a loss.[161] The reasons for this are readily apparent. First, the projected income and expenses were only estimates. Second, vital areas of income were not included. The same is true of the Templar commandery of Le Mas-Déu in Roussillon in 1264,[162] where the commandery and its seven dependencies had an income of around 350 metric tonnes of barley, 100 tonnes of wheat, 150 tonnes of grapes, 5,815 litres of oil, 364 hens, 50 geese, 9 pigs, 4 lambs, 115 eggs, and a small quantity of broad beans and peas. This gave a revenue of 6,246

Templari: mito e storia. Atti del convegno internazionale di studi alla magione Templare di Poggibonsi-Siena, 29–31 Maggio 1987, G. Minnucci and F. Sardi (eds.), Siena, 1989, pp. 41–65.

[157] See Riley-Smith, *Knights*, p. 347.

[158] *CH*, III, no. 3534, pp. 305–306 (1274); no. 3614, p. 344 (1276); no. 3646, p. 356 (1278); no 3754, p. 412 (1281); no. 4017, p. 522 (1288); H27 (1276); H28 (1278); H29 (1281); H30 (1288, 1290, 1290).

[159] H115 (1304).

[160] Analysed in G. Duby, 'La Seigneurie at l'économie paysanne. Alpes du sud, 1338', *Etudes rurales* 2(1961), pp. 2–36 and reprinted in *idem, Seigneurs et paysans*, Saint-Amand-Montrond, 1988, pp. 20–60. See also, *idem*, 'Techniques et rendements agricoles dans les Alpes du sud en 1338', *AM* 70(1958), pp. 404–413.

[161] B. Beaucage, 'Une Enigme des Hospitaliers de Saint-Jean de Jérusalem: le Déficit chronique des commanderies du moyen Rhône, au prieuré de Provence, en 1338', *PH* 30(1980), p. 160; J. Durbec, 'L'Exploitation des biens d'un baillage provençal des Hospitaliers de Saint-Jean-de-Jérusalem en 1338. Le Baillage de Beaulieu, entre Solliès et Hyères', *PH* 25(1975), p. 253.

[162] L. Verdon, 'Les Revenues de la commanderie templière du Mas Déu (Roussillon) d'après le terrier de 1264', *AM* 107(1995), p. 168.

sous of Melgueil. Nevertheless, there was a projected deficit of 239 *sous*.[163] This list is deficient in that it refers only to those sources of income which are related to agricultural activities. There is no mention of the Order's largest sources of revenue: neither rent nor any other financial income such as fines levied in the seigneurial court, specifically mentioned as payable to Jerusalem in 1262.[164] There are similar omissions in the Hospitaller inventory of 1338. Especially noticeable is the lack of reference to livestock.[165] Templar land was highly productive, as the Hospitallers who assimilated formerly Templar lands into their commandery of Beaulieu in the early fourteenth century were to discover, for 56 per cent of their cereals, 72 per cent of their hay, 60 per cent of their wine and around 80 per cent of their financial income came from previously Templar lands, and not their own.[166]

When the requisite provisions for the East had been assembled, they had to be shipped, and the next section will examine how this was effected. Although there is no documentation of specific cargoes being shipped from Occitania, by analogy with Apulia, where records have survived, it is quite clear that the Orders' vessels were being used to ship the resources so far discussed.[167]

Shipping

Shipping carried risks. The Military Orders did not generally have to concern themselves with the hazards of unsatisfactory contracts of carriage,[168] for they had their own ships by the thirteenth century. Shipping was especially dangerous in the Mediterranean, as piracy was rife, particularly that by Italians and Muslims,[169] and shipwreck put an end to many a Crusader's voyage.[170] There was no real distinction between a warship and a merchant ship. All had to be able to defend themselves. Mediterranean shipping was well developed by the

---

[163] *ibid.*, p. 168.

[164] *CH*, III, *Statutes of Brother Hugh Revel* (1262), no. 3039, cap. 2, p. 44.

[165] Beaucage, 'Enigme', p. 160.

[166] Durbec, 'L'Exploitation', p. 254.

[167] *inter alia*: *CH*, III, no. 3401, p. 231 (1270); III, no. 3466, p. 273 (1272); III, no. 3609, p. 342 (1276).

[168] C. Dufourcq, *La Vie quotidienne dans les ports méditerranéens au moyen age (Provence, Languedoc, Catalogne)*, Biarritz, 1975, p. 35 *et seq.*

[169] *Les Miracles de Notre-Dame de Roc-Amadour au XIIe siècle*, E. Albe (ed and tr.), Paris, 1907, pp. 240–242; R. Unger, *The Ship in the Medieval Economy*, London, 1980, pp. 122, 123, 128, 131, 132, 149.

[170] G. Constable, 'Medieval Charters as a Source for the History of the Crusades', *Crusade and Settlement: Papers read at the First Conference of the Society for the Study of the Crusades and the Latins East and presented to R. C. Smail*, P. Edbury (ed.), Cardiff, 1985, p. 79.

time of the Crusades, and fleets could be immense.[171] Of the ships which plied the Mediterranean in the period of the Crusades, the two main types were the cargo-ship and the galley.

The cargo-ship was the biggest of all ships, with a capacity of up to six hundred tons. An example from Marseille in 1330 measured over 30 metres in length, had a beam of 9.5 metres and was over 5 metres in height.[172] The cargo-ship was a sailing ship, its oars served for navigation. Twin masted, each around 20 metres high with the mainmast raked forward, these ships were rigged with lateen sails and two or three bridges. The cargo-ship continued to develop, and by 1331 Alfonso of Aragon promulgated naval ordinances which distinguished six types.[173] The complement of such a ship was around one hundred sailors, and it could carry over a thousand passengers.[174] By contrast, the galley was small and fast. Whilst it could use a square sail in the right conditions, it was principally rigged with a lateen sail set onto a raked mainmast, although its propulsion was provided by oarsmen. It was only 12 to 25 feet in length, never more than 2 metres in height, and its hull was long relative to its beam.[175]

Special ships were given over to transporting horses.[176] The horse-transports used by Crusaders were loaded via stern doors, caulked below the water line during the passage,[177] allowing the discharge of mounted knights direct onto the beaches. The capacity of these ships was large.[178] For Richard the Lion-Heart's Crusade fourteen horse transports put to sea from Marseille, each capable of carrying forty horses, forty foot-soldiers, all their arms and thirty oarsmen.[179] By the time of Saint Louis' attack on Tunis, the transports

[171] As early as 963 Emperor Nicephorus Phocas had captured Crete using an armada of three thousand ships, A. Lewis and T. Runyan, *European Naval and Maritime History, 300–1500*, Bloomington, 1985, p. 31.
[172] Dufourcq, *Vie*, p. 57.
[173] *ibid.*, p. 58.
[174] Unger, *Ship*, pp. 123–125; Dufourcq, *Vie*, pp. 57–58.
[175] Unger, *Ship*, pp. 121–122; Dufourcq, *Vie*, p. 59.
[176] This was an old science. In 762 Emperor Constantine V had assembled a fleet of eight hundred χελάνδια, each carrying twelve horses, Pryor, 'Transportation of Horses', p. 9; Robert Guiscard had also used extensive horse-transports for his attack on Dyrrachium, Anna Comnena, *The Alexiad*, E. Dawes (tr.), London, 1928, pp. 95–96.
[177] Joinville, *Histoire*, p. 36.
[178] For an illustration of one of Charles of Anjou's 1278 horse-transports, see that by J. Pryor in R. Davis, *The Medieval Warhorse, Origin, Development and Redevelopment*, London, 1989, p. 62.
[179] Richard of Devizes, *Chronicon de rebus gestis Ricardi primis regis Angliæ*, J. Stevenson (ed.), London, 1838, cap. 20, p. 17.

ordered from the Venetians and Genoese could each carry one hundred horses, their knights and attendants.[180]

In the twelfth century the Military Orders relied on the ships of others, notably the large maritime interests of the Italian peninsula,[181] but by the early thirteenth century they had their own ships.[182] It is not coincidental that at this time the strain of finding resources in the Holy Land was forcing many Latin nobles into impecunity.[183] The Military Orders were thus not only consolidating their independence in the Mediterranean, but also providing a steady stream of military traffic and hardware, as distinct from the principally commercial activities of the Pisans, Genoese and Venetians.

Barcelona and Marseille were the two greatest ports to the west of the Alps, and in Crusading ventures Marseille was preferred for the shorter voyage. It became even more important for the Temple after 1220, owing to quarrels with Frederick II which put the Adriatic off limits.[184] The Hospitallers had plans to construct hostels in Marseille and Tarascon for brethren preparing to sail to Outremer,[185] whilst the Templar official known as the 'master of the passages' was based in Marseille.[186] Also, the city provided at least one Templar ship's captain: Brother Vassayl.[187] Records of passages are scarce, but one example of the Orders' Mediterranean traffic is an affair in 1230 which demonstrates the solidarity of the Temple and Hospital when their privileges were brought into question.

The Temple and Hospital lodged a joint complaint against the commune of Marseille for its refusal to respect their maritime privileges. They petitioned Odo of Montbéliard, constable of the kingdom of Jerusalem, that he might sequester the ships and merchandise coming from Marseille to Acre, and award it to the Orders in satisfaction for their claim that the commune had occasioned them 2,000 marks worth of lost income. They claimed that they were not being permitted to exercise their privileges from the viscounts of Marseille, and others, to keep their own ships in Marseille for importing and exporting merchandise, and the carriage of pilgrim traffic. Following this hearing, and

---

180 Unger, *Ship*, p. 123.
181 An 1162 contract with the Mairano family of Venice is an example, Barber, 'Supplying', p. 323.
182 One of the first known Templar ships was at Constantinople in 1207, *ibid.*, p. 323.
183 J. Riley-Smith, *The Feudal Nobility and the Latin Kingdom of Jerusalem, 1174–1277*, London, 1973, pp. 28–32; Barber, 'Supplying', p. 315.
184 Barber, *Knighthood*, pp. 238–239.
185 *CH*, III, no. 4284 (1295), p. 667; Riley-Smith, *Knights*, p. 362.
186 'qui tunc erat magister passagii, cujus nomen ignorat, existens Marsillie', *Procès des Templiers*, J. Michelet (ed.), I, Paris, 1841, p. 458.
187 Ramon Muntaner, *Chronique du très magnifique seigneur en Ramon Muntaner*, in *Collection des chroniques nationales françaises*, J. Buchon (ed.), VI, Paris, 1827, ch. 94, p. 112.

the submissions of John of Saint-Hilaire, the consul of Marseille to Acre, the Orders had their privileges restored to them, but with restrictions. Henceforward, the Orders would be limited to two annual passages, Easter and August, and each Order would be permitted only two ships for each passage. Moreover, although they could carry as many merchants as they wished, they would be limited to 1,500 passengers per ship.[188] To demonstrate the importance of these privileges, the act was ratified in Marseille in the presence of the masters of both Orders: Brother Herman of Périgord and Brother Gerinus, as well as various other officials including the 'masters of the marines' (*commendatores navium*) of both Orders: Brother William of Valencia of the Hospital and Brother William of Capmeillier of the Temple. These were not regional posts, but offices within the main hierarchy.[189] Present also was the Templars' other main nautical officer, the sergeant-commander of the Vault of Acre.[190] Prior to this ratification, and as a gesture of the re-establishment of good will, a treaty was signed in 1233 between the masters of the Temple and the Hospital and the deputy of the commune of Marseille stipulating in favour of the Orders the exemption of all tolls in the port of Marseille.[191]

The subsequent size of the Orders' marines in Marseille remained around the limit stipulated by Odo of Montbéliard. Fourteen years later Girard Amalric, a public notary of Marseille, recorded the number of ships riding at anchor in the port, their owners and their destinations.[192] Of the 115 ships that harboured in Marseille between January and July, only 4 cargo-ships belonged to the Orders. The Hospital had moored *The Countess*, *The Falcon*,[193] and *The Griffin*, all with no indication of their destination, whilst the Temple had berthed only *The Good Adventure* bound for Acre. To give an idea of the maritime competition directed to Outremer, of the remaining 111 ships, 17 were bound for Cyprus, Syria or Acre.[194]

---

[188] *Codice diplomatico del sacro militare ordine Gerosolimitano*, S. Paoli (ed.), I, Lucca, 1733, no. 116, pp. 124–127; *Inventaire chronologique et analytique des chartes de la maison de Baux*, L. Barthélemy (ed.), Marseille, 1882, Suppl. no. 10, p. 523; *CH*, II, no. 2067, pp. 462–464 (1233).

[189] Another Templar commander of the Marine, Brother William Nigro, appeared in Cyprus in 1300, 'Actes passés à Famagouste de 1299–1301 par devant le notaire genois Lamberto di Sambuceto', C. Desimoni (ed.), *Revue de l'orient latin* 1(1893), no. 221, p. 58 (1300).

[190] *RTemp.*, *Hierarchical Statutes*, caps. 119 and 143, pp. 99–100, 113.

[191] 56H4054 (1233).

[192] Record of Giraud Amalric, in J. Pryor, *Business Contracts of Medieval Provence*, Toronto, 1981, pp. 70–72.

[193] Later the Temple had a similarly named ship, constructed by the Genoese; it was the pride of their marine, and entrusted to Brother Roger of Flor. For his extraordinary career see Ramon Muntaner, *Chronique*, VI, ch. 94, pp. 111–116.

[194] Pryor, *Business*, pp. 70–72.

These Templar and Hospitaller ships were regulars in Marseille, and commercial documents demonstrate their use by merchants. In August 1229 Stephen Manduel[195] entrusted Bertrand of Cavaillon with ninety Saracen bezants of Acre to be taken to Outremer for valuation on a Templar ship.[196] In 1229 and 1238 Stephen and Bernard Manduel used two un-named Templars ships as couriers.[197] In April 1238 a similar arrangement to that of 1229 was undertaken, but with *The Falcon* of the Hospital as courier.[198] In August 1244 John Manduel entrusted cloth to be shipped on the Hospitaller ship *The Griffin*,[199] whilst in the two previous years he had used unnamed Hospitaller ships.[200] Towards the end of the century, a Templar ship, *The Rose*, also plied between Marseille and Acre.[201]

More broadly, the Orders possessed substantial maritime privileges around the Gulf of the Lion. As early as 1178, when Frederick II was crowned in Arles, Viscount Bertrand of Marseille and his nephews, William the Fat and Raymond Barral, granted the Hospital the right to relief from all quay taxes and other maritime and terrestrial duties.[202] In 1188 Farald Ferréol exempted the Hospital from all taxes which he levied in the port of Avignon;[203] and in 1209 Viscount Hugh of Baux of Marseille accorded the Order the free traffic of their goods in the ports of Trinquetaille, the Petit Rhône, Saint-Gilles and others besides.[204]

As the case in front of Odo of Montbéliard demonstrates, the Marseille shipping connection was administered from both Europe and Outremer. Another such intervention from Outremer occurred in 1216, when the Hospitaller Brother William of Antioch journeyed to Aldenbourg for an audience with the Emperor Frederick II. He obtained a confirmation of the privilege from the viscounts of Marseille to build and keep all manner of ships at

---

[195] A study of this family and its commerce appears in D. Abulafia, 'Marseilles, Acre and the Mediterranean, 1200–1291', *Coinage in the Latin East: the Fourth Oxford Symposium on Coinage and Monetary History*, P. Edbury and D. Metcalf (eds.), Oxford, 1980, pp. 19–39.

[196] 'hanc quidem comandam portabo in hoc viagio Surie, in nave Templi', *Documents inédits sur le commerce de Marseille au moyen age*, L. Blancard (ed.), I, Marseille, 1884, no. 22, pp. 28–29 (August 1229).

[197] *ibid.*, I, no. 22, pp. 28–29 (August 1229); no. 68, pp. 102–102 (August 1235).

[198] *ibid.*, I, no. 80, pp. 120–122 (April 1238).

[199] *ibid.*, I, no. 101, pp. 162–162 (August 1244).

[200] *ibid.*, I, no. 96, pp. 155–156 (August 1243); no. 94, pp. 153–154 (August 1242).

[201] *ibid.*, II, no. 49, p. 436 (May 1288); no. 79, p. 446 (April 1290).

[202] 'quando imperator Alemanie venit Arelaten', *Actes concernant les vicomtes de Marseille*, H. Gérin-Ricard and E. Isnard (eds.), Paris, 1926, no. 265, p. 75; 56H4054 (1178); *CH*, I, no. 542, p. 369 (1178).

[203] 56H4224 (1188).

[204] *Actes concernant*, no. 335, p. 162 (1209); 56H4054 (1209).

Marseille and places under its jurisdiction. Also, that the Orders' ships might sail wherever they wished, and welcome on board both pilgrims and merchants 'in the defence of Christendom'.[205]

The vulnerability of Toulon had been demonstrated by its sack in 1178 at the hands of Muslims from Mallorca,[206] and in 1224 the seigneurs of Toulon gave the Templars the right to build houses and fortification wherever they wished in Toulon, so that their cargo-ships, galleys and other ships might harbour safely. The enclosure still bears the name: the *Carrièro del Temple*. Their ships were to be allowed to be loaded and unloaded without incurring any tax, and pilgrims and merchants were welcome on board free of tax, although merchants had to pay the ancient customary tax. The Order was also given the right to transport its own animals free of financial levy.[207]

It appears from the geography of the Orders' commanderies that they shared the maritime traffic in ports where they both had commanderies, as at Montpellier, Narbonne, Nice and Saint-Gilles.[208] In Marseille both Orders had major commanderies around the *Vieux port*, although the Temple had a secondary commandery on one of the many islands in the bay, for in 1288 two knights 'were received together on a certain island near Marseille in the chapel of the house of the Temple of the said island'.[209]

---

[205] *Acta imperii inedita, seculi XIII*, E. Winkelmann (ed.), Innsbruck, 1880, no. 139, p. 117.

[206] *GCN(Toulon)*, no. 93, col. 62. (1178).

[207] *ibid.*, no. 146, cols. 89–92 (1224).

[208] Saint-Gilles was on the Petit-Rhône, which flowed into the Mediterranean where La Grande-Motte stands today. Saint-Gilles had more than one port, linked by a channel running from Beaucaire, passing by the walls of Saint-Gilles along the route which the Canal du Midi now takes, *Les Coutumes de Saint-Gilles*, E. Bligny-Bondurand (ed.), Paris, 1915; 'La Leude et les péages de Saint-Gilles au xiie siècles, Textes en langue d'Oc et en Latin', E. Bondurand (ed.), *Mémoire de l'académie de Nîmes* 24(1901), pp. 267–291. My thanks also to P. Santoni for a private communication concerning this. The major port was where the Orders had their primary emplacements, but in 1177 the Temple developed another, Pelamorgues (citadel of the monks), and followed a concerted policy of acquisition here throughout the 1190s. It has been wrongly claimed that these acquisitions began in 1189, R Jéolas, *Bulletin de l'association d'histoire et d'archéologie de Saint-Gilles, Exposition 1984, Les ordres religieux militaires à Saint-Gilles au XIIe siècle*, They actually began in 1177, *Saint-Gilles(Temple)*, fol. 39r (1177). For the further expansion, *Saint-Gilles(Temple)*, fols. 34v–35r; 40rv (1189); 40rv (1192); 42v–43r (1193); 42rv; 41v (1194). The paradox is that already, in the act of 1177, it was called *Pela Monachos*.

[209] 'fuerunt simul recepti in quadam insula prope Massiliam, in capella domus Templi dicte insule', *Procès des Templiers*, II, p. 243.

Conclusion

The Hospital and the Temple provided a link between East and West that not only benefited themselves and the Crusade effort, but also others who were able to profit from their varied expertise. For example, not only did the Orders act as official collectors and transporters of papal taxes,[210] but when Alfonso of Poitiers was preparing the materials for the 1270 Tunis Crusade, he entrusted two Templars with purchasing the provisions for his fleet, hiring the Genoese and Catalan boats, and ensuring that all was ready at Aigues-Mortes by the right date.[211]

The advantages of the intensive contact that the Military Orders had between East and West was also used by those in need of eastern products. When the Cluniac abbot of Saint-Gilles requested in 1157 that the Order of the Hospital present him with one pound of incense every year, he had very good reason to ask this.[212] Likewise did his successor twelve years later when he requested the same of the Temple.[213] Good incense was produced in the near-East, and who better to procure this than Orders which operated large scale trading networks across the Mediterranean. Not all of the Orders' cargoes were as sweet-smelling, however, for the Temple also brought Muslim slaves to southern Europe.[214]

Once the Military Orders possessed their own marines the benefits accrued to a far larger circle than just the Orders alone, for they served three major functions. First, they enabled the Orders to swap information and to act as a reliable channel of communication between East and West.[215] This was not only internal communication, but was put to the service of the Latin East. For instance, letters of import to those in Europe, including to the Pope, were frequently entrusted to the Military Orders, even by the Kings of Jerusalem.[216]

---

210 See above, p. 187.
211 *Correspondance administrative d'Alfonse de Poitiers*, A. Molinier (ed.), Collection des documents inédits sur l'histoire de France, Paris, 1894–1900, i, no. 1134, p. 747; ii, no. 1759, p. 361; no. 1779, pp. 374–375; no. 1796, pp. 385–386; no. 1801, pp. 390–392; no. 1814, pp. 399–400; no. 1815, pp. 400–401 (1269); no. 1832, pp. 411–412 (1270). His brother, Saint Louis, had also used the Templars for transporting money to the Holy Land for the 1248 Crusade, J. Le Goff, *Saint Louis*, Paris, 1996, p. 177.
212 56H4101 (1157); Ménard, *Histoire*, pp. 35–36.
213 56H5289 (1169).
214 Barber, 'Supplying', p. 325.
215 Generally, S. Menache, *The Vox Dei*, New York and Oxford, 1990, pp. 33–35 for the importance of shipping as a conduit of information; *ibid.*, p. 235 for a man who supported his story by saying it came from the Hospitallers to lend it authenticity.
216 Phillips, *Defenders*, pp. 27, 53, 104–105, 145–146, 151–152, 246, 268.

Likewise, information which needed dissemenating was entrusted to them, as when Pope Hadrian IV informed Brother Peter of Rovira, the Templars Master in Spain, of his plans following the defeat at Jacob's Ford in November 1157.[217] And some two decades later Pope Alexander III had his crusading proposals revealed to the kings of England and France by the Templars and Hospitallers at a meeting at Nonancourt.[218]

Second, the Military Orders were able to offer expert assistance and information to the large number of pilgrims they transported. And third, their extensive awareness of events in the East, and their military reputation, made them ideal couriers for merchants to use in international trading ventures. Indicative of the importance the Orders attached to their trade, when the War of Saint Sabas (1256–1261) sparked civil war in Acre, the Templars and Hospitallers were in opposing camps, but both were intermeshed enough in the mercantile policies of the city to become involved. Paradoxically, the Temple sided with the Venetians, aided by Pisan and Provençal merchants, whilst the Hospital allied itself with the Genoese and Catalan merchants.[219] No conclusions can be drawn from these Templar-Provençal and Hospitaller-Catalan alliances, for the Hospital, at least, was motivated by its belief in the cause of the Genoese.[220]

The natural progression from this naval expertise was that in the 1290s both Orders, with papal encouragement, began to orient themselves towards being primarily naval powers.[221] In the case of the Hospital, their maritime vocation did not die with the Crusading movement of the central Middle Ages, for after its contribution to the Smyrna campaign of 1344,[222] its victory with the Triple Alliance against 'Ali Pasha in 1571 is possibly the best known engagement of any Military Order against Islam, the greatest naval battle since Actium: Lepanto.[223]

[217] *Papsturkunden in Spanien: Vorarbeiten zur Hispania Pontificia*, P. Kehr (ed.), II, no. 78, Berlin, 1926, pp. 360–362; Phillips, *Defenders*, p. 129.

[218] *ibid.*, p. 247.

[219] Mayer, *Crusades*, p. 263.

[220] Riley-Smith, *Knights*, pp. 184–185.

[221] *ibid.*, pp. 6, 200–201; Barber, *Knighthood*, pp. 183, 287, 293–294; Mayer, *Crusades*, p. 276.

[222] *ibid.*

[223] Porter, *History*, II, p. 170.

CHAPTER VII

Portrait of a Commandery:
Saint Eulalia

'Here you are, written on me, O Lord,
I like to read these traits, which
mark your victories, O Christ!
The same purple blood which is being taken from my body
pronounces your sacred name.'[1]

Prudentius, *Hymnus in honorem passionibus Eulaliæ beatissimæ
martyris*, in *Œuvres*, M. Lavarenne (ed.), IV, Paris, 1951,
verse 28, p. 58

APPROXIMATELY equidistant between Albi and Nîmes, lying on the
limestone plateaux of the Causses du Larzac in the Aveyron, rising above
the valleys of the Cernon and the Dourbie, stands the Templar commandery
of Saint Eulalia. One of the Temple's most important commanderies in Occitania,[2] it controlled the dependent commanderies of La Cavalerie, La Couvertoirade, Fraissinel, Gals, Millau and La Salvatge. It was joined to the Order's
coastal centre at Saint-Gilles by the well-trodden *Cami romieu* (pilgrim's
way),[3] which also connected it to the commanderies of Millau and La Couvertoirade.[4]

The patron saint of the commandery was the fourth century Spanish twelve
year old martyr Saint Eulalia.[5] According to a powerful legend she was a virgin

---

[1] 'Scribens ecce mihi, Domine,/ quam iuuat hos apices legere,/ qui tua, Christe, tropæa
notant!/ Nomen et ipsa sacrum loquitur/ purpura sanguinis eciliti.'
[2] A. du Bourg, *Histoire du grand-prieuré de Toulouse*, Toulouse, 1883, p. 376.
[3] J. Cabot, *Anciens ports et moulins de petite Camargue*, Montpellier, 1991, p. 38; Carcenac,
Larzac, p. 73.
[4] J.-P. Amalvy and A. Salsac, *La Couvertoirade: Guide de visite*, Montpellier, 1986, p. 19.
[5] Properly speaking Saint Eulalia of Mérida (Feast day, 10 December). Saint Eulalia of
Barcelona, although given a separate feast day (February 12), was a later creation, based
entirely on Saint Eulalia of Mérida, H. Moretus, 'Les Saintes-Eulalies', *Revue des questions
historiques* 89(1911), pp. 85–119; A. Butler, *Butler's Lives of the Saints*, H. Thirston and D.
Attwater (eds.), IV, Aberdeen, 1956, pp. 530–531.

persecuted under the edicts of Diocletian.[6] Martyred after pronouncing her judge to be destroying souls by forcing them to renounce God, she was first excoriated with iron hooks, then her wounds were fired. Her hair caught light and burnt. As she died, a dove flew from her mouth, and her body lay covered by snow until buried by Christians.[7] Her cult spread rapidly all over Europe. A hymn by Prudentius (b.348) and the oldest surviving French poem, the ninth century *Cantilène de Sainte-Eulalie*, were both written in her honour. She had a reputation for purity. In the words of the *Cantilène*: 'Buona pulcella fut Eulalia. Bel auret corps bellezour anima.'[8] She was also respected for her courage and strength, 'a true soldier of Christ'.[9] All are qualities which would have been cherished by a Military Order, qualities in which it could project an image of itself.[10]

We are fortunate to have a fourteenth century Latin inventory of the moveable possessions of the commandery of Saint Eulalia.[11] It was compiled in 1308 by two commissioners deputed by the seneschal of Rouergue and the *viguier* of Figeac in the wake of the arrest of the Templars on 13 October 1307. This short chapter reconstructs the aspect and furnishings of the Saint Eulalia, giving a visual portrait of a rural commandery.

The Commandery

The history of the Temple's acquisition of the patrimony of Saint Eulalia began in 1140 when Raymond of Luzençon granted the Order land at Saint-Georges in the vale of Cernon.[12] The Order was leased the church of Saint Eulalia with its tithes and appurtenances by the Benedictine abbey of Gellone

---

[6] H. Delehaye, *Les Légendes hagiographiques*, Brussels, 1905, *passim*, especially pp. 241–260 has highlighted the need for caution when handling the traditional details of the lives of saints.

[7] Her *passio* is in *España Sagrada, theatro geographico-historico de la Iglesia de España*, H. Florez (ed.), XIII, Madrid, 1756, pp. 398–406; see also Gregory of Tours, *De sancta Eulalia*, in *España Sagrada*, Florez (ed.), XIII, p. 407; *Butler's Lives*, pp. 530–531.

[8] *Cantilène de Sainte-Eulalie*, in *Les Carlovingiennes*, A. Krafft (ed.), Paris, 1899, verse 1, p. 31.

[9] 'Oubliant son âge et son sexe elle agit avec fierté comme véritable soldat de Christ', *Histoire des saints et de la sainteté chrétienne*, F. Chiovaro *et al.* (eds.), II, Paris, 1987, p. 148.

[10] The Templars also dedicated the commandery chapel at Béziers to Saint Eulalia, A. Soucaille, 'Les Templiers et les Hospitaliers à Béziers', *Bulletin de la société archéologique, scientifique et littéraire de Béziers* 13(1885), p. 156.

[11] H, Sainte-Eulalie 1 (1308). It has been published in *Saint Eulalia(1308)*.

[12] Published in A. du Bourg, 'Etablissement des chevaliers du Temple et de Saint-Jean de Jérusalem en Rouergue', *Mémoires de la société des lettres* 13(1886), p. 179.

in 1152.[13] Only in 1161 was the yearly rent of 80 *sous* of Melgueil and six cheeses commuted into a lump sum payment of 2,000 *sous*.[14] Meanwhile, in 1159 the *villa* of Sainte-Eulalie was presented to Brother Elias of Montbrun, master of the Temple in Rouergue, by Count Raymond Berenger IV of Barcelona (also count of Millau).[15]

The pattern of donations to the commandery reflects the habitual trend towards an initial period of intensity followed by the establishment of a more restrained rhythm. From 1140 to 1200 there were over 300 transactions concerning the commandery, 53 of these between 1171 and 1180, whilst from 1200 to the turn of the following century there were only 111 transactions.[16] An example of one of Saint Eulalia's dependent commanderies was Gals. It comprised three *mas*, units of old Gallo-Roman *villæ*, and its first mention came in 1150. However, its chapel pre-dated the advent of the Templars, for it was dedicated to Saint Martin.[17]

The core complex of buildings at Saint Eulalia comprised the conventual house, the chapel, a dormitory, a wardrobe, a large and a small store-room, a grange with a tool-shed, a work-shop and substantial stables. The commandery was fortified, and the Order built ramparts around it, as it did at its dependency of La Cavalerie.[18] The commandery's shape was square. It was walled with ramparts, and each corner had a tower, save the north-eastern corner which housed the chapel. The castle was built into the wall running south from the chapel, and its façade constituted the eastern fortification. The main southern gateway was heavily fortified with a portcullis, loopholes, and perhaps a drawbridge.[19]

The scale of the internal fortifications is hard to ascertain, but in other commanderies in this area heavy fortification was common. Both the twelfth century Templar castle at La Couvertoirade, and the fortified Templar chapel at Vaour, attest to the Templars' expertise in military architechture in this part of the Aveyron.[20] Such solid structures were needed not only as protection from hostile forces, but also from looters, as the destruction in the fourteenth century of the prestigious Hospitaller commandery of Trinquetaille by

---

[13] H, Sainte-Eulalie 15 (1152).

[14] H, Sainte-Eulalie 23 (1161).

[15] du Bourg, 'Etablissement', p. 180.

[16] Carcenac, *Larzac*, pp. 29–31.

[17] B. Bourgeois, 'A la Recherche de la grange templière de Gals en haut Rouergue', *AM* 100(1988), pp. 81–86; *Prov*, ii, no. 429, pp. 67–68; no. 430, pp. 68–69 (1178).

[18] Carcenac, *Larzac*, p. 38.

[19] *Sainte-Eulalie de Cernon*, Editione Nove 12100, Millau, p. 7.

[20] C. Higounet and J. Gardelles, *L'Architecture des ordres militaires dans le sud-ouest de la France*, p. 175 in E. Delaruelle, 'Templiers et Hospitaliers en Languedoc pendant la croisade des Albigeois', *CF* 4(1969), p. 322.

PLATE VI: Commandery of Saint Eulalia. A Templar tower (exterior).

brigands demonstrates all too well.[21] The heaviest fortifications were to be found on seafronts, as the mighty Templar tower of Saint Blaise at Hyères demonstrates. It is a single structure, with a chapel on the ground floor, a large *aula* on the first, and a fortified terrace on the third.[22]

The decorations and furnishings in the main body of the commandery were comfortable, clearly designed to fend off the bitter cold of winter. The walls were covered with hangings, curtains and cloths, whilst the rooms contained a lamp, 6 quilts, 5 mattresses, 26 cushions, 4 small pillows, 23 woollen wraps covered in rabbit-fur, 76 blankets, 120 lambskins. Presumably for important visitors, they also had a folding bed. They also kept a small armoury stocked with 30 iron helmets and 5 crossbows for their personal protection.[23]

The chapel at Saint Eulalia was a small, rectangular, Romanesque edifice, built of stone and volcanic tuff. Almost all of the Military Orders' chapels in Occitania were Romanesque, save the Hospitaller commandery of Aix, which is strikingly northern-Gothic. The conventual door was in the south side of the chapel by the apse and perhaps, as at Montsaunès, it connected with the castle, allowing direct entry for the brethren down an internal staircase.[24] The nave is still original, with typically Templar capitals: frusta, shells, *feuilles d'eau* and bovine heads. It was well stocked with sacerdotal vestments: 17 processional copes, 24 surplices, 5 sets of festal vestments, 2 samite chasubles, 4 sets of priests' vestments embroidered with golden thread, an alb, 3 deacons' dalmatics and 3 sub-deacons' dalmatics.[25] For the celebration of Mass, the chapel had 3 silver chalices, 2 bowls and a silver thurible.[26] The interior was visually rich, adorned with both silk and woollen hangings, a cross inlaid with gold, silver and precious stones, 2 golden altar-cloths, 6 other altar-frontals, a golden pall, 2 brass cases, and 9 reliquaries and caskets.[27] One of these may have been used for storing important charters, for at the Hospitaller commandery of Aix all papal bulls and the commandery's privileges were kept in a wooden casket in the chapel.[28]

A fourteenth century inventory from the time of the Trial of the Templars

---

21 E. Cahen *at al.* (eds.), *Archéologie*, in *Les Bouches-du-Rhône, encyclopédie départemetal*, IV, Marseille, 1932, p. 196.

22 M. Vecchione, 'Un Edifice templier: la tour Saint-Blaise d'Hyères', *PH* 40(1990), pp. 57–75.

23 *Sainte Eulalia(1308)*, pp. 258–259.

24 A. du Mège, 'Notes sur quelque monuments de l'ordre de la milice du Temple et sur l'église de Montsaunès', *Mémoires de la société archéologique du Midi de la France* 5(1842), p. 304.

25 *Saint Eulalia(1308)*, p. 258.

26 *ibid.*, p. 258.

27 *ibid.*

28 *CH*, IV, no. 4708, p. 123 (early fourteenth century).

also exists from the Toulouse Temple, and this showpiece urban chapel out-shone that of Saint Eulalia in its opulence. It housed numerous crosses of valu-able metals and stones (one particularly large wooden and silver one having two shards of the True Cross inlaid into it amongst forty-five precious stones), pyxes, hanging-basins with Holy Water, copper and iron standing- and hanging-candelabra, shrouds emblazoned with the Templar cross, a battle-standard, and even vestments embroidered with the device of the counts of Toulouse. Overlooking all, from above the high altar, was an image of the Templars' patron: the Blessed Virgin.[29]

The chapel at Saint Eulalia also served as a library for the commandery's twenty-one books.[30] Whilst we do not possess the titles, comparison with an inventory of some forty books from the Hospital at Aix is instructive. Half of these were liturgical, as were the additional books chained in the choir. The remainder included *peciæ* of biblical books, Papias' glossary, John Beleth's *Summa de ecclesiasticis officiis*,[31] a martyrology, a book of sermons, a book of charts for astronomical calculations, and notably a Hospitaller Rule and the Rule of Saint Augustine.[32] None of these works are extraordinary, although the *peciæ* perhaps indicate a connection with traffic from the world of the uni-versities.[33] At Templar Saint Lucy of Arles there were forty-one itemized books,[34] and lists of books from La Cavalerie, Grasse and Limaye have also remained.[35] They demonstrate a similar reading taste. Few examples of Templar liturgical books have survived, although among those which have, a vernacular bible, a psalter and a breviary are now all kept in Paris.[36] The practi-cal nature of the commanderies' books fits in with the general trend of Occita-nian monasticism, which was not known for its scholarship. The library of the

---

[29] du Bourg, *Histoire*, no. 23, pp. xv–xvi.

[30] *Saint Eulalia(1308)*, p. 258.

[31] John Beleth, *Summa de ecclesiasticis officiis*, H. Douteil (ed.), Corpus christianorum. Continuatio Mediævalis 41–41A, 2 vols., Turnhout, 1976.

[32] *CH*, IV, no. 4708, p. 123 (early fourteenth century).

[33] G. Fink-Errara, 'Une Institution du monde médiéval: la "pecia" ', *Revue philosophique de Louvain* 60(1962), pp. 184–243; J.-A. Destrez, 'La "Pecia" dans les manuscrits du moyen âge', *Revue des sciences philosophiques et théologiques* 13(1924), pp. 182–197. Generally, *La Production du livre universitaire au moyen âge: exemplar et pecia*, L. Bataillon *et al.* (eds.), Paris, 1988.

[34] 56H5170; A.-M. Legras and J.-L. Lemaitre, 'La Pratique liturgique des Templiers et des Hospitaliers de Saint-Jean de Jérusalem', *L'Ecrit dans la société médiévale, Textes en hommage à Lucie Fossier*, A. Dufour and C. Bourlet (eds.), Paris, 1991, pp. 121–122.

[35] *ibid.*, pp. 123–125.

[36] Paris, National library of France, nouv. acq. fr. 1404, lat. 1079 and lat. 10478. For a full catalogue of the few remaining liturgical books, see Legras and Lemaitre, 'Pratique', pp. 77–137.

great Saint Victor of Marseille only contained some three hundred books, although it included Cicero, Seneca and Aristotle.[37]

Life at Saint Eulalia

Gathering for the Office in the chapel formed the heart of the community's life. Templars celebrated the morning Offices of Matins, Lauds, Prime, Terce and Sext, and the afternoon and evening Offices of Nones, Vespers and Compline.[38] Communal Mass followed Prime,[39] but any other Masses being celebrated in the chapel were open to the brethren.[40] Additionally, vigils for the dead were held daily between Nones and Vespers, and the brethren's attendance was encouraged, although not compulsory.[41] Moreover, orders and appeals were issued at the end of the Offices, save Compline after which a light collation was taken, and thus attendance had a practical, as well as spiritual, value.[42]

The brothers were to say those parts of the Offices which required their participation,[43] although they were permitted to listen attentively in silence until such time as they had learnt them.[44] Unlike monastic houses, the majority of Templar brethren were not permitted to enter the choir, so as not to obstruct the ministering priests and servers.[45] Rather, they congregated in the nave, with the old and infirm kept apart with the new brethren, who had to stay at the back until they had learnt when to stand, kneel and genuflect.[46] Seating was provided, and there were detailed rules for when to sit and stand. For example, at Matins they were to sit for the invitatory (Psalm 94, *Venite exultemus Domino*) and the hymn, but in reverence to the Trinity were to rise and bow during the *Gloria Patri* at the end of psalms. They were to stand again at the end of Matins during the explanation of the Gospels and the *Te Deum* which closed the Office, and remain standing whilst Lauds and the hours of the Virgin were sung.[47]

---

[37] E. Baratier, 'Marquisat et comtés en Provence', *Histoire de la Provence*, E. Baratier (ed), Toulouse 1969, p. 159.
[38] *The Rule of the Templars*, J. Upton-Ward (ed. and tr.), Woodbridge, 1992, p. 14.
[39] *RTemp., Conventual Life*, cap. 284, pp. 171–172.
[40] *ibid.*, cap. 284, pp. 171–172.
[41] *ibid.*, cap. 356, pp. 202–203; cap. 359, p. 204.
[42] *ibid.*, cap. 309, p. 481.
[43] *ibid., Hierarchical Statutes*, cap. 146, p. 115.
[44] *ibid., Conventual Life*, cap. 282, p. 171; cap. 307, p. 180.
[45] *ibid.*, cap. 363, pp. 205–206.
[46] *ibid., Hierarchical Statutes*, cap. 147, p. 115; *Conventual Life*, cap. 307, p. 180; cap. 340, p. 195.
[47] *ibid., Primitive Rule*, cap. 15, p. 26; cap. 16, p. 27.

As with Carthusian *conversi*,[48] Templars who could not hear the Office and the hours of Our Lady were to say fixed numbers of the *Pater noster*.[49] Reflective of the work which made up the lives of many of the Templars, brethren were excused attendance at Nones and Vespers (i.e., attending chapel between lunch and Compline) if they were working with a hot oven, had their hands in pastry, were washing their hair, were working at a forge, or were shoeing an animal.[50] In addition to the Divine Office, after all meals the brethren retired to the chapel to give thanks.[51]

The brethren ate together in the refectory in silence to the accompaniment of readings from the Scripture,[52] using the normal monastic hand signals to express their requirements.[53] These would have been similiar to those listed by Udalric of Cluny in his *De signis loquendi*.[54] They ate in pairs, sharing bowls,[55] save those on penance who ate on the floor.[56] The listing of eight bowls in Saint Eulalia's inventory may suggest a community of around sixteen brethren,[57] a number which concurs with the seventeen processional copes in the chapel.[58] Paupers also ate in the refectory on various occasions. Following the death of a brother a pauper was to be fed a brother's ration of meat and wine for forty days,[59] and on visits of the master when five paupers were to be fed every day of his presence.[60]

The first meal of the day followed Sext, and the second Vespers. The last meal of the day was a light collation which included wine, and was taken immediately before Compline.[61] The food permitted to the brethren depended on a weekly cycle, with special provisions for feasts and fasts. Generally, brethren were permitted meat three times a week, rationed according to rank.[62] On

---

[48] C. Lawrence, *Medieval Monasticism*, London and New York, 1989, p. 162.

[49] The numbers evolved over time, *RTemp., Primitive Rule*, cap. 10, p. 22; *Conventual Life*, cap. 306, p. 180.

[50] *RTemp., Hierarchical Statutes*, cap. 146, p. 115; *Conventual Life*, cap. 300, p. 178; cap. 302, p. 179.

[51] *ibid., Primitive Rule*, cap. 29, pp. 37–38.

[52] *ibid.*, cap. 24, p. 34; *Conventual Life*, cap. 288, pp. 173–174.

[53] *ibid., Primitive Rule*, cap. 23, pp. 33–34.

[54] Udalric of Cluny, *Antiquores consuetudines Cluniacensis monasterii*, in *PL* 149, book 2, ch. 4, *De signis loquandi*, cols. 703–704.

[55] *RTemp. Primitive Rule*, cap. 25, p. 35.

[56] *ibid., Ordinary Chapters*, cap. 470, p. 254; cap. 512, p. 271.

[57] *Sainte Eulalia(1308)*, p. 258.

[58] *ibid.*

[59] *RTemp., Further Penances*, cap. 621, p. 321; *Hierarchical Statutes*, cap. 189, pp. 137–138.

[60] *ibid.*, cap. 94, pp. 83–84.

[61] *The Rule*, Upton-Ward (ed. and tr.), pp. 14–15; *RTemp., Primitive Rule*, cap. 30, pp. 38–39; *Conventual Life*, cap. 309, p. 181.

[62] *ibid., Primitive Rule*, cap. 26, pp. 35–36.

Fridays Lenten meat (*viande de karesme*) was given to all.[63] On Sundays all were permitted two meals, save the sergeants and squires who had one.[64] On all other days two or three meals of vegetables and bread were served to all.[65] Wine was drunk, and although there were strict rules concerning its consumption, persistent over-indulgence was recorded on at least one occasion in the Barcelona Rule.[66]

There were two sittings for meals. The first bell summoned the knights, chaplains and paupers to table, the second the sergeants.[67] Varying amounts of food were granted, depending on the rank of the brother.[68] The meal was begun by a blessing from a chaplain, after which all would say a private *Pater noster* before cutting their bread.[69] Meals were prepared in a kitchen equipped with two tripods for cooking over the fire, an iron spit, two pothooks, four knives, seven axes, a copper bottle, and an assortment of bowls, cauldrons and steaming basins.

The food eaten by the brethren was the produce of their own lands. The plateau of Larzac was given over to agriculture, whilst the valleys of the Cernon, Tarn and Dourbie were fertile enough for the cultivation of vines, gardens and meadows.[70] Both winter and spring cereals were cultivated, notably corn and rye in the winter, and the later crops of oats and spring barley.[71] Moreover, these crops were alternated such that the fields could have periods of fallow between the harvest and sowing,[72] as well as a cycle of fallow,[73] which in the eighteenth century gave a four-yearly cycle of corn, barley, oats and fallow.[74]

Their holdings of livestock were large. Saint Eulalia, La Cavalerie and Fraissinel together possessed 1,725 sheep, 160 goats, 24 pigs, 146 cattle (of which 63 were beasts of burden), 35 horses and 8 donkeys.[75] Some of these horses were for riding, as the commandery possessed three saddles and a spare girth-strap. The animals were raised on the plateaux of the Causses and the

---

63 *ibid.*, cap. 28, p. 37.
64 *ibid.*, cap. 26, pp. 35–36.
65 *ibid.*, cap. 27, p. 36.
66 'Un Nouveau manuscrit de la règle du Temple', J. Delaville le Roulx (ed.), *Annuaire-bulletin de la société de l'histoire de France* 26(1889), cap. 7, p. 196.
67 *RTemp, Conventual Life*, cap. 286, pp. 172–173; cap. 294, pp. 175–176; cap. 302, p. 170.
68 *ibid., Hierarchical Statutes*, cap. 153, p. 119.
69 *ibid., Conventual Life*, cap. 287, p. 173; *Reception*, cap. 681, pp. 347–348.
70 Carcenac, *Larzac*, p. 37.
71 *ibid.*, p. 125.
72 P. Marres, *Les Grands Causses*, ii, Tours, 1935, p. 33.
73 The terms *cultum* and *incultum* refer to this, but it is impossible to determine the exact duration of this period of fallow, Carcenac, *Larzac*, pp. 125–126.
74 *ibid.*, p. 126.
75 *Sainte Eulalia(1308)*, pp. 259–260.

fallow lands of the commandery, and used for their milk, meat, skin and wool. Hare was a delicacy they enjoyed, for they possessed four hare-snares. Milk was especially important, as cheese-making was a central activity in the area, and the Templars had property at nearby Roquefort.[76] The responsibility for these animals was entrusted to a Commander of Animals.[77]

The commandery had a milling complex at Saint-George de Luzençon, and archæological evidence suggests that its construction began soon after the foundation of the commandery.[78] Grain was vital for the large amount of bread eaten by the brethren,[79] and was kept in the *Tour de Quarante* on the western extreme of the north wall.[80] It was here that payments in kind were brought by tenants on the Feast of Saint Julian.[81] In 1308 the mill had 30 sextaries of corn in it,[82] and stored in the commandery were a further 82 sextaries of oats and 16 sextaries of spring barley.[83] More was stored in the other dependent commanderies. At Fraissinel a distinction was made between the 62 sextaries of spring barley and 32 of corn from rents, and the 214 sextaries of oats, 180 sextaries of rye, and 3 of spring barley which had come from the mill.[84]

The tools used for the working of the fields were stored in the commandery. Metal for the making of implements was purchased, as witnessed in the list of tolls of Millau for iron, steel and tin.[85] At Saint Eulalia were to be found an impressive array of agricultural implements. The storeroom housed a mason's hammer, 2 axes, 10 gimlets of varying sizes, 6 mattocks, spades, shovels, forks, baskets, rope, axes, adzes, drills, files, forks, hoes, saws, lamps and a scythe, as well as the hardware necessary for the beasts of burden to pull their wooden swing ploughs.[86]

[76] Carcenac, *Larzac*, p. 142.

[77] *ibid.*, p. 98.

[78] A. Soutou, 'Les Moulins des Templiers à Sainte-Eulalie de Cernon (Aveyron)', *AM* 103(1991), pp. 369–378.

[79] For medieval bread consumption, see G. Duby, *Guerriers et paysans VIIe–XIIe siècle*, Paris 1973, pp. 211–212.

[80] *Sainte Eulalie de Cernon*, p. 3.

[81] J. Miquel, *Cités Templières du Larzac*, Millau, 1989, p. 16.

[82] *Saint Eulalia(1308)*, p. 259.

[83] *ibid.*

[84] *ibid.*

[85] *Le Livre de l'Epervier*, L. Constans (ed.), Paris, 1882, pp. 64–66.

[86] *Saint Eulalia(1308)*, p. 259.

Conclusion

Along with the entire Order, the brethren living at Saint Eulalia were arrested by edict of King Philip IV of France in 1307. Those from Saint Eulalia were taken to the castle of Najac.[87] As with most Templar possessions in Occitania, Saint Eulalia was transferred to the Order of the Hospital, which took on its administration. The Hundred Years War took its toll in the Rouergue, and the Hospitallers enlarged and built new ramparts around Sainte Eulalia in 1442x1450 as a defence against the prevailing anarchy. Just over a century later, during the Wars of Religion, the commandery was sacked by protestants, but remained in the hands of the Hospitallers until the 1789 Revolution, when it was destroyed, divided into thirty-two plots and sold off.[88] So ended 639 years of control by the two principal Military and Religious Orders of the Crusades, Orders which had shaped, governed, controlled, worked and integrated themselves into the area to the extent that its history is inseparable from theirs.

[87] Miquel, *Cités Templières*, p. 15.
[88] *Sainte Eulalie de Cernon*, pp. 12–13.

CONCLUSION

Their arms the rust hath eaten.
Their statues none regard:
Arabia shall not sweeten
Their dust, with all her nard.

A. E. Housman, *More Poems*, III, v. 4, in
Collected Poems and Selected Prose, C. Ricks (ed.),
Harmondsworth, 1988, p. 149

THIS study has attempted to re-create the world within which the Military Orders lived in a European outpost, supporting their brethren in the East. All available material, of many differing types, has been used; but it remains to be said that some matters will forever be lost to us, and they will remain unknown. Nevertheless, as this work has attempted to demonstrate, Occitania was a highly important region for both Military Orders, an area where heightened sensibilities to Islam, concern about the control of Mediterranean shores, enthusiasm for Crusade, and rich agricultural produce were easily harnessed and utilized.

Why the Military Orders succeeded while other twelfth century Orders and congregations were not able to gain a foothold in Occitania is a complex question, the answer to which lies as much in the composition and history of Occitanian culture as in the strenuous efforts made by the Military Orders to achieve implantation there. Nevertheless, some factors are immediately apparent.

Sensibility to Crusade had been strong in the Midi from the beginnings of the Crusading project. Occitania despatched the largest contingent on the First Crusade, retained firm links with the Occitanian house of Tripoli (the castle of Tripoli still bears the name Qal'at Sandjil, the 'Castle of Saint-Gilles'), provided several clerics to fill benefices in the Holy Land, continued to send pilgrim-Crusaders for the entire duration of the Jerusalem Crusades, and encouraged mercantile trade between Europe and the near-East. The Military Orders were ambassadors of Crusade, and their presence was a daily reminder of the ambitions of the Latins in Outremer. They bore the Cross on their habits, and offered a continuous link, even for those who could not travel in person. The Temple and Hospital caught the imaginations of the Occitanians. They represented not only the martial side of Crusading, but also its piety, as well as the inseparability of the concepts of pilgrim and armed-pilgrim/ Crusader. This image was recognized and used by others in the furtherance of

Crusade, as King Baldwin's mission of 1184–1185 demonstrates. The kingdom was in a precarious state, with an infirm ruler facing the increasing threat posed by Saladin. Chosen to accompany Patriarch Heraclius to Europe were the Masters of the Temple and Hospital. This was an unprecedentd but clear attempt to harness Euopean support by using the appeal and popularity of the Military Orders.[1]

Within Occitania, the most important feature of the Orders' activities was recruitment, for nothing was possible without personnel. The timing was fortuitous, for by the time the Orders moved to Occitania, the momentum had gone out of the Benedictine internal reforms, and local society as a whole was ready to embrace new modes of religious life. Their ensuing success is attributable to a number of features, but two fundamental factors underpinned their policies.

First, the Military Orders created mechanisms and structures to provide possibilities for all members of society to attach themselves to commanderies. Non-nobles could benefit from, and contribute to, this military monasticism in a way that the mainstream monastic world never provided. The Cistercian reforms had broken the aristocratic stranglehold on monasticism, but not that fundamentally. Whilst a Cistercian *conversus* was forbidden ever to become a choir-monk,[2] and thus could not aspire to higher spiritual or administrative responsibilities, a sergeant of the Military Orders, by definition a non-knight, could rise to a position of real power (such as commanding a house or shipyard). Moreover, confraternity with the Cistercians was a rare privilege,[3] yet the Military Orders created a breathtakingly flexible system, looser even than that which was to be adopted by the mendicants in the thirteenth century.

Second, recruitment was a very localized phenomenon. This policy enabled the laity to develop particularly durable links with the various commanderies from their inceptions. Locals were not only permitted to share in the benefits of the Orders' prayers and works, but they established and manned the commanderies themselves. These two characteristics bred strength and loyalty.

The Military Orders would have been disadvantaged, perhaps fatally, without the support of the indigenous Church in Occitania. The reaction of the Occitanian Church to their presence is striking, for it demonstrates, contrary to expectations, their acceptance of the Military Orders. When disagreements did arise between the Church and the Military Orders, they related to

[1] J. Phillips, *Defenders of the Holy Land, Relations between the Latin East and the West 1119–1187*, Oxford, 1996, pp. 253–255.
[2] *Carta caritatis*, in *Documenta pro Cisterciensis ordinis historiæ ac juris studio*, J.-B. Van Damme (ed.), Westmalle, 1959, ch. 11, p. 21; *Exordium Cistercii*, in *Documenta*, J.-B. Van Damme (ed.), cap. 22, p. 28.
[3] L. Gougaud, *Dévotions et pratiques ascétiques du moyen âge*, Paris, 1925, p. 133.

the establishment of Templar and Hospitaller 'parishes', and the subsequent competition for the attentions of the laity. Church attacks on the Military Orders were not directed at the acceptability of warrior-monks, but at the possibility that they might abuse their privileges, or monopolize the gifts of the faithful. This was a genuine concern; and rightly so, for the charters demonstrate that the twin appeal of donating both to a spiritually meritorious Order, and also directly to the war-effort in the East, held powerful promises.

Two popular cults helped the Orders focus this appeal. The Temple dedicated all its churches to the Blessed Virgin, who was enjoying general popularity in the twelfth century. Another cult strongly linked to Crusade was that of the Magdalene, for she was especially linked to the Passion, as was Crusade by the centrality of the Holy Sepulchre. According to Occitanian tradition, she had landed near Marseille, evangelized Gaul, and was buried in Provence.[4] She was generally popular in the twelfth century, and became ever more so in Provence throughout the central Middle Ages.[5] Even the Cathar heretics accorded her pride of place.[6] In this context the exhibition of a finger of the Magdalene by the Hospitallers of Aix can be seen, as in so many other fields, as an instance of the Military Orders evoking images associated with the Holy Land, and therefore Crusade.[7]

The fundamental feature which distinguished life in a commandery from that in a monastery was one of vision. The monk looked no further than the Order's Rule and into himself to understand his purpose. His world ended at the monastery gate, for beyond it lay the world he had renounced. By contrast, the brother of the Military Order additionally looked daily to another continent for the purpose of his religious life. The Crusader states were at the root of a vocation lived fully in Europe.

The constant ebb and flow of manpower, provisions, arms, armour, horses and money being dispatched across the Mediterranean by the Military Orders in Occitania is testimony to the importance they placed on the survival of Latin rule in the Holy Land. It reflects the fact that brethren who professed in Europe recognized that despite their overwhelming numerical superiority, they were part of a support structure.

Whereas the Crusades originated in Europe, but were fought in Outremer, the Military Orders were founded in the Holy Land, and as such were not

---

4   Aix, Vézelay and Ephesus all claim to house her relics, H. Garth, *Saint Mary Magdalene in Mediaeval Literature*, Baltimore, 1950, pp. 101–104; J.-R. Palanque, 'Sur les origines du culte de la Madeleine en Provence', *PH* 9(1959), pp. 193–200; V. Saxer, *Le Culte de Marie Madeleine en Occident*, Paris, 1959, pp. 6–9, 46, 230, 264.
5   *ibid.*, maps.
6   B. Neipp, *Marie-Madeleine; femme et âpotre*, Renens, 1991, p. 74.
7   56H4175 (1286).

European institutions. The story related by Usāmah ibn Munqidh of how the Templars in Jerusalem, who used to let him pray in the al-Aqsa, ejected a brother who was trying to force Usāmah to pray the *Allāhu akbar* facing east, and not the *qiblah*, explaining:

> this is a stranger who has only recently arrived from the land of the Franks and he has never before seen anyone praying except eastwards,[8]

is revealing, for it demonstrates the gulf that divided European brothers from those in Jerusalem. The tone is almost parental. The Templars being embarrassed at the bad-manners of their young recruit, but knowing that in time he would become 'civilized' to the ways of the East.

Underscoring all of the analysis of the Military Orders as new forms of religious life incorporated into the thoughts and hearts of the people, the economy, and the identity of central-southern Occitania, has been the suggestion of a rhythmic heart-beat of two Orders more closely linked than the activities and policies of individual brethren might suggest. No-one would doubt that the Temple and the Hospital fought with similar military equipment. This study has sought to demonstrate that their spiritual equipment, and the uses to which they put it in attracting the money and manpower necessary to sustain their armies in the Holy Land, was no less similar in its construction. This comes across strongly in all of their Occitanian activities.

The Orders were created in the twelfth century atmosphere of rebirth and renewal, at a time when an emphasis on poverty and a return to the *Ecclesia primitiva* attracted many intent on a religious life. Both Orders emphasized poverty. The Templars styled themselves the 'Poor knights of the Temple of Solomon', and the Hospital stressed its poverty by its subservience to the poor. Poverty was an intrinsic part of their vocations, vowed in the reception ceremonies. Yet, unlike the mendicants who were to strive for corporate poverty, this would have been inimical to the vocations of the Military Orders, which required wealth to fulfill their combat and hospitalling functions.

The impact of all these facets of their existence meant that the relationships between the Military Orders and the laity at large deflected much of the hostility which might be directed towards new religious establishments. Such was, for example, the hostility felt towards the Cistercians at Silvacane, that one Brother Raymond was subjected to abuse, taunted, and maliciously harassed by the locals' dogs.[9]

More generally, perceptions of the brethren of the Military Orders were in stark contrast to those of monks or clerics. Although accused of pride, the

---

[8]   Usāmah ibn Munqidh, *Kitāb al l'tibār*, in *An Arab-Syrian Gentleman and Warrior in the Time of the Crusades*, P. Hitti (ed. and tr.), New York, 1929, p. 164.
[9]   3H31 (1268).

Military Orders were not prone to intellectual arrogance. Those who professed as brethren were not, in the main, lettered, and thus did not become embroiled in debates which rocked other Orders throughout the twelfth, and especially, thirteenth centuries. Further, most commanderies were much smaller than monasteries, and unlikely to excite strong feelings of local resentment for being pampered havens for the indolent.

In this Occitanian society made up of burgeoning towns, and a disproportionate number of castles, the Military Orders were representatives of the new knighthood: the *militia*. In a southern climate where the legitimation of knighthood was to culminate in the knightly virtues of *pretz* and *paratge*, the Orders can properly be seen as the incarnations of the heroes of courtly tales of pure, knightly virtues, as embodied in the twelfth century Occitan Arthurian epic, *Jaufre*.[10] Moreover, unlike a Saint Bernard, who abandoned his knightly inheritance at the doors of Cîteaux on entering the Order, those who professed as knights of the Military Orders could glory in their knighthood, for the Temple, and later the Hospital, had crystallized the ethos of the Gregorian reform of the *bellatores* into a knighthood 'worthy and so holy . . . founded by the grace of the Holy Spirit'.[11]

The Military Orders were thus not in a traditional manner monastic. They formed a bridge that spanned a century of experimentation with new forms of religious life, and which culminated in the mendicant friars. One can discern in the Military Orders aspects that would be deemed hallmarks of the mendicants' break from the cloister. For example, it was the Military Orders who first organized their structures in geographical zones and were, truly, international religious Orders. It was also part of the Military Orders' vision to cultivate relationships with the inhabitants of the expanding towns, and to this end they built commanderies in urban centres, as well as in rural areas. Also, it is the mendicants who are credited with the mass use of receptions *ad succurrendum*,[12] but the Military Orders were the first to use this method of attracting the faithful on such a large scale. But, in common with monasticism, the Military Orders looked rather to their own salvation than that of others, and they were for the most part unordained, cœnobitic landholders. Further, they were not traditionally monastic in that they laid no claim to be following an Apostolic life, and they did not engage in any theological or moral debate.

That which the charters and the sheer scale of the success of the Military Orders demonstrate best is that Occitanian society of the twelfth and thirteenth century felt a pull so strong to these Orders, that their success should

---

[10] *Jaufre*, in *Les Troubadours*, R. Lavaud and R. Nelli (eds. and trs.), Bruges, 1960, pp. 40–609.

[11] *RTemp.*, *Primitive Rule*, cap. 2, p. 12.

[12] Gougaud, *Dévotions*, p. 133.

rightly be placed alongside that of Cîteaux. Perhaps they were even more successful than the white monks. For whilst the impact of other Orders in Occitania was limited, it is no exaggeration to state that the Temple and Hospital changed the face of twelfth century Occitanian religious life: a dominant position not to be rivalled by the mendicants until the end of the thirteenth century, when the smaller of the two mendicant Orders, the Dominicans, could claim forty-nine convents in greater Occitania.[13]

The success of the Temple and the Hospital in this world 'across the sea' is testimony to the religious power of the image of the Jerusalem pilgrimage throughout the central Middle Ages. Notwithstanding military defeats, the loss of prized territory, and the mounting odds against the re-establishment of Latin rule in the near-East, patrons in the West continued to support and identify with these Orders. They best represented the fusion of the aspirations of a Church militant and the currents which had, for the previous two centuries, sought to re-invent, reform and create anew expressions and manifestations of the religious life. The Military Orders evolved from being institutions designed to aid pilgrimage, to becoming themselves pilgrims. The European commandery, where the vast majority of brethren lived, was a place where those who could not experience the pale glory of the earthly Jerusalem might experience its heavenly counterpart. But, unlike any Orders which had come before, the Orders of the Temple and the Hospital defied Saint Anselm's distinction of the spiritual value of the two Jerusalems,[14] and permitted an unprecedented number of people, lay and clerical, to share in their aspirations of the dual nature of:

the Holy city, new Jerusalem, coming down out of heaven from God, prepared as a bride adorned for her husband (Revelations XXI, 2).

---

[13] C. Ribaucourt, 'Les Mendiants du Midi d'après la cartographie de "l'enquête" 146, CF 8(1973), pp. 25–33, maps, pp. 30–31; M.-H. Vicaire, 'Le Développement de la province dominicaine de Provence', CF 8(1973), p. 36.
[14] Anselm of Canterbury, Opera omnia, in PL 158, book 2, letter 19, col. 1169.

BIBLIOGRAPHY

Manuscript Sources

Arles
Municipal archives
  ms. GG 89, *Authenticum domus Hospitalis prioratus Sancti Egidii*
  ms. GG 90, *Authenticum domus militie Templi Sancti Egidii*

Marseille
Departmental archives of the Bouches-du-Rhône
  1G, bundles 1–503, charters of the archbishopric of Aix-en-Provence
  3H, bundles 1–69, charters of the Cistercian abbey of Silvacane
  56H, bundles 1–5325, charters of the Hospital and Temple

Paris
National archives
  ms. S5512, late Hospitaller register
National Library of France
  ms. lat. 1079, Templar Psalter
  ms. lat. 10478, Templar Breviary
  ms. lat. 11082, *Chartularium domus Templi Hierosolymitani de Roais*
  ms. lat. 14045, Templar Rule
  ms. nouv. acq. fr. 1404, Templar vernacular Bible
  nouv. acq. lat., books 1–71, collected papers of the Marquis of Albon

Toulouse
Departmental archives of the Haute-Garonne
  H, bundles, charters of the Hospital and Temple

Printed Sources

Primary Sources: Individual Authors

Aimatus of Monte Cassino, *L'Ystoire de li Norman*s, F. Champollion-Figeac (ed.), Paris, 1835.
Anna Comnena, *The Alexiad*, E. Dawes (tr.), London, 1928.
Anselm of Canterbury, *Opera omnia*, in *PL* 158–159.
Aubri of Trois Fontaines, *Chronica*, in *MGHSS* 23, G.-H. Pertz (ed.), pp. 893–894.
Bartholemew of Neocastro, *Historia Sicula*, in *Rerum italicarum scriptores*, L. Muratori (ed.), Milan, 1928, cols. 1013–1194.
Benjamin of Tudela, *The Itinery of Benjamin of Tudela*, M.-N. Amor (tr.), London, 1907.
Bernard of Clairvaux, *Liber ad milites Templi de laude novæ militiæ*, in *Sources Chrétiennes* 367, P.-Y. Emery (ed.), Paris, 1990.
Bernard Sicard of Marvejols, 'Ab greu cossire', in *Choix des poésies originales des troubadours*, M. Renouard (ed.), IV, Paris, 1819, no. 27, pp. 191–193.

Cæsarius of Heisterbach, *Dialogus miraculorum*, J. Strange (ed.), Cologne, Bonn, Brussels, 2 vols., 1851.

Clement VI, *Clément VI, 1342–1352, Lettres closes, patentes et curiales se rapportant à la France*, E Déprez (ed.), Bibliothèque des Ecoles françaises d'Athènes et de Rome 1, Paris, 1901.

Eberhard, *Annales*, in *MGHSS* 17, P. Jaffé (ed.), pp. 591–605.

Gervase of Dover, *Chronico de regibus Angliæ*, in *Recueil des Historiens des Gaules* 17, M.-J.-J. Brial (ed.), Paris, 1818, pp. 660–679.

Gregory IX, *Les Registres de Grégoire IX, Recueil des bulles de ce Pape*, L. Auvray (ed.), 4 vols., Paris, 1890.

Gregory of Tours, *De sancta Eulalia*, in *España Sagrada, theatro geographico-historico de la Iglesia de España*, H. Florez (ed.), Madrid, XIII, 1756, p. 407.

Housman A, *Collected Poems and Selected Prose*, C. Ricks (ed.), Harmondsworth, 1988.

Ibn al-Athīr, *al-Kāmil fi at-Ta'rīkh*, in *RHC Or.* 1, pp. 189–744.

Ibn al-Qalānisī, *Dhail Ta'rīkh Dimashq*, in *The Damascus Chronicle of the Crusades*, H. Gibb (tr.), London, 1932.

'Imād ad-Din al-Iṣfahāni, *al-Fath al qussī fi l-fath al-qudsī*, in *Conquète de la Syrie et de la Palestine par Saladin*, H. Massé (tr.), Documents relatifs à l'histoire des croisades 10, Paris, 1972.

Innocent III, *Opera omnia*, in *PL* 214–217.

——— *Die Register Innocenz' III*, O. Hageneder et al. (eds.), 2 vols., Grasse and Cologne 1964, Rome and Vienna, 1979.

——— *The Letters of Pope Innocent III (1198–1216) Concerning England and Wales: A Calender with an Appendix of Texts*, A. and M. Cheney (eds. and trs.), Oxford, 1967.

James of Molay, *De unione Templi et Hospitalis ordinum*, in *Le Dossier de l'affaire des Templiers*, G. Lizerand (ed. and tr.), Paris, 1923, pp. 2–15.

James of Vitry, *Historia Hierosolymitana*, in *Gesta Dei per Francos*, J. Bongars (ed.), Hanover, 1611, pp. 1047–1124.

——— *Sermones vulgares*, in *Analecta novissima: Spicilegii Solesmensis altera continuatio*, J. Pitra (ed.), 2 vols., Paris, 1888.

John Beleth, *Summa de ecclesiasticis officiis*, H. Douteil (ed.), Corpus christianorum. Continuatio Mediævalis 41–41A, 2 vols., Turnhout, 1976.

John of Joinville, *Histoire de Saint-Louis*, N. de Wailly (ed.), Paris, 1868.

John of Würzburg, *Descriptio Terræ Sanctæ*, in *Descriptiones Terræ Sanctæ ex sæc. VIII. IX. XII. et XV.*, T. Tobler (ed.), Leipzig, 1874, pp. 108–192.

John of Ypres, *Chronicon Sythiense S. Bertini*, in *Thesaurus novus anecdotorum*, E. Martène (ed.), III, Paris, 1717, cols. 440–775.

Juvenal, *D. Iunii Iuvenalis saturæ*, A. Housman (ed.), Cambridge, 1931.

Marcabru, 'Pax in Nomine Domini', in *La Poesia dell'antica Provenza*, G. Sansone (ed.), Milan, 1984, pp. 112–117.

Matthew Paris, *Historia Anglorum*, Rolls Series 44, F. Madden (ed.), 3 vols., London, 1866–1869.

——— *Chronica majora*, Rolls Series 57, H. Luard (ed.), 7 vols., London 1872–1883.

Nicholas IV, *Registres de Nicholas IV, Recueil des bulles de ce pape*, E. Langlois (ed.), Paris, 1886.

Olivier del Temple, 'Estat aurai', in *Das Altprovenzalische Kreuzlied*, K. Lewent (ed.), Geneva, 1976, pp. 439–441.

Orderic Vitalis, *The Ecclesiastical History of Orderic Vitalis*, M. Chibnall (ed. and tr.), 6 vols., Oxford, 1968–1980.

Peter of les Vaux-de-Cernay, *Hystoria albigensis*, P. Guébins and E. Lyon (eds.), 3 vols., Paris, 1926–1939.

Peter William, *Miracula beati Egidii*, in *MGHSS* 12, P. Jaffé (ed.), pp. 316–323.

Prudentius, *Hymnus in honorem passionibus Eulaliæ beatissimæ martyris*, in *Œuvres*, M. Lavarenne (ed.), IV, Paris, 1951, pp. 54–61.

Ralph of Caen, *Gesta Tancredi in expeditione Hierosolymitana*, in *RHC Occ.* 3, pp. 603–716.

Ralph of Diceto, *Opera historica*, Rolls Series 68, W. Stubbs (ed.), 2 vols., London, 1876.

Ramon Muntaner, *Chronique du très magnifique seigneur en Ramon Muntaner*, in *Collection des chroniques nationales françaises*, J. Buchon (ed.), V–VI, Paris, 1827.

Richard Bonomel, 'Ir'e dolors s'es mon cor asseza', in *Choix des poésies originales des troubadours*, M. Renouard (ed.), IV, 1819, no. 22, pp. 131–133.

Richard of Devizes, *Chronicon de rebus gestis Ricardi primis regis Angliæ*, J. Stevenson (ed.), London, 1838.

Richard the Pilgrim, *La Chanson d'Antioche*, P. Paulin (ed.), 2 vols., Paris, 1848.

Robert of Torigny, *Chronica*, Rolls Series 82, R. Howlett (ed.), IV, London, 1889.

Roger of Hovendon, *Chronica*, Rolls Series 51, W. Stubbs (ed.), 4 vols., London, 1868–1887.

Rorgo Fretellus, *Rorgo Fretellus de Nazareth et sa description de la Terre Sainte. Histoire et édition du texte*, P. Boeren (ed.), Amsterdam, 1980.

Salimbene de Adam, *Cronica*, G. Scalia (ed.), 2 vols., Bari, 1966.

Sicard of Cremona, *Chronicon*, in *Rerum italicarum scriptores*, L. Muratori (ed.), VII, Milan, 1725.

Smith A, *An Enquiry into the Wealth of Nations*, Edinburgh, 1850.

Theodoric, *Libellus de locis sanctis*, M.-L. and W. Bulst (eds.), Heidleberg, 1976.

Thomas of Aquinas, *Summa theologiæ*, Brothers of the English Dominican Province (eds.), 61 vols, London, 1964–1980.

Thomas of Cantimpré, *Bonum universale de apibus*, G. Colverinus (ed.), Douai, 1627.

Udalric of Cluny, *Antiquores consuetudines Cluniacensis monasterii*, in *PL* 149, cols. 635–778.

Usāmah ibn Munqidh, *Kitāb al l'tibār*, in *An Arab-Syrian Gentleman and Warrior in the Time of the Crusades*, P. Hitti (ed. and tr.), New York, 1929.

Walter Daniel, *Vita Ailredi abbatis Rievall'*, F. Powicke (ed.), London, 1950.

Walter Map, *De nugis curialium*, M. James (ed. and tr.), revised by C. Brooke and R. Mynors, Oxford, 1983.

William Armoricus, *Gesta Philippi Augusti Francorum regis*, in *Recueil des Historiens des Gaules* 17, M.-J.-J. Brial (ed.), Paris, 1818, pp. 62–116.

William of Puylaurens, *Historia albigensium*, in *Recueil des Historiens des Gaules et de la France* 19, M.-J.-J. Brial (ed.), Paris, 1880, pp. 193–225.

William of Tudela, *La Chanson de la croisade albigeoise*, H. Gougaud (ed.), Paris, 1989.

William of Tyre, *Chronicon*, R. Huygens (ed.), Corpus Christianorum. Continuatio Mediævalis, 2 vols., Turnhout, 1986.

Primary Sources: Collections and Anonymous

Actes concernant les vicomtes de Marseille, H. Gérin-Ricard and E. Isnard (eds.), Paris, 1926.

Acta imperii inedita, seculi XIII, E. Winkelmann (ed.), 2 vols., Innsbruck, 1880–1885.

Acta pontificum romanorum inedita, J. Pflugk-Harttung (ed.), 3 vols., Tübingen, 1881, Stuttgart, 1884–1888.

'Actes passés à Famagouste de 1299–1301 par devant le notaire genois Lamberto di Sambuceto', C. Desimoni (ed.), *Archives de l'orient latin* 2(1884), pp. 3–120 and *Revue de l'orient latin* 1(1893), pp. 59–139, 225–353.

The Anglo-Saxon Chronicle, D. Whitelock (tr.), London, 1961.

Annales prioratus de Dunstaplia, Rolls Series 36, H. Luard (ed.), III, London, 1866.

Arab Historians of the Crusades, F. Gabrieli (ed.), E. Costello (tr.), New York, 1989.

Bullarium Franciscanum, J. Sbaraglia (ed.), 4 vols., Rome, 1759–1768.

Bullaire de l'église de Maguelone (1030–1303), J. Rouquette and A. Villemagne (eds.), 2 vols., Montpellier, 1911.

Cantilène de Sainte-Eulalie, in *Les Carlovingiennes*, A. Krafft (ed.), Paris, 1899, p. 31.

Carta caritatis, in *Documenta pro Cisterciensis ordinis historiæ ac juris studio*, J.-B. Van Damme (ed.), Westmalle, 1959, pp. 15–21.

Cartulaire de l'abbaye de Saint-Victor de Marseille, B. Guérard (ed.), Collection des cartulaires de France 9, 2 vols., Paris, 1857.

Cartulaire de la commanderie de Richerenches de l'ordre du Temple (1136–1214), Marquis de Ripert-Monclar (ed.), Marseille, 1978.

Le Cartulaire de La Selve, P. Ourliac and A. Magnou (eds.), Paris, 1985.

Cartulaire de l'ordre du Temple 1119?–1150. Recueil des chartes et des bulles relatives à l'ordre du Temple, Marquis d'Albon (ed.), Paris, 1913.

Cartulaires des Templiers de Douzens, P. Gérard and E. Magnou (eds.), Collection des documents inédite sur l'histoire de la France 3, Paris 1965.

'Cartulaire des Templiers de Montsaunès', C. Higounet (ed.), *Bulletin philologique et historique*, Paris, 1957, pp. 225–293.

Cartulaire des Templiers de Vaour (Tarn), C. Portal and E. Cabié (eds.), Albi, 1894.

Cartulaire de Trinquetaille, P. Amargier (ed.), Aix-en-Provence, 1972.

Le Cartulaire du chapitre du Saint-Sépulcre de Jérusalem, G. Bresc-Bautier (ed.), Documents relatifs à l'histoire des croisades 15, Paris, 1984.

Cartulaire général de l'ordre des Hopitaliers de Saint-Jean de Jérusalem (1100–1310), J. Delaville le Roulx (ed.), 4 vols., Paris, 1894–1906.

'Charte de la communauté de Montsaunès', A. du Mège (ed.), *Mémoires de la société archéologique du Midi de la France* 5(1842), pp. 210–222.

Chartularium domus Hospitalis Hierosolymitani Sancti Pauli prope Romanis, in *Cartulaires des Hospitaliers et des Templiers en Dauphiné* 3, U. Chevalier (ed.), Vienne, 1975, pp. 3–58.

Chartularium domus Templi Hierosolymitani de Roais diocesis Vasionensis, in *Cartulaires des Hospitaliers et des Templiers en Dauphiné* 3, U. Chevalier (ed.), Vienne, 1975, pp. 61–136.

La Chastelaine de Vergy, R. Stuip (ed.), Saint-Amand-Montrond, 1985.

La Châtelaine de Saint-Gilles, in *Les Amours du bon vieux tems*, de Sainte Palaye (ed.), Paris, 1756, pp. 66–80.

Choix des poésies originales des troubadours, M. Renouard (ed.), 6 vols, Paris, 1816–1821.

Chronica Adefonsi imperatoris, L. Sánchez Belda (ed.), Escuela de estudios medievales, textos 14, Madrid, 1950.

Chronica magistrorum defunctorum, in *Monasticon Anglicanum*, W. Dugdale (ed.), VI(II), London, 1830, pp. 796–798.

Cîteaux. Documents primitifs, F. de Place (ed.), Cîteaux, 1988.

Codice diplomatico del sacro militare ordine Gerosolimitano, S. Paoli (ed.), 2 vols., Lucca, 1733–1737.

Conciliorum œcumenicorum decreta, J. Alberigo *et al.* (eds.), Freiburg im Breisgau, 1962.

Correspondance administrative d'Alfonse de Poitiers, A. Molinier (ed.), Collection des documents inédits sur l'histoire de France, 2 vols., Paris, 1894–1900.

Les Coutumes de Saint-Gilles, E. Bligny-Bondurand (ed.), Paris, 1915.

Crónicas anónimas de Sahagún, A. Ubierto Arteta (ed.), Textos Medievales 75, Zaragoza, 1987.

De excidio urbis Acconis, in *Veterum scriptorum et monumentorum amplissima collectio*, E. Martène and U. Durand (eds.), v, Paris, 1729, cols. 758–786.

Documents inédits sur le commerce de Marseille au moyen age, L. Blancard (ed.), 2 vols., Marseille, 1884.

Epistola a. dapiferi militiæ Templi, in *Recueil des historiens des Gaules et de la Frence* 15, M. Bouquet *et al.* (eds.), Paris, pp. 540–541.

España sagrada, theatro geographico-historico de la Iglesia de España, H. Florez (ed.), Madrid, 1747–1918.

Exordium Cistercii, in *Documenta pro Cisterciensis ordinis historiæ ac juris studio*, J.-B. Van Damme (ed.), Westmalle, 1959, pp. 22–28.

Exordium parvum, in *Documenta pro Cisterciensis ordinis historiæ ac juris studio*, J.-B. Van Damme (ed.), Westmalle, 1959, pp. 5–15.

Flores historiarum, Rolls Series 95, H. Luard (ed.), 3 vols., London, 1890.

Gallia christiana, D de Sainte-Marthe *et al.* (eds.), 16 vols., Paris, 1812–1896.

Gallia christiana novissima, U. Chevalier and J. H. Albanès (eds.), 7 vols., Montbéliard and Valence, 1895–1920.

Gesta comitum Barchionensium, L. Barrau Dihigo and J. Massó Torrents (eds.), Barcelona, 1925.

Gesta Dagoberti, in *MGHSS rerum Merovingicarum* 2, B. Krush (ed.), pp. 396–426.

Le Guide du pèlerin de Saint-Jacques de Compostelle, J. Vielliard (ed. and tr.), Macon, 1950.

Histoire des Saints et de la sainteté chrétienne, F. Chiovaro *et al.* (eds.), 11 vols., Paris, 1986–1988.

Inventaire chronologique et analytique des chartes de la maison de Baux, L. Barthélemy (ed.), Marseille, 1882.

'L'Inventaire des biens de la commanderie du Temple de Sainte-Eulalie du Larzac en 1308', A. Higounet-Nadal (ed.), *AM* 68(1956), pp. 255–262.

Jaufre, in *Les Troubadours*, R. Lavaud and R. Nelli (eds. and trs.), Bruges, 1960, pp. 40–609.

The Knights Hospitallers in England; the Report of Prior Philip de Thames to the Great Master Elyan de Villanova for A.D. *1338*, L. Larking and J. Kemble (eds.), London, 1856.

'Lettre d'un Templier trouvée récemment à Jerusalem', F. Abel (ed.), *Revue biblique* 35(1926), pp. 288–295.

'La Leude et les péages de Saint-Gilles au xiie siècles, Textes en langue d'Oc et en Latin', E. Bondurand (ed.), *Mémoire de l'académie de Nîmes* 24(1901), pp. 267–291.

Liber memorandorum ecclesie de Bernewell, J. Clark (ed.), Cambridge, 1907.

Le Livre de l'Epervier, L. Constans (ed.), Paris, 1882.

'Los LXXII noms de nostre senhor Jhesu Crist, trobat escrig per salut de tots fidelz crestians', *Ecrivains anticonformistes du moyen-âge occitan, hérétiques et politiques*, R. Nelli (ed. and tr.), Paris, 1977, pp. 137–141.

Les Miracles de Notre-Dame de Roc-Amadour au XIIᵉ *siècle*, E. Albe (ed. and tr.), Paris, 1907.

Missau e rituau en lengo nostro, Traductions officielles A.E.L. (ed.), Marseille, 1976.

Monasticon Anglicanum, W. Dugdale (ed.), 6 vols., London, 1817–1830.

Monumenta Germaniæ historica scriptores, G. H. Pertz *et al.* (eds.), Hanover, 1896– .

'Un Nouveau manuscit de la règle du Temple', J. Delaville le Roulx (ed.), *Annuaire-bulletin de la société de l'histoire de France* 26(1889), pp. 185–214.

'Un Nouveau texte du traité "De constructione castri Safet" ', R. Huygens (ed.), *Studi medievali* 6(1965), pp. 355–387.

'Papst- Kaiser- und Normannenurkunden aus Unteritalien', W. Holtzman (ed.), *Quellen und Forschungen aus italienischen Archiven und Bibliotheken* 35(1955), pp. 46–85.

Papsturkunden in Spanien: Vorarbeiten zur Hispania Pontificia, P. Kehr (ed.), 2 vols., Berlin, 1926–1928.

Papsttum und Untergang der Templerordens, H. Finke (ed.), 2 vols., Münster, 1907.

Papsturkunden für Templer und Johanniter, R. Hiestand (ed.), Göttingen, 1972.

Parliament Acts, The Statutes of the Realm, 10 vols., London, 1810–1828.

Patrologiæ cursus completus. series latina, J.-P. Migne (ed.), 221 vols., Paris, 1844–1865.

Les Plus anciennes chartes en langue provençale; Recueil des pièces originales antérieures au XIIIe siècle, C. Brunel (ed.), Paris, 1926 and Supplement 1952.

'La Prière des malades dans les hôpitaux de l'ordre de Saint-Jean', L. Le Grand (ed.), *Bibliothèque de l'Ecole des Chartes* 57(1896), pp. 325–338.

Procès des Templiers, J. Michelet (ed.), 2 vols., Paris, 1861.

Recueil des actes des comtes de Provence appartenant à la maison de Barcelona, F. Benoit (ed.), 2 vols., Paris, 1925.

Recueil des historiens des croisades. Historiens occidentaux, Académie des inscriptions et belles lettres (ed.), 5 vols., Paris, 1844–1895.

Recueil des historiens des croisades. Historiens orientaux, Académie des inscriptions et belles lettres (ed.), 5 vols., Paris, 1872–1906.

Recueil des historiens des Gaules et de la Frence, M. Bouquet *et al.* (eds), 24 vols., Paris, 1737–1904.

Regesta pontificum romanorum, P. Jaffé (ed.), Berlin, 1851.

Regesta pontificum romanorum ab condita ecclesia ad annum post Christum natun MCXCVIII, P. Jaffé (ed.), 2 vols., Leipzig, 1885–1888.

Regesta pontificum romanorum inde ab anno 1198 ad annum 1304, A. Potthast (ed.), 2 vols., Berlin, 1874–1875.

Regesta regni Hierosolymitani, R Röhricht (ed.), 2 vols., Innsbruck, 1893–1904.

La Règle des Templiers, L. Daillez (ed. and tr.), Nice, 1977.

La Règle du Temple, H de Curzon (ed.), Paris, 1886.

The Rule of the Templars, J. Upton-Ward (ed. and tr.), Woodbridge, 1992.

The Rule, Statutes and Customs of the Hospitallers, E. King (ed. and tr.), London, 1934.

Statuta capitulorum generalium ordinis Cisterciensis, J. Canivez (ed.), 8 vols., Louvain, 1933–1941.

Statuts d'hotels-Dieu et de léproseries, L. Le Grand (ed.), Paris, 1904.

Storia del musulmani di Sicilia, M. Amari (ed.), 8 vols., Catania, 1930–1939.

Veterum scriptorum et monumentorum historicum, dogmaticorum, moralium, amplissima collectio, E. Martène and U. Durand (eds.), 9 vols., Paris, 1724–1733.

Visites générales des commanderies de l'ordre des Hospitaliers dépendantes du grand prieuré de Saint-Gilles (1338), B. Beaucage (ed.), Aix-en-Provence, 1982.

Ysengrimus, J. Mann (ed.), Mittellateinische Studien und Texte 12, Leiden, 1987.

Secondary Sources

Abulafia, D., 'Marseilles, Acre and the Mediterranean, 1200–1291', *Coinage in the Latin East: the Fourth Oxford Symposium on Coinage and Monetary History*, P. Edbury and D. Metcalf (eds.), Oxford, 1980, pp. 19–39.

Aitkin, R., 'The Knights Templars in Scotland', *Scottish Review* 32(1898), pp. 1–36.

Albanès, J., *Le Couvent royal de Saint-Maximin en Provence de l'ordre des frères prêcheurs*, Marseille, 1882.

Amalvy, J.-P. and A. Salsac, *La Couvertoirade: Guide de visite*, Montpellier, 1986.

Amargier, P., 'La Situation hospitalière à Marseille', *CF* 13(1978), pp. 239–260.

Amblard Larolphie, P., 'Le Crédit à Toulouse et dans le Toulousain (1140–1208)', *AM* 10(1944), pp. 5–23.

Ambraziejuté, M., *Studien über die Johanniterregel*, Freiburg, 1929.

Annales du Midi, Toulouse, 1889– .

L'Art de Vérifier les dates des faits historiques, des inscriptions, des chroniques, et autres monumens, depuis la naissance de notre-Seigneur, a Benedictine (ed.), 3 vols., Paris, 1883–1887.

Aubenas, R., *Etude sur le notariat provençal*, Aix-en-Provence, 1951.

Aurell i Cardona, M., 'Le Personnel politique Catalan et Aragonais d'Alphonse ier en Provence (1166–1196)', *AM* 93(1981), pp. 121–139.

Baratier, E., *La Démographie provençale du XIIᵉ au XVIᵉ siècle*, Paris, 1961.

―――― 'Marquisat et comtés en Provence', *Histoire de la Provence*, E. Baratier (ed.), Toulouse, 1969, pp. 123–169.

―――― 'Rois Angevins et papes d'Avignon (xiiie–xve siècles), *Histoire de la Provence*, E. Baratier (ed.), Toulouse, 1969, pp. 169–217.

―――― 'Les Communautés de Haute-Provence au moyen age: problèmes d'habitat de population', *PH* 21(1971), pp. 237–248.

Barber, M., 'James of Molay, the last Grand Master of the Order of the Temple', *Studia monastica* 14(1972), pp. 91–124.

―――― *The Trial of the Templars*, Cambridge, 1993.

―――― 'Catharism and the Occitan Nobility: the Lordships of Cabaret, Minerve and Termes', *The Ideals and Practice of Medieval Knighthood* 3, Papers from the Fourth Strawberry Hill Conference (1988), C. Harper-Bill and R. Harvey (eds.), Woodbridge, 1990, pp. 1–19.

―――― 'Supplying the Crusader States: The Role of the Templars', *The Horns of Ḥaṭṭīn*, B. Kedar (ed.), London, 1992, pp. 314–326.

―――― *The New Knighthood*, Cambridge, 1994.

Bautier, R.-H., 'Recherches sur les routes de l'Europe médiévale. I. De Paris et de foires de Champagne à la Méditerranée par le Massif Central', *Bulletin philologique et historique* (1960), pp. 99–143.

―――― 'Recherches sur les routes de l'Europe médiévale. II. Le grand axe routier est-ouest du Midi de la France: d'Avignon à Toulouse', *Bulletin philologique et historique* (1961), pp. 277–308.

―――― *The Economic Development of Medieval Europe*, H. Karolyi (tr.), London, 1971.

Beaucage, B., 'Une Enigme des Hospitaliers de Saint-Jean de Jérusalem: le Déficit chronique des commanderies du moyen Rhône, au prieuré de Provence, en 1338', *PH* 30(1980), pp. 137–164.

Benjamin, R., 'A Forty Years War: Toulouse and the Plantagenets, 1156–96', *Historical Research, The Bulletin of the Institute of Historical Research*, 61(1988), pp. 270–285.

Benoit, F., *et al.*, *Villes épiscopales de Provence: Aix, Arles, Fréjus, Marseille et Riez de l'époque gallo-romaine au moyen-age*, Paris, 1954.

Bensch, S. P., *Barcelona and its Rulers, 1096–1291*, Cambridge, 1995.

Berlière, U., 'La Familia dans les monastères bénédictins au moyen âge', *Mémoires de l'Académie royale de Belgique* 29(1930), pp. 3–123.

Bisson, T., *Medieval France and her Pyrenean Neighbours*, London, 1989.

―――― *The Medieval Crown of Aragon*, Oxford, 1991.

Blanc, C., 'Les Pratiques de piété des laïcs dans les pays du Bas-Rhone aux xie et xiie siècles', *AM* 72(1960), pp. 139–147.

Blancard, L., *Inventaire-sommaire des archives départementales antérieures à 1799, Bouches-du-Rhone, archives écclésiastiques, série H*, Paris, 1869.

Blaquière, H., 'Les Hospitaliers en Albigeois à l'époque de la croisade: la commanderie de Rayssac', *CF* 4(1969), pp. 335–351.

Blès, A., *Dictionnaire historique des rues de Marseille*, Marseille, 1989.

Bonnet, E., 'Les Maisons de l'ordre du Temple dans le Languedoc méditerranéen', *Cahiers d'histoire et d'archéologie* 7(1934), pp. 513–525.

Bourgeois, B., 'A la Recherche de la grange templière de Gals en haut Rouergue', *AM* 100(1988), pp. 81–86.

Brundage, J., 'A Twelfth-Century Oxford Disputation Concerning the Privileges of the Knights Hospitalers', *Mediæval Studies* 24(1962), pp. 153–160.

——— 'The Votive Obligations of Crusaders: the Development of a Canonistic Doctrine', *Traditio* 24(1968), pp. 77–118.

——— *Medieval Canon Law and The Crusader*, Madison, Milwaukee and London, 1969.

——— 'The Lawyers of the Military Orders', in *The Military Orders. Fighting for the Faith and Caring for the Sick*, M. Barber (ed.), Aldershot, 1994, pp. 346–357.

Bull, M., *Knightly Piety and the Lay Response to the First Crusade, The Limousin and Gascony c.970–c.1130*, Oxford, 1993.

Bulst-Thiele, M.-L., *Sacræ domus militiæ Templi Hierosolymitani magistri, Untersuchungen zur Geschichte des Templerordens*, Göttingen, 1974.

Busquet, R., *Histoire de Provence des origines à la révolution française*, Monaco, 1954.

Butler, A., *Butler's Lives*, of the Saints, H. Thirston and D. Attwater (eds.), 4 vols., Aberdeen, 1956.

Cabié, E., 'Sur trois chartes albigeoises concernant les origines de l'ordre de Saint-Jean de Jérusalem', *AM* 10(1891), pp. 145–156.

Cabot, J., *Anciens ports et moulins de petite Camargue*, Montpellier, 1991.

Cahen, E., *et al.* (eds.), *Archéologie*, in *Les Bouches-du-Rhône, encyclopédie départemetal*, IV, Marseille, 1932.

Cahiers de Fanjeaux, Toulouse, 1966– .

Camera, M., *Memorie storico-diplomatiche dell'antica città e ducato di Amalfi*, 2 vols., Salerno, 1876–1881.

Carcenac, A.-R., *Les Templiers du Larzac*, Nîmes, 1994.

Carrière, V., 'Les Débuts de l'ordre du Temple', *Le Moyen Age* 18(1914), pp. 308–335.

Castaing-Sicard, M., *Monnaies féodales et circulation monétaire en Languedoc (Xe-XIIIe siècles)*, Toulouse, 1967.

Caster, G., 'Le Vignoble suburbain de Toulouse au XIIe siècle', *AM* 78(1966), pp. 201–207.

Castro, S., *Los Comendadores de la ordern de Santiago*, Madrid, 1949.

Cazel, F., 'The Tax of 1185 in Aid of the Holy Land', *Speculum* 30(1955), pp. 385–392.

Chailan, M., *L'Ordre de Malte dans la ville d'Arles*, Marseille, 1974.

Chartrou, J., *L'Anjou de 1109 à 1151*, Paris, 1928.

Clerc, M., *Aquae Sextiae, histoire d'Aix-en-Provence dans l'antiquité*, Aix-en-Provence, 1916.

Cole, P., *The Preaching of the Crusades to the Holy Land, 1095–1270*, Cambridge (Mass.), 1991.

Combes, J., 'Les Foires en Languedoc au moyen âge', *Annales* 13(1958), pp. 231–259.

Constable, G., 'Monasteries, Rural Churches and the Cura Animarum in the Early Middle Ages', *Settimane di studio del centro italiano de studi sull'altro medioevo, XXVIII: Cristainizzazione ad organizzazione ecclesiastica delle compagne nell'alto medioevo: espansione e resistenze*, II, Spoleto, 1982, pp. 349–389.

———— 'The Financing of the Crusades in the Twelfth Century', *Outremer – Studies in the History of the Crusading Kingdom of Jerusalem presented to Joshua Prawer*, B. Kedar *et al.* (eds.), Jerusalem, 1982, pp. 64–88.

———— 'The Authority of Superiors in Religious Communities', *La Notion d'autorité au moyen age: Islam, Byzance, Occident. Colloques internationaux de la Napoule*, G. Makdisi *et al.* (eds.), Paris, 1982, pp. 189–210.

———— 'Papal, Imperial and Monastic Propaganda in the Eleventh and Twelfth Centuries', *Prédication et propagande au Moyen Age: Islam, Byzance, Occident. Penn-Paris-Dumbarton Oaks Colloquia (20–25 octobre 1980)* III, G. Makdisi (ed.), Paris, 1983, pp. 179–198.

———— 'Medieval Charters as a Source for the History of the Crusades', *Crusade and Settlement: Papers read at the First Conference of the Society for the Study of the Crusades and the Latin East and presented to R. C. Smail*, P. Edbury (ed.), Cardiff, 1985, pp. 73–89.

Coulet, N., 'Hôpitaux et œuvres d'assistance dans le diocèse et la ville d'Aix-en-Provence XIIIe–mi-XIVe siècles', *CF* 13 (1978), pp. 213–237.

Cousin, P., 'Les Débuts de l'ordre des Templiers et Saint-Bernard', *Melanges Saint Bernard, XXIVᵉ congrès de l'association Bourguignonne des sociétés savantes*, Dijon, 1953, pp. 41–52.

Crozet, R., 'Le Voyage d'Urbain II en France', *AM* 49(1937), pp. 42–69.

d'Abdal, R., 'A Propos de la domination de la maison de Barcelone sur le Midi français', *AM* 76(1964), pp. 315–345.

Daillez, L., *Les Templiers et l'agriculture ou les composts Templiers*, Nice, 1981.

Davis, R., 'The Warhorses of the Normans', *Anglo-Norman Studies*, 10, *Proceedings of the Battle Conference*, R. Allen Brown (ed.), Woodbridge, 1987, pp. 67–81.

———— *The Medieval Warhorse, Origin, Development and Redevelopment*, London, 1989.

de Fontette, M., 'Les Mendiants supprimés au 2e concile de Lyon (1274). Frères sachets et frères pies', *CF* 8(1973), pp. 193–217.

de La Coste-Messelière, R. and G. Jugnot, 'L'Acceuil des pèlerins à Toulouse', *CF* 15(1980), pp. 117–135.

Delaruelle, E., 'La Ville de Toulouse vers 1200 d'après quelques travaux récents', *CF* 1(1966), pp. 107–122.

———— 'Templiers et Hospitaliers en Languedoc pendant la croisade des Albigeois', *CF* 4(1969), pp. 315–334.

Delaville le Roulx, J., *Les Hospitaliers en Terre Sainte et à Chypre (1100–1310)*, Paris, 1904.

Delehaye, H., *Les Légendes hagiographiques*, Brussels, 1905.

Demurger, A., *Vie et mort de l'ordre du Temple, 1120–1314*, Paris, 1989.

de Saint-Paul, F., *Jean de Matha, un fondateur d'avant-garde*, Paris, Montreal, 1960.

de Santi, L., 'Relations du comte de Toulouse Raymond VII avec la ville de Marseille', *AM* 11(1899), pp. 200–207.

Deschamps, P., 'Raymond de St Gilles et sa sépulture au chateau de Tripoli (Liban)', *Etudes de civilisation médiévale (XIᵉ–XIIᵉ siècles), Mélanges offerts à E.-R. Labande*, CESM (ed.), Poitiers, 1975, pp. 209–217.

Destrez, J.-A., 'La "Pecia" dans les manuscrits du moyen âge', *Revue des sciences philosophiques et théologiques* 13(1924), pp. 182–197.

de Tarde, H., 'La Rédaction des coutumes de Narbonne', *AM* 85(1973), pp. 371–395.

de Valous, G., 'Quelques observations sur la toute primitive observance des Templiers et la *Regula pauperum commilitonum Christi Templi Salomonici* rédigée par Saint-Bernard au concile de Troyes (1128)', *Mélanges Saint Bernard, 24e congrès de l'association Bourguignonne des sociétés savantes*, Dijon, 1953, pp. 32–40.

Devic, C., and J. Vaissete, *Histoire générale de Languedoc*, 5 vols., Toulouse, 1872–1904.

Diago, F., *Historia de la provincia de Aragón de la orden de Predicadores*, Barcelona, 1599.

Dictionnaire de biographie française, J. Baltheau, M. Barroux and M. Prevost (eds.), Paris, 1929– .

Dorland's Illustrated Medical Dictionary (28th edition), Philadelphia, 1994.

Dossat, Y., 'La Société méridionale à la veille de la croisade albigeoise', *Revue historique et littéraire de Languedoc* 1(1944).

du Bourg, A., *Histoire du grand-prieuré de Toulouse*, Toulouse, 1883.

—— 'Établissement des chevaliers du Temple et de Saint-Jean de Jérusalem en Rouergue', *Mémoires de la société des lettres* 13(1886), pp. 141–181.

Duby, G., 'Techniques et rendements agricoles dans les Alpes du sud en 1338', *AM* 70(1958), pp. 404–413.

—— 'La Seigneurie at l'économie paysanne. Alpes du sud, 1338', *Etudes rurales* 2 (1961), pp. 2–36.

—— *Guerriers et paysans VIIᵉ–XIIᵉ siècle*, Paris, 1973.

—— *Le Moyen âge*, Paris, 1987.

—— *Seigneurs et paysans*, Saint-Amand-Montrond, 1988.

du Cange, C., *Glossarium mediæ et infimæ latinitatis*, 7 vols., Paris, 1840–1850.

Dufourcq, C., *La Vie quotidienne dans les ports méditerranéens au moyen age (Provence, Languedoc, Catalogne)*, Biarritz, 1975.

—— *La Vie quotidienne dans l'Europe médiévale sous domination arabe*, Biarritz, 1978.

du Mège, A., 'Notes sur quelque monuments de l'ordre de la milice du Temple et sur l'église de Montsaunès', *Mémoires de la société archéologique du Midi de la France* 5(1842), pp. 187–209.

Dunbabin, J., *France in the Making, 843–1180*, Oxford, 1985.

—— *A Hound of God. Pierre de La Palud and the Fourteenth Century Church*, Oxford, 1991.

Dupont, A., 'L'Exploitation du sel sur les étangs de Languedoc (ixe-xiiie siècles)', *AM* 70(1958), pp. 7–25.

—— 'Un Aspect du commerce du sel en Languedoc oriental au xiiie siècle: la Rivalité entre Lunel et Aigues-Mortes', *PH* 18(1968), pp. 101–112.

Dupront, A., *Du sacré, croisades et pèlerinages, images et langages*, Mayenne, 1987.

Durand, G., 'L'Architecture grandmontaine dans le Midi Languedocien entre 1150 et 1250', *AM* 107(1995), pp. 5–34.

Durbec, J., 'Les Templiers en Provence. Formation des commanderies et répartitions géographique de leurs biens', *PH* 8(1959), pp. 3–37, 97–132.

—— 'L'Exploitation des biens d'un baillage provençal des Hospitaliers de Saint-Jean-de-Jérusalem en 1338. Le Baillage de Beaulieu, entre Solliès et Hyères', *PH* 25(1975), pp. 243–254.

Edwards, J., 'The Templars in Scotland in the Thirteenth Century', *Scottish Historical Review* 5(1907), pp. 13–25.

Elm, K., 'Ausbreitung, Wirksamkeit und Ende des provençalischen Sackbrüder (*Fratres de poenitentia Jesu Christi*) in Deutschland und den Niederlanden. Ein Beitrag zur kurialen und konziliaren Ordenspolitik des 13. Jahrhunderts', *Francia. Forschungen zur Westeuropäischen Geschichte* 1(1973), pp. 257–324.

Emery, R., *Heresy and Inquisition in Narbonne*, New York, 1941.

—— 'The Friars of the Blessed Virgin Mary and the Pied Friars', *Speculum* 24(1949), pp. 228–238.

—— 'The Friars of the Sack', *Speculum* 18(1943), pp. 323–334.

────── *The Friars in Medieval France*, New York, 1962.

Fedden, R., and J. Thomas, *Crusader Castles*, London, 1950.

Fink-Errara, G., 'Une Institution du monde médiéval: la "pecia" ', *Revue philosophique de Louvain* 60(1962), pp. 184–243.

Fletcher, R., *Moorish Spain*, London, 1994.

Fliche, A., *Aigues-Mortes et Saint-Gilles*, Paris 1934.

Flipo, V., *Mémento pratique d'archéologie française*, Paris, 1929.

Forey, A., 'The Order Of Mountjoy', *Speculum* 46(1971), pp. 250–266.

────── *The Templars in the Corona de Aragón*, Oxford, 1973.

────── 'The Military Orders in the Crusading Proposals of the late-Thirteenth and early-Fourteenth Centuries', *Traditio* 36(1980), pp. 317–345.

────── 'The Will of Alfonso I of Aragon and Navarre', *Durham University Journal* (1980), pp. 59–65.

────── 'A Rejoinder', *Durham University Journal* (1981), p. 173.

────── 'The Military Orders and the Spanish Reconquest in the Twelfth and Thirteenth Centuries', *Traditio* 40(1984), pp. 197–234.

────── 'The Militarisation of the Hospital of Saint John', *Studia Monastica* 26(1984), pp. 75–89.

────── 'The Emergence of the Military Order in the Twelfth Century', *Journal of Ecclesiastical History* 36(1985), pp. 175–195.

────── 'Novitiate and Instruction in the Military Orders in the Twelfth and Thirteenth Centuries', *Speculum* 61(1986), pp. 1–17.

────── 'Recruitment to the Military Orders (Twelfth to mid-Fourteenth centuries)', *Viator* 17(1986), pp. 141–71.

────── 'Women and the Military Orders in the Twelfth and Thirteenth Centuries', *Studia monastica* 29(1987), pp. 63–93.

────── 'The Military Orders and Holy War against Christians', *English Historical Review* 104(1989), pp. 1–24.

────── 'The Military Orders and the Ransoming of Captives from Islam (Twelfth to Early Fourteenth Centuries)', *Studia monastica* 33(1991), pp. 259–279.

────── *The Military Orders*, Basingstoke, 1992.

Fournier, P., *Le Royaume d'Arles et de Vienne*, Grenoble, 1884.

Gagnière, S., 'Les Moulins à bateaux sur le Rhône à Avignon et dans les environs', *PH* 1(1950), pp. 75–87.

Gams, P., *Series episcoporum*, Ratisbon, 1873.

García Larragueta, S., 'La Orden de San Juan en la crisis del imperio hispánico del siglo XII', *Hispania* 12(1952), pp. 483–524.

────── *El Gran priorado de Navarra de la orden de San Juan de Jerusalén*, 2 vols., Pamplona, 1957.

Garrigues, J., 'Les Styles du commencement de l'année dans le Midi. L'Emploi de l'année pisane en pays Toulousain et Languedoc', *AM* 53(1941), pp. 237–270, 336–362.

Garth, H., *Saint Mary Magdalene in Mediaeval Literature*, Baltimore, 1950.

Gasquet, F., *English Monastic Life*, London, 1904.

Germain, A., *Histoire du commerce de Montpellier*, 3 vols., Montpellier, 1861.

Gervers, M., '*Pro defensionis Terre Sancte*: the Development and Exploitation of the Hospitallers' Landed Estate in Essex', in *The Military Orders. Fighting for the Faith and Caring for the Sick*, M. Barber (ed.), Aldershot, 1994, pp. 3–20.

Gilles, H., 'A Propos des dîmes monastiques', *CF* 19(1984), pp. 287–308.

Giordanengo, G., 'Les Hôpitaux arlésiens du xiie au xive siècle', *CF* 13(1978), pp. 189–212.

———— *Le Droit féodal dans les pays du droit écrit. L'Exemple de la Provence et du Dauphiné XIIᵉ–début XIVᵉ siècle*, Rome, 1988.

Gmelin, J., 'Die Regel des Templeordens kritisch untersucht', *Mitteilungen des Instituts für Österreichische Geschichsforschung* 14(1893), pp. 237–284.

Gougaud, L., *Dévotions et pratiques ascétiques du moyen âge*, Paris, 1925.

Gouron, A., 'Les Etapes de la pénétration du droit romain au xiie siècle dans l'ancienne Septimanie', *AM* 69(1957), pp. 103–120.

———— 'Diffusion des consulats méridionaux et expansion du droit romainaux xiie et xiiie siècles', *Bibliothèque de l'Ecole des Chartes* 121(1963), Paris, pp. 26–77.

———— 'Le Rôle social des juristes dans les villes méridionales au Moyen Age', *Annales de la Faculté des Lettres et Sciences humaines de Nice* 9–10(1969), pp. 55–67.

———— ' "Libertas hominium Montispessulani", Rédaction et diffusion des coutumes de Montpellier', *AM* 90(1978), pp. 289–318.

———— 'Aux Origines de l'"émergence" du droit; glossateurs et coutumes méridionales (xiie – milieu du xiiie siècle)', *La Société du droit dans le Midi de la France au Moyen Age*, Variorum (ed.), London, 1984, pp. 255–270.

———— 'The Training of Southern French Lawyers during the Thirteenth and Fourteenth Centuries', *La Société du droit dans le Midi de la France au Moyen Age*, Variorum (ed.), London, 1984, pp. 219–227.

———— *La Science du droit dans le Midi de la France au Moyen Age*, London, 1984.

Gouron, M., 'Découverte du tympan de l'église Saint-Martin à Saint-Gilles', *AM* 62(1950), pp. 115–120.

Grand, R., 'Justice criminelle, procèdure et peines dans les villes aux xiiie et xive siècles', *Bibliothèque de l'Ecole des Chartes* 102(1941), pp. 51–108.

Guerreau, A., 'Observations statistiques sur les créations de couvents franciscains en France, xiiie-xve siècles', *Mouvements franciscains et société française XIIᵉ–XXᵉ siècles*, A. Vauchez (ed.), Paris, 1984, pp. 27–60.

Guimbail, R., 'Les Hommes et la terre dans une communauté du Lauraguais: Puysubran (Pexiora) du xiie au début du xvie siècle', *AM* 99(1987), pp. 429–452.

Gutton, F., *L'Ordre de Calatrava*, Paris, 1955.

———— *L'Ordre d'Alcantara*, Paris, 1975.

Hamilton, B., *The Albigensian Crusade*, London, 1974.

———— *The Latin Church in the Crusader States: The Secular Church*, London, 1980.

Hiestand, R., 'Chronologisches zur Geschichte des Königreiches Jerusalem um 1130', *Deutsches Archiv* 26(1970), pp. 220–229.

———— 'Saint-Ruf d'Avignon, Raymond de Saint-Gilles et l'Eglise Latine du comtée de Tripoli', *AM* 98(1986), pp. 327–336.

Higounet, C., 'Les Origines d'une commanderie de l'ordre de Malte: le Burgaud (Haute-Garonne)', *AM* 44(1932), pp. 129–141.

———— 'Le Peuplement de Toulouse au xiie siècle', *AM* 55(1943), pp. 490–498.

———— 'L'Occupation du sol du pays entre Tarn et Garonne au Moyen Age', *AM* 65(1953), pp. 301–330.

———— 'Observations sue la seigneurie rurale et l'habitat en Rouergue du ixe au xive siècle', *AM* 62(1954), pp. 121–134.

Hildesheimer, F., *Notre-Dame de la Garde, la bonne mère de Marseille*, Marseille, 1985.

Hill, J. and L., 'Justification historique du titre de Raymond de Saint-Gilles: "Christiane milicie excellentissimus princeps" ', *AM* 66(1954), pp. 102–112.

────── *Raymond IV Count of Toulouse*, Syracuse, 1962.

Hitti, P., *History of the Arabs*, Basingstoke, 1994.

Hodgett, G., *A Social and Economic History of Medieval Europe*, London, 1972.

Holt, R., *The Mills of Medieval England*, Oxford, 1988.

Housely, N. *The Later Crusades, 1274–1580*, Oxford, 1992.

Hunt, N. (ed.), *Cluniac Monasteries in the central Middle Ages*, London and Basingstoke, 1971.

Hyland, A., *The Medieval Warhorse from Byzantium to the Crusades*, Stroud, 1994.

Jaspert, N., 'La Estructuración de las primeras posesiones del capítulo del Santo Sepolcro en la península Ibérica: la génesis del priorado de Santa Ana en Barcelona y sus dependencias', *I. Jornadas de estudio la orden del Santo Sepulcro*, Calatayud – Zaragoza, 1991, pp. 93–108.

Jéolas, R., *Bulletin de l'association d'histoire et d'archéologie de Saint-Gilles, Exposition 1984, Les ordres militaires à Saint-Gilles au XIIe siècle*, 1984.

Jotischky, A., *The Perfection of Solitude. Hermits and Monks in the Crusader States*, Pennsylvania, 1995.

Katsura, H., 'Serments, hommages et fiefs dans la seigneurie des Guilhem de Montpellier (fin XIe-début XIIIe siècle)', *AM* 104(1992), pp. 141–161.

King, E., *The Knights Hospitallers in the Holy Land*, London, 1931.

Knöpfler, Dr, 'Die Ordensregel der Tempelherren', *Historisches Jahrbuch* 8(1877), pp. 666–695.

Knowles, D., *Thomas Beckett*, London, 1970.

Lafont, R., *Histoire d'Occitanie*, Paris, 1979.

Lavoie, R., 'Les Statistiques criminelles et le visage du justicier: Justice royale et justice seigneuriale en Provence au Moyen Age', *PH* 28(1979), pp. 3–20.

Lawrence, C., *Medieval Monasticism*, London and New York, 1989.

────── *The Friars*, London, 1994.

Le Blévec, D., 'Aux Origines des Hospitaliers de Saint-Jean de Jérusalem: Gérard dit "Tenque" et l'établissement de l'ordre dans le Midi', *AM* 89(1977), pp. 137–151.

────── 'Les Templiers en Vivarais: Les Archives de la commanderie de Jalèz et l'implantation de l'ordre du Temple en Cévennes', *Revue du Vivarais* 84(1980), pp. 36–49.

Le Blévec, D., and A. Venturini, 'Cartulaires des ordres militaires XIIe–XIIIe siècles (Provence occidentale – basse vallée du Rhône)', *Mémoires et documents de l'Ecole des Chartes* 39(1993), pp. 451–465.

Leclercq, J., 'La Vêture "ad succurrendum" d'après le moine Raoul', *Analecta monastica, Studia Anselmiana* 37(1955), pp. 158–168.

Ledesma, M., 'Notas sobre la actividad militar de los hospitalarios', *Principe de Viana* 25(1964), pp. 51–56.

Lees, B., *Records of the Templars in England in the Twelfth Century*, London, 1935.

Le Goff, J., *La Naissance du purgatoire*, Paris, 1981.

────── *Saint Louis*, Paris, 1996.

Legras, A.-M., and J.-L. Lemaitre, 'La Pratique liturgique des Templiers et des Hospitaliers de Saint-Jean de Jérusalem', *L'Ecrit dans la société médiévale, Textes en hommages à Lucie Fossier*, C. Bourlet and A. Dufour (eds.), Paris, 1991, pp. 77–137.

Lejeune, R., 'L'Esprit de croisade dans l'épopée occitane', *CF* 4(1969), pp. 143–173.

Léonard, E., *Gallicarum militiae Templi domorum eorumque præceptorum seriem secundum Albonensia apographa in bibliotheca nationali Parisiensi asservata*, Paris, 1930.

────── *Les Angevins de Naples*, Paris, 1954.

Le Roy Ladurie, E., *Montaillou, village occitane de 1294 à 1324*, Paris, 1975.

Levy, E., *Petit dictionnaire Provençal-Français*, Heidelberg, 1973.

Lewis, A., 'Patterns of Economic Development in Southern France, 1050–1271', *Studies in Medieval and Renaissance History* 3(1980), pp. 55–83.

Lewis, A. and T. Runyan, *European Naval and Maritime History, 300–1500*, Bloomington, 1985.

Lomas, D., *La Orden de Santiago 1170–1275*, Madrid, 1965.

Lourie, E., 'The Will of Alfonso I, "El Batallador',' King of Aragon and Navarre: a Reassessment', *Speculum* 50(1975), pp. 635–651.

—— 'The Will of Alfonso I of Aragon and Navarre. A Reply to Dr Forey', *Durham University Journal* (1981), pp. 165–172.

Lunt, W., *Papal Revenue in the Middle Ages*, 2 vols., Baltimore, 1934.

Lynch, J., *Simoniacal Entry into Religious Life from 1000 to 1260*, Columbia, 1976.

Macalister, R., *Ecclesiastical Vestments*, London, 1896.

Madaule, J., *Le Drame albigeois et l'unité française*, Saint-Amand, 1973.

Magnou, E., 'Oblature, classe chevaleresque et servage dans les maisons méridionales du Temple au xiie siècle', *AM* 73(1961), pp. 377–397.

Magnou-Nortier, E., 'Fidélité et féodalité méridionales d'après les serments de fidélité (xe–début xiie siècle), *AM* 80(1968), pp. 457–484.

Mandonnet, P., *Saint Dominique, l'idée, l'homme et l'œuvre*, 2 vols., Paris, 1937.

Marres, P., *Les Grands Causses*, 2 vols., Tours, 1935.

Mayer, H., *The Crusades*, J. Gillingham (tr.), Oxford, 1972.

—— *Marseilles Levantehandel und ein akkonensisches Fälscheratelier des XIII. Jahrhunderts*, Tübingen, 1972.

Meersseman, G., 'Etudes sur les anciennes confréries dominicaines, 4, Les milices de Jésus-Christ', *Archivum fratrum predicatorum* 23(1953), pp. 175–308.

Melville, M., 'Les Débuts de l'ordre du Temple', *Die geistlichen Ritterordern Europas, Vorträge und Forschungen* 26(1980), pp. 23–31.

Menache, S., *The Vox Dei*, New York and Oxford, 1990.

Ménard, M., *Histoire civile, écclesiastique, et litteraire de la ville de Nismes avec les preuves*, Paris, 1744.

Menéndez Pidal, J., 'Noticias acerca de la Orden militar de Santa Maria de España', *Revista de archivos, bibliotecas y museos* 17(1907), pp. 161–207.

Metcalf, D., 'The Templars as Bankers and Monetary Transfers between West and East in the Twelfth Century', *Coinage in the Latin East: the Fourth Oxford Symposium on Coinage and Monetary History*, P. Edbury and D. Metcalf (eds.), Oxford, 1980, pp. 1–17.

Miquel, J., *Cités Templières du Larzac*, Millau, 1989.

Miret y Sans, J., *Les Cases de Templers y Hospitalers en Catalunya*, Barcelona, 1910.

Moorman, J., *A History of the Franciscan Order*, Oxford, 1968.

Moretus, H., 'Les Saintes-Eulalies', *Revue des questions historiques* 89(1911), pp. 85–119.

Morris, C., '*Equestris Ordo*: Chivalry as a Vocation in the Twelfth Century', *Studies in Church History* 15(1978), pp. 87–96.

Morris, R. (Rear Admiral), *The Hydrographer of the Navy, Ocean Passages for the World*, Crown Copyright, 1987.

Mourre, M., *Dictionnaire encyclopédique d'histoire*, Paris, 1978.

Mundy, J., *Liberty and Political Power in Toulouse 1050–1230*, New York, 1954.

Murray, A., *Reason and Society in the Middle Ages*, Oxford, 1978.

Neipp, B., *Marie-Madeleine; femme et apôtre*, Renens, 1991.

Nelli, R., 'Le Vicomte de Béziers (1185–1209) vu par les Troubadours', *CF* 4(1969), pp. 303–314.

Nicholson, H., *Templars, Hospitallers and Teutonic Knights: Images of the Military Orders 1128–1291*, Leicester, 1993.

Nicolle, D., 'Arms and Armor Illustrated in the Art of the Latin East', *The Horns of Ḥaṭṭīn*, B. Kedar (ed.), Jerusalem and London, 1992, pp. 327–340.

O'Callaghan, J., *The Spanish Military Order of Calatrava and its Affiliates*, London, 1975.

Odriozola y Grimaud, C., *Ramón Berenguer IV, conde de Barcelona, caballero del Santo Sepulcro de Jerusalén. Memorias históricas referentes a la cesión en su favor de la Corona de Aragón, hecha por la Orden militar del Santo Sepulcro, la del Hospital y del Temple en el año 1140*, Barcelona, 1911.

Ourliac, P., 'Le Pays de La Selve à la fin du xiie siècle', *AM* 80(1968), pp. 581–602.

Pacaut, M., 'Structures monastiques, société et l'Eglise en Occident aux xie et xiie siècles', *Cahiers d'histoire 20, Aspects de la vie conventuelle aux XIe et XIIe siècles. Actes du Ve congrès de la société des historiens médiévistes (St-Etienne, 1974)*, Lyons, 1975, pp. 191–131.

Palanque, J.-R., 'Sur les origines du culte de la Madeleine en Provence', *PH* 9(1959), pp. 193–200.

Pallarés Gil, M., 'La Frontera sarracena en tiempo de Berenguer IV', *Boletin de historia y geografia del Bajo-Barcelona* 1(1907), pp. 150–151.

Pallenberg, C., *La Crociata dei bambini*, Milan, 1983.

Paterson, L., 'The Occitan Squire in the Twelfth and Thirteenth Centuries', *The Ideals and Practice of Medieval Knighthood, Papers from the First and Second Strawberry Hill Conferences*, C. Harper-Bill and R. Harvey (eds.), Woodbridge, 1986, pp. 133–152.

——— *The World of the Troubadours, Medieval Occitan Society, c.1100–1300*, Cambridge, 1993.

Paul, J., 'La Signification sociale du Franciscanisme', *Mouvements franciscains et société française XIIe–XXe siècles*, A. Vauchez (ed.), Paris, 1984, pp. 9–25.

Phillips, J., 'Hugh of Payns and the 1129 Damascus Crusade', in *The Military Orders. Fighting for the Faith and Caring for the Sick*, M. Barber (ed.), Aldershot, 1994, pp. 346–357.

——— *Defenders of the Holy Land, Relations between the Latin East and the West 1119–1187*, Oxford, 1996.

Poly, J.-P., *La Provence et la société féodale (879–1166)*, Paris, 1976.

Portal, F., *La République marseillaise du XIIIe siècle*, Marseille, 1907.

Porter, W., *A History of the Knights of Malta*, 2 vols., London, 1858.

Prawer, J., *The Latin Kingdom of Jerusalem*, London, 1972.

La Production du livre universitaire au moyen âge: exemplar et pecia, L. Bataillon *et al.* (eds.), Paris, 1988.

Provence Historique, Marseille, 1950– .

Prütz, H., *Die Anatomie der Templerordens*, Sitzungsberichte der Münchner Academie, 1903.

——— *Die geistlichen Ritterorden, Ihre Stellung zur kirchlichen, politischen, gesellschaftlichen und wirtschaftlichen Entwicklung des Mittelalters*, Berlin, 1908.

Pryor, J., *Business Contracts of Medieval Provence*, Toronto, 1981.

——— 'Transportation of Horses by Sea During the Era of the Crusades: Eighth Century to 1265 A.D.', *The Mariner's Mirror* 68(1982), pp. 9–27, 103–125.

——— 'In subsidiam Terræ Sanctæ: Exports of Foodstuffs and War Materials from the Kingdom of Sicily to the Kingdom of Jerusalem, 1285–1284', *Asian and African Studies* 22(1988), pp. 127–146.

Puig y Puig, S., *Episcopologio de la sede Barcinonense*, Barcelona, 1929.

Rassow, P., 'La Cofradia de Belchite', *Anuario de historia del derecho Español* 3(1926), pp. 200–226.

Remensnyder, A., *Remembering Kings Past, Monastic Foundation Legends in Medieval Southern France*, Ithaca, 1995.

Renouard, Y., 'Le Vin vieux au Moyen Age', *AM* 76(1964), pp. 448–455.

Reynaud, F., *La Commanderie de l'Hôpital de Saint-Jean de Jérusalem de Rhodes et de Malte à Manosque*, Gap, 1981.

Ribaucourt, C., 'Les Mendiants du Midi d'après la cartographie de "l'enquête" 146', *CF* 8(1973), pp. 25–33.

Richard, J., 'Le Milieu famial', *Bernard de Clairvaux*, Commission d'Histoire de l'ordre de Cîteaux (ed.), Paris, 1953, pp. 3–15.

———— *The Latin Kingdom of Jerusalem*, J. Shirley (tr.), Amsterdam, 1979.

———— 'Les Saint-Gilles et le comté de Tripoli', *CF* 18(1983), pp. 65–75.

Riley-Smith, J., *The Knights of Saint John in Jerusalem and Cyprus 1050–1310*, London, 1967.

———— *The Feudal Nobility and the Latin Kingdom of Jerusalem, 1174–1277*, London, 1973.

————*The First Crusade and the Idea of Crusading*, London, 1986.

Rocacher, J., *Rocamadour et son pèlerinage, étude historique et archéolgique*, 2 vols., Toulouse, 1979.

Rolland, H., 'La Monnaie de Saint-Gilles', *PH* 5(1955), pp. 32–38.

Rubin, M., *Corpus Christi, The Eucharist in Late Medieval Culture*, Cambridge, 1991.

Runciman, S., *A History of the Crusades*, Harmondsworth, 3 vols., 1990–1991.

———— *The Sicilian Vespers*, Cambridge, 1992.

Russell, J., *Medieval Demography*, New York, 1987.

Sainte-Eulalie de Cernon, Editions Nove 1211, Millau.

Saint-Jean, R., 'L'Abbaye cistercienne de Mazan (Ardèche) et ses filles provençales: Sénanque et Thoronet', *AM* 18(1968), pp. 77–100.

———— 'Les Origines du consulat en Vivarais méridional au Moyan Age', *AM* 88(1965), pp. 353–370.

Santoni, P., 'Les Deux premiers siècles du prieuré de Saint-Gilles de l'ordre de l'Hôpital de Saint-Jean de Jérusalem', *Actes du colloque de Barroux, Des Hospitaliers de Saint-Jean de Jérusalem, de Chypre et de Rhodes hier aux chevaliers de Malte aujourd'hui*, Paris, 1983, pp. 114–183.

Saxer, V., *Le Culte de Marie Madeleine en Occident*, Paris, 1959.

Schatzmiller, J., 'Structures communales juives à Marseille. Autour d'un contrat de 1278', *PH* 28(1979), pp. 33–45.

Schmid, P., 'Die Entstehung des Marseiller Kirchenstaates', *Archiv für Urkundenforschung* 10(1928), pp. 176–207.

Schnürer, G., *Die ursprüngliche Templerregel*, Freiburg, 1908.

Selwood, D., '*Quidem autem dubitaverunt*: The Saint, the Sinner, the Temple and a Possible Chronology', *Autour de la première croisade, Actes du colloque de la Society for the Study of the Crusades and the Latin East (Clermont-Ferrand, 22–25 juin 1995)*, M. Balard (ed.), Paris, 1996, pp. 221–230.

———— '*Ultra vel Citra Mare?* The Expansion of the Orders of the Temple and the Hospital into Occitania', *I. Templari: La Guerra è la Santità*, S. Cerrini (ed.), Piacenza, forthcoming.

Sery, L., 'Constance, fille de France, "Reine d'Angleterre",' Comtesse de Toulouse', *AM* 63(1951), pp. 193–209.

Sigal, P.-A., 'L'Ex-voto au Moyen Age dans les régions Nord-Ouest de la Méditeranée (XIIe-XVe siècles)', *PH* 33(1983), pp. 13–31.

Smith, G., *The Historical Geography of the Holy Land*, London, 1908.

Soucaille, A., 'Les Templiers et les Hospitaliers à Béziers', *Bulletin de la société archéologique, scientifique et littéraire de Béziers* 13(1885), pp. 154–163.

Southern, R., *Western Society and the Church in the Middle Ages*, Harmondsworth, 1990.

Soutou, A., 'Trois chartes occitanes du XIIIe siècle concernant les Hospitaliers de la Bastide-Pradines (Aveyron)', *AM* 79(1967), pp. 121–172.

——— *La Couvertoirade*, Millau, 1973.

——— 'Les Moulins des Templiers à Sainte-Eulalie de Cernon (Aveyron)', *AM* 103(1991), pp. 369–378.

Spicciani, A., 'Papa Innocenzo IV e i Templari', *I. Templari: mito e storia. Atti del convegno internazionale di studi alla magione Templare di Poggibonsi-Siena, 29–31 Maggio 1987*, G. Minnucci and F. Sardi (eds.), Siena, 1989, pp. 41–65.

Sternfeld, R., *Karl von Anjou als Graf von Provence*, Berlin, 1888.

Stouff, L., 'La Commune d'Arles au XIIIe siècle', *PH* 11(1961), pp. 294–316.

Strayer, J., *The Albigensian Crusades*, Ann Arbor, 1992.

Thomas, A., and F. Olivier-Martin, 'Un Document inédit sur la procédure accusatoire dans la châtellenie de Bellac au XIVe siècle', *Revue historique de droit français et etranger* 14(1935), pp. 707–732.

Toepfer, M., *Die Konversen der Zisterzienser. Untersuchungen über Ihren Beitrag zur mittelalterlichen Blüte des Ordens*, Berlin, 1983.

Torres-Fontes, J., 'La Orden de Santa Maria de España', *Miscelánea medieval Murciana*, 3(1977), pp. 73–119.

Treuille, H., 'Autour d'une variante du chemin de Saint Jacques de Toulouse vers le haut Comminges', *CF* 15(1980), pp. 99–116.

Trudon des Ormes, A., *Liste des maisons et de quelques dignitaires de l'ordre du Temple en Syrie, en Chypre et en France d'après les pièces du procès*, Paris, 1900.

Unger, R., *The Ship in the Medieval Economy*, London, 1980.

Vecchione, M., 'Un Edifice templier: la tour Saint-Blaise d'Hyères', *PH* 40(1990), pp. 57–75.

Ventura, J., *Alfons el Cast*, Barcelona, 1961.

Verdon, L., 'Les Revenues de la commanderie templière du Mas Déu (Roussillon) d'après le terrier de 1264', *AM* 107(1995), pp. 168–193.

Vicaire, M.-H., 'Le Développement de la province dominicaine de Provence', *CF* 8(1973), pp. 35–77.

Viguier, M.-C., 'Le "Sermon des juifs" à Carpentras: Carnaval ou pourim', *AM* 101(1989), pp. 279–287.

Vilar Bonet, M., 'Actividades financieras de la orden del Templo en la Corona de Aragón', *VIIe Congreso de historia de la Corona de Aragón*, Barcelona, 1962.

Le Village de Provence au bas moyen age, Cahiers du centre d'études des sociétés méditeranéens, Série no. 2, Aix en Provence, 1987.

Villanueva, J., *Viage literario á las iglesias de España*, 22 vols., Madrid, 1803–1852.

Wakefield, W., *Heresy, Crusade and Inquisition in Southern France 1100–1250*, London, 1974.

Weinburger, S., 'Les Conflits entre clercs et laïcs dans la Provence du XIe siècle', *AM* 92(1980), pp. 269–279.

Wollasch, J., 'A Cluniac Necrology from the Time of Abbot Hugh', *Cluniac Monasticism in the central Middle Ages*, N. Hunt (ed.), London and Basingstoke, 1971, pp. 143–190.

Zacour, N., 'The Children's Crusade', *A History of the Crusades*, K. Setton (ed.), II, Madison, Milwaukee and London, 1969, pp. 325–342.

Theses or Otherwise Unpublished Works

Rovik, S., 'The Templars in the Holy Land in the Twelfth Century', Oxford D.Phil. thesis, 1986.

INDEX

Abbreviations

(T)   Templar

(TCfra) Templar *confrater*

(TCsor) Templar *consoror*

(H)   Hospitaller

(HS)   Hospitaller sister

(HCfra) Hospitaller *confrater*

(HCsor) Hospitaller *consoror*

Notes to index

Templar and Hospitaller properties (castles, commanderies, properties &c.) appear as individual entries, as do other monastic and ecclesiastical properties.

Matters relating to Templars and Hospitallers appear as individual entries.

Titles (*i.e.*, Commander, Prior &c.) have been omitted. As Chapter Five explains, the variations were multifarious.